MEMOIRS

OF

NAPOLEON BONAPARTE

JOSEPHINE

MEMOIRS

OF

NAPOLEON BONAPARTE

BY

LOUIS ANTOINE FAUVELET DE BOURRIENNE

HIS PRIVATE SECRETARY

TO WHICH ARE ADDED AN ACCOUNT OF THE IMPORTANT EVENTS OF THE HUNDRED
DAYS, OF NAPOLEON'S SURRENDER TO THE ENGLISH, AND OF HIS
RESIDENCE AND DEATH AT ST. HELENA, WITH ANECDOTES
AND ILLUSTRATIVE EXTRACTS FROM ALL THE
MOST AUTHENTIC SOURCES

EDITED BY R. W. PHIPPS

COLONEL, LATE ROYAL ARTILLERY

New and Revised Edition

WITH NUMEROUS ILLUSTRATIONS

VOL. II.

NEW YORK

CHARLES SCRIBNER'S SONS

1891

TROW'S
PRINTING AND BOOKBINDING COMPANY,
NEW YORK.

CONTENTS.

CHAPTER I.

1800.

CHAPTER II.

1800.

CHAPTER III.

1800–1801.

CHAPTER IV.

1800–1801.

CHAPTER V.

1801–1802.

CHAPTER VI.

1802.

CHAPTER VII.

1802.

CHAPTER VIII.

1802–1803.

CHAPTER IX.

1802.

CHAPTER X.

1802.

CHAPTER XI.

1802.

CHAPTER XII.

1802.

CHAPTER XIII.

1802–1803.

CHAPTER XIV.

1802–1803.

CHAPTER XV.

1802.

CHAPTER XVI.

1802.

CHAPTER XVII.

1803.

CHAPTER XVIII.

1803.

CHAPTER XIX.

1803.

CHAPTER XX.

1803.

CHAPTER XXI.

1804.

CHAPTER XXII.

1804.

CHAPTER XXIII.

1804.

CHAPTER XXIV.

1804.

CHAPTER XXV.

1804.

CHAPTER XXVI.

1804.

CHAPTER XXVII.

1804.

CHAPTER XXVIII.

1804.

CHAPTER XXIX.

1804.

CHAPTER XXX.

1805.

CHAPTER XXXI.

1805.

CHAPTER XXXII.

1805.

CHAPTER XXXIII.

1805.

CHAPTER XXXIV.

1805.

LIST OF ILLUSTRATIONS.

LIST OF ILLUSTRATIONS

MEMOIRS

OF

NAPOLEON BONAPARTE.

CHAPTER I.

1800.

Bonaparte's confidence in the army—*Ma belle France*—The convent of Bernardins—Passage of Mont St. Bernard—Arrival at the convent—Refreshments distributed to the soldiers—Mont Albaredo—Artillery dismounted—The fort of Bard—Fortunate temerity—Bonaparte and Melas—The spy—Bonaparte's opinion of M. Necker—Capitulation of Genoa—Intercepted despatch—Lannes at Montebello—Boudet succeeded by Desaix—Coolness of the First Consul to M. Collot—Conversation and recollections—The battle of Marengo—General Kellerman—Supper sent from the Convent del Bosco—Particulars respecting the death of Desaix—The Prince of Lichtenstein—Return to Milan—Savary and Rapp.

It cannot be denied that if, from the 18th Brumaire to the epoch when Bonaparte began the campaign, innumerable improvements had been made in the internal affairs of France, foreign affairs could not be seen with the same satisfaction. Italy had been lost, and from the frontiers of Provence the Austrian camp fires were seen. Bonaparte was not ignorant of the difficulties of his position, and it was even on account of these very difficulties that, whatever might be the result of his hardy enterprise, he wished to escape from it as quickly as possible. He cherished no illusions, and often said all must be staked to gain all.

The army which the First Consul was preparing to attack was numerous, well disciplined, and victorious.

His, with the exception of a very small number of troops, was composed of conscripts; but these conscripts were commanded by officers whose ardour was unparalleled. Bonaparte's fortune was now to depend on the winning or losing of a battle. A battle lost would have dispelled all the dreams of his imagination, and with them would have vanished all his immense schemes for the future of France. He saw the danger, but was not intimidated by it; and trusting to his accustomed good fortune, and to the courage and fidelity of his troops, he said, " I have, it is true, many conscripts in my army, but they are Frenchmen. Four years ago did I not with a feeble army drive before me hordes of Sardinians and Austrians, and scour the face of Italy? We shall do so again. The sun which now shines on us is the same that shone at Arcola and Lodi. I rely on Massena. I hope he will hold out in Genoa. But should famine oblige him to surrender, I will retake Genoa in the plains of the Scrivia. With what pleasure shall I then return to my dear France! *Ma belle France.*"

At this moment, when a possible, nay, a probable chance, might for ever have blasted his ambitious hopes, he for the first time spoke of France as *his.* Considering the circumstances in which we then stood, this use of the possessive pronoun " *my* " describes more forcibly than anything that can be said the flashes of divination which crossed Bonaparte's brain when he was wrapped up in his chimerical ideas of glory and fortune.

In this favourable disposition of mind the First Consul arrived at Martigny on the 20th of May. Martigny is a convent of Bernardins, situated in a valley where the rays of the sun scarcely ever penetrate. The army was in full march to the Great St. Bernard. In this gloomy solitude did Bonaparte wait three days, expecting the fort of Bard, situated beyond the mountain and covering the road to Yvrée, to surrender. The town was carried on the 21st of May, and on the third day he learned that the fort still held out, and that there were no indications of its surrender. He launched into complaints against the commander of the siege, and said, " I am weary of staying in this convent ; those fools will never take Bard ; I must go myself and see what can be done. They cannot even settle so contemptible an affair without me ! " He immediately gave orders for our departure.

The grand idea of the invasion of Italy by crossing Mont St. Bernard emanated exclusively from the First Consul. This miraculous achievement justly excited the admiration of the world. The incredible difficulties it presented did not daunt the courage of Bonaparte's troops. His generals, accustomed as they had been to brave fatigue and danger, regarded without concern the gigantic enterprise of the modern Hannibal.

A convent or hospice, which had been established on the mountain for the purpose of affording assistance to solitary travellers, sufficiently bespeaks the dangers of these stormy regions. But the St. Bernard was now to be crossed, not by solitary travellers, but by an army. Cavalry, baggage, limbers, and artillery were now to wend their way along those narrow paths where the goat-herd cautiously picks his footsteps. On the one hand masses of snow, suspended above our heads, every moment threatened to break in avalanches, and sweep us away in their descent. On the other, a false step was death. We all passed, men and horse, one by one, along the goat-paths. The artillery was dismounted, and the guns, put into excavated trunks of trees, were drawn by ropes.

I have already mentioned that the First Consul had transmitted funds to the hospice of the Great St. Bernard. The good fathers had procured from the two valleys a considerable supply of cheese, bread, and wine. Tables were laid out in front of the hospice, and each soldier as he defiled past took a glass of wine and a piece of bread and cheese, and then resigned his place to the next. The fathers served, and renewed the portions with admirable order and activity.

The First Consul ascended the St. Bernard with that calm self-possession and that air of indifference for which he was always remarkable when he felt the necessity of setting an example and exposing himself to danger. He asked his guide many questions about the two valleys, inquired what were the resources of the inhabitants, and whether accidents were as frequent as they were said to be. The guide informed him that the experience of ages enabled the inhabitants to foresee good or bad weather, and that they were seldom deceived.

Bonaparte, who wore his gray greatcoat, and had his whip in his hand, appeared somewhat disappointed at not seeing any one come from the valley of Aosta to inform him of the taking of the fort of Bard. I never left him for a moment during the ascent. We encountered no personal danger, and escaped with no other inconvenience than excessive fatigue.

On his arrival at the convent the First Consul visited the chapel and the three little libraries. He had time to read a few pages of an old book, of which I have forgotten the title.[1]

Our breakfast-dinner was very frugal. The little garden was still covered with snow, and I said to one of the fathers, "You can have but few vegetables here."—"We get our vegetables from the valleys," he replied ; "but in the month of August, in warm seasons, we have a few lettuces of our own growing."

When we reached the summit of the mountain we seated ourselves on the snow and slid down. Those who went first smoothed the way for those who came behind them.

---

[1] The Vallaisians afterwards erected a tablet in honour of Napoleon in the Convent of the Great St. Bernard, inscribing it in terse, if not elegant, Latin :— "NAPOLEONI . . . . ÆGYPTIACO, BIS ITALICO, SEMPER INVICTO . . . . GRATA RESPUBLICA."

This rapid descent greatly amused us, and we were only stopped by the mud which succeeded the snow at the distance of five or six hundred toises down the declivity.

We crossed, or rather climbed up, Mont Albaredo to avoid passing under the fort of Bard, which closes the valley of Aosta. As it was impossible to get the artillery up this mountain it was resolved to convey it through the town of Bard, which was not fortified. For this operation we made choice of night, and the wheels of the cannon and caissons, and even the horses' feet, being wrapped in straw, the whole passed quietly through the little town. They were, indeed, under the fire of the fort; however, it did not so completely command the street but that the houses would have protected them against any very fatal consequences. A great part of the army had passed before the surrender of the fort, which so completely commands the narrow valley leading to Aosta that it is difficult to comprehend the negligence of the Austrians in not throwing up more efficient works; by very simple precautions they might have rendered the passage of St. Bernard unavailing.

On the 23d we came within sight of the fort of Bard, which commands the road bounded by the Doria Baltea on the right and Mont Albaredo on the left. The Doria Baltea is a small torrent which separates the town of Bard from the fort. Bonaparte, whose retinue was not very numerous, crossed the torrent. On arriving within gunshot of the fort he ordered us to quicken our pace to gain a little bridle-path on the left, leading to the summit of Mont Albaredo, and turning the town and fort of Bard. We ascended this path on foot with some difficulty. On reaching the summit of the mountain, which commands the fort, Bonaparte levelled his telescope on the grass, and stationing himself behind some bushes, which served at once to shelter and conceal him, he attentively reconnoitred the fort. After addressing several questions to the persons who had come to give him information, he mentioned, in a tone of dissatisfaction, the faults that had been committed, and ordered the erection of a new battery to attack a point which he marked out, and from whence, he guaranteed, the firing of a few shots would oblige the fort to surrender. Having given these orders he descended the mountain and went to sleep that night at Yvrée. On the 2d of June he learned that the fort had surrendered the day before.

The passage of Mont St. Bernard must occupy a great place in the annals of successful temerity. The boldness of the First Consul seemed, as it were, to have fascinated the enemy, and his enterprise was so unexpected that not a single Austrian corps defended the approaches of the fort of Bard. The country was entirely exposed, and we only encountered here and there a few feeble parties, who were incapable of checking our march upon Milan. Bonaparte's advance astonished and confounded the enemy, who thought of nothing but marching back the way he came, and renouncing the invasion of France. The bold genius which actuated Bonaparte did not inspire General Melas, the commander-in-chief of the Austrian forces. If Melas had had the firmness which ought to belong to the leader of an army—if he had compared the respective positions of the two parties—if he had considered that there was no longer time to regain his line of operations and recover his communication with the Hereditary States, that he was master of all the strong places in Italy, that he had nothing to fear from Masséna, that Suchet could not resist him :—if, then, following Bonaparte's example, he had marched upon Lyons, what would have become of the First Consul? Melas would have found few obstacles, and almost everywhere open towns, while the French army would have been exhausted without having an enemy to fight. This is, doubtless, what Bonaparte would have done had he been Melas ; but, fortunately for us, Melas was not Bonaparte.

We arrived at Milan on the 2d of June, the day on which the First Consul heard that the fort of Bard was taken. But little resistance was opposed to our entrance into the capital of Lombardy, and the term "engagements" can scarcely be applied to a few affairs of advance posts, in which success could not be for a moment doubtful. The fort of Milan was immediately blockaded. Murat was sent to Piacenza, of which he took possession without difficulty, and Lannes beat General Ott at Montebello. He was far from imagining that by that exploit he conquered for himself a future duchy!

The First Consul passed six days at Milan. On the day after our arrival there a spy who had served us very well in the first campaign in Italy was announced. The First Consul recollected him, and ordered him to be shown into his cabinet. "What, are you here?" he exclaimed; "so you are not shot yet!"—"General," replied the spy, "when the war recommenced I determined to serve the Austrians because you were far from Europe. I always follow the fortunate; but the truth is, I am tired of the trade. I wish to have done with it, and to get enough to enable me to retire. I have been sent to your lines by General Melas, and I can render you an important service. I will give an exact account of the force and the position of all the enemy's corps, and the names of their commanders. I can tell you the situation in which Alessandria now is. You know me: I will not deceive you; but, I must carry back some report to my general. You need not care for giving me some true particulars which I can communicate to him."—"Oh! as to that," resumed the First Consul, "the enemy is welcome to know my forces and my positions, provided I know his, and he be ignorant of my plans. You shall be satisfied; but do not deceive me: you ask for 1000 louis, you shall have them if you serve me well."

I then wrote down, from the dictation of the spy, the names of the corps, their amount, their positions, and the names of the generals commanding them. The Consul stuck pins in the map to mark his plans on places respecting which he received information from the spy. We also learned that Alessandria was without provisions, that Melas was far from expecting a siege, that many of his troops were sick, and that he wanted medicines. Berthier was ordered to draw up for the spy a nearly accurate statement of our positions.

The information given by this man proved so accurate and useful that on his return from Marengo Bonaparte ordered me to pay him the 1000 louis. The spy afterwards informed him that Melas was delighted with the way in which he had served him in this affair, and had rewarded him handsomely. He assured us that he had bidden farewell to his odious profession. The First Consul regarded this little event as one of the favours of fortune.

In passing through Geneva the First Consul had an interview with M. Necker.[1] I know not how it happened, but at the time he did not speak to me of this interview. However, I was curious to know what he thought of a man who had acquired so much celebrity in France. One evening, when we were talking of one thing and another, I managed to turn the conversation on that subject. "M. Necker," said he, "appears to me very far below his reputation. He did not equal the idea I had formed of him. I tried all I could to get him to talk ; but he said nothing remarkable. He is an ideologist[2]—a banker. It is impossible that such a man can have any but narrow views ; and, besides, most celebrated people lose on a close view."

---

[1] Madame de Staël briefly mentions this interview in her *Considèrations sur la Rèvolution Française.* "M. Necker," she says, "had an interview with Bonaparte, when he was on his way to Italy by the passage of Mont. St. Bernard, a few days before the battle of Marengo. During this conversation, which lasted two hours, the First Consul made a very favourable impression on my father by the confident way he spoke of his future projects."—*Bourrienne.*

[2] This was a constant term of reproach with Bonaparte. He set all the metaphysicians of the Continent against him by exclaiming, " Je ne veux point d'idéologues."

—"Not always, General," observed I.—"Ah!" said he, smiling, "that is not bad, Bourrienne. You are improving. I see I shall make something of you in time!"

The day was approaching when all was to be lost or won. The First Consul made all his arrangements, and sent off the different corps to occupy the points he had marked out. I have already mentioned that Murat's task was the occupation of Piacenza. As soon as he was in possession of that town he intercepted a courier of General Melas. The despatch, which was addressed to the Aulic Council of Vienna, was delivered to us on the night of the 8th of June. It announced the capitulation of Genoa, which took place on the 4th, after the long and memorable defence which reflected so much honour on Masséna. Melas in his despatch spoke of what he called our pretended army of reserve with inconceivable contempt, and alluded to the presence of Bonaparte in Italy as a mere fabrication. He declared he was still in Paris. It was past three in the morning when Murat's courier arrived. I immediately translated the despatch, which was in German. About four o'clock I entered the chamber of the First Consul, whom I was obliged to shake by the arm in order to wake him. He had desired me, as I have already mentioned, never to respect his repose on the arrival of bad news ; but on the receipt of good news to let him sleep. I read to him the despatch, and so much was he confounded by this unexpected event that his first exclamation was, "Bah! you do not understand German." But hardly had he uttered these words when he arose, and by eight o'clock in the morning orders were despatched for repairing the possible consequences of this disaster, and countermanding the march of the troops on the Scrivia. He himself proceeded the same day to Stradella.

I have seen it mentioned in some accounts that the First Consul in person gained the battle of Montebello. This is a mistake. He did not leave Milan until the 9th of June, and that very day Lannes was engaged with the enemy. The conflict was so terrible that Lannes, a few days after, describing it in my presence to M. Collot, used these remarkable words, which I well remember : "Bones were cracking in my division like a shower of hail falling on a skylight."

By a singular chance Desaix, who was to contribute to the victory and stop the rout of Marengo, arrived from Egypt at Toulon, on the very day on which we departed from Paris. He was enabled to leave Egypt in consequence of the capitulation of El-Arish, which happened on the 4th of January 1800. He wrote me a letter, dated 16th Floréal, year VIII. (6th of May 1800), announcing his arrival. This letter I did not receive until we reached Martigny. I showed it to the First Consul. "Ah !" exclaimed he, " Desaix in Paris ! " and he immediately despatched an order for him to repair to the headquarters of the army of Italy wherever they might be. Desaix arrived at Stradella on the morning of the 11th of June. The First Consul received him with the warmest cordiality, as a man for whom he had a high esteem, and whose talents and character afforded the fairest promise of what might one day be expected of him. Bonaparte was jealous of some generals, the rivalry of whose ambition he feared ; but on this subject Desaix gave him no uneasiness; equally remarkable for his unassuming disposition, his talent, and information, he proved by his conduct that he loved glory for her own sake, and that every wish for the possession of political power was foreign to his mind. Bonaparte's friendship for him was enthusiastic. At this interview at Stradella Desaix was closeted with the First Consul for upwards of three hours. On the day after his arrival an order of the day communicated to the army that Desaix was appointed to the command of Boudet's division.[1]

---

[1] Boudet was on terms of great intimacy with Bonaparte, who, no doubt, was much affected at his death. However, the only remark he made on receiving the

DESAIX.

I expressed to Bonaparte my surprise at his long interview with Desaix. "Yes," replied he, "he has been a long time with me; but you know what a favourite he is. As soon as I return to Paris I will make him War Minister. I would make him a prince if I could. He is quite an antique character." Desaix died two days after he had completed his thirty-third year, and in less than a week after the above observations.

About this time M. Collot came to Italy and saw Bonaparte at Milan. The latter received him coldly, though he had not yet gained the battle of Marengo. M. Collot had been on the most intimate footing with Bonaparte, and had rendered him many valuable services. These circumstances sufficiently accounted for Bonaparte's coolness, for he would never acknowledge himself under obligations to any one, and he did not like those who were initiated into certain family secrets which he had resolved to conceal.[1]

intelligence, was "Who the devil shall I get to supply Boudet's place?"—*Bourrienne.*

The command given to Desaix was a corps especially formed of the two divisions of Boudet and Monnier (*Savary,* tome i. p. 262). Boudet was not killed at Marengo, still less before (see *Erreurs,* tome i. p. 14).

[1] The day after the interview I had a long conversation with M. Collot while Bonaparte was gone to review some corps stationed at Milan. M. Collot perfectly understood the cause of the unkind treatment he had experienced, and of which he gave me the following explanation:—

Some days before the Consulate—that is to say, two or three days after our return from Egypt,—Bonaparte, during his jealous fit, spoke to M. Collot about his wife, her levities, and their publicity. "Henceforth," said Bonaparte, "I will have nothing to do with her."—"What, would you part from her?"—"Does not her conduct justify me in so doing?"—"I do not know; but is this the time to think of such a thing, when the eyes of all France are fixed upon you? These domestic squabbles will degrade you in the eyes of the people, who expect you to be wholly devoted to their interests; and you will be laughed at, like one of Molière's husbands. If you are displeased with your wife's conduct you can call her to account when you have nothing better to do. Begin by raising up the State. After that you may find a thousand reasons for your resentment when now you would not find one. You know the French people well enough to see how important it is that you should not commence with this absurdity."

By these and other similar remarks M. Collot thought he had produced some impression, when Bonaparte suddenly exclaimed: "No, my determination is fixed; she shall never again enter my house. I care not what people say. They will gossip about the affair for two days, and on the third it will be forgotten. She shall

On the 13th the First Consul slept at Torre di Galifolo. During the evening he ordered a staff-officer to ascertain whether the Austrians had a bridge across the Bormida. A report arrived very late that there was none. This information set Bonaparte's mind at rest, and he went to bed very well satisfied ; but early next morning, when a firing was heard, and he learned that the Austrians had debouched on the plain, where the troops were engaged, he flew into a furious passion, called the staff-officer a coward, and said he had not advanced far enough. He even spoke of bringing the matter to an investigation.

go to Malmaison, and I will live here. The public know enough, not to be mistaken as to the reasons of her removal."

M. Collot vainly endeavoured to calm his irritation. Bonaparte vented a torrent of reproaches upon Josephine. "All this violence," observed M Collot, "proves that you still love her. Do but see her ; she will explain the business to your satisfaction, and you will forgive her."—"I forgive her! Never! Collot, you know me. If I were not sure of my own resolution, *I would tear out this heart, and cast it into the fire.*" Here anger almost choked his utterance, and he made a motion with his hand as if tearing his breast.

When this violent paroxysm had somewhat subsided M. Collot withdrew; but before he went away Bonaparte invited him to breakfast on the following morning.

At ten o'clock M. Collot was there, and as he was passing through the courtyard he was informed that Madame Bonaparte, who, as I have already mentioned, had gone to Lyons without meeting the General, had returned during the night. On M. Collot's entrance Bonaparte appeared considerably embarrassed. He led him into a side room, not wishing to bring him into the room where I was writing. "Well," said Bonaparte to M. Collot, "she is here."—"I rejoice to hear it. You have done well for yourself as well as for us."—"But do not imagine I have forgiven her. As long as I live I shall suspect. The fact is, that on her arrival I desired her to be gone; but that fool Joseph was there. What could I do, Collot ? I saw her descend the staircase followed by Eugène and Hortense. They were all weeping; and I have not a heart to resist tears. Eugène was with me in Egypt. I have been accustomed to look upon him as my adopted son. He is a fine brave lad. Hortense is just about to be introduced into society, and she is admired by all who know her. I confess, Collot, I was deeply moved ; I could not endure the distress of the two poor children. 'Should they,' thought I, 'suffer for their mother's faults?' I called back Eugène and Hortense, and their mother followed them. What could I say, what could I do ? I should not be a man without some weakness."—"Be assured they will reward you for this."—"They ought, Collot, they ought ; for it has cost me a hard struggle." After this dialogue Bonaparte and M. Collot entered the breakfast-parlour, where I was then sitting. Eugène breakfasted with us, but neither Josephine nor Hortense. I have already related how I acted the part of mediator in this affair. Next day nothing was wanting to complete the reconciliation between the Conqueror of Egypt and the charming woman who conquered Bonaparte.—*Bourrienne.*

From motives of delicacy I refrain from mentioning the name of the officer here alluded to.

Bonaparte mounted his horse and proceeded immediately to the scene of action. I did not see him again until six in the evening. In obedience to his instructions I repaired to San Giuliano, which is not above two leagues from the place where the engagement commenced. In the course of the afternoon I saw a great many wounded passing through the village, and shortly afterwards a multitude of fugitives. At San Giuliano nothing was talked of but a retreat, which, it was said, Bonaparte alone firmly opposed. I was then advised to leave San Giuliano, where I had just received a courier for the General-in-Chief. On the morning of the 14th General Desaix was sent towards Novi to observe the road to Genoa, which city had fallen several days before, in spite of the efforts of its illustrious defender, Masséna. I returned with this division to San Giuliano. I was struck with the numerical weakness of the corps which was marching to aid an army already much reduced and dispersed. The battle was looked upon as lost, and so indeed it was. The First Consul having asked Desaix what he thought of it, that brave General bluntly replied, "The battle is completely lost; but it is only two o'clock, we have time to gain another to-day." I heard this from Bonaparte himself the same evening. Who could have imagined that Desaix's little corps, together with the few heavy cavalry commanded by General Kellerman, would, about five o'clock, have changed the fortune of the day? It cannot be denied that it was the instantaneous inspiration of Kellerman that converted a defeat into a victory, and decided the battle of Marengo.

That memorable battle, of which the results were incalculable, has been described in various ways. Bonaparte had an account of it commenced no less than three times; and I must confess that none of the narratives are more correct than that contained in the *Memoirs of the Duke of Rovigo.* The Emperor Napoleon became dissatisfied with what had been said by the First Consul Bonaparte. For my part, not having had the honour to bear a sword, I cannot say that I saw any particular movement executed this or that way ; but I may mention here what I heard on the evening of the battle of Marengo respecting the probable chances of that event. As to the part which the First Consul took in it, the reader, perhaps, is sufficiently acquainted with his character to account for it. He did not choose that a result so decisive should be attributed to any other cause than the combinations of his genius ; and if I had not known his insatiable thirst for glory I should have been surprised at the sort of half satisfaction evinced at the cause of the success amidst the joy manifested for the success itself. It must be confessed that in this he was very unlike Jourdan, Hoche, Kléber, and Moreau, who were ever ready to acknowledge the services of those who had fought under their orders.

Within two hours of the time when the divisons commanded by Desaix left San Giuliano I was joyfully surprised by the triumphant return of the army, whose fate, since the morning, had caused me so much anxiety. Never did fortune within so short a time show herself under two such various faces. At two o'clock all denoted the desolation of a defeat, with all its fatal consequences ; at five victory was again faithful to the flag of Arcola. Italy was reconquered by a single blow, and the crown of France appeared in the perspective.

At seven in the evening, when I returned with the First Consul to headquarters, he expressed to me his sincere regret for the loss of Desaix, and then he added, "Little Kellerman made a lucky charge. He did it at just the right moment. We are much indebted to him. You see what trifling circumstances decide these affairs."

These few words show that Bonaparte sufficiently appreciated the services of Kellerman.   However, when that officer approached the table at which were seated the First Consul and a number of his generals, Bonaparte merely said, "You made a pretty good charge."   By way of counterbalancing this cool compliment he turned towards Bessières, who commanded the horse grenadiers of the Guard, and said, "Bessières, the Guard has covered itself with glory."   Yet the fact is, that the Guard took no part in the charge of Kellerman, who could assemble only 500 heavy cavalry ; and with this handful of brave men he cut in two the Austrian column, which had overwhelmed Desaix's division, and had made 6000 prisoners.   The Guard did not charge at Marengo until nightfall.

Next day it was reported that Kellerman, in his first feeling of dissatisfaction at the dry congratulation he had received, said to the First Consul, "I have just placed the crown on your head !"   I did not hear this, and I cannot vouch for the truth of its having been said.   I could only have ascertained that fact through Bonaparte, and of course I could not, with propriety, remind him of a thing which must have been very offensive to him.   However, whether true or not, the observation was circulated about, verbally and in writing, and Bonaparte knew it.   Hence the small degree of favour shown to Kellerman, who was not made a general of division on the field of battle as a reward for his charge at Marengo.[1]

---

[1] If Savary's story be correct, and he was then *aide de camp* to Desaix, and Bourrienne acknowledges his account to be the best, the inspiration of the charge did not come from the young Kellerman.   Savary says that Desaix sent him to tell Napoleon that he could not delay his attack, and that he must be supported by some cavalry. Savary was then sent by Napoleon to a spot where he was told he would find Kellerman, to order him to charge in support of Desaix.   Desaix and Kellerman were so placed as to be out of sight of each other (*Savary*, tome i. pp. 274-279).   Thiers (tome i. p. 445) follows Savary.

It may here be mentioned that Savary, in his account of the battle, expressly states that he carried the order from Bonaparte to Kellerman to make this charge. He also makes the following observations on the subject :—

"After the fall of the Imperial Government some pretended friends of General Kellerman have presumed to claim for him the merit of originating the charge of

M. Delaforêt, the Postmaster-general, sometimes *transacted business* with the First Consul. The nature of this secret business may easily be guessed at.[1] On the occasion of one of their interviews the First Consul saw a letter from Kellerman to Lasalle, which contained the following passage : "Would you believe, my friend, that Bonaparte has not made me a general of division though I have just placed the crown on his head ?" The letter was sealed again and sent to its address ; but Bonaparte never forgot its contents.

Whether Kellerman did or did not give the crown of France to the First Consul, it is very certain that on the evening of the battle of Marengo he gave him a supper,

cavalry. That general, whose share of glory is sufficently brilliant to gratify his most sanguine wishes, can have no knowledge of so presumptuous a pretension. I the more readily acquit him from the circumstance that, as we were conversing one day respecting that battle, I called to his mind my having brought to him the First Consul's orders, and he appeared not to have forgotten that fact. I am far from suspecting his friends of the design of lessening the glory of either General Bonaparte or General Desaix ; they know as well as myself that theirs are names so respected that they can never be affected by such detractions, and that it would be as vain to dispute the praise due to the Chief who planned the battle as to attempt to depreciate the brilliant share which General Kellerman had in its successful result. I will add to the above a few observations.

"From the position which he occupied General Desaix could not see General Kellerman ; he had even desired me to request the First Consul to afford him the support of some cavalry. Neither could General Kellerman, from the point where he was stationed, perceive General Desaix's division ; it is even probable that he was not aware of the arrival of that General, who had only joined the army two days before. Both were ignorant of each other's position, which the First Consul was alone acquainted with ; he alone could introduce harmony into their movements ; he alone could make their efforts respectively conduce to the same object.

" The fate of the battle was decided by Kellerman's bold charge ; had it, however, been made previously to General Desaix's attack, in all probability it would have had a quite different result. Kellerman appears to have been convinced of it, since he allowed the Austrian column to cross our field of battle and extend its front beyond that of the troops we had still in line without making the least attempt to impede its progress. The reason of Kellerman's not charging it sooner was that it was too serious a movement, and the consequences of failure would have been irretrievable ; that charge, therefore, could only enter into a general combination of plans, to which he was necessarily a stranger" (*Memoirs of the Duke of Rovigo*, tome i. pp. 278-280).

[1] When M. Delaforêt was replaced soon after this by Lavalette, Napoleon ordered the discontinuance of the practice followed until then of allowing letters to be opened by subordinate officials. This right was restricted, as in England, to the Minister. However bad this practice, it was limited, not extended, in his reign. See *Meneval*, tome iii. pp. 60-62, and *Lavalette*, tome ii. p. 10.

of which his famishing staff and the rest of us partook. This was no inconsiderable service in the destitute condition in which we were. We thought ourselves exceedingly fortunate in profiting by the precaution of Kellerman, who had procured provisions from one of those pious retreats which are always well supplied, and which soldiers are very glad to fall in with when campaigning. It was the convent del Bosco which on this occasion was laid under contribution; and in return for the abundance of good provisions and wine with which they supplied the commander of the heavy cavalry the holy fathers were allowed a guard to protect them against pillage and the other disastrous concomitants of war.

After supper was over the First Consul dictated to me the bulletin of the battle. When we were alone I said to him, " General, here is a fine victory ! You recollect what you said the other day about the pleasure with which you would return to France after striking a grand blow in Italy ; surely you must be satisfied now ? "—" Yes, Bourrienne, I am satisfied. But Desaix ! . . . Ah, what a triumph would this have been if I could have embraced him to-night on the field of battle ! " As he uttered these words I saw that Bonaparte was on the point of shedding tears, so sincere and profound was his grief for the death of Desaix. He certainly never loved, esteemed, or regretted any man so much.

The death of Desaix has been variously related, and I need not now state that the words attributed to him in the bulletin were imaginary. Neither did he die in the arms of his *aide de camp*, Lebrun, as I wrote from the dictation of the First Consul. The following facts are more correct, or at all events more probable :—the death of Desaix was not perceived at the moment it took place. He fell without saying a word, at a little distance from Lefebvre-Desnouettes. A sergeant of battalion of the 9th brigade of light infantry, commanded by Barrois, seeing him extended on the ground, asked permission to pick up his cloak. It was found to be perforated behind; and this circumstance leaves it doubtful whether Desaix was killed by some unlucky inadvertency, while advancing at the head of his troops, or by the enemy when turning towards his men to encourage them. However, the event was so instantaneous, the disorder so complete, and the change of fortune so sudden, that it is not surprising there should be no positive account of the circumstances which attended his death.[1]

Early next morning the Prince of Liechtenstein came from General Melas with negotiations to the First Consul. The propositions of the General did not suit Bonaparte, and he declared to the Prince that the army shut up in Alessandria should evacuate freely, and with the honours of war; but on those conditions, which are well known, and by which Italy was to be fully restored to the French domination. That day were repaired the faults of Scherer, whose inertness and imbecility had paralysed everything, and who had fled, and been constantly beaten, from the Adriatic to Mont Cenis. The Prince of Liechtenstein begged to return to render an account of his mission to General Melas. He came back in the evening, and made many observations on the hard nature of the conditions. "Sir," replied the First Consul, in a tone of marked impatience, "carry my final determination to your General, and return quickly. It is irrevocable! Know that I am as well acquainted with your position as you are yourselves. I did not begin to learn the art of war yesterday. You are

[1] Savary, though Desaix's *aide de camp*, throws no light on the cause of that General's death. He says :—" As soon as the Austrian column was dis; ersed I quitted General Kellerman's cavalry, and was returning to meet General Desaix, whose troops were debouching in my view, when the Colonel of the 9th regiment informed me that he had been killed. I was at the distance of only a hundred paces from the spot where I had left him. I hastened to it, and found the General stretched upon the ground, completely stripped of his clothes, and surrounded by other naked bodies. I recognised him notwithstanding the darkness, owing to the thickness of his hair, which still retained its tie " (*Memoirs of the Duke of Rovigo*, tome i. p. 277).

blocked up in Alessandria; you have many sick and
wounded; you are in want of provisions and medicines. I
occupy the whole of your rear. Your finest troops are
among the killed and wounded. I might insist on harder
conditions; my position would warrant me in so doing;
but I moderate my demands in consideration of the gray
hairs of your General, whom I respect."

This reply was delivered with considerable dignity and
energy. I showed the Prince out, and he said to me,
"These conditions are very hard, especially that of giving
up Genoa, which surrendered to us only a fortnight ago,
after so long a siege." It is a curious fact that the Emperor of Austria received intelligence of the capitulation
and restitution of Genoa at the same time.

When the First Consul returned to Milan he made Savary and Rapp his *aides de camp.* They had previously
served in the same rank under Desaix. The First Consul
was at first not much disposed to take them, alleging that
he had *aides de camp* enough. But his respect for the
choice of Desaix, added to a little solicitation on my part,
soon removed every obstacle. These two officers served
him to the last hour of his political career with unfailing
zeal and fidelity.

I have seen nothing in the *Memoirs of the Duc de Rovigo*
(Savary) about my having had anything to do with his admission to the honour. I can probably tell the reason
why one of the two *aides de camp* has risen higher than
the other. Rapp had an Alsacian frankness which always
injured him.[1]

[1] Several instances of this will be found in Rapp's Memoirs, which may indeed
partly explain why he was only count when Savary was a duke. A Corsican connection being introduced into Napoleon's room, Rapp, as in the case of Georges Cadoudal (see *ante*), would not at first withdraw, and when ordered out left the door
ajar, telling Napoleon afterwards, "I do not like your Corsicans." On another occasion, "Rapp," said Napoleon, having a quantity of French gold before him, "do
not the Germans like these little napoleons?"—"Yes, Sire, much more than they do
the great one."—"See," answered Napoleon, "what may be called German frankness" (*Rapp*, p. 25).

CHAPTER II.

1800.

WHAT little time, and how few events sometimes suffice to
change the destiny of nations! We left Milan on the 13th
of June, Marengo on the 14th, and on the 15th Italy was
ours! A suspension of hostilities between the French
and Austrian armies was the immediate result of a single
battle; and by virtue of a convention, concluded between
Berthier and Melas, we resumed possession of all the
fortified places of any importance, with the exception of
Mantua. As soon as this convention was signed Bonaparte dictated to me at Torre di Galifolo the following
letter to his colleagues :—

The day after the battle of Marengo, CITIZENS CONSULS, General
Melas transmitted a message to our advance posts requesting permission to send General Skal to me. During the day the convention, of which I send you a copy, was drawn up, and at night it was

signed by Generals Berthier and Melas. I hope the French people will be satisfied with the conduct of their army.[1]

(Signed) BONAPARTE.

The only thing worthy of remark in this letter would be the concluding sentence, in which the First Consul still affected to acknowledge the sovereignty of the people, were it not that the words " Citizens Consuls " were evidently foisted in with a particular design. The battle was gained ; and even in a trifling matter like this it was necessary that the two other Consuls should feel that they were not so much the colleagues as the subordinates of the First Consul.

We returned to Milan, and our second occupation of that city was marked by continued acclamations wherever the First Consul showed himself. At Milan the First Consul now saw Masséna for the first time since our departure for Egypt. Bonaparte lavished upon him the highest praises, but not higher than he deserved, for his admirable defence of Genoa. He named him his successor in the command of the army of Italy. Moreau was on the Rhine, and therefore none but the conqueror of Zurich could properly have succeeded the First Consul in that command. The great blow was struck ; but there might still occur an emergency requiring the presence of a skilful experienced general, well acquainted with the country. And besides, we could not be perfectly at ease, until it was ascertained what conditions would be adhered to by the Cabinet of Vienna, which was then entirely under the influence of the Cabinet of London.

After our return from the battle the popular joy was general and heartfelt, not only among the higher and

---

[1] The nephew of Cambacérès points out that Bourrienne has omitted the heading of this letter, " *To the Consuls of the Republic,*" and also its ending, " *I shall be at Milan this evening,*" " *I salute you affectionately.*" This last formula, he says, Napoleon seems to have attached some importance to, as in other original letters, where Bourrienne in his haste had omitted it, Napoleon had added it with his own hands (*Erreurs,* tome ii. p. 185).

middle ranks of society, but in all classes ; and the affection evinced from all quarters to the First Consul was unfeigned. In what a tone of sincerity did he say to me one day, when returning from the parade, " Bourrienne, do you hear the acclamations still resounding ? That noise is as sweet to me as the sound of Josephine's voice. How happy and proud I am to be loved by such a people ! "

During our stay at Milan Bonaparte had arranged a new government for Piedmont ; he had ever since cherished the wish to unite that rich and fertile country to the French territory because some Piedmontese provinces had been possessed by Louis XIV. That monarch was the only king whom the First Consul really admired. "If," said he one day, "Louis XIV. had not been born a king, he would have been a great man. But he did not know mankind ; he could not know them, for he never knew misfortune." He admired the resolution of the old King, who would rather bury himself under the ruins of the monarchy than submit to degrading conditions, after having commanded the sovereigns of Europe. I recollect that Bonaparte was extremely pleased to see in the reports which he ordered to be made that in Casal, and in the valleys of Pignerol, Latour, and Luzerne, there still existed many traces of the period when those countries belonged to France ; and that the French language was yet preserved there. He already began to identify himself with the past ; and abusing the old kings of France was not the way to conciliate his favour.

The First Consul appointed for the government of Piedmont a Council which, as may naturally be imagined, he composed of those Piedmontese who were the declared partisans of France. He stated as the grounds of this arrangement that it was to give to Piedmont a new proof of the affection and attachment of the French people. He afterwards appointed General Dupont President of the Council, with the title of Minister-Extraordinary of the

French Government. I will here mention a secret step taken by Bonaparte towards the overthrowing of the Republic. In making the first draught of General Dupont's appointment I had mechanically written, " Minister-Extraordinary of the French Republic."—"No ! no ! " said Bonaparte, "not of the *Republic ;* say of the *Government.*"

On his return to Paris the First Consul gave almost incredible proofs of his activity. The day after his arrival he promulgated a great number of decrees, and afterwards allotted the rewards to his soldiers. He appointed Kellerman a general of division which, on every principle of justice, he ought to have done on the field of battle. He distributed sabres of honour, with the following inscription, highly complimentary to himself :—

" *Battle of Maringo,*[1] *commanded in person by the First Consul.— Given by the Government of the Republic to General Lannes.*"

Similar sabres where presented to Generals Victor, Watrin, Gardanne, and Murat ; and sabres of less value to other officers : and also muskets and drumsticks of honour to the soldiers and drummers who had distinguished themselves at Marengo, or in the army of the Rhine ; for Bonaparte took care that the officers and men who had fought under Moreau should be included among those to whom the national rewards were presented. He even had a medal struck to perpetuate the memory of the entry of the French army into Munich. It is worthy of remark that while official fabrications and exaggerated details of facts were published respecting Marengo and the short campaign of Italy, by a feigned modesty the victorious army of Marengo received the unambitious title of *Army of Reserve.* By this artifice the honour of the Constitution was saved. The First Consul had not violated it. If he had marched to the field, and staked everything on a chance, it was merely accidentally, for he commanded only

---

[1] Spelt for some time, I do not know why, as Marìngo.—*Bourrienne.*

an "Army of Reserve," which nevertheless he had greeted
with the title of *Grand Army* before he entered upon the
campaign.   It is scarcely conceivable that Bonaparte, possessing as he did an extraordinary mind, should have descended to such pitiful artifices.[1]

Even foreigners and prisoners were objects of Bonaparte's designing intentions.   I recollect one evening his
saying to me, " Bourrienne, write to the Minister of War,
and tell him to select a fine brace of pistols, of the Versailles manufacture, and send them, in my name, to General Zach.   He dined with me to-day, and highly praised
our manufacture of arms.   I should like to give him a
token of remembrance ; besides,—the matter will be talked
of at Vienna, and may perhaps do good !"

As soon as the news of the battle of Marengo reached
Paris Lucien Bonaparte, Minister of the Interior, ordered
preparations for the festival, fixed for the 14th of July, in
commemoration of the first Federation.   This festival and
that of the 1st Vendémiaire were the only ones preserved
by the Consular Government.   Indeed, in those memorable days, when the Revolution appeared in its fairest
point of view, France had never known such joy as that to
which the battle of Marengo gave rise.   Still, amidst all
this popular transport there was a feeling of regret.   The
fame of Desaix, his heroic character, his death, the words
attributed to him and believed to be true, caused mourning to be mingled with joy.   It was agreed to open a sub-
scription for erecting a national monument to his memory.
A reflection naturally arises here upon the difference
between the period referred to and the present time.
France has endowed with nearly a million the children of
one of her greatest orators and most eloquent defenders
of public liberty, yet, for the monument to the memory

[1] Thiers (tome vi. p. 70) says the title *Grande Armée* was first given by Napoleon
to the force prepared in 1805 for the campaign against Austria. The Constitution
forbad the First Consul to command the armies in person. Hence the title, "*Army
of Reserve*," given to the force which fought Marengo.

of Desaix scarcely 20,000 francs were subscribed. Does not this form a singular contrast with the patriotic munificence displayed at the death of General Foy? The pitiful monument to Desaix, on the Place Dauphine, sufficiently attests the want of spirit on the part of the subscribers. Bonaparte, who was much dissatisfied with it, gave the name of Desaix to a new quay, the first stone of which was laid with great solemnity on the 14th of July.

On that day the crowd was immense in the Champ-de-Mars and in the Temple of Mars, the name which at that time the Church of the Invalides still preserved. Lucien delivered a speech on the encouraging prospects of France, and Lannes made an appropriate address on presenting to the Government the flags taken at Marengo. Two more speeches followed; one from an *aide de camp* of Masséna, and the other from an *aide de camp* of Lecourbe; and after the distribution of some medals the First Consul then delivered the following address :—

CITIZENS! SOLDIERS!—The flags presented to the Government, in the presence of the people of this immense capital, attest at once the genius of the Commanders-in-Chief Moreau, Masséna, and Berthier; the military talents of the generals, their lieutenants; and the bravery of the French soldiers.

On your return to the camp tell your comrades that for the 1st Vendémiaire, when we shall celebrate the anniversary of the Republic, the French people expect either peace or, if the enemy obstinately refuse it, other flags, the fruit of fresh victories.

After this harangue of the First Consul, in which he addressed the military in the name of the people, and ascribed to Berthier the glory of Marengo, a hymn was chanted, the words of which were written by M. de Fontanes, and the music composed by Méhul. But what was most remarkable in this *fête* was neither the poetry, the music, nor even the panegyrical eloquence of Lucien, —it was the arrival at the Champ-de-Mars, after the ceremony at the Invalides, of the Consular Guard re-

turning from Marengo. I was at a window of the
École-Militaire, and I can never forget the commotion,
almost electrical, which made the air resound with cries of
enthusiasm at their appearance. These soldiers did not
defile before the First Consul in fine uniforms as at a review. Leaving the field of battle when the firing ceased,
they had crossed Lombardy, Piedmont, Mont Cenis,
Savoy, and France in the space of twenty-nine days.
They appeared worn by the fatigue of a long journey,
with faces browned by the summer sun of Italy, and with
their arms and clothing showing the effects of desperate
struggles. Do you wish to have an idea of their appearance? You will find a perfect type in the first grenadier
put by Gérard at one side of his picture of the battle of
Austerlitz.

At the time of this *fête*, that is to say, in the middle of
the month of July, the First Consul could not have imagined that the moderate conditions he had proposed
after the victory would not be accepted by Austria. In
the hope, therefore, of a peace which could not but be
considered probable, he, for the first time since the establishment of the Consular Government, convoked the
deputies of the departments, and appointed their time of
assembling in Paris for the 1st Vendémiaire, a day which
formed the close of one remarkable century and marked
the commencement of another.

The remains of Marshal Turenne, to which Louis XIV.
had awarded the honours of annihilation by giving them a
place among the royal tombs in the vaults of St. Denis,
had been torn from their grave at the time of the sac-
rilegious violation of the tombs. His bones, mingled in-
discriminately with others, had long lain in obscurity in
a garret of the College of Medicine when M. Lenoir collected and restored them to the ancient tomb of Turenne
in the Musée des Petits Augustins. Bonaparte resolved
to enshrine these relics in that sculptured marble with

which the glory of Turenne could so well dispense. This was, however, intended as a connecting link between the past days of France and the future to which he looked forward. He thought that the sentiments inspired by the solemn honours rendered to the memory of Turenne would dispose the deputies of the departments to receive with greater enthusiasm the pacific communications he hoped to be able to make.

However, the negotiations did not take the favourable turn which the First Consul had expected ; and, notwithstanding all the address of Lucien, the communication was not heard without much uneasiness. But Lucien had prepared a speech quite to the taste of the First Consul. After dilating for some time on the efforts of the Government to obtain peace he deplored the tergiversations of Austria, accused the fatal influence of England, and added in a more elevated and solemn tone, " At the very moment when the Consuls were leaving the Palace of the Government a courier arrived bearing despatches which the First Consul has directed me to communicate to you." He then read a note declaring that the Austrian Government consented to surrender to France the three fortresses of Ulm, Philipsburg, and Ingolstadt. This was considered as a security for the preliminaries of peace being speedily signed. The news was received with enthusiasm, and that anxious day closed in a way highly gratifying to the First Consul.

Whilst victory confirmed in Italy the destinies of the First Consul, his brothers were more concerned about their own interests than the affairs of France. They loved money as much as Bonaparte loved glory. A letter from Lucien to his brother Joseph, which I shall subjoin, shows how ready they always were to turn to their own advantage the glory and fortune of him to whom they were indebted for all their importance. I found this letter among my papers, but I cannot tell why and how I

preserved it.   It is interesting, inasmuch as it shows the
opinion that family of future kings entertained of their
own situation, and of what their fate would have been had
Bonaparte, like Desaix, fallen on the field of Marengo.   It
is, besides, curious to observe the philosopher Lucien
causing *Te Deum* to be chanted with the view of influencing the public funds.   At all events I copy Lucien's
letter as he wrote it, giving the words marked in italics,
and the numerous notes of exclamation which distinguish
the original.

24th June.

My Brother—I send you a courier; I particularly wish that
the First Consul would give me notice of his arrival twenty-four
hours beforehand, and that he would inform *me alone* of the barrier by which he will enter.   The city wishes to prepare triumphal
arches for him, and it deserves not to be disappointed.

At my request a Te Deum was chanted yesterday.   There were
60,000 persons present.

The intrigues of Auteuil [1] continue.   It has been found difficult
to decide between C—— and La F——.   The latter has proposed
his daughter in marriage to me.   Intrigue has been carried to the
last extreme.   I do not know yet whether the High Priest has
decided for one party or the other.   I believe that he would cheat
them both for an Orleans, and your friend of Auteuil was at the
bottom of it all.   The news of the battle of Marengo petrified them,
and yet next day the High Priest certainly spent three hours with
your friend of Auteuil.   As to us, had the victory of Marengo

---

[1] This intrigue, so called from Talleyrand, one of its heads, living in the suburb
of Auteuil, arose from the wish of many of the most influential men to be prepared in case of the death of Napoleon in any action in Italy.   It was simply a con-
tinuation of the same combinations which had been attempted or planned in 1799,
till the arrival of Bonaparte from Egypt made the party choose him as the instrument for the overthrow of the Directors.   There was little secrecy about their
plans; see Miot de Melito (tome i. p. 276), where Joseph Bonaparte tells his friends
all that was being proposed in case his brother fell.   Carnot seems to have been
the most probable choice as leader and replacer of Bonaparte.   In the above letter
" C——," stands for Carnot, "La F——," for La Fayette, the "High Priest "
is Siéyès, and the " friend of Auteuil" is Talleyrand; see Iung's *Lucien*, tome i.
p. 411.   The postscript seems to refer to a wretched scandal about Caroline and
Lucien; see Iung's *Lucien*, tome i. pp. 411, 432–433.   The reader should remark
the retention of this and other documents by Bourrienne, which forms one of the
charges brought against him farther on.

closed the First Consul's career we should now have been proscribed.

Your letters say nothing of what I expected to hear. I hope at
least to be informed of the answer from Vienna before any one. I
am sorry you have not paid me back for the battle of Marengo.

The festival of the 14th of July will be very gratifying. We expect peace as a certainty, and the triumphant return of the First
Consul. The family is all well. Your wife and all her family are
at Morfontaine. Ney is at Paris. Why do you return with the First
Consul ? Peace ! and Italy ! ! Think of our last interview. I
embrace you.

(Signed) Lucien.

On the margin is written—

P.S.—Read the letter addressed to the Consul, and give it to
him *after you have carefully closed it.*

Forward the enclosed. Madame Murat never lodged in my
house. Her husband is a fool, whom his wife ought to punish by
not writing to him for a month.

(Signed) Lucien Bonaparte.

Bonaparte, confirmed in his power by the victory of
Marengo, remained some days longer at Milan to settle
the affairs of Italy. He directed me to furnish Madame
Grassini with money to pay her expenses to Paris.[1] We
departed amidst the acclamations of the inhabitants, and
took the road to Turin. The First Consul stopped at
Turin for some hours, and inspected the citadel, which
had been surrendered to us in pursuance of the capitulation of Alessandria. In passing over Mont Cenis we observed the carriage of Madame Kellerman, who was going
to meet her husband. Bonaparte on recognizing the lady
stopped his carriage and congratulated her on the gallant
conduct of her husband at the battle of Marengo.

On our arrival at Lyons we alighted at the Hôtel des

---

[1] The First Consul saw Madame Grassini at a concert at Milan, and was struck
with her beauty. He was introduced to her, and at the expiration of a few weeks
the Conqueror of Italy counted one conquest more. Madame Grassini proceeded to
Paris, where she subsequently became one of the singers of the Court concerts
(*Mémoires de Constant*).

Célestins, and the loud acclamations of a numerous multitude assembled round the hotel obliged Bonaparte to show himself on the balcony. Next day he proceeded to the Square of Bellecour, where, amidst the plaudits of the people, he laid the first stone of some new buildings destined to efface one of the disasters of the Revolution.

We left Lyons that evening and continued our journey by way of Dijon. On our arrival in that town the joy of the inhabitants was very great. I never saw a more graceful and captivating sight than that which was presented by a group of beautiful young females,[1] crowned with flowers, who accompanied Bonaparte's carriage, and which at that period, when the Revolution had renewed all the republican recollections of Greece and Rome, looked like the chorus of females dancing around the victor at the Olympic games.

But all our journey was not so agreeable. Some accidents awaited us. The First Consul's carriage broke down between Villeneuve-le-Roi and Sens. He sent a courier to inform my mother that he would stop at her house till his carriage was repaired. He dined there, and we started again at seven in the evening.

But we had other disasters to encounter. One of our off-wheels came off, and as we were driving at a very rapid pace the carriage was overturned on the bridge at a short distance from Montreau-Faut-Yonne. The First Consul, who sat on my left, fell upon me, and sustained no injury. My head was slightly hurt by striking against some things which were in the pocket of the carriage ; but this accident was not worth stopping for, and we arrived at Paris on the same night, the 2d of July. Duroc, who was the third in the carriage, was not hurt.

I have already mentioned that Bonaparte was rather

---

[1] Savary (tome i. p. 287), remarking on the extreme joy shown by the ladies of Dijon, remarks, " One of the most beautiful became, later, one of the ornaments of the Court as the Duchess of Bassano," *i.e.* Madame Maret.

talkative when travelling ; and as we were passing through
Burgundy, on our return to Paris from Marengo, he said
exultingly, "Well, a few more events like this campaign,
and I may go down to posterity."—"I think," replied I,
"that you have already done enough to secure great and
lasting fame."—"Yes," resumed he, "I have done enough,
it is true. In less than two years I have won Cairo, Paris,
and Milan ; but for all that, my dear fellow, were I to die
to-morrow I should not at the end of ten centuries occupy
half a page of general history !"

On the very day when Desaix fell on the field of Marengo Kléber was assassinated by a fanatical Mussulman,
named Soleiman Haleby,[1] who stabbed him with a dagger,
and by that blow decided the fate of Egypt. Thus was
France, on the same day, and almost at the same hour, deprived of two of her most distinguished generals. Menou,
as senior in command, succeeded Kléber, and the First
Consul confirmed the appointment. From that moment
the loss of Egypt was inevitable.

I have a few details to give respecting the tragical death
of Kléber. The house of Elfy Bey, which Bonaparte occupied at Cairo, and in which Kléber lived after his departure, had a terrace leading from a *salon* to an old
ruined cistern, from which, down a few steps, there was
an entrance into the garden. The terrace commanded a
view of the grand square of El Beguyeh, which was to the
right on coming out of the *salon*, while the garden was on
the left. This terrace was Bonaparte's favourite prome-

---

[1] "This fellah was, at most, eighteen or twenty years of age : he was a native of
Damascus, and declared that he had quitted his native city by command of the
grand vizier, who had entrusted him with the commission of repairing to Egypt and
killing the grand sultan of the French [Bonaparte being probably intended]. That
for this purpose alone he had left his family, and performed the whole journey on
foot, and had received from the grand vizier no other money than what was absolutely requisite for the exigences of the journey. On arriving at Cairo he had gone
forthwith to perform his devotions in the great mosque, and it was only on the eve
of executing his project that he confided it to one of the scherifs of the mosque "
(*Duc de Rovigo's Memoirs,* tome i. p. 367).

nade, especially in the evenings, when he used to walk up and down and converse with the persons about him. I often advised him to fill up the reservoir, and to make it level with the terrace. I even showed him, by concealing myself in it, and coming suddenly behind him, how easy it would be for any person to attempt his life and then escape, either by jumping into the square, or passing through the garden. He told me I was a coward, and was always in fear of death ; and he determined not to make the alteration I suggested, which, however, he acknowledged to be advisable. Kléber's assassin availed himself of the facility which I so often apprehended might be fatal to Bonaparte.

I shall not stop to refute all the infamous rumours which were circulated respecting Kléber's death. When the First Consul received the unexpected intelligence he could scarcely believe it. He was deeply affected ; and on reading the particulars of the assassination he instantly called to mind how often he had been in the same situation as that in which Kléber was killed, and all I had said respecting the danger of the reservoir—a danger from which it is inconceivable he should have escaped, especially after his Syrian expedition had excited the fury of the natives. Bonaparte's knowledge of Kléber's talents—the fact of his having confided to him the command of the army, and the aid which he constantly endeavoured to transmit to him, repel at once the horrible suspicion of his having had the least participation in the crime, and the thought that he was gratified to hear of it.

It is very certain that Bonaparte's dislike of Kléber was as decided as the friendship he cherished for Desaix. Kléber's fame annoyed him, for he was weak enough to be annoyed at it. He knew the manner in which Kléber spoke of him, which was certainly not the most respectful. During the long and sanguinary siege of St. Jean d'Acre Kléber said to me, " That little scoundrel Bonaparte, who is no higher than my boot, will enslave France. See what a villainous expedition he has succeeded in involving us in." Kléber often made the same remark to others as well as to me. I am not certain that it was ever reported to Bonaparte ; but there is reason to believe that those who found it their interest to accuse others did not spare Kléber.

Kléber, who was a sincere republican, saw and dreaded for his country's sake the secret views and inordinate ambition of Bonaparte. He was a grumbler by nature ; yet he never evinced discontent in the discharge of his duties as a soldier. He swore and stormed, but marched bravely to the cannon's mouth : he was indeed courage personified. One day when he was in the trench at St. Jean d'Acre, standing up, and by his tall stature exposed to every shot, Bonaparte called to him, "Stoop down, Kléber, stoop down ! "—" Why," replied he, " your confounded trench does not reach to my knees." He never regarded the Egyptian expedition with a favourable eye. He thought it too expensive, and utterly useless to France. He was convinced that in the situation in which we stood, without a navy or a powerful Government, it would have been better to have confined our attention to Europe than to have wasted French blood and money on the banks of the Nile, and among the ruined cities of Syria. Kléber, who was a cool, reflecting man, judged Bonaparte without enthusiasm, a thing somewhat rare at that time, and he was not blind to any of his faults.[1]

Bonaparte alleged that Kléber said to him, " *General, you are as great as the world !* " Such a remark is in direct opposition to Kléber's character. He was too sincere to

---

[1] *Erreurs* (tome i. p. 6) suggests that *Moreau* should be substituted here for *Kléber*, as the letters of Kléber show that Kléber did not and that Moreau did dislike the expedition. Thiers (*Consulat*, tome ii. p. 4) describes Kléber as at first "*ardently*" wishing to take part in the expedition, and when in Egypt wishing to return. Kléber was a man disliking command, and not liking to obey.

say anything against his conviction.   Bonaparte, always anxious to keep Egypt, of which the preservation alone could justify the conquest, allowed Kléber to *speak* because he *acted* at the same time.   He knew that Kléber's sense of military duty would always triumph over any opposition he might cherish to his views and plans.   Thus the death of his lieutenant, far from causing Bonaparte any feeling of satisfaction, afflicted him the more, because it almost totally deprived him if the hope of preserving a conquest which had cost France so dear, and which was his work.

The news of the death of Kléber arrived shortly after our return to Paris.   Bonaparte was anxiously expecting accounts from Egypt, none having been received for a considerable time.   The arrival of the courier who brought the fatal intelligence gave rise to a scene which I may relate here.   It was two o'clock in the morning when the courier arrived at the Tuileries.   In his hurry the First Consul could not wait to rouse any one to call me up.   I had informed him some days before that if he should want me during the night he should send for me to the corridor, as I had changed my bedchamber on account of my wife's accouchement.   He came up himself, and instead of knocking at my door knocked at that of my secretary.   The latter immediately rose, and opening the door to his surprise saw the First Consul with a candle in his hand, a Madras handkerchief on his head, and having on his gray greatcoat.   Bonaparte, not knowing of the little step down into the room, slipped and nearly fell.   "Where is Bourrienne?" asked he.   The surprise of my secretary at the apparition of the First Consul can be imagined.   "What, General, is it you?"—"Where is Bourrienne?"   Then my secretary, in his shirt, showed the First Consul my door.   After having told him that he was sorry at having called him up, Napoleon came to me.[1]   I dressed in a hurry, and

[1] After such a circumstantial account it is odd that Miot de Melito (tome i. p. 290) places the reception of this news at Morfontaine, where he himself apparently

we went downstairs to my usual room. We rang several times before they opened the door for us. The guard were not asleep, but having heard so much running to and fro feared we were thieves. At last they opened the door, and the First Consul threw on the table the immense packet of despatches which he had just received. They had been fumigated and steeped in vinegar. When he read the announcement of the death of Kléber the expression of his countenance sufficiently denoted the painful feelings which arose in his mind. I read in his face, *Egypt is lost!*

was. He says that Joseph did not conceal that his brother looked on this as a fresh favour of fortune. Kléber, says Miot, was the personal enemy of Bonaparte, who did not pardon him for abandoning him in Egypt, and as Kléber had a great reputation in the army, if he had returned to France he would have been a redoubtable obstacle to the designs of the First Consul. Savary (tome i. p. 368) describes Napoleon as having already forgotten his grievances against Kléber, and as showing much regret at losing him in such an unfortunate manner.

A similar respect for the slumbers of others will be found in the experience of Meneval (tome i. p. 135 and tome iii. p. 124).

CHAPTER III.

1800–1801.

THE happy events of the campaign of Italy had been
crowned by the armistice, concluded on the 5th of July.
This armistice was broken on the 1st of September, and
renewed after the battle of Hohenlinden.   On his return
from Marengo Bonaparte was received with more enthusiasm than ever.   The rapidity with which, in a campaign
of less than two months, he had restored the triumph of
the French standard, excited universal astonishment.   He
then actively endeavoured to open negotiations with England and Austria ; but difficulties opposed him in every
direction.   He frequently visited the theatre, where his
presence attracted prodigious throngs of persons, all eager
to see and applaud him.

The immense number of letters which were at this time
addressed to the First Consul is scarcely conceivable.

They contained requests for places, protestations of fidelity, and, in short, they were those petitionary circulars that are addressed to all persons in power. These letters were often exceedingly curious, and I have preserved many of them ; among the rest was one from Durosel Beaumanoir, an emigrant who had fled to Jersey. This letter contains some interesting particulars relative to Bonaparte's family. It is dated Jersey, 12th July 1800, and the following are the most remarkable passages it contains :—

I trust, General, that I may, without indiscretion, intrude upon your notice, to remind you of what, I flatter myself, you have not totally forgotten, after having lived eighteen or nineteen years at Ajaccio. But you will, perhaps, be surprised that so trifling an affair should be the subject of the letter which I have the honour to address to you. You cannot have forgotten, General, that when your late father was obliged to take your brothers from the college of Autun, from whence he went to see you at Brienne, he was unprovided with money, and he asked me for twenty-five louis, which I lent him with pleasure. After his return he had no opportunity of paying me, and when I left Ajaccio your mother offered to dispose of some plate in order to pay the debt. To this I objected, and told her that I would wait until she could pay me at her convenience, and previous to the breaking out of the Revolution I believe it was not in her power to fulfil her wish of discharging the debt.

I am sorry, General, to be obliged to trouble you about such a trifle. But such is my unfortunate situation that even this trifle is of some importance to me. Driven from my country, and obliged to take refuge in this island, where everything is exceedingly expensive, the little sum I have mentioned, which was formerly a matter of indifference, would now be of great service to me.

You will understand, General, that at the age of eighty-six, after having served my country well for sixty years, without the least interruption, not counting the time of emigration, chased from every place, I have been obliged to take refuge here, to subsist on the scanty succour given by the English Government to the French emigrant. I say *emigrant* because I have been forced to be one. I had no intention of being one, but a horde of brigands, who came from Caen to my house to assassinate me, considered I had committed a great crime in being the senior general of the canton and in having the Grand Cross of St. Louis: this was too much for them; if it had not been for the cries of my neighbours, my door would have been broken open, and I should have been assassinated; and I had but time to fly by a door at the back, only carrying away what I had on me. At first I retired to Paris, but there they told me that I could do nothing but go into a foreign country, so great was the hate entertained for me by my fellow-citizens, although I lived in retirement, never having any discussion with any one. Thus, General, I have abandoned all I possessed, money and goods, leaving them at the mercy of what they call the nation, which has profited a good deal by this, as I have nothing left in the world, not even a spot to put my foot on. If even a house had been reserved for me, General, I could ask for what depends on you, for I have heard it said that some emigrants have been allowed to return home. I do not even ask this favour, not having a place to rest my foot. And, besides, I have with me here an exiled brother, older than I am, very ill and in perfect second childhood, whom I could not abandon. I am resigned to my own unhappy fate, but my sole and great grief is that not only I myself have been ill-treated, but that my fate has, contrary to the law, injured relations whom I love and respect. I have a mother-in-law, eighty years old, who has been refused the dower I had given her from my property, and this will make me die a bankrupt if nothing is changed, which makes me miserable.

I acknowledge, General, that I know little of the new style, but, according to the old form, I am your humble servant,

DUROSEL BEAUMANOIR.

I read this letter to the First Consul, who immediately said, "Bourrienne, this is sacred! Do not lose a minute. Send the old man ten times the sum. Write to General Durosel that he shall be immediately erased from the list of emigrants. What mischief those brigands of the Convention have done! I can never repair it all." Bonaparte uttered these words with a degree of emotion which I rarely saw him evince. In the evening he asked me whether I had executed his orders, which I had done without losing a moment. The death of M. Frotté had given me a lesson as to the value of time!

Availing myself of the privilege I have already fre-

quently taken of making abrupt transitions from one
subject to another, according as the recollection of past
circumstances occurs to my mind, I shall here note down
a few details, which may not improperly be called *domestic*, and afterwards describe a conspiracy which was
protected by the very man against whom it was hatched.

At the Tuileries, where the First Consul always resided
during the winter and sometimes a part of the summer,
the grand *salon* was situated between his cabinet and the
room in which he received the persons with whom he had
appointed audiences. When in this audience-chamber,
if he wanted anything or had occasion to speak to anybody, he pulled a bell which was answered by a confidential servant named Landoire, who was the messenger
of the First Consul's cabinet. When Bonaparte's bell
rung it was usually for the purpose of making some in-
quiry of me respecting a paper, a name, a date, or some
matter of that sort; and then Landoire had to pass
through the cabinet and *salon* to answer the bell and
afterwards to return and to tell me I was wanted. Impatient at the delay occasioned by this running about,
Bonaparte, without saying anything to me, ordered the
bell to be altered so that it should ring within the cabinet,
and exactly above my table. Next morning when I entered the cabinet I saw a man mounted upon a ladder.
"What are you doing here?" said I. "I am hanging a
bell, sir." I called Landoire and asked him who had
given the order. "The First Consul," he replied. I
immediately ordered the man to come down and remove the ladder, which he accordingly did. When I
went, according to custom, to awaken the First Consul
and read the newspapers to him I said, "General, I found
a man this morning hanging a bell in your cabinet. I was
told it was by your orders; but being convinced there
must be some mistake I sent him away. Surely the bell
was not intended for you, and I cannot imagine it was in-

tended for me : who then could it be for ? "—" What a stupid fellow that Landoire is ! " said Bonaparte. " Yesterday, when Cambacérès was with me, I wanted you. Landoire did not come when I touched the bell. I thought it was broken, and ordered him to get it repaired. I suppose the bell-hanger was doing it when you saw him, for you know the wire passes through the cabinet." I was satisfied with this explanation, though I was not deceived by it. For the sake of appearance he reproved Landoire, who, however, had done nothing more than execute the order he had received. How could he imagine I would submit to such treatment, considering that we had been friends since our boyhood, and that I was now living on full terms of confidence and familiarity with him ?

Before I speak of the conspiracy of Céracchi, Aréna, Topino-Lebrun, and others, I must notice a remark made by Napoleon at St. Helena. He said, or is alleged to have said, " The two attempts which placed me in the greatest danger were those of the sculptor Céracchi and of the fanatic of Schœnbrun." I was not at Schœnbrun at the time ; but I am convinced that Bonaparte was in the most imminent danger. I have been informed on unquestionable authority that Staps set out from Erfurth with the intention of assassinating the Emperor ; but he wanted the necessary courage for executing the design. He was armed with a large dagger, and was twice sufficiently near Napoleon to have struck him. I heard this from Rapp, who seized Staps, and felt the hilt of the dagger under his coat. On that occasion Bonaparte owed his life only to the irresolution of the young *illuminato* who wished to sacrifice him to his fanatical fury. It is equally certain that on another occasion, respecting which the author of the St. Helena narrative observes complete silence, another fanatic more dangerous than Staps attempted the life of Napoleon.[1]

[1] At the time of this second attempt I was not with Napoleon ; but he directed me

The following is a correct statement of the facts relative to Céracchi's conspiracy. The plot itself was a mere shadow ; but it was deemed advisable to give it substance, to exaggerate, at least in appearance, the danger to which the First Consul had been exposed :—

There was at that time in Paris an idle fellow called Harrel ; he had been a *chef de bataillon,* but he had been dismissed the service, and was consequently dissatisfied. He became connected with Cérracchi, Aréna, Topino-Lebrun, and Demerville. From different motives all these individuals were violently hostile to the First Consul, who, on his part, was no friend to Cérracchi and Aréna, but scarcely knew the two others. These four individuals formed, in conjunction with Harrel, the design of assassinating the First Consul, and the time fixed for the perpetration of the deed was one evening when Bonaparte intended to visit the opera.

On the 20th of September 1800 Harrel came to me at the Tuileries. He revealed to me the plot in which he was engaged, and promised that his accomplices should be apprehended in the very act if I would supply him with money to bring the plot to maturity. I knew not how to act upon this disclosure, which I, however, could not reject without incurring too great a responsibility. I immediately communicated the business to the First Consul, who ordered me to supply Harrel with money ; but not to mention the affair to Fouché, to whom he wished to prove that he knew better how to manage the police than he did.

Harrel came nearly every evening at eleven o'clock to inform me of the progress of the conspiracy, which I immediately communicated to the First Consul, who was not sorry to find Aréna and Céracchi deeply committed. But the time passed on, and nothing was done. The First

---

to see the madman who had formed the design of assassinating him. It will be seen in the course of these Memoirs what were his plans, and what was the result of them.—*Bourrienne.*

Consul began to grow impatient. At length Harrel came to say that they had no money to purchase arms. Money was given him. He, however, returned next day to say that the gunsmith refused to sell them arms without authority. It was now found necessary to communicate the business to Fouché in order that he might grant the necessary permission to the gunsmith, which I was not empowered to do.

On the 10th of October the Consuls, after the breaking up of the Council, assembled in the cabinet of their colleague. Bonaparte asked them in my presence whether they thought he ought to go to the opera. They observed that as every precaution was taken no danger could be apprehended, and that it was desirable to show the futility of attempts against the First Consul's life. After dinner Bonaparte put on a greatcoat over his green uniform and got into his carriage accompanied by me and Duroc. He seated himself in front of his box, which at that time was on the left of the theatre between the two columns which separated the front and side boxes. When we had been in the theatre about half an hour the First Consul directed me to go and see what was doing in the corridor. Scarcely had I left the box than I heard a great uproar, and soon discovered that a number of persons, whose names I could not learn, had been arrested. I informed the First Consul of what I had heard, and we immediately returned to the Tuileries.

It is certain that the object of the conspiracy was to take the First Consul's life, and that the conspirators neglected nothing which could further the accomplishment of their atrocious design. The plot, however, was known through the disclosures of Harrel ; and it would have been easy to avert instead of conjuring up the storm. Such was, and such still is, my opinion. Harrel's name was again restored to the army list, and he was appointed commandant of Vincennes. This post he held at the time of the Duc d'Enghien's assassination. I was afterwards told that his wife was foster-sister to the unfortunate prince, and that she recognised him when he entered the prison which in a few short hours was to prove his grave.

Carbonneau, one of the individuals condemned, candidly confessed the part he had taken in the plot, which he said was brought to maturity solely by the agents of the police, who were always eager to prove their zeal to their employers by some new discovery.

Although three months intervened between the machinations of Céracchi and Aréna and the horrible attempt of the 3d Nivôse, I shall relate these two events in immediate succession ; for if they had no other points of resemblance they were at least alike in their object. The conspirators in the first affair were of the revolutionary faction. They sought Bonaparte's life as if with the view of rendering his resemblance to Cæsar so complete that not even a Brutus should be wanting. The latter, it must with regret be confessed, were of the Royalist party, and in their wish to destroy the First Consul they were not deterred by the fear of sacrificing a great number of citizens.

The police knew nothing of the plot of the 3d Nivôse for two reasons ; first, because they were no parties to it, and secondly, because two conspirators do not betray and sell each other when they are resolute in their purpose. In such cases the giving of information can arise only from two causes, the one excusable, the other infamous, viz. the dread of punishment, and the hope of reward. But neither of these causes influenced the conspirators of the 3d Nivôse, the inventors and constructors of that machine which has so justly been denominated *infernal!*

On the 3d Nivôse (24th December 1800) the first performance of Haydn's magnificent oratorio of the "Creation" took place at the opera, and the First Consul had expressed his intention of being present. I did not dine with him that day, but as he left me he said, "Bourrienne, you know I am going to the opera to-night, and you may go too ; but I cannot take you in the carriage, as Lannes, Berthier, and Lauriston are going with me." I was very glad of this, for I much wished to hear one of the master-pieces of the German school of composition. I got to the opera before Bonaparte, who on his entrance seated himself, according to custom, in front of the box. The eyes of all present were fixed upon him, and he appeared to be perfectly calm and self-possessed. Lauriston, as soon as he saw me, came to my box, and told me that the First Consul, on his way to the opera, had narrowly escaped being assassinated in the Rue St. Nicaise by the explosion of a barrel of gunpowder, the concussion of which had shattered the windows of his carriage. " Within ten seconds after our escape," added Lauriston, " the coachman having turned the corner of the Rue St. Honoré, stopped to take the First Consul's orders ; and he coolly said, ' To the opera.' "[1]

[1] The following particulars respecting the affair of the infernal machine are related by Rapp, who attended Madame Bonaparte to the opera. He differs from Bour-rienne as to the total ignorance of the police :—

" The affair of the infernal machine has never been properly understood by the public. The police had intimated to Napoleon that an attempt would be made against his life, and cautioned him not to go out. Madame Bonaparte, Mademoi-selle Beauharnais, Madame Murat, Lannes, Bessières, the *aide de camp* on duty, Lieutenant Lebrun, now Duke of Piacenza, were all assembled in the *salon*, while the First Consul was writing in his cabinet. Hadyn's oratorio was to be performed that evening ; the ladies were anxious to hear the music, and we also expressed a wish to that effect. The escort piquet was ordered out ; and Lannes requested that Napoleon would join the party. He consented ; his carriage was ready, and he took along with him Bessières and the *aide de camp* on duty. I was directed to attend the ladies. Josephine had received a magnificent shawl from Constantinople, and she that evening wore it for the first time. ' Permit me to observe,' said I, ' that your shawl is not thrown on with your usual elegance.' She good-humouredly begged that I would fold it after the fashion of the Egyptian ladies. While I was engaged in this operation we heard Napoleon depart. ' Come, sister,' said Madame Murat, who was impatient to get to the theatre ; ' Bonaparte is going.' We stepped into the carriage : the First Consul's equipage had already reached the middle of the Place du Carrousel. We drove after it, but we had scarcely entered the place when the machine exploded. Napoleon escaped by a singular chance. St. Régent, or his servant François, had stationed himself in the middle of the Rue Nicaise. A grena-dier of the escort, supposing he was really what he appeared to be, a water-carrier, gave him a few blows with the flat of his sabre and drove him off. The cart was turned round, and the machine exploded, between the carriages of Napoleon and

On hearing this I left the theatre and returned to the Palace, under the expectation that I should speedily be wanted. Bonaparte soon returned home, and as intelligence of the affair had spread through Paris the grand *salon* on the ground-floor was filled with a crowd of functionaries, eager to read in the eye of their master what they were to think and say on the occasion. He did not keep them long in suspense. "This," exclaimed he vehemently, "is the work of the Jacobins: they have attempted my life! . . . There are neither nobles, priests, nor Chouans in this affair! . . . I know what I am about, and they need not think to impose on me. These are the Septembrizers who have been in open revolt and conspiracy, and arrayed against every succeeding Government. It is scarce three months since my life was attempted by Céracchi, Aréna, Topino-Lebrun, and Demerville. They all belong to one gang! The cut-throats of September, the assassins of Versailles, the brigands of the 31st of May, the conspirators of Prairial are the authors of all the crimes committed against established Governments! If they cannot be checked they must be crushed! France must be purged of these ruffians!" It is impossible to form any idea of the bitterness with which Bonaparte pronounced these words. In vain did some of the Councillors of State, and Fouché in particular, endeavour to point out to him that there was no evidence against any one, and that before he pronounced people to be guilty it would be right to ascertain

Josephine. The ladies shrieked on hearing the report; the carriage windows were broken, and Mademoiselle Beanharnais received a slight hurt on her hand. I alighted and crossed the Rue Nicaise, which was strewed with the bodies of those who had been thrown down, and the fragments of the walls that had been shattered by the explosion. Neither the Consul nor any individual of his suite sustained any serious injury. When I entered the theatre Napoleon was seated in his box, calm and composed, and looking at the audience through his opera-glass. Fouché was beside him, 'Josephine?' said he, as soon as he observed me. She entered at that moment, and he did not finish his question. 'The rascals,' said he very coolly, 'wanted to blow me up. Bring me a book of the oratorio'" (*Memoirs of General Count Rapp*, p. 19).

the fact. Bonaparte repeated with increased violence what he had before said of the Jacobins; thus adding, not without some ground of suspicion, one crime more to the long catalogue for which they had already to answer.

Fouché had many enemies, and I was not, therefore, surprised to find some of the Ministers endeavouring to take advantage of the difference between his opinion and that of the First Consul; and it must be owned that the utter ignorance of the police respecting this event was a circumstance not very favourable to Fouché. He, however, was like the reed in the fable—he bent with the wind, but was soon erect again. The most skilful actor could scarcely imitate the inflexible calmness he maintained during Bonaparte's paroxysm of rage, and the patience with which he allowed himself to be accused.

Fouché, when afterwards conversing with me, gave me clearly to understand that he did not think the Jacobins guilty. I mentioned this to the First Consul, but nothing could make him retract his opinion. " Fouché," said he, " has good reason for his silence. He is serving his own party. It is very natural that he should seek to screen a set of men who are polluted with blood and crimes ! He was one of their leaders. Do not I know what he did at Lyons and the Loire ? That explains Fouché's conduct now ! "

This is the exact truth ; and now let me contradict one of the thousand fictions about this event. It has been said and printed that "the dignitaries and the Ministers were assembled at the Tuileries. 'Well,' said the First Consul, advancing angrily towards Fouché, 'will you still say that this is the Royalist party?' Fouché, better informed than was believed, answered coolly, ' Yes, certainly, I shall say so ; and, what is more, I shall prove it.' This speech caused general astonishment, but was afterwards fully borne out." This is pure invention. The First Consul only said to Fouché, "I do not trust to your police; I guard myself, and I watch till two in the morning." This however, was very rarely the case.

On the day after the explosion of the infernal machine a considerable concourse assembled at the Tuileries. There was absolutely a torrent of congratulations. The prefect of the Seine convoked the twelve mayors of Paris and came at their head to wait on the First Consul. In his reply to their address Bonaparte said, " As long as this gang of assassins confined their attacks to me personally I left the law to take its course ; but since, by an unparalleled crime, they have endangered the lives of a portion of the population of Paris, their punishment must be as prompt as exemplary. A hundred of these wretches who have libelled liberty by perpetrating crimes in her name must be effectually prevented from renewing their atrocities." He then conversed with the Ministers, the Councillors of State, etc., on the event of the preceding day ; and as all knew the First Consul's opinion of the authors of the crime each was eager to confirm it. The Council was several times assembled when the Senate was consulted, and the adroit Fouché, whose conscience yielded to the delicacy of his situation, addressed to the First Consul a report worthy of a Mazarin. At the same time the journals were filled with recollections of the Revolution, raked up for the purpose of connecting with past crimes the individuals on whom it was now wished to cast odium. It was decreed that a hundred persons should be banished ; and the Senate established its character for complaisance by passing a *Sénatus-consulte* conformable to the wishes of the First Consul.

A list was drawn up of the persons styled Jacobins, who were condemmed to transportation. I was fortunate enough to obtain the erasure of the names of several whose opinions had perhaps been violent, but whose education and private character presented claims to recommendation. Some of my readers may probably recollect them without my naming them, and I shall only mention M. Tissot, for the purpose of recording, not the service I rendered him, but an instance of grateful acknowledgment.

When in 1815 Napoleon was on the point of entering Paris M. Tissot came to the prefecture of police, where I then was, and offered me his house as a safe asylum, assuring me I should there run no risk of being discovered. Though I did not accept the offer yet I gladly seize on this opportunity of making it known. It is gratifying to find that difference of political opinion does not always exclude sentiments of generosity and honour! I shall never forget the way in which the author of the essays on Virgil uttered the words *Domus mea.*

But to return to the fatal list. Even while I write this I shudder to think of the way in which men utterly innocent were accused of a revolting crime without even the shadow of a proof. The name of an individual, his opinions, perhaps only assumed, were sufficient grounds for his banishment. A decree of the Consuls, dated 4th of January 1801, confirmed by a *Sénatus-consulte* on the next day, banished from the territory of the Republic, and placed under special inspectors, 130 individuals, nine of whom were merely designated in the report as Septembrizers.

The exiles, who in the reports and in the public acts were so unjustly accused of being the authors of the infernal machine, were received at Nantes, with so much indignation that the military were compelled to interfere to save them from being massacred.

In the discussions which preceded the decree of the Consuls few persons had the courage to express a doubt respecting the guilt of the accused. Truguet was the first to mount the breach. He observed that without denying the Government the extraordinary means for getting rid of its enemies he could not but acknowledge that the emigrants threatened the purchasers of national domains, that the public mind was corrupted by pamphlets, and that——Here the First Consul, interrupting him, exclaimed, "To what pamphlets do you allude?"—"To pamphlets which are publicly circulated."—"Name them!"—"You know them as well as I do."[1]

After a long and angry ebullition the First Consul abruptly dismissed the Council. He observed that he would not be duped; that the villains were known; that they were Septembrizers, the hatchers of every mischief. He had said at a sitting three days before, "If proof should fail, we must take advantage of the public excitement. The event is to me merely the opportunity. They shall be banished for the 2d September, for the 31st May, for Babœuf's conspiracy—or anything else."

On leaving one of the sittings of the Council, at which the question of a special tribunal had been discussed, he told me that he had been a little ruffled; that he had said a violent blow must be struck; that blood must be spilt; and that as many of the guilty should be shot as there had been victims of the explosion (from fifteen to twenty); that 200 should be banished, and the Republic purged of these scoundrels.

The arbitrariness and illegality of the proceeding were so evident that the *Sénatus-consulte* contained no mention of the transactions of the 3d Nivôse, which was very remarkable. It was, however, declared that the measure of the previous day had been adopted with a view to the preservation of the Constitution. This was promising.

The First Consul manifested the most violent hatred of the Jacobins; for this he could not have been blamed if under the title of Jacobins he had not comprised every devoted advocate of public liberty. Their opposition annoyed him, and he could never pardon them for having presumed to condemn his tyrannical acts, and to resist the

---

[1] The *Parallel between Cæsar, Cromwell, and Bonaparte,* of which I shall speak a little farther on, is here alluded to.—*Bourrienne.*

destruction of the freedom which he had himself sworn to
defend, but which he was incessantly labouring to overturn.   These were the true motives of his conduct ; and,
concious of his own faults, he regarded with dislike those
who saw and disapproved of them.   For this reason he
was more afraid of those whom he called Jacobins than
of the Royalists.

I am here recording the faults of Bonaparte, but I excuse him ; situated as he was, any other person would
have acted in the same way.   Truth now reached him
with difficulty, and when it was not agreeable he had no
disposition to hear it.   He was surrounded by flatterers ;
and the greater number of those who approached him, far
from telling him what they really thought, only repeated
what he had himself been thinking.   Hence he admired
the wisdom of his Counsellors.   Thus Fouché, to maintain himself in favour, was obliged to deliver up to his
master 130 names chosen from among his own most intimate friends as objects of proscription.

Meanwhile Fouché, still believing that he was not deceived as to the real authors of the attempt of the 3d Nivôse, set in motion with his usual dexterity all the springs
of the police.   His efforts, however, were for some time
unsuccessful ; but at length on Saturday, the 31st January
1801, about two hours after our arrival at Malmaison,
Fouché presented himself and produced authentic proofs
of the accuracy of his conjectures.   There was no longer
any doubt on the subject ; and Bonaparte saw clearly
that the attempt of the 3d Nivôse was the result of a plot
hatched by the partisans of royalty.   But as the act of
proscription against those who were jumbled together
under the title of *the Jacobins* had been executed, it was
not to be revoked.

Thus the consequence of the 3d Nivôse was that both
the innocent and guilty were punished ; with this difference,
however, that the guilty at least had the benefit of a trial.

When the Jacobins, as they were called, were accused with such precipitation, Fouché had no positive proofs of their innocence ; and therefore their illegal condemnation ought not to be attributed to him. Sufficient odium is attached to his memory without his being charged with a crime he never committed. Still, I must say that had he boldly opposed the opinion of Bonaparte in the first burst of his fury he might have averted the blow. Every time he came to the Tuileries, even before he had acquired any traces of the truth, Fouché always declared to me his conviction of the innocence of the persons first accused. But he was afraid to make the same observation to Bonaparte. I often mentioned to him the opinion of the Minister of Police ; but as proof was wanting he replied to me with a triumphant air, " Bah! bah ! This is always the way with Fouché. Besides, it is of little consequence. At any rate I shall get rid of them. Should the guilty be discovered among the Royalists they also shall be punished."

The real criminals being at length discovered through the researches of Fouché, St. Régent and Carbon expiated their crimes by the forfeit of their heads. Thus the First Consul gained his point, and justice gained hers.[1]

I have often had occasion to notice the multifarious means employed by Bonaparte to arrive at the possession of supreme power, and to prepare men's minds for so great a change. Those who have observed his life must have also remarked how entirely he was convinced of the truth that public opinion wastes itself on the rumour of a project, and possesses no energy at the moment of its execution. In order, therefore, to direct public attention to the

[1] It was St. Régent, or St. Réjeant, who fired the infernal machine. The violence of the shock flung him against a post and part of his breast bone was driven in. He was obliged to resort to a surgeon, and it would seem that this man denounced him (*Memoirs of Miot de Melito*, tome i. p. 354).

The discussions which took place in the Council of State on this affair are remarkable, both for the violence of Napoleon and for the resistance made in the Council, to a great extent successfully, to his views as to the plot being one of the Jacobin party.

question of hereditary power a pamphlet was circulated about Paris, and the following is the history of it :—

In the month of December 1800, while Fouché was searching after the real authors of the attempt of the 3d Nivôse, a small pamphlet, entitled "*Parallel between Cæsar, Cromwell, and Bonaparte,*" was sent to the First Consul. He was absent when it came. I read it, and perceived that it openly advocated hereditary monarchy. I then knew nothing about the origin of this pamphlet, but I soon learned that it issued from the office of the Minister of the Interior [Lucien Bonaparte], and that it had been largely circulated. After reading it I laid it on the table. In a few minutes Bonaparte entered, and taking up the pamphlet pretended to look through it : "Have you read this ? " said he.—"Yes, General."—"Well! what is your opinion of it ? "—"I think it is calculated to produce an unfavourable effect on the public mind : it is ill-timed, for it prematurely reveals your views." The First Consul took the pamphlet and threw it on the ground, as he did all the stupid publications of the day after having slightly glanced over them. I was not singular in my opinion of the pamphlet, for next day the préfets in the immediate neighbourhood of Paris sent a copy of it to the First Consul, complaining of its mischievous effect ; and I recollect that in one of their letters it was stated that such a work was calculated to direct against him the poniards of new assassins. After reading this correspondence he said to me, "Bourrienne, send for Fouché ; he must come directly, and give an account of this matter." In half an hour Fouché was in the First Consul's cabinet. No sooner had he entered than the following dialogue took place, in which the impetuous warmth of the one party was strangely contrasted with the phlegmatic and rather sardonic composure of the other.

"What pamphlet is this? What is said about it in Paris?"—"General, there is but one opinion of its dangerous tendency."—"Well, then, why did you allow it to appear?"—"General, I was obliged to show some consideration for the author!"—"Consideration for the author! What do you mean? You should have sent him to the Temple."—"But, General, your brother Lucien patronises this pamphlet. It has been printed and published by his order. In short, it comes from the office of the Minister of the Interior."—"No matter for that! Your duty as Minister of Police was to have arrested Lucien, and sent him to the Temple. The fool does nothing but contrive how he can commit me!"

With these words the First Consul left the cabinet, shutting the door violently behind him. Being now alone with Fouché, I was eager to get an explanation of the suppressed smile which had more than once curled his lips during Bonaparte's angry expostulation. I easily perceived that there was something in reserve. "Send the author to the Temple!" said Fouché; "that would be no easy matter! Alarmed at the effect which this parallel between Cæsar, Cromwell, and Bonaparte was likely to produce, I went to Lucien to point out to him his imprudence. He made me no answer, but went and got a manuscript, which he showed me, and which contained corrections and annotations in the First Consul's handwriting."

When Lucien heard how Bonaparte had expressed his displeasure at the pamphlet, he also came to the Tuileries to reproach his brother with having thrust him forward and then abandoned him. "'Tis your own fault," said the First Consul. "You have allowed yourself to be caught! So much the worse for you! Fouché is too cunning for you! You are a mere fool compared with him!" Lucien tendered his resignation, which was accepted, and he departed for Spain. This diplomatic mission turned to his advantage. It was necessary that time should veil the Machiavelian invention of the *Par-*

allel.[1] Lucien, among other instructions, was directed to use all his endeavours to induce Spain to declare against Portugal in order to compel that power to separate herself from England.

The First Consul had always regarded Portugal as an English colony, and he conceived that to attack it was to assail England. He wished that Portugal should no longer favour England in her commercial relations, but that, like Spain, she should become dependent on him. Lucien was therefore sent as ambassador to Madrid, to second the Ministers of Charles IV. in prevailing on the King to invade Portugal. The King declared war, but it was not of long duration, and terminated almost without a blow being struck, by the taking of Olivenza. On the 6th of June 1801 Portugal signed the treaty of Badajoz, by which she promised to cede Olivenza, Almeida, and some other fortresses to Spain, and to close her ports against England. The First Consul, who was dissatisfied with the treaty, at first refused to ratify it. He still kept his army in Spain, and this proceeding determined Portugal to accede to some slight alterations in the first treaty. This business proved very advantageous to Lucien and Godoy.

The cabinet of the Tuileries was not the only place in which the question of hereditary succession was discussed. It was the constant subject of conversation in the *salons*

---

[1] The *Parallel* has been attributed to different writers; some phrases seemed the work of Lucien, but, says Thiers (tome ii. p. 210), its rare elegance of language and its classical knowledge of history should attribute it to its real author, Fontanes. Joseph Bonaparte (*Erreurs*, tome i. p. 270) says that Fontanes wrote it, and Lucien Bonaparte corrected it. See *Meneval*, tome iii. p. 105. Whoever wrote it, Napoleon certainly planned its issue. "It was," said he to Rœderer, "a work of which he himself had given the idea, but the last pages were by a fool" (*Miot*, tome i. p. 318). See also *Lanfrey*, tome ii. p. 208; and compare the story in Iung's *Lucien*, tome ii. p. 490. Miot, then in the confidence of Joseph, says, that Lucien's removal from office was the result of an angry quarrel between him and Fouché in the presence of Napoleon, when Fouché attacked Lucien, not only for the pamphlet, but also for the disorder of his public and his private life; but Miot (tome i. p. 319) fixes the date of this as the 3d November, while Bourrienne dates the disapproval of the pamphlet as in December.

of Paris, where a new dynasty was already spoken of.
This was by no means displeasing to the First Consul;
but he saw clearly that he had committed a mistake in
agitating the question prematurely; for this reason he
waged war against the *Parallel*, as he would not be suspected of having had any share in a design that had failed.
One day he said to me, "I believe I have been a little too
precipitate. The pear is not quite ripe!" The Consulate
for life was accordingly postponed till 1802, and the hereditary empire till 1804.

After the failure of the artful publication of the pamphlet Fouché invited me to dine with him. As the First
Consul wished me to dine out as seldom as possible, I informed him of the invitation I had received. He was,
however, aware of it before, and he very readily gave me
leave to go. At dinner Joseph was placed on the right
of Fouché, and I next to Joseph, who talked of nothing
but his brother, his designs, the pamphlet, and the bad
effect produced by it. In all that fell from him there was
a tone of blame and disapproval. I told him my opinion,
but with greater reserve than I had used towards his
brother. He seemed to approve of what I said; his
confidence encouraged me, and I saw with pleasure that
he entertained sentiments entirely similar to my own.
His unreserved manner so imposed upon me that, notwithstanding the experience I had acquired, I was far from
suspecting myself to be in the company of a spy. Next
day the First Consul said to me very coldly, "Leave my
letters in the basket, I will open them myself." This unexpected direction surprised me exceedingly, and I determined to play him a trick in revenge for his unfounded
distrust. For three mornings I laid at the bottom of the
basket all the letters which I knew came from the Ministers, and all the reports which were addressed to me for the
First Consul. I then covered them over with those which,
judging from their envelopes and seals, appeared to be

of that trifling kind with which the First Consul was daily overwhelmed : these usually consisted of requests that he would name the number of a lottery ticket, so that the writer might have the benefit of *his* good luck—solicitations that he would stand godfather to a child—petitions for places—announcements of marriages and births—absurd eulogies, etc. Unaccustomed to open the letters, he became impatient at their number, and he opened very few. Often on the same day, but always on the morrow, came a fresh letter from a Minister, who asked for an answer to his former one, and who complained of not having received one. The First Consul unsealed some twenty letters and left the rest.

The opening of all these letters, which he was not at other times in the habit of looking at, annoyed him extremely ; but as I neither wished to carry the joke too far, nor to remain in the disagreeable position in which Joseph's treachery had placed me, I determined to bring the matter to a conclusion. After the third day, when the business of the night, which had been interrupted by little fits of ill-humour, was concluded, Bonaparte retired to bed. Half an hour after I went to his chamber, to which I was admitted at all hours. I had a candle in my hand, and, taking a chair, I sat down on the right side of the bed, and placed the candle on the table. Both he and Josephine awoke. "What is the matter?" he asked with surprise. "General, I have come to tell you that I can no longer remain here, since I have lost your confidence. You know how sincerely I am devoted to you ; if you have, then, anything to reproach me with, let me at least know it, for my situation during the last three days has been very painful."—"What has Bourrienne done?" inquired Josephine earnestly. "That does not concern you," he replied. Then turning to me he said, "'Tis true, I have cause to complain of you. I have been informed that you have spoken of important affairs in a very indiscreet manner."—"I can assure you that I spoke to none but your brother. It was he who led me into the conversation, and he was too well versed in the business for me to tell him any secret. He may have reported to you what he pleased, but could not I do the same by him? I could accuse and betray him as he has accused and betrayed me. When I spoke in confidence to your brother, could I regard him as an inquisitor?"—"I must confess," replied Bonaparte, "that after what I heard from Joseph I thought it right to put my confidence in quarantine."—"The quarantine has lasted three days, General; surely that is long enough."—"Well, Bourrienne, let us say no more about it. Open my letters as usual; you will find the answers a good deal in arrear, which has much vexed me; and besides, I was always stumbling on some stupid nonsense or other!"

I fancy I still see and hear the amiable Josephine sitting up in bed and saying, in her gentle way, "What! Bonaparte, is it possible you could suspect Bourrienne, who is so attached to you, and who is your only friend? How could you suffer such a snare to be laid for him? What! a dinner got up on purpose! How I hate these odious police manœuvres!"—"Go to sleep," said Bonaparte; let women mind their gewgaws, and not interfere with politics." It was near two in the morning before I retired.

When, after a few hours' sleep, I again saw the First Consul, he was more kind to me than ever, and I perceived that for the present every cloud had dispersed.[1]

---

[1] Joseph Bonaparte (*Erreurs*, tome i. p. 273) says what he reported to his brother was Bourrienne's conversation to him in the First Consul's cabinet during Napoleon's absence. It is curious that at the only time when Napoleon became dissatisfied with Meneval (Bourrienne's successor), and ordered him not to open the letters, he used the same expression when returning to the usual order of business, which in this case was in a few hours. "My dear Meneval," said he, "there are circumstances in which I am forced to put my confidence in quarantine" (*Meneval*, tome i. p. 123). For any one who has had to manage an office it is pleasant to find that even Napoleon was much dependent on a good secretary. In an illness of his second secretary he said, showing the encumbrance of his desk, "With Meneval I should soon clear off all that" (*Meneval, tomo* i. p. 151).

CHAPTER IV.

1800–1801.

THE armistice concluded after the battle of Marengo,
which had been first broken and then resumed, continued
to be observed for some time between the armies of the
Rhine and Italy and the Imperial armies.   But Austria,
bribed by a subsidy of 2,000,000 sterling, would not treat
for peace without the participation of England.   She did
not despair of recommencing the war successfully.

M. de St. Julien had signed preliminaries at Paris ; but
the Court of Vienna disavowed them, and Duroc, whom
Bonaparte sent to convey the preliminaries to Vienna for
the Imperial ratification, was not permitted to pass the
Austrian advance posts.   This unexpected proceeding,
the result of the all-powerful influence of England, justly
incensed the First Consul, who had given decided proofs
of moderation and a wish for peace.   "I want peace,"
said he to me, " to enable me to organise the interior ;
the people also want it.   You see the conditions I offer.
Austria, though beaten, obtains all she got at Campo-
Formio.   What can she want more ?   I could make fur-

ther exactions; but, without fearing the reverses of 1799, I must think of the future. Besides, I want tranquillity, to enable me to settle the affairs of the interior, and to send aid to Malta and Egypt. But I will not be trifled with. I will force an immediate decision!"

In his irritation the First Consul despatched orders to Moreau, directing him to break the armistice and resume hostilities unless he regained possession of the bridges of the Rhine and the Danube by the surrender of Philipsburg, Ulm, and Ingolstadt. The Austrians then offered to treat with France on new bases. England wished to take part in the Congress, but to this the First Consul would not consent until she should sign a separate armistice and cease to make common cause with Austria.

The First Consul received intelligence of the occupation of the three garrisons on the 23d of September, the day he had fixed in his ultimatum to England for the renewal of hostilities. But for the meanwhile he was satisfied with the concessions of Austria : that power, in the expectation of being supported by England, asked her on what terms she was to treat.

During these communications with Austria M. Otto was in London negotiating for the exchange of prisoners. England would not hear of an armistice by sea like that which France had concluded with Austria by land. She alleged that, in case of a rupture, France would derive from that armistice greater advantage than Austria would gain by that already concluded. The difficulty and delay attending the necessary communications rendered these reasons plausible. The First Consul consented to accept other propositions from England, and to allow her to take part in the discussions of Luneville, but on condition that she should sign a treaty with him without the intervention of Austria. This England refused to do. Weary of this uncertainty, and the tergiversation of Austria, which was still under the influence of England, and feeling that

the prolongation of such a state of things could only turn
to his disadvantage, Bonaparte broke the armistice. He
had already consented to sacrifices which his successes in
Italy did not justify. The hope of an immediate peace
had alone made him lose sight of the immense advantages
which victory had given him.

Far from appearing sensible to the many proofs of
moderation which the First Consul evinced, the combined
insolence of England and Austria seemed only to increase.
Orders were immediately given for resuming the offensive in Germany and Italy, and hostilities then recommenced.

The chances of fortune were long doubtful. After a re-
verse Austria made promises, and after an advantage she
evaded them ; but finally, fortune proved favourable to
France. The French armies in Italy and Germany crossed
the Mincio and the Danube, and the celebrated battle of
Hohenlinden brought the French advanced posts within
ten leagues of Vienna. This victory secured peace ; for,
profiting by past experience, the First Consul would not
hear of any suspension of arms until Austria should consent to a separate treaty. Driven into her last intrench-
ments, Austria was obliged to yield. She abandoned England ; and the English Cabinet, in spite of the subsidy of
2,000,000 sterling, consented to the separation. Great
Britain was forced to come to this arrangement in consequence of the situation to which the successes of the army
of Moreau had reduced Austria, which it was certain would
be ruined by longer resistance.

England wished to enter into negotiations at Luneville.
To this the First Consul acceded ; but, as he saw that
England was seeking to deceive him, he required that
she should suspend hostilities with France, as Austria had
done. Bonaparte very reasonably alleged that an indefinite armistice on the Continent would be more to the disadvantage of France than a long armistice by sea would

MOREAU.

be unfavourable to England.   All this adjourned the preliminaries to 1801 and the peace to 1802.

The impatience and indignation of the First Consul had
been highly excited by the evasions of Austria and the
plots of England, for he knew all the intrigues that were
carrying on for the restoration of the Bourbons.   His joy
may be therefore conceived when the battle of Hohenlinden
balanced the scale of fortune in his favour.   On the 3d of
December 1800 Moreau gained that memorable victory
which at length put an end to the hesitations of the Cabinet of Vienna.[1]

On the 6th of December the First Consul received intelligence of the battle of Hohenlinden.   It was on a
Saturday, and he had just returned from the theatre when
I delivered the despatches to him.   He literally danced
for joy.   I must say that he did not expect so important
a result from the movements of the army of the Rhine.
This victory gave a new face to his negotiations for peace,
and determined the opening of the Congress of Luneville,
which took place on the 1st of January following.

On receiving information of the battle of Hohenlinden,
Madame Moreau came to the Tuileries to call on the First
Consul and Madame Bonaparte.   She did not see them,
and repeated her calls several times with no better success.   The last time she came she was accompanied by her
mother, Madame Hulot.   She waited for a considerable
time in vain, and when she was going away her mother,
who could no longer restrain her feelings, said aloud, before me and several persons of the household, that "it ill
became the wife of the conqueror of Hohenlinden to dance
attendance in this way."   This remark reached the ears of

---

[1] On the eve of the battle of Hohenlinden Moreau was at supper with his *aides de
camp* and several general officers, when a despatch was delivered to him.   After he
had read it he said to his guests, though he was far from being in the habit of boasting, "I am here made acquainted with Baron Kray's movements.   They are all I
could wish.   To-morrow we will take from him 10,000 prisoners."   Moreau took 40,-
000, besides a great many flags.—*Bourrienne.*

those to whom it was directed. Madame Moreau shortly after rejoined her husband in Germany ; and some time after her departure Madame Hulot came to Malmaison to solicit promotion for her eldest son, who was in the navy. Josephine received Madame Hulot very kindly, and requested her to stay to dinner. She accepted the invitation. The First Consul, who did not see her until the hour of dinner, treated her very coolly : he said little to her, and retired as soon as dinner was over. His rudeness was so marked and offensive that Josephine, who was always kind and amiable, thought it necessary to apologise, by observing that his mind was disturbed by the non-arrival of a courier whom he expected.

Bonaparte entertained no dislike of Moreau, because he did not fear him ; and after the battle of Hohenlinden he spoke of him in the highest terms, and frankly acknowledged the services he had rendered on that important occasion ; but he could not endure his wife's family, who, he said, were a set of intriguers.[1]

Luneville having been fixed upon for the Congress, the First Consul sent his brother Joseph to treat with Count Louis de Cobentzel. On his way Joseph met M. de Cobentzel, who had passed Luneville, and was coming to Paris to sound the sentiments of the French Government. Joseph returned to Paris with him. After some conversation with the First Consul they set out next day for Luneville, of which place Bonaparte appointed General Clarke governor. This appeared to satisfy Clarke, who was very anxious to be something, and had long been importuning Bonaparte for an appointment.

A day or two after the news of the battle of Hohen-

---

[1] Napoleon had good reason for his opinion. " Moreau had a mother-in-law and a wife lively and given to intrigue. Bonaparte could not bear intriguing women. Besides, on one occasion Madame Moreau's mother, when at Malmaison, had indulged in sharp remarks on a suspected scandalous intimacy between Bonaparte and his young sister Caroline, then just married. The Consul had not forgiven such conversation" (*Rémusat*, tome i. p. 192). See also *Meneval*, tome iii. p. 57, as to the mischief done by Madame Hulot.

linden M. Maret came to present for Bonaparte's signature some decrees made in Council. While affixing the signatures, and without looking up, the First Consul said to M. Maret, who was a favourite with him, and who was standing at his right hand, "Are you rich, Maret?"—"No, General."—"So much the worse : a man should be independent."—"General, I will never be dependent on any one but you." The First Consul then raised his eyes to Maret and said, "Hem! that is not bad!" and when the secretary-general was gone he said to me, "Maret is not deficient in cleverness : he made me a very good answer."

On the 9th of February 1801, six weeks after the opening of the Congress of Luneville, peace was signed between Austria and France. This peace—the fruit of Marengo and Hohenlinden—restored France to that honourable position which had been put in jeopardy by the feeble and incapable government of the pentarchy and the reverses of 1799. This peace, which in the treaty, according to custom, was called perpetual, lasted four years.

Joseph Bonaparte, while treating for France at Luneville, was speculating on the rise of the funds which he thought the peace would produce. Persons more wise, who were like him in the secret, sold out their stock at the moment when the certainty of the peace became known. But Joseph purchased to a great extent, in the hope of selling to advantage on the signature of peace. However, the news had been discounted, and a fall took place. Joseph's loss was considerable, and he could not satisfy the engagements in which his greedy and silly speculations had involved him. He applied to his brother, who neither wished nor was able to advance him the necessary sum. Bonaparte was, however, exceedingly sorry to see his elder brother in this embarrassment. He asked me what was to be done. I told him I did not know ; but I advised him to consult M. de Talleyrand, from whom he had often received good advice. He did so, and M. de

Talleyrand replied, with that air of coolness which is so peculiar to him, "What! is that all? Oh! that is nothing. It is easily settled. You have only to raise the price of the funds."—"But the money?"—"Oh, the money may be easily obtained. Make some deposits in the Mont-de-Piété, or the sinking fund. That will give you the necessary money to raise the funds; and then Joseph may sell out, and recover his losses." M. de Talleyrand's advice was adopted, and all succeeded as he had foretold. None but those who have heard M. de Talleyrand converse can form an accurate idea of his easy manner of expressing himself, his imperturbable coolness, the fixed unvarying expression of his countenance, and his vast fund of wit.[1]

During the sitting of the Congress the First Consul learnt that the Government couriers conveyed to favoured individuals in Paris various things, but especially the delicacies of the table, and he ordered that this practice should be discontinued. On the very evening on which this order was issued Cambacérès entered the *salon*, where I was alone with the First Consul, who had already been laughing at the mortification which he knew this regulation would occasion to his colleague : " Well, Cambacérès, what brings you here at this time of night?"—" I come to solicit an exception to the order which you have just given to the Director of the Posts. How do you think a man can make friends unless he keeps a good table? You know very well how much good dinners assist the business of Government." The First Consul laughed, called him a gourmand, and, patting him on the shoulder, said, " Do not distress yourself, my dear Cambacérès; the couriers shall continue to bring *you* your *dindes aux truffes*, your Strasburg *pâtés*, your Mayence hams, and your other titbits."

---

[1] Talleyrand had a large experience in all sorts of speculation. When old he gave this counsel to one of his *protégés:* " Do not speculate. I have always speculated on assured information, and that has cost me *so many* millions ; " and he named his losses. We may believe that in this reckoning he rather forgot the amount of his gains (Sainte-Beuve, *Talleyrand*, 93).

Those who recollect the magnificent dinners given by
Cambacérès and others, which were a general topic of
conversation at the time, and who knew the ingenious calculation which was observed in the invitation of the
guests, must be convinced of the vast influence of a good
dinner in political affairs. As to Cambacérès, he did not
believe that a good government could exist without good
dinners ; and his glory (for every man has his own particular glory) was to know that the luxuries of his table
were the subject of eulogy throughout Paris, and even
Europe. A banquet which commanded general suffrage
was to him a Marengo or a Friedland.[1]

At the commencement of 1801 Fulton presented to

[1] Bourrienne does not exaggerate this excellent quality of the worthy Cambacérès.
When Beugnot was sent to administer the Grand Duchy of Berg, Cambacérès said
to him, "My dear Beugnot, the Emperor arranges crowns as he chooses ; here is
the Grand Duke of Berg (Murat) going to Naples ; he is welcome, I have no objection, but every year the Grand Duke sent me a couple of dozen hams from his Grand
Duchy, and I warn you I do not intend to lose them, so you must make your preparations. . . . I never once omitted to acquit myself of the obligation, . . .
and if there were any delay, . . . his Highness never failed to cause one of his
secretaries to write a good scolding to my house steward ; but when the hams
arrived exactly, his Highness never failed to write to my wife himself to thank her.
. . . This was not all ; the hams were to come carriage free. This petty job-
bery occasioned discontent, . . . and it would not have cost me more to pay the
carriage. The Prince would not allow it. There was an agreement between him
and Lavalette (the head of the Posts), . . . And my Lord appeared to lay as
much stress on the performance of this treaty as on the procuring of the hams"
(*Beugnot*, tome i. p. 262).

Cambacérès never suffered the cares of Government to distract his attention from
the great object of life. On one occasion, for example, being detained in consultation with Napoleon beyond the appointed hour of dinner—it is said that the fate of
the Duc d'Enghien was the topic under discussion—he was observed, when the hour
became very late, to show great symptoms of impatience and restlessness. He at
last wrote a note which he called a gentleman usher in waiting to carry. Napoleon,
suspecting the contents, nodded to an *aide de camp* to intercept the despatch. As he
took it into his hands Cambacérès begged earnestly that he would not read a trifling
note upon domestic matters. Napoleon persisted, and found it to be a note to the
cook containing only the following words, " *Gardez les entremets—les rôtis sont
perdus.*" When Napoleon was in good humor at the result of a diplomatic conference he was accustomed to take leave of the plenipotentiaries with, "Go and dine
with Cambacérès." His table was in fact an important state engine, as appears from
the anecdote of the trout sent to him by the municipality of Geneva, and charged
300 francs in their accounts. The Imperial *Cour des Comptes* having disallowed
the item, was interdicted from meddling with similar municipal affairs in future
(Hayward's *Art of Dining*, p. 20).

Bonaparte his memorial on steamboats. I urged a serious examination of the subject. "Bah!" said he, "these projectors are all either intriguers or visionaries. Don't trouble me about the business." I observed that the man whom he called an intriguer was only reviving an invention already known, and that it was wrong to reject the scheme without examination. He would not listen to me; and thus was adjourned, for some time, the practical application of a discovery which has given such an important impulse to trade and navigation.

Paul I. fell by the hands of assassins on the night of the 24th of March 1801. The First Consul was much shocked on receiving the intelligence. In the excitement caused by this unexpected event, which had so important an influence on his policy, he directed me to send the following note to the *Moniteur :—*

Paul I. died on the night of the 24th of March, and the English squadron passed the Sound on the 30th. History will reveal the connection which probably exists between these two events.

Thus were announced the crime of the 24th of March and the not ill-founded suspicions of its authors.[1]

The amicable relations of Paul and Bonaparte had been daily strengthened. "In concert with the Czar," said Bonaparte, "I was sure of striking a mortal blow at the English power in India. A palace revolution has overthrown all my projects." This resolution, and the admiration of the Autocrat of Russia for the head of the French Republic, may certainly be numbered among the causes of Paul's death. The individuals generally accused at the time were those who were violently and perseveringly threatened, and who had the strongest interest in the succession of a new Emperor. I have seen a letter from a northern sovereign which in my mind leaves no

[2] We do not attempt to rescue the fair fame of our country. This is one among many instances in which Bourrienne was misled.—*Editor of 1836 edition.*

doubt on this subject, and which specified the reward of
the crime, and the part to be performed by each actor.
But it must also be confessed that the conduct and character of Paul I., his tyrannical acts, his violent caprices,
and his frequent excesses of despotism, had rendered him
the object of accumulated hatred, for patience has its
limit. These circumstances did not probably create the
conspiracy, but they considerably facilitated the execution
of the plot which deprived the Czar of his throne and his
life.

As soon as Alexander ascended the throne the ideas of
the First Consul respecting the dismemberment of Poland were revived, and almost wholly engrossed his mind.
During his first campaign in Italy, and several times when
in Egypt, he told Sulkowsky that it was his ardent wish
to re-establish Poland, to avenge the iniquity of her dismemberment, and by that grand reparatory act to restore
the former equilibrium of Europe. He often dictated to
me for the *Moniteur* articles tending to prove, by various
arguments, that Europe would never enjoy repose until
those great spoliations were avenged and repaired ; but
he frequently destroyed these articles instead of sending
them to press. His system of policy towards Russia
changed shortly after the death of Paul. The thought of
a war against that empire unceasingly occupied his mind,
and gave birth to the idea of that fatal campaign which
took place eleven years afterwards, and which had other
causes than the re-establishment of Poland. That object
was merely set forward as a pretext.

Duroc was sent to St. Petersburg to congratulate the
Emperor Alexander on his accession to the throne. He
arrived in the Russian capital on the 24th of May. Duroc,
who was at this time very young, was a great favourite of
the First Consul. He never importuned Bonaparte by his
solicitations, and was never troublesome in recommending
any one or busying himself as an agent for favour ; yet he

warmly advocated the cause of those whom he thought
injured, and honestly repelled accusations which he knew
to be false.   These moral qualities, joined to an agreeable
person and elegant manners, rendered him a very superior
man.

The year 1801 was, moreover, marked by the fatal creation of special tribunals, which were in no way justified
by the urgency of circumstances.   This year also saw the
re-establishment of the African Company, the treaty of
Luneville (which augmented the advantages France had
obtained by the treaty of Campo-Formio), and the peace
concluded between Spain and Portugal by means of Lucien.
On the subject of this peace I may mention that Portugal,
to obtain the cession of Olivenza, secretly offered Bonaparte, through me, 8,000,000 of francs if he would contribute his influence towards the acquisition of that town
by Portugal.   He rejected this offer indignantly, declaring
that he would never sell honour for money.   He has been
accused of having listened to a similar proposition at Pas-
seriano, though in fact no such proposition was ever made
to him.   Those who bring forward such accusations little
know the inflexibility of his principles on this point.

One evening in April 1801 an English paper—the *London
Gazette*—arrived at Malmaison.   It announced the landing
in Egypt of the army commanded by Abercromby, the
battle given by the English, and the death of their General.   I immediately translated the article, and presented
it to the First Consul, with the conviction that the news
would be very painful to him.   He doubted its truth, or
at least pretended to do so.   Several officers and *aides de
camp* who were in the *salon* coincided in his opinion, especially Lannes, Bessières, and Duroc.   They thought by
so doing to please the First Consul, who then said to me,
in a jeering tone, "Bah! you do not understand English.
This is the way with you: you are always inclined to believe bad news rather than good!"   These words, and the

approving smiles of the gentlemen present, ruffled me, and I said with some warmth, "How, General, can you believe that the English Government would publish officially so important an event if it were not true? Do you think that a Government that has any self-respect would, in the face of Europe, state a falsehood respecting an affair the truth of which cannot long remain unknown? Did you ever know an instance of so important an announcement proving untrue after it had been published in the *London Gazette?* I believe it to be true, and the smiles of these gentlemen will not alter my opinion." On these observations the First Consul rose and said, "Come, Bourrienne, I want you in the library." After we had left the *salon* he added, "This is always the way with you. Why are you vexed at such trifles? I assure you I believe the news but too confidently, and I feared it before it came. But they think they please me by thus appearing to doubt it. Never mind them."—"I ask your pardon," said I, "but I conceive the best way of proving my attachment to you is to tell you what I believe to be true. You desire me not to delay a moment in announcing bad news to you. It would be far worse to disguise than to conceal it."

CHAPTER V.

1801–1802.

BEFORE he placed two crowns on his own head Bonaparte
thought it would promote the interests of his policy to
place one on the head of a prince, and even a prince of the
House of Bourbon.   He wished to accustom the French to
the sight of a king.   It will hereafter be seen that he
gave sceptres, like his confidence, conditionally, and that
he was always ready to undo his own work when it became
an obstacle to his ambitious designs.

In May 1801 the Infanta of Spain, Maria Louisa, third
daughter of Charles IV., visited Paris.   The Infante Louis
de Bourbon, eldest son of the Duke of Parma, had gone to
Madrid in 1798 to contract a marriage with Maria Amelia,
the sister of Maria Louisa ; but he fell in love with the
latter.   Godoy favoured the attachment, and employed all
his influence to bring about the marriage.   The son who,
six years later, was born of this union, was named Charles
Louis, after the King of Spain.   France occupied the
Duchy of Parma, which, in fulfilment of the conventions
signed by Lucien Bonaparte, was to belong to her after
the death of the reigning Duke.   On the other hand,

France was to cede the Grand Duchy of Tuscany to the
son of the Duke of Parma; and Spain paid to France,
according to stipulation, a considerable sum of money.
Soon after the treaty was communicated to Don Louis and
his wife they left Madrid and travelled through France.
The prince took the title of Count of Leghorn. All accounts are unanimous as to the attentions which the Prince
and Princess received on their journey. Among the *fêtes*
in honour of the illustrious couple that given by M. de
Talleyrand at Neuilly was remarkable for magnificence.[1]

When the Count of Leghorn was coming to pay his first
visit to Malmaison Bonaparte went into the drawing-room
to see that everything was suitably prepared for his reception. In a few minutes he returned to his cabinet and
said to me, somewhat out of humour, " Bourrienne, only
think of their stupidity ; they had not taken down the
picture representing me on the summit of the Alps pointing to Lombardy and commanding the conquest of it. I
have ordered its removal. How mortifying it would have
been if the Prince had seen it ! "

Another picture in the drawing-room at Malmaison
represented the First Consul sleeping on the snow on the
summit of the Alps before the battle of Marengo.

The Count of Leghorn's visit to Paris imparted brilliancy
to the first years of the reign of Bonaparte, of whom it was
at that time said, " He made kings, but would not be one ! "

At the representation of *Œdipus*, the following expression of Philactetes was received with transport :—

> " J'ai fait des Souverains, et n'ai pas voulu l'être."
> " Monarchs I've made, but one I would not be."

The First Consul, on leaving the theatre, did not conceal his satisfaction. He judged, from the applause with
which that verse had been received, that his pamphlet was
forgotten. The manner, moreover, in which a king,

[1] A full account of these *fêtes* appears in the *Memoirs of Madame Junot, Duchesse
d'Abrantès*, vol. ii. p. 220.

crowned by his hands, had been received by the public, was no indifferent matter to him, as he expected that the people would thus again become familiar with what had been so long proscribed.

This King, who, though well received and well entertained, was in all respects a very ordinary man, departed for Italy. I say very ordinary, not that I had an opportunity of judging of his character myself, but the First Consul told me that his capabilities were extremely limited; that he even felt repugnance to take a pen in his hand; that he never cast a thought on anything but his pleasures: in a word, that he was a fool.

One day, after the First Consul had spent several hours in company with him and his consort, he said to me, "I am quite tired. He is a mere automaton. I put a number of questions to him, but he can answer none. He is obliged to consult his wife, who makes him understand as well as she is able what he ought to say." The First Consul added, "The poor Prince will set off to-morrow, without knowing what he is going to do." I observed that it was a pity to see the happiness of the people of Tuscany entrusted to such a prince. Bonaparte replied, "Policy requires it. Besides, the young man is not worse than the usual run of kings." The Prince fully justified in Tuscany the opinion which the First Consul formed of him.[1]

[1] This unfortunate Prince was very ill-calculated to recommend, by his personal character, the institutions to which the nobility clung with so much fondness. Nature had endowed him with an excellent heart, but with very limited talents; and his mind had imbibed the false impress consequent upon his monastic education. He resided at Malmaison nearly the whole time of his visit to Paris. Madame Bonaparte used to lead the Queen to her own apartments; and as the First Consul never left his closet except to sit down to meals, the *aides de camp* were under the necessity of keeping the King company, and of endeavoring to entertain him, so wholly was he devoid of intellectual resources. It required, indeed, a great share of patience to listen to the frivolities which engrossed his attention. His turn of mind being thus laid open to view, care was taken to supply him with the playthings usually placed in the hands of children; he was, therefore, never at a loss for occupation. His nonentity was a source of regret to us: we lamented to see a tall handsome youth, destined to rule over his fellow-men, trembling at the sight of a horse, and wasting his time in the game of hide-and-seek, or at leap-frog, and whose whole information consisted in knowing his prayers, and in saying grace before and after

In order to show still further attention to the King of Etruria, after his three weeks' visit to Paris, the First Consul directed him to be escorted to Italy by a French guard, and selected his brother-in-law Murat for that purpose.

The new King [1] of a new kingdom entered Florence on the 12th of April 1801 ; but the reception given him by the Tuscans was not at all similar to what he had experienced at Paris. The people received the royal pair as sovereigns imposed on them by France. The ephemeral kingdom of Etruria lasted scarcely six years. The King died in 1803, in the flower of his age, and in 1807 the Queen was expelled from her throne by him who had constructed it for her.

At this period a powerful party urged Bonaparte to break with the Pope, and to establish a Gallican Church, the head of which should reside in France. They thought to flatter his ambition by indicating to him a new source of power which might establish a point of comparison between him and the first Roman emperors. But his ideas did not coincide with theirs on this subject. "I am con-

---

meals. Such, nevertheless, was the man to whom the destinies of a nation were about to be committed ! When he left France to repair to his kingdom, "Rome need not be uneasy," said the First Consul to us after the farewell audience, "there is no danger of *his* crossing the Rubicon" (*Memoirs of the Duke of Rovigo*, vol. i. p. 363).

I once heard the First Consul, in a conversation with his colleague, Cambacérès, treat his royal *protégé*, the King of Etruria, very severely. Of course his Majesty was not present. "This good King," said he, "evinces no great concern for his dear and well-beloved subjects. He spends his time in gossiping with old women, to whom he is very lavish of his praise to me, though in secret he murmurs bitterly at the thought of owing his elevation to the hateful French Republic."—"It is alleged," observed M. Cambacérès, "that you wished to disgust the French people with kings by showing them this fine specimen of royalty, as the Spartans used to disgust their children with intoxication by showing them a drunken slave."—"Not at all, not at all," resumed the First Consul, "I have no wish to excite a distaste for royalty: but the presence of his Majesty, the King of Etruria, will vex a good many worthy folks who are striving hard to revive a taste for the Bourbons" (*Mémoires de Constant*).

[1] Louis de Bourbon (1773–1803), Prince of Parma, son of Ferdinand, Duke of Parma. Given Tuscany in 1801 as kingdom of Etruria in return for Parma taken from his father. Died 1803. His wife, Maria Louisa (1782–1824), daughter of Charles IV. of Spain, governed as Regent in the name of her son, Charles Louis, till 1807, when Etruria was annexed to France. In 1815 she was given the Duchy of Lucca.

vinced," said he, "that a part of France would become
Protestant, especially if I were to favour that disposition.
I am also certain that the much greater portion would
remain Catholic, and would oppose, with the greatest zeal
and fervour, the schism of a part of their fellow-citizens.
I dread the religious quarrels, the family dissensions, and
the public distractions, which such a state of things would
inevitably occasion. In reviving a religion which has
always prevailed in the country, and which still prevails in
the hearts of the people, and in giving the liberty of ex-
ercising their worship to the minority, I shall satisfy
every one."

The First Consul, taking a superior view of the state
of France, considered that the re-establishment of religious worship would prove a powerful support to his Government : and he had been occupied ever since the commencement of 1801 in preparing a *Concordat* with the
Pope. It was signed in the month of July in the same
year. It required some time to enable the parties to come
to an understanding on the subject.

Cardinal Consalvi arrived, in the month of June 1801,
at Paris, to arrange matters on the part of the Pope.
Cardinal Caprara and M. de Spina also formed part of the
embassy sent by the Holy Father. There were, besides,
several able theologians, among whom Doctor C——[1] was

---

[1] The "Doctor C——" was *Caselli*, later Archbishop of Parma. Bernier was
given the Bishopric of *Orleans*, not *Versailles;* see *Erreurs*, tome i. p. 275. The
details of the surprise attempted at the last moment by putting before Cardinal
Consalvi for his signature an altered copy of the *Concordat* should be read in his
Memoirs (tome i. p. 355), or in *Lanfrey* (tome ii. p. 357). As for Napoleon's belief
that part of the nation might become Protestant, Narbonne probably put the matter
truly when he said there was not religion enough in France to stand a division. It
should be noted that the *Concordat* did not so much restore the Catholic Church as
destroy the old Gallican Church, with all its liberties, which might annoy either
Pope or Emperor. But on this point see *The Gallican Church and the Revolution*,
by Jervis : London, Kegan Paul, Trench and Co., 1882. The clergy may, it is true,
have shown wisdom in acceding to any terms of restoration. Rénan (*Souvenirs*,
p. 212), speaking of M. Émery of St. Sulpice, and obviously thinking of the resistance of the French clergy of the present day, says that Émery would have been
astonished if told that a request for authority to re-open the great seminary of St.
Sulpice was a base concession to the civil power, and a sort of impiety.

distinguished. He was a member of the Pope's chancery; his knowledge gave him so much influence over his colleagues that affairs advanced only as much as he pleased. However, he was gained over by honours conferred on him, and promises of money. Business then went on a little quicker. The *Concordat* was signed on the 15th of July 1801, and made a law of the State in the following April. The plenipotentiaries on the part of Bonaparte were Joseph Bonaparte, Cretet, and the Abbé Bernier, afterwards Bishop of Versailles.

A solemn *Te Deum* was chanted at the cathedral of Notre Dame on Sunday, the 11th of April. The crowd was immense, and the greater part of those present stood during the ceremony, which was splendid in the extreme; but who would presume to say that the general feeling was in harmony with all this pomp? Was, then, the time for this innovation not yet arrived? Was it too abrupt a transition from the habits of the twelve preceding years? It is unquestionably true that a great number of the persons present at the ceremony expressed, in their countenances and gestures, rather a feeling of impatience and displeasure than of satisfaction or of reverence for the place in which they were. Here and there murmurs arose expressive of discontent. The whispering, which I might more properly call open conversation, often interrupted the divine service, and sometimes observations were made which were far from being moderate. Some would turn their heads aside on purpose to take a bit of chocolate-cake, and biscuits were openly eaten by many who seemed to pay no attention to what was passing.

The Consular Court was in general extremely irreligious; nor could it be expected to be otherwise, being composed chiefly of those who had assisted in the annihilation of all religious worship in France, and of men who, having passed their lives in camps, had oftener entered a church in Italy to carry off a painting than to hear the

Mass. Those who, without being imbued with any religious ideas, possessed that good sense which induces men
to pay respect to the belief of others, though it be one in
which they do not participate, did not blame the First
Consul for his conduct, and conducted themselves with
some regard to decency. But on the road from the Tuileries to Notre Dame, Lannes and Augereau wanted to
alight from the carriage as soon as they saw that they were
being driven to Mass, and it required an order from the
First Consul to prevent their doing so. They went therefore to Notre Dame, and the next day Bonaparte asked
Augereau what he thought of the ceremony. "Oh ! it was
all very fine," replied the General ; "there was nothing
wanting, except the million of men who have perished
in the pulling down of what you are setting up." [1]   Bonaparte was much displeased at this remark. [2]

During the negotiations with the Holy Father Bonaparte one day said to me, "In every country religion is
useful to the Government, and those who govern ought to
avail themselves of it to influence mankind. I was a Ma-
hometan in Egypt; I am a Catholic in France. With
relation to the police of the religion of a state, it should be
entirely in the hands of the sovereign. Many persons have
urged me to found a Gallican Church, and make myself its
head ; but they do not know France. If they did, they
would know that the majority of the people would not like
a rupture with Rome. Before I can resolve on such a
measure the Pope must push matters to an extremity ; but
I believe he will not do so."—" You are right, General,
and you recall to my memory what Cardinal Consalvi said :
' The Pope will do all the First Consul desires.' "—"That

---

[1] This remark has been attributed elsewhere to General Delmas.

[2] According to a gentleman who played a part in this empty pageantry, Lannes
at one moment did get out of the carriage, and Augereau kept swearing *in no low
whisper* during the whole of the chanted Mass. Most of the military chiefs who
sprung out of the Revolution had no religion at all, but there were some who were
Protestants, and who were irritated by the restoration of Catholicism as the national
faith.—*Editor of 1836 edition.*

is the best course for him. Let him not suppose that he has to do with an idiot. What do you think is the point his negotiations put most forward? The salvation of my soul! But with me immortality is the recollection one leaves in the memory of man. That idea prompts to great actions. It would be better for a man never to have lived than to leave behind him no traces of his existence."

Many endeavours were made to persuade the First Consul to perform in public the duties imposed by the Catholic religion. An influential example, it was urged, was required. He told me once that he had put an end to that request by the following declaration : "Enough of this. Ask me no more. You will not obtain your object. You shall never make a hypocrite of me. Let us remain where we are."

I have read in a work remarkable on many accounts that it was on the occasion of the *Concordat* of the 15th July 1801 that the First Consul abolished the republican calendar and re-established the Gregorian. This is an error. He did not make the calendar a religious affair. The *Sénatus-consulte*, which restored the use of the Gregorian calendar, to commence in the French Empire from the 11th Nivôse, year XIV. (1st January 1806), was adopted on the 22d Fructidor, year XIII. (9th September 1805), more than four years after the *Concordat*. The re-establishment of the ancient calendar had no other object than to bring us into harmony with the rest of Europe on a point so closely connected with daily transactions, which were much embarrassed by the decadary calendar.[1]

Bonaparte at length, however, consented to hear Mass, and St. Cloud was the place where this ancient usage was first re-established. He directed the ceremony to commence sooner than the hour announced in order that those who would only make a scoff at it might not arrive until the service was ended.

[1] See the end of the second volume.

Whenever the First Consul determined to hear Mass publicly on Sundays in the chapel of the Palace a small altar was prepared in a room near his cabinet of business. This room had been Anne of Austria's oratory. A small portable altar, placed on a platform one step high, restored it to its original destination. During the rest of the week this chapel was used as a bathing-room. On Sunday the door of communication was opened, and we heard Mass sitting in our cabinet of business. The number of persons there never exceeded three or four, and the First Consul seldom failed to transact some business during the ceremony, which never lasted longer than twelve minutes. Next day all the papers had the news that the First Consul had heard Mass in his apartments. In the same way Louis XVIII. has often heard it in his!

On the 19th of July 1801 a papal bull absolved Talleyrand from his vows. He immediately married Madame Grandt, and the affair obtained little notice at the time. This statement sufficiently proves how report has perverted the fact. It has been said that Bonaparte on becoming Emperor wished to restore that decorum which the Revolution had destroyed, and therefore resolved to put an end to the improper intimacy which subsisted between Talleyrand and Madame Grandt. It is alleged that the Minister at first refused to marry the lady, but that he at last found it necessary to obey the peremptory order of his master. This pretended resurrection of morality by Bonaparte is excessively ridiculous. The bull was not registered in the Council of State until the 19th of August 1802.[1]

---

[1] The First Consul had on several occasions urged M. de Talleyrand to return to holy orders. He pointed out to him that that course would be most becoming his age and high birth, and promised that he should be made a cardinal, thus raising him to a par with Richelieu, and giving additional lustre to his administration (*Memoirs of the Duke of Rovigo*, vol. i. p. 426).

In a recently-published work, entitled, *Echoes from Old Calcutta*, the author, Dr. Busteed, gives an account of Madame Grandt which is obtained entirely from original sources. Married to a gentleman in the Civil Service before she was fifteen years of age, Madame Grandt was, within eighteen months of her marriage, the

I will end this chapter by a story somewhat foreign to the preceding transactions, but which personally concerns myself. On the 20th of July 1801 the First Consul, *ex proprio motu,* named me a Councillor of State extraordinary. Madame Bonaparte kindly condescended to have an elegant but somewhat ideal costume made for me. It pleased the First Consul, however, and he had a similar one made for himself. He wore it a short time and then left it off. Never had Bonaparte since his elevation shown himself so amiable as on this occasion.

heroine of a *crim. con.* case against Sir Philip Francis, in which her husband laid the damages at 1,500,000 sicca rupees. The facts relating to this remarkable action are republished by Dr. Busteed from the notes of one of the judges who presided at the trial—Mr. Justice Hyde. Eventually judgment was pronounced for the plaintiff by the majority of the judges, with damages at 50,000 sicca rupees. After living for a short time under the protection of Francis, Madame Grandt went to Europe, and ultimately emerged from obscurity as the wife of Talleyrand. Her extraordinary beauty—which lasted till late in life—has been perpetuated by a painting by Gerard, which hangs between the portraits of Madame Récamier and Prince de Talleyrand in the Musée at Versailles. The following is the description given of her by Francis to his second wife :—

" She was tall, most elegantly formed, with the stature of a nymph, a complexion of unequalled delicacy, and auburn hair of the most luxuriant profusion ; fine blue eyes with black eyelashes and brows gave her countenance a most piquant singularity."

And so Madame de Rémusat writes of her in later life in her recently-published *Memoirs,* vol. ii. p. 183 :—

" She was tall, and her figure had all the suppleness and grace so common to women born in the East. Her complexion was dazzling, her eyes of the brightest blue, and her slightly turned-up nose gave her, singularly enough, a look of Talleyrand himself. Her fine golden hair was of proverbial beauty."

Another French writer says that she possessed " la plus belle chevelure blonde qui ait peut-être jamais existé." Like many other reigning beauties, however, she was credited with dullness. The Robinson Crusoe incident (when Sir George Robinson was asked about " his man Friday ")—" Vous avez du être bien content le jour où vous avez trouvé Vendredi "—which is usually cited in evidence of the prevailing belief, did not actually happen. " It was guessed at," said Talleyrand, " and that was enough ; the blunder was ascribed to her without compunction." The real hero of the incident is supposed to have been a French abbé. But it matters not who it was, for the fact is undeniable that the lady's understanding was not equal to her beauty ; and as the story is an excellent one it will doubtless always be associated with the name of the Princesse de Talleyrand, *née* Catherine Noel Worlée, some time Madame Grandt (*The Academy*).

But M. de Talleyrand vindicated his choice, saying, " A clever wife often compromises her husband ; a stupid one only compromises herself " (*Historical Characters,* p. 122, Bulwer, Lord Dalling).

CHAPTER VI.

1802.

For the last time in these Memoirs I shall return to the
affairs of Egypt—to that episode which embraces so short
a space of time and holds so high a place in the life of
Bonaparte. Of all his conquests he set the highest value
on Egypt, because it spread the glory of his name throughout the East. Accordingly he left nothing unattempted
for the preservation of that colony. In a letter to General
Kléber he said, "You are as able as I am to understand
how important is the possession of Egypt to France. The
Turkish Empire, in which the symptoms of decay are
everywhere discernible, is at present falling to pieces, and
the evil of the evacuation of Egypt by France would now
be the greater, as we should soon see that fine province
pass into the possession of some other European power."
The selection of Gantheaume, however, to carry assistance
to Kléber was not judicious. Gantheaume had brought
the First Consul back from Egypt, and though the success
of the passage could only be attributed to Bonaparte's own
plan, his determined character, and superior judgment,
yet he preserved towards Gantheaume that favourable disposition which is naturally felt for one who has shared a
great danger with us, and upon whom the responsibility
may be said to have been imposed.

This confidence in mediocrity, dictated by an honourable feeling, did not obtain a suitable return. Gantheaume, by his indecision and creeping about in the Mediterranean, had already failed to execute a commission entrusted to him. The First Consul, upon finding he did not leave Brest after he had been ordered to the Mediterranean, repeatedly said to me, "What the devil is Gantheaume about?" With one of the daily reports sent to the First Consul he received the following quatrain, which made him laugh heartily:—

> "Vaisseaux lestés, tête sans lest,
> Ainsi part l'Amiral Gantheaume;
> Il s'en va de Brest à Bertheaume,
> Et revient de Bertheaume à Brest!"

> "With ballast on board, but none in his brain,
> Away went our gallant Gantheaume,
> On a voyage from Brest to Bertheaume,
> And then from Bertheaume—to Brest back again!"

Gantheaume's hesitation, his frequent tergiversations, his arrival at Toulon, his tardy departure, and his return to that port on the 19th of February 1801, only ten days prior to Admiral Keith's appearance with Sir Ralph Abercromby off Alexandria, completely foiled all the plans which Bonaparte had conceived of conveying succour and reinforcements to a colony on the brink of destruction.

Bonaparte was then dreaming that many French families would carry back civilisation, science, and art to that country which was their cradle. But it could not be concealed that his departure from Egypt in 1799 had prepared the way for the loss of that country, which was hastened by Kléber's death and the choice of Menou as his successor.

A sure way of paying court to the First Consul and gaining his favour was to eulogise his views about Egypt, and to appear zealous for maintaining the possession of that country. By these means it was that Menou gained his confidence. In the first year of the occupation of that country he laid before him his dreams respecting Africa. He spoke of the negroes of Senegal, Mozambique, Mehedie, Marabout, and other barbarous countries which were all at once to assume a new aspect, and become civilised, in consequence of the French possession of Egypt. To Menou's adulation is to be attributed the favourable reception given him by the First Consul, even after his return from Egypt, of which his foolish conduct had allowed the English to get possession. The First Consul appointed him Governor of Piedmont, and at my request gave my elder brother the situation of Commissary-General of Police in that country; but I am in candour obliged to confess that the First Consul was obliged to retract this mark of his favour in consequence of my brother's making an abuse of it.

It was also by flattering the First Consul on the question of the East that Davoust, on his return from Egypt in 1800 in consequence of the Convention of El-Arish, insinuated himself into Bonaparte's good graces and, if he did not deserve, obtained his favour.[1] At that time Davoust certainly had no title whatever to the good fortune which he suddenly experienced. He obtained, without first serving in a subordinate rank, the command-in-chief of the grenadiers of the Consular Guard; and from that time commenced the deadly hatred which Davoust bore towards me. Astonished at the great length of time that Bonaparte had been one day conversing with him I said, as soon as he was gone, "How could you talk so long with a man whom you have always called a stupid fellow?"—"Ah! but I did not know him well enough before. He is a better man, I assure you, than he is thought; and you will come over to my opinion."—"I hope so." The First Consul, who was often extremely indiscreet, told Davoust

---

[1] It is difficult to imagine a man of Davoust's determined character playing the *rôle* of a sycophant. Allowance must be made for M. de Bourrienne's evident bias.

my opinion of him, and his hostility against me ceased but with his life.

The First Consul could not forget his cherished conquest in the East. It was constantly the object of his thoughts. He endeavoured to send reinforcements to his army from Brest and Toulon, but without success. He soon had cause to repent having entrusted to the hands of Menou the command-in-chief, to which he became entitled only by seniority, after the assassination of Kléber by Soleiman Heleby. But Bonaparte's indignation was excited when he became acquainted with Menou's neglect and mismanagement, when he saw him giving reins to his passion for reform, altering and destroying everything, creating nothing good in its stead, and dreaming about forming a land communication with the Hottentots and Congo instead of studying how to preserve the country. His pitiful plans of defence, which were useless from their want of combination, appeared to the First Consul the height of ignorance. Forgetful of all the principles of strategy, of which Bonaparte's conduct afforded so many examples, he opposed to the landing of Abercromby a few isolated corps, which were unable to withstand the enemy's attack, while the English army might have been entirely annihilated had all the disposable troops been sent against it.

The great admiration which Menou expressed at the expedition to Egypt; his excessive fondness for that country, the religion of which he had ridiculously enough embraced under the name of Abdállah ; the efforts he made, in his sphere, to preserve the colony ; his enthusiasm and blind attachment to Bonaparte ; the flattering and encouraging accounts he gave of the situation of the army, at first had the effect of entirely covering Menou's incapacity.[1] This alone can account for the First Consul's

---

[1] For a ludicrous description of Menou see the *Memoirs of Marmont :*—" Clever and gay, he was an agreeable talker, but a great liar. He was not destitute of some

preference of him. But I am far from concurring in what
has been asserted by many persons, that France lost
Egypt at the very moment when it seemed most easy of
preservation. Egypt was conquered by a genius of vast
intelligence, great capacity, and profound military science.
Fatuity, stupidity, and incapacity lost it. What was the
result of that memorable expedition? The destruction of
one of our finest armies; the loss of some of our best
generals; the annihilation of our navy ; the surrender of
Malta ; and the sovereignty of England in the Mediterranean. What is the result at present? A scientific
work. The gossiping stories and mystifications of Herod-
otus, and the reveries of the good Rollin, are worth as
much, and have not cost so dear.

The First Consul had long been apprehensive that the
evacuation of Egypt was unavoidable. The last news he
had received from that country was not very encouraging,
and created a presentiment of the approach of the dreaded
catastrophe. He, however, published the contrary ; but
it was then of great importance that an account of the
evacuation should not reach England until the preliminaries of peace were signed, for which purpose M. Otto was
exerting all his industry and talent. We made a great
merit of abandoning our conquests in Egypt ; but the
sacrifice would not have been considered great if the
events which took place at the end of August had been
known in London before the signing of the preliminaries
on the 1st of October. The First Consul himself answered
M. Otto's last despatch, containing a copy of the prelim-

education. His character, one of the oddest in the world, came very near to lunacy.
Constantly writing, always in motion in his room, riding for exercise every day, he
was never able to start on any necessary or useful journey. . . . When, later,
Bonaparte, then First Consul, gave him by special favour the administration of
Piedmont, he put off his departure from day to day for six months ; and then he
only did start because his friend Maret himself put him into his carriage, with post-
horses already harnessed to it. . . . When he left this post they found in his
cabinet 900 letters which he had not opened. He was an eccentric lunatic, amusing
enough sometimes, but a curse to everything which depended on him " (*Memoirs of
the Duc de Raguse*, tome i. p. 410).

inaries ready to be adopted by the English Ministry.
Neither this despatch nor the answer was communicated
to M. de Talleyrand, then Minister for Foreign Affairs.
The First Consul, who highly appreciated the great talents
and knowledge of that Minister, never closed any diplomatic arrangement without first consulting him ; and he
was right in so doing. On this occasion, however, I told
him that as M. de Talleyrand was, for his health, taking the
waters of Bourbon-l'Archambault, four days must elapse
before his reply could be received, and that the delay might
cause the face of affairs to change. I reminded him that
Egypt was on the point of yielding. He took my advice,
and it was well for him that he did, for the news of the
compulsory evacuation of Egypt arrived in London the
day after the signing of the preliminaries. M. Otto informed the First Consul by letter that Lord Hawkesbury,
in communicating to him the news of the evacuation, told
him he was very glad everything was settled, for it would
have been impossible for him to have treated on the same
basis after the arrival of such news. In reality we consented at Paris to the voluntary evacuation of Egypt, and
that was something for England, while Egypt was at that
very time evacuated by a convention made on the spot.
The definitive evacuation of Egypt took place on the 30th
of August 1801 ; and thus the conquest of that country,
which had cost so dear, was rendered useless, or rather
injurious.[1]

[1] *Erreurs* (tome i. p. 94) attacks the correctness of this paragraph, but it appears
to be right. See *Thiers*, tome iii. p. 184. The French had consented to evacuate Egypt, but neither side knew of the surrender of Alexandria when the preliminaries were signed.

CHAPTER VII.

1802.

The epoch of the peace of Amiens must be considered as
the most glorious in the history of France, not excepting
the splendid period of Louis XIV.'s victories and the more
brilliant era of the Empire.   The Consular glory was then
pure, and the opening prospect was full of flattering hope ;
whereas those who were but little accustomed to look
closely into things could discern mighty disasters lurking
under the laurels of the Empire.

The proposals which the First Consul made in order to
obtain peace sufficiently prove his sincere desire for it.
He felt that if in the commencement of his administration
he could couple his name with so hoped for an act he
should ever experience the affection and gratitude of the
French.   I want no other proof of his sentiments than
the offer he made to give up Egypt to the Grand Seignior,
and to restore all the ports of the Gulf of Venice and of
the Mediterranean to the States to which they had previously belonged ; to surrender Malta to the order of the
Knights of St. John, and even to raze its fortifications if
England should think such a measure necessary for her

interests. In the Indies, Ceylon was to be left to him,[1]
and he required the surrender of the Cape of Good Hope
and all the places taken by the English in the West Indies.

England had firmly resolved to keep Malta, the Gibraltar of the Mediterranean, and the Cape of Good Hope, the
caravanserai of the Indies. She was therefore unwilling
to close with the proposition respecting Malta; and she
said that an arrangement might be made by which it
would be rendered independent both of Great Britain and
France. We clearly saw that this was only a lure, and
that, whatever arrangements might be entered into,
England would keep Malta, because it was not to be expected that the maritime power would willingly surrender
an island which commands the Mediterranean. I do not
notice the discussions respecting the American islands,
for they were, in my opinion, of little consequence to us.[2]

[1] Ceylon belonged to Holland, but was retained by England under the treaty of Amiens.

[2] It is strange that Bourrienne does not allude to one of the first arbitrary acts of Napoleon, the discussions on which formed part of those conversations between Napoleon and his brother Lucien of which Bourrienne complained to Josephine he knew nothing. In 1763 France had ceded to England the part of Louisiana on the east of the Mississippi, and the part on the west of that river, with New Orleans, to Spain. By the treaty negotiated with Spain by Lucien Bonaparte in 1800 her share was given back to France. On the 30th April 1803 Napoleon sold the whole to the United States for 80,000,000 francs (£3,250,000), to the intense anger of his brothers Joseph and Lucien. Lucien was especially proud of having obtained the cession for which Napoleon was, at that time, very anxious; but both brothers were horrified when Napoleon disclosed how little he cared for constitutional forms by telling them that if the Legislature, as his brothers threatened, would not ratify the treaty, he would do without the ratification; see Iung's *Lucien*, tome ii. p. 126.

Napoleon's most obvious motives were want of money and the certainty of the seizure of the province by England, as the rupture with her was now certain. But there was perhaps another cause. The States had already been on the point of seiz-ing the province from Spain, which had interfered with their trade (Hinton's *United States*, p. 435, and *Thiers*, tome iv. p. 320).

Of the sum to be paid, 20,000,000 were to go to the States, to cover the illegal seiz-ures of American ships by the French navy, a matter which was not settled for many years later. The remaining 60,000,000 were employed in the preparations for the invasion of England; see *Thiers*, tome iv. pp. 320 and 325, and *Lanfrey*, tome iii. p. 48. The transaction is a remarkable one, as forming the final withdrawal of France from North America (with the exception of some islands on the Newfoundland coast), where she had once held such a proud position. It also eventually made an addition to the number of slave States.

There seems to have been some difficulty about handing over the country; see

They cost more than they produce ; and they will escape
from us, some time or other, as all colonies ultimately do
from the parent country. Our whole colonial system is
absurd ; it forces us to pay for colonial produce at a rate
nearly double that for which it may be purchased from
our neighbours.

When Lord Hawkesbury consented to evacuate Malta,
on condition that it should be independent of France and
Great Britain, he must have been aware that such a condition would never be fulfilled. He cared little for the
order of St. John, and he should have put, by way of
postscript, at the bottom of his note, " We will keep Malta
in spite of you." I always told the First Consul that if he
were in the situation of the English he would act the
same part ; and it did not require much sagacity to fore-
tell that Malta would be the principal cause of the rupture
of peace. He was of my opinion ; but at that moment he
thought everything depended on concluding the negotiations, and I entirely agreed with him. It happened, as
was foreseen, that Malta caused the renewal of war. The
English, on being called upon to surrender the island,
eluded the demand, shifted about, and at last ended by
demanding that Malta should be placed under the protection of the King of Naples,—that is to say, under the
protection of a power entirely at their command, and to
which they might dictate what they pleased. This was
really too cool a piece of irony !

I will here notice the quarrel between the First Consul
and the English newspapers, and give a new proof of his
views concerning the freedom of the press. However,
liberty of the press did *once* contribute to give him infi-
nite gratification, namely, when all the London journals
mentioned the transports of joy manifested in London on

Martens, tome ix. p. 302, where the States, on 27th October 1810, announce their
intention of annexing certain lands to the eastwards and southwards of the Spanish
portion, which they had not received.

the arrival of General Lauriston, the bearer of the ratification of the preliminaries of peace.

The First Consul was at all times the declared enemy of the liberty of the press, and therefore he ruled the journals with a hand of iron.[1] I have often heard him say, " Were I to slacken the reins, I should not continue three months in power." He unfortunately held the same opinion respecting every other prerogative of public freedom. The silence he had imposed in France he wished, if he could, to impose in England. He was irritated by the calumnies and libels so liberally cast upon him by the English journals, and especially by one written in French, called *L'Ambigu*, conducted by Peltier, who had been the editor of the *Actes des Apôtres* in Paris. The *Ambigu* was constantly teeming with the most violent attacks on the First Consul and the French nation. Bonaparte could never, like the English, bring himself to despise newspaper libels, and he revenged himself by violent articles which he caused to be inserted in the *Moniteur*. He directed M. Otto to remonstrate, in an official note, against a system of calumny which he believed to be authorised by the English Government. Besides this official proceeding he applied personally to Mr. Addington, the

[1] An incident, illustrative of the great irritation which Bonaparte felt at the plain speaking of the English press, also shows the important character of Coleridge's writings in the *Morning Post*. In the course of a debate in the House of Commons Fox asserted that the rupture of the truce of Amiens had its origin in certain essays which had appeared in the *Morning Post*, and which were known to have proceeded from the pen of Coleridge. But Fox added an ungenerous and malicious hint that the writer was at Rome, within the reach of Bonaparte. The information reached the ears for which it was uttered, and an order was sent from Paris to compass the arrest of Coleridge. It was in the year 1806, when the poet was making a tour in Italy. The news reached him at Naples, through a brother of the illustrious Humboldt, as Mr. Gillman says—or in a friendly warning from Prince Jerôme Bonaparte, as we have it on the authority of Mr. Cottle—and the Pope appears to have been reluctant to have a hand in the business, and, in fact, to have furnished him with a passport, if not with a carriage for flight. Coleridge eventually got to Leghorn, where he got a passage by an American ship bound for England ; but his escape coming to the ears of Bonaparte, a look-out was kept for the ship, and she was chased by a French cruiser, which threw the captain into such a state of terror that he made Coleridge throw all his journals and papers overboard (Andrews' *History of Journalism*, vol. ii. p. 28).

Chancellor of the Exchequer, requesting him to procure the adoption of legislative measures against the licentious writings complained of; and, to take the earliest opportunity of satisfying his hatred against the liberty of the press, the First Consul seized the moment of signing the preliminaries to make this request.

Mr. Addington wrote a long answer to the First Consul, which I translated for him. The English Minister refuted, with great force, all the arguments which Bonaparte had employed against the press. He also informed the First Consul that, though a foreigner, it was competent in him to institute a complaint in the courts of law; but that in such case he must be content to see all the scandalous statements of which he complained republished in the report of the trial. He advised him to treat the libels with profound contempt, and do as he and others did, who attached not the slightest importance to them. I congratulate myself on having in some degree prevented a trial taking place at that time.

Things remained in this state for the moment; but after the peace of Amiens the First Consul prosecuted Peltier, whose journal was always full of violence and bitterness against him. Peltier was defended by the celebrated Mackintosh, who, according to the accounts of the time, displayed great eloquence on this occasion, yet, in spite of the ability of his counsel, he was convicted. The verdict, which public opinion considered in the light of a triumph for the defendant, was not followed up by any judgment, in consequence of the rupture of the peace occurring soon after. It is melancholy to reflect that this nervous susceptibility to the libels of the English papers contributed certainly as much as, and perhaps more than, the consideration of great political interests to the renewal of hostilities. The public would be astonished at a great many things if they could only look under the cards.

I have anticipated the rupture of the treaty of Amiens

that I might not interrupt what I had to mention respecting Bonaparte's hatred of the liberty of the press. I now return to the end of the year 1801, the period of the expedition against St. Domingo.

The First Consul, after dictating to me during nearly the whole of one night instructions for that expedition, sent for General Leclerc, and said to him in my presence, "Here, take your instructions; you have a fine opportunity for filling your purse. Go, and no longer tease me with your eternal requests for money." The friendship which Bonaparte felt for his sister Pauline had a good deal of influence in inducing him to take this liberal way of enriching her husband.

The expedition left the ports of France on the 14th of December 1801, and arrived off Cape St. Domingo on the 1st of February 1802. The fatal result of the enterprise is well known, but we are never to be cured of the folly of such absurd expeditions. In the instructions given to Leclerc everything was foreseen; but it was painful to know that the choice of one of the youngest and least capable of all the generals of the army left no hope of a successful result.[1]

The expedition to St. Domingo was one of Bonaparte's great errors. Almost every person whom he consulted endeavoured to dissuade him from it. He attempted a justification through the medium of his historians of St. Helena; but does he succeed when he says, "that he was

---

[1] This attack on Leclerc is met by *Erreurs* (tome ii. p. 247), which details the previous distinguished services of that general, and points out that the First Consul could have easily found quicker means of enriching Leclerc than by sending him and Pauline to St. Domingo; see also Iung's *Lucien*, tome ii. p. 160, where both Napoleon and Lucien seem to agree as to the expedition. As for Madame Leclerc, Madame Junot says that Napoleon strongly urged her going out, which he would hardly have done unless he had believed in the success of the expedition. "I believe," says the Duchesse d'Abrantès (tome ii. p. 234), "General Leclerc would willingly have dispensed with this addition to his baggage, for it was a positive calamity, after the first quarter of an hour's interview had exhausted the pleasure of surveying her really beautiful person, to have the burden of amusing, occupying, and taking care of Madame Leclerc."

obliged to yield to the advice of his Council of State?"
He, truly, was a likely man to submit a question of war to
the discussion of the Council of State, or to be guided in
such an affair by any Council! We must believe that no
other motive influenced the First Consul but the wish, by
giving him the means of enriching himself, to get rid of a
brother-in-law who had the gift of specially annoying him.
The First Consul, who did not really much like this expedition, should have perhaps reflected longer on the difficulties of attempting to subdue the colony by force.
He was shaken by this argument, which I often repeated
to him, and he agreed with it, but the inconceivable influence which the members of his family exercised on him
always overcame him.

Bonaparte dictated to me a letter for Toussaint, full of
sounding words and fine promises, informing him that his
two children, who had been educated in Paris, were sent
back to him, offering him the title of vice-governor, and
stating that he ought readily to assist in an arrangement
which would contribute to reconnect the colony with the
mother-country. Toussaint, who had at first shown a
disposition to close with the bargain, yet feeling afraid of
being deceived by the French, and probably induced by
ambitious motives, resolved on war. He displayed a great
deal of talent ; but, being attacked before the climate had
thinned the French ranks, he was unable to oppose a fresh
army, numerous and inured to war. He capitulated, and
retired to a plantation, which he was not to leave without
Leclerc's permission. A feigned conspiracy on the part
of the blacks formed a pretence for accusing Toussaint,
and he was seized and sent to France.

Toussaint was brought to Paris in the beginning of
August. He was sent, in the first instance, to the Temple,
whence he was removed to the Château de Joux. His imprisonment was rigorous ; few comforts were allowed him.
This treatment, his recollection of the past, his separation

from the world, and the effects of a strange climate, accelerated his death, which took place a few months after his arrival in France. The reports which spread concerning his death, the assertion that it was not a natural one, and that it had been caused by poison, obtained no credit. I should add that Toussaint wrote a letter to Bonaparte; but I never saw in it the expression attributed to him—"The first man of the blacks to the first man of the whites!" Bonaparte acknowledged that the black leader possessed energy, courage, and great skill. I am sure that he would have rejoiced if the result of his relations with St. Domingo had been something else than the kidnapping and transportation of Toussaint.

Leclerc, after fruitless efforts to conquer the colony, was himself carried off by the yellow fever. Rochambeau succeeded him by right of seniority, and was as unsuccessful as Menou had been in Egypt. The submission of the blacks, which could only have been obtained by conciliation, he endeavoured to compel by violence. At last, in December 1803, he surrendered to an English squadron, and abandoned the island to Dessalines.

Bonaparte often experienced severe bodily pain, and I have now little doubt, from the nature of his sufferings, that they were occasioned by the commencement of that malady which terminated his life at St. Helena. These pains, of which he frequently complained, affected him most acutely on the night when he dictated to me the instructions for General Leclerc. It was very late when I conducted him to his apartment. We had just been taking a cup of chocolate, a beverage of which we always partook when our business lasted longer than one o'clock in the morning. He never took a light with him when he went up to his bedroom. I gave him my arm, and we had scarcely got beyond the little staircase which leads to the corridor, when he was rudely run against by a man who was endeavouring to escape as quickly as possible by the

staircase. The First Consul did not fall because I supported him. We soon gained his chamber, where we
found Josephine, who, having heard the noise, awoke
greatly alarmed. From the investigations which were
immediately made it appeared that the uproar was occasioned by a fellow who had been keeping an assignation
and had exceeded the usual hour for his departure.[1]

On the 7th of January 1802 Mademoiselle Hortense was
married to Louis Bonaparte. As the custom was not yet
resumed of adding the religious ceremony to the civil contract, the nuptial benediction was on this occasion
privately given by a priest at the house Rue de la Victoire.
Bonaparte also caused the marriage of his sister Caroline,[2]
which had taken place two years earlier before a mayor,
to be consecrated in the same manner; but he and his
wife did not follow the example. Had he already, then,
an idea of separating from Josephine, and therefore an
unwillingness to render a divorce more difficult by giving
his marriage a religious sanction? I am rather inclined
to think, from what he said to me, that his neglecting to
take a part in the religious ceremony arose from indifference.

Bonaparte said at St. Helena, speaking of Louis and
Hortense, that " they loved each other when they married :
they desired to be united. The marriage was also the
result of Josephine's intrigues, who found her account in
it." I will state the real facts. Louis and Hortense did
not love one another at all. That is certain. The First

---

[1] In speaking of an accident, when Napoleon had a dangerous fall at St. Cloud,
having been thrown out of a carriage on to a great block of stone, narrowly escaping
severe injury to his stomach, Metternich says, " I could almost imagine that this
accident may have assisted to develop the germ of the malady to which Napoleon
succumbed at St. Helena, and I am surprised that this has not been already remarked. It is true, however, that he has often told me that this malady was hereditary in his family " (*Metternich*, tome i. p. 278). His father and several other
members of the family died of the same disease. This accident appears to have
happened in an unsuccessful attempt to drive himself in 1802 ; see Iung's *Lucien*,
tome ii. p. 259.

[2] The wife of Murat, and the cleverest of Bonaparte's sisters.

HORTENSE BEAUHARNAIS,
QUEEN OF HOLLAND

Consul knew it, just as he well knew that Hortense had a
great inclination for Duroc, who did not fully return it.
The First Consul agreed to their union, but Josephine
was troubled by such a marriage, and did all she could to
prevent it. She often spoke to me about it, but rather
late in the day. She told me that her brothers-in-law
were her declared enemies, that I well knew their intrigues, and that I well knew there was no end to the annoy-
ances they made her undergo. In fact, I did know all
this perfectly. She kept on repeating to me that with
this projected marriage she would not have any support ;
that Duroc was nothing except by the favour of Bonaparte ; that he had neither fortune, fame, nor reputation,
and that he could be no help to her against the well-known
ill-will of the brothers of Bonaparte. She wanted some
assurance for the future. She added that her husband
was very fond of Louis, and that if she had the good
fortune to unite him to her daughter this would be a
counterpoise to the calumnies and persecutions of her
other brothers-in-law. I answered her that she had concealed her intentions too long from me, and that I had
promised my services to the young people, and the more
willingly as I knew the favourable opinion of the First
Consul, who had often said to me, "My wife has done
well ; they suit one another, they shall marry one another.
I like Duroc ; he is of good family. I have rightly given
Caroline to Murat, and Pauline to Leclerc, and I can well
give Hortense to Duroc, who is a fine fellow. He is worth
more than the others. He is now general of a division :
there is nothing against this marriage. Besides, I have
other plans for Louis." In speaking to Madame Bonaparte I added that her daughter burst into tears when
spoken to about her marriage with Louis.

The First Consul had sent a brevet of general of division
to Duroc by a special courier, who went to Holland,
through which the newly-made general had to pass on his

return from St. Petersburg, where, as I have already said, he had been sent to compliment the Emperor Alexander on his accession to the throne. The First Consul probably paid this compliment to Duroc in the belief that the marriage would take place.

During Duroc's absence the correspondence of the lovers passed, by their consent, through my hands. Every night I used to make one in a party at billiards, at which Hortense played very well. When I told her, in a whisper, that I had got a letter for her, she would immediately leave off playing and run to her chamber, where I followed and gave her Duroc's epistle. When she opened it her eyes would fill with tears, and it was some time before she could return to the *salon.* All was useless for her. Josephine required a support in the *family* against the *family.* Seeing her firm resolution, I promised to no longer oppose her wishes, which I could not disapprove, but I told her I could only maintain silence and neutrality in these little debates, and she seemed satisfied.

When we were at Malmaison those intrigues continued. At the Tuileries the same conduct was pursued, but then the probability of success was on Duroc's side ; I even congratulated him on his prospects, but he received my compliments in a very cold manner. In a few days after Josephine succeeded in changing the whole face of affairs. Her heart was entirely set on the marriage of Louis with her daughter ; and prayers, entreaties, caresses, and all those little arts which she so well knew how to use, were employed to win the First Consul to her purpose.

On the 4th of January the First Consul, after dinner, entered our cabinet, where I was employed. "Where is Duroc ? " he inquired.—"He has gone to the opera, I believe."—"Tell him, as soon as he returns, that I have promised Hortense to him, and he shall have her. But I wish the marriage to take place in two days at the latest. I will give him 500,000 francs, and name him command-

ant of the eighth military division ; but he must set out
the day after his marriage with his wife for Toulon. We
must live apart ; I want no son-in-law at home. As I wish
to come to some conclusion, let me know to-night whether
this plan will satisfy him."—"I think it will not."—"Very
well ! then she shall marry Louis."—"Will she like that ?"
—"She must like it." Bonaparte gave me these directions in a very abrupt manner, which made me think that
some little domestic warfare had been raging, and that to
put an end to it he had come to propose his ultimatum.
At half-past ten in the evening Duroc returned ; I reported
to him, word for word, the proposition of the First Consul. "Since it has come to that, my good friend," said
he, "tell him he may keep his daughter for me. I am
going to see the ———," and, with an indifference for
which I cannot account, he took his hat and went off.[1]
The First Consul, before going to bed, was informed of
Duroc's reply, and Josephine received from him the promise that Louis and Hortense should be married. The
marriage took place a few days after, to the great regret
of Hortense, and probably to the satisfaction of Duroc.
Louis submitted to have forced on him as a wife a woman
who had hitherto avoided him as much as possible. She
always manifested as much indifference for him as he displayed repugnance for her, and those sentiments have not
been effaced.[2]

Napoleon said at St. Helena that he wished to unite

[1] Duroc eventually married a Mademoiselle Hervas d'Alménara, the daughter of a
Spanish banker, who was later Minister of Joseph, and was created Marquis of
Abruenara. The lady was neither handsome nor amiable, but she possessed a vast
fortune, and Bonaparte himself solicited her hand for his *aide de camp*. After the
death of Duroc his widow married a M. Fabvier, and Napoleon gave his Duchy of
Frioul to his daughter.

[2] The marriage of Louis Bonaparte took place on the 7th January. The bride and
bridegroom were exceedingly dull, and Mademoiselle Hortense wept during the whole
of the ceremony. Josephine, knowing that this union, which commenced so inaus-
piciously, was her own work, anxiously endeavoured to establish a more cordial feeling between her daughter and son-in-law. But all her efforts were vain, and the
marriage proved a very unhappy one (*Mémoires de Constant*).

Napoleon III. was the son of the Queen of Holland (Hortense Beauharnais).

Louis with a niece of Talleyrand. I can only say that I never heard a word of this niece, either from himself, his wife, or his daughter ; and I rather think that at that time the First Consul was looking after a royal alliance for Louis. He often expressed regret at the precipitate marriages of his sisters. It should be recollected that we were now in the year which saw the Consulship for life established, and which, consequently, gave presage of the Empire. Napoleon said truly to the companions of his exile that "Louis' marriage was the result of Josephine's intrigues," but I cannot understand how he never mentioned the intention he once had of uniting Hortense to Duroc. It has been erroneously stated that the First Consul believed that he reconciled the happiness of his daughter with his policy. Hortense did not love Louis, and dreaded this marriage. There was no hope of happiness for her, and the event has proved this. As for the policy of the First Consul, it is not easy to see how it was concerned with the marriage of Louis to Hortense, and in any case the grand policy which professed so loudly to be free from all feminine influences would have been powerless against the intrigues of Josephine, for at this time at the Tuileries the boudoir was often stronger than the cabinet. Here I am happy to have it in my power to contradict most formally and most positively certain infamous insinuations which have prevailed respecting Bonaparte and Hortense. Those who have asserted that Bonaparte ever entertained towards Hortense any other sentiments than those of a father-in-law for a daughter-in-law have, as the ancient knights used to say, "lied in their throats." We shall see farther on what he said to me on this subject, but it is never too soon to destroy such a base calumny. Authors unworthy of belief have stated, without any proof, that not only was there this criminal *liaison*, but they have gone so far as to say that Bonaparte was the father of the eldest son of Hortense. It is a lie, a vile lie.

And yet the rumour has spread through all France and all Europe.   Alas! has calumny such powerful charms that, once they are submitted to, their yoke cannot be broken?[1]

---

[1] Bourrienne's account of this marriage, and his denial of the vile calumny about Napoleon, is corroborated by Madame Rémusat. After saying that Hortense had refused to marry the son of Rewbell and also the Comte de Mun, she goes on: " A short time afterwards Duroc, then *aide de camp* to the Consul, and already noted by him, fell in love with Hortense. She returned the feeling, and believed she had found that other half of herself which she sought. Bonaparte looked favourably on their union, but Madame Bonaparte in her turn was inflexible. 'My daughter,' said she, 'must marry a gentleman or a Bonaparte.' Louis was then thought of. He had no fancy for Hortense ; detested the Beauharnais family, and had a supreme contempt for his sister-in-law.   But as he was silent, he was believed to be gentle ; and as he was severe by character, he was believed to be upright. Madame Louis told me afterwards that at the news of this arrangement she experienced violent grief. Not only was she forbidden to think of the man she loved, but she was about to be given to another of whom she had a secret distrust " (*Rémusat*, tome i. p. 156). For the cruel treatment of Hortense by Louis see the succeeding pages of *Rémusat.* As for the vile scandal about Hortense and Napoleon, there is little doubt that it was spread by the Bonapartist family for interested motives. "Madame Louis became *enceinte* soon after her marriage. The Bonapartists, and especially Madame Murat (Caroline); had disliked this marriage because Joseph having only daughters, it was forseen that the first son of Louis and the grandson of Madame Bonaparte would be the object of great interest. They therefore spread the revolting story that this was the result of a connection of the First Consul with his daughter-in-law, encouraged by the mother herself. 'The public willingly believed this suspicion.' Madame Murat told Louis," etc. (*Rémusat*, tome i. p. 159). This last sentence is corroborated by Miot de Melito (tome ii. p. 170), who, speaking of the later proposal of Napoleon to adopt this child, says that Louis "remembered the damaging stories which ill-will had tried to spread among the public concerning Hortense Beauharnais before he married her, and although a comparison of the date of his marriage with that of the birth of his son must have shown him that these tales were unfounded, he felt that they would be revived by the adoption of this child by the First Consul." Thus this wretched story did harm in every way. The conduct of Josephine must be judged with leniency, engaged as she was in a desperate struggle to maintain her own marriage,—a struggle she kept up with great skill ; see *Metternich*, tome ii. p. 295.   " She baffled all the calculations, all the manœuvres of her adversaries."   But she was foolish enough to talk in her anger as if she believed some of the disgraceful rumours of Napoleon. "Had he not seduced his sisters, one after the other?" (*Rémusat*, tome i. p. 204). As to how far this scandal was really believed by the brothers of Napoleon, see Iung's *Lucien* (tome ii. pp. 268-269), where Lucien describes Louis as coming three times to him for advice as to his marriage with Hortense, both brothers referring to this rumour. The third time Louis announces he is in love with Hortense. " You are in love? Why the devil, then, do you come to me for advice? If so, forget what has been rumoured, and what I have advised you. Marry, and may God bless you."

Thiers (tome iii. p. 303) follows Bourrienne's account. Josephine, alluding to Louis Bonaparte, said, " *His family* have maliciously informed him of the disgraceful stories which have been spread on the conduct of my daughter and on the birth of her son. Hate assigns this child to Napoleon " (*Rémusat*, tome i. p. 205). The child in question was Napoléon Charles (1802-1807).

CHAPTER VIII.

1802–1803.

Bonaparte President of the Cisalpine Republic—Meeting of the deputation at Lyons—Malta and the English—My immortality—*Fête* given
by Madame Murat—Erasures from the emigrant list—Restitution of
property—General Sebastiani—Lord Whitworth—Napoleon's first
symptoms of disease—Corvisart—Influence of physical suffering on
Napoleon's temper—Articles for the *Moniteur*—General Andréossi
—M. Talleyrand's pun—Jerôme Bonaparte—Extravagance of Bonaparte's brothers—M. Collot and the navy contract.

BONAPARTE was anxious to place the Cisalpine Republic on
a footing of harmony with the Government of France.
It was necessary to select a President who should perfectly agree with Bonaparte's views; and in this respect
no one could be so suitable as Bonaparte himself. The
two Presidencies united would serve as a transition to the
throne. Not wishing to be long absent from Paris, and
anxious to avoid the trouble of the journey to Milan, he
arranged to meet the deputation half-way at Lyons. Before our departure I said to him, "Is it possible that you
do not wish to revisit Italy, the first scene of your glory,
and the beautiful capital of Lombardy, where you were
the object of so much homage?"—"I certainly should,"
replied the First Consul, "but the journey to Milan would
occupy too much precious time. I prefer that the meeting should take place in France. My influence over the
deputies will be more prompt and certain at Lyons than
at Milan; and then I should be glad to see the noble
wreck of the army of Egypt, which is collected at Lyons."

On the 8th of January 1802 we set out. Bonaparte
who was now ready to ascend the throne of France,

wished to prepare the Italians for one day crowning him King of Italy, in imitation of Charlemagne, of whom in anticipation he considered himself the successor. He saw that the title of President of the Cisalpine Republic was a great advance towards the sovereignty of Lombardy, as he afterwards found that the Consulate for life was a decisive step towards the throne of France. He obtained the title of President without much difficulty on the 26th of January 1802. The journey to Lyons and the conferences were only matters of form; but high-sounding words and solemn proceedings were required for the public mind.[1]

The attempts which had been made on the life of the First Consul gave rise to a report that he took extraordinary precautions for his safety during this journey to Lyons. I never saw those precautions, and Bonaparte was at all times averse to adopt any. He often repeated "That whoever would risk his own life might take his." It is not true that guards preceded his carriage and watched the roads. The Consul travelled like a private person, and very rarely had arms in his carriage.[2]

---

[1] Ugo Foscolo, the author of the *Ultime Lettere di Jacopo Ortis*, a work which enjoys great and merited reputation in Italy, was at Lyons at the time of the meeting of the Cisalpine Senate.—*Bourrienne.*

[2] Bonaparte may have been careless of his own safety, but that he took great pains in regard to his brother's may be inferred from the following letter, written a few years later:—

"Take care that your *valets de chambre*, your cooks, the guards that sleep in your apartments, and those who come during the night to awaken you with despatches, are all Frenchmen. No one should enter your room during the night except your *aide de camp*, who should sleep in the chamber that precedes your bedroom. Your door should be fastened inside, and you ought not to open it, even to your *aide de camp*, until you have recognised his voice; he himself should not knock at your door until he has locked that of the room which he is in, to make sure of being alone, and of being followed by no one. These precautions are important; they give no trouble, and they inspire confidence—besides, they may really save your life. You should establish these habits immediately and permanently; you ought not to be obliged to have resource to them on some emergercy, which would hurt the feelings of those around you. Do not trust only to your own experience. The Neapolitan character has been notorious in every age, and you have to do with a woman [Queen of Naples] who is the impersonation of crime" (*Napoleon to Joseph*, May 31, 1806.—*Du Casse*, tome ii. p. 260).

At this time, when the ambition of Bonaparte every day took a farther flight, General Clarke took it into his head to go into the box of the First Consul at the "Français," and to place himself in the front seat. By chance the First Consul came to the theatre, but Clarke, hardly rising, did not give up his place. The First Consul only stayed a short time, and when he came back he showed great discontent at this affectation of pride and of vanity. Wishing to get rid of a man whom he looked on as a blundering flatterer and a clumsy critic, he sent him away as *chargé d'affaires* to the young extemporised King of Etruria, where Clarke expiated his folly in a sort of exile. This is all the " *great disfavour* " which has been so much spoken about, In the end General Clarke returned to favour. Berlin knows and regrets it.

On the 25th of March of the same year England signed, at Amiens, a suspension of arms for fourteen months, which was called a treaty of peace. The clauses of this treaty were not calculated to inspire the hope of a very long peace. It was evident, as I have already said, that Engg-gland would not evacuate Malta ; and that island ultimately proved the chief cause of the rupture of the treaty of Amiens. But England, heretofore so haughty in her bearing to the First Consul, had at length treated with him as the Head of the French Government. This, as Bonaparte was aware, boded well for the consolidation of his power.

At that time, when he saw his glory and power augmenting, he said to me in one of our walks at Malmaison, in a moment of hilarity, and clapping me on the shoulder, " Well, Bourrienne, you also will be immortal ! "—" Why, General ? "—" Are you not my secretary ? "—"Tell me the name of Alexander's,"[1] said I. Bonaparte then turned to

---

[1] Bonaparte did not know the name of Alexander's secretary, and I forgot at the moment to tell him it was Callisthenes. He wrote Alexander's Memoirs, as I am writing Bonaparte's ; but, notwithstanding this coincidence, I neither expect nor desire the immortality of my name.—*Bourrienne.*

me and laughing, said, "Hem! that is not bad." There
was, to be sure, a little flattery conveyed in my question,
but that never displeased him, and I certainly did not in
that instance deserve the censure he often bestowed on me
for not being enough of a courtier and flatterer.

Madame Murat gave a grand *fête* in honour of Bonaparte
at her residence at Neuilly.   At dinner Bonaparte sat opposite Madame Murat at the principal table, which was appropriated to the ladies.   He ate fast, and talked but little.
However, when the dessert was served, he put a question
to each lady.   This question was to inquire their respective ages.   When Madame Bourrienne's turn came he
said to her, "Oh! I know yours."   This was a great deal
for his gallantry, and the other ladies were far from being
pleased at it.

Next day, while walking with me in his favourite alley
at Malmaison, he received one of those stupid reports of
the police which were so frequently addressed to him.   It
mentioned the observations which had been made in Paris
about a green livery he had lately adopted.   Some said
that green had been chosen because it was the colour of
the House of Artois.   On reading that a slight sneer was
observable in his countenance, and he said, "What are
these idiots dreaming of?   They must be joking, surely.
Am I no better than M. d'Artois?   They shall soon see
the difference."

Until the middle of the year 1801 the erasures from the
emigrant list had always been proposed by the Minister of
Police.   The First Consul having been informed that intrigue and even bribery had been employed to obtain
them, determined that in future erasures should be part
of the business of his cabinet.   But other affairs took up
his attention, and a dozen or fifteen erasures a week were
the most that were made.   After *Te Deum* had been
chanted at Malmaison for the *Concordat* and the peace, I
took advantage of that moment of general joy to propose

to Bonaparte the return of the whole body of emigrants. "You have," said I in a half-joking way, "reconciled Frenchmen to God—now reconcile them to each other. There have never been any real emigrants, only absentees; and the proof of this is, that erasures from the list have always been, and will always be, made daily." He immediately seized the idea. "We shall see," said he; "but I must except a thousand persons belonging to high families, especially those who are or have been connected with royalty or the Court."

I said in the Chamber of Deputies, and I feel pleasure in repeating here, that the plan of the *Sénatus-consulte,* which Bonaparte dictated to me, excepted from restitution only such mansions as were used for public establishments. These he would neither surrender nor pay rent for. With those exceptions he was willing to restore almost all that was possessed by the State and had not been sold.

The First Consul, as soon as he had finished this plan of a decree, convoked a Grand Council to submit it to their consideration. I was in an adjoining room to that in which they met, and as the deliberations were carried on with great warmth, the members talking very loudly, sometimes even vociferating, I heard all that passed. The revolutionary party rejected all propositions of restitution. They were willing to call back their victims, but they would not part with the spoil.

When the First Consul returned to his cabinet, dissatisfied with the ill success of his project, I took the liberty of saying to him, "You cannot but perceive, General, that your object has been defeated, and your project unsuccessful. The refusal to restore to the emigrants all that the State possesses takes from the recall all its generosity and dignity of character. I wonder how you could yield to such an unreasonable and selfish opposition."—"The revolutionary party," replied he, "had the majority in the

Council. What could I do? Am I strong enough to overcome all those obstacles?"—"General, you can revive the question again, and oppose the party you speak of."—"That would be difficult," he said; "they still have a high hand in these matters. Time is required. However, nothing is definitively arranged. We shall see what can be done." The *Sénatus-consulte*, published on the 6th Floréal, year X. (26th of April 1802), a fortnight after the above conversation took place, is well known. Bonaparte was then obliged to yield to the revolutionary party, or he would have adhered to his first proposition.[1]

Napoleon referred to this matter at St. Helena. He himself says that he "would have been able" (he should have said that he wished) to grant everything, that for a moment he thought of doing so, and that it was a mistake not to do so. "This limitation on my part," he adds, "destroyed all the good effect of the return of the emigrants. The mistake was the greater since I thought of doing it, but I was alone, surrounded by oppositions and by spies: all were against your party. You cannot easily picture the matter to yourself, but important affairs hurried me, time pressed, and I was obliged to act differently." Afterwards he speaks of a syndicate he wished to form, but I have never heard a word of that. I have said how things really happened, and what has been just read confirms this.[2]

The Royalists, dissatisfied with the state of political affairs, were not better pleased with the illiberal conditions of the recall of the emigrants. The friends of public lib-

---

[1] The *Sénatus-consulte* retained the woods and forests of the emigrants, and made their recall an "*amnesty.*" In the end this retention of the forests was used by Napoleon with great dexterity as a means of recalling the emigrant nobility and placing them under personal obligations to him for restoring this species of property. See *Thiers*, tome iii. p. 458, livre xiv.

[2] This was by no means the only time that Napoleon's wishes were opposed successfully in his Council of State. On such occasions he used to describe himself as "*repulsed with loss.*" See the interesting work of St. Hilaire, *Napoléon au Conseil d'État.*

erty, on the other hand, were far from being satisfied with the other acts of the First Consul, or with the conduct of the different public authorities, who were always ready to make concessions to him. Thus all parties were dissatisfied.

Bonaparte was much pleased with General Sebastiani's conduct when he was sent to Constantinople, after the peace of Amiens, to induce the Grand Seignior to renew amicable relations with France.[1]

At the period here alluded to, namely, before the news of the evacuation of Egypt, that country greatly occupied Bonaparte's attention. He thought that to send a man like Sebastiani travelling through Northern Africa, Egypt, and Syria might inspire the sovereigns of those countries with a more favourable idea of France than they now entertained, and might remove the ill impressions which England was endeavouring to produce. On this mission Sebastiani was accordingly despatched. He visited all the Barbary States, Egypt, Palestine, and the Ionian Isles. Everywhere he drew a highly-coloured picture of the power of Bonaparte, and depreciated the glory of England.[2] He strengthened old connections, and contracted new ones with the chiefs of each country. He declared to the authorities of the Ionian Isles that they might rely on the powerful protection of France. Bonaparte, in my opinion, expected too much from the labours of a single individual furnished with but vague instructions. Still Sebastiani did all that could be done. The interesting details of his proceedings were published in the *Moniteur.* The secret information respecting the means of successfully attack-

---

[1] There appears to be some confusion of dates here. The preliminaries of peace between Turkey and France were signed on 9th October 1801, and the definitive treaty 25th June 1802. Sebastiani only left Toulon for Tunis on 16th September 1802, and did not arrive at Alexandria till 16th October 1802. See *Erreurs*, tome i. p. 14; *Thiers*, tome iv. pp. 212 and 291; *Alison*, chap. xxxvi. paragraph 97.

[2] This General, or Count Sebastiani, was afterwards ambassador for Louis Philippe at our Court.

ing the English establishments in India was very curious, though not affording the hope of speedy success.

The published abstract of General Sebastiani's report was full of expressions hostile to England. Among other things it was stated that Egypt might be conquered with 6000 men, and that the Ionian Isles where disposed to throw off the yoke. There can be little doubt that this publication hastened the rupture of the treaty of Amiens.

England suspended all discussions respecting Malta, and declared that she would not resume them till the King of Great Britain should receive satisfaction for what was called an act of hostility. This was always put forward as a justification, good or bad, for breaking the treaty of Amiens, which England had never shown herself very ready to execute.

Bonaparte, waiving the usual forms of etiquette, expressed his wish to have a private conference with Lord Whitworth, the ambassador from London to Paris, and who had been the English ambassador at St. Petersburg previous to the rupture which preceded the death of Paul I. Bonaparte counted much on the effect he might produce by that captivating manner which he so well knew how to assume in conversation ; but all was in vain. In signing the treaty of Amiens the British Minister was well aware that he would be the first to break it.

About the commencement of the year 1802 Napoleon began to feel acute pains in his right side. I have often seen him at Malmaison, when sitting up at night, lean against the right arm of his chair, and unbuttoning his coat and waistcoat exclaim, " What pain I feel ! " I would then accompany him to his bedchamber, and have often been obliged to support him on the little staircase which led from his cabinet to the corridor. He frequently used to say at this time, "I fear that when I am forty I shall become a great eater : I have a foreboding that I shall grow very corpulent." This fear of obesity, though it

annoyed him very much, did not appear to have the least
foundation, judging from his habitual temperance and
spare habit of body. He asked me who was my physician.
I told him M. Corvisart, whom his brother Louis had recommended to me. A few days after he called in Corvisart, who three years later was appointed first physician
to the Emperor. He appeared to derive much benefit
from the prescriptions of Corvisart, whose open and good-
humoured countenance at once made a favourable impression on him.

The pain which the First Consul felt at this time increased his irritability. Perhaps many of the acts of this
epoch of his life should be attributed to this illness. At
the time in question his ideas were not the same in the
evening as they had been in the morning ; and often in
the morning he would tear up, even without the least remark, notes he had dictated to me at night and which he
had considered excellent. At other times I took on myself not to send to the *Moniteur*, as he wished me to do,
notes which, dictated by annoyance and irascibility, might
have produced a bad effect in Europe. When the next
day he did not see the article, I attributed this to the note
being too late, or to the late arrival of the courier. But
I told him it was no loss, for it would be inserted the next
day. He did not answer at once, but a quarter of an hour
afterwards he said to me, " Do not send my note to the
Moniteur without showing it to me." He took it and re-
read it. Sometimes he was astonished at what he had
dictated to me, and amused himself by saying that I had
not understood him properly. " That is not much good,
is it ? "—" 'Pon my word, I don't quite know."—" Oh no,
it is worthless ; what say you ? " Then he bowed his head
a little, and tore up the paper. Once when we were at the
Tuileries he sent me at two o'clock in the morning a small
note in his own writing, in which was, " To Bourrienne.
Write to Maret to make him erase from the note which

Fleurieu has read to the Tribunate the phrase (spelt *frase*) concerning Costaz, and to soften as much as possible what concerns the reporter of the Tribunate."

This change, after time for reflection, arose, as often happened with him, from observations I had made to him, and which he had at first angrily repulsed.

After the peace of Amiens the First Consul, wishing to send an ambassador to England, cast his eyes—for what reason I know not—on General Andréossi. I took the liberty of making some observation on a choice which did not appear to me to correspond with the importance of the mission. Bonaparte replied, "I have not determined on it; I will talk to Talleyrand on the subject." When we were at Malmaison in the evening M. de Talleyrand came to transact business with the First Consul. The proposed appointment of an ambassador to England was mentioned. After several persons had been named the First Consul said, "I believe I must send Andréossi." M. de Talleyrand, who was not much pleased with the choice, observed in a dry sarcastic tone, " You must send André *aussi!* Pray, who is this André?"—"I did not mention any André; I said Andréossi. You know Andreossi, the general of artillery?"—"Ah! true; Andréossi: I did not think of him: I was thinking only of the diplomatic men, and did not recollect any of that name. Yes, yes; Andréossi is in the artillery!" The general was appointed ambassador, and went to London after the treaty of Amiens; but he returned again in a few months. He had nothing of consequence to do, which was very lucky for him.

In 1802 Jérôme was at Brest in the rank of *enseigne de vaisseau.*[1] He launched into expenses far beyond what his fortune or his pay could maintain. He often drew upon me for sums of money which the First Consul paid with much unwillingness. One of his letters in particular excited

[1] A rank in the navy equivalent to that of our lieutenant.

Napoleon's anger. The epistle was filled with accounts of the entertainments Jérôme was giving and receiving, and ended by stating that he should draw on me for 17,000 francs. To this Bonaparte wrote the following reply :—

I have read your letter, Monsieur l'Enseigne de Vaisseau ; and I am waiting to hear that you are studying on board your corvette a profession which you ought to consider as your road to glory. Die young, and I shall have some consolatory reflection ; but if you live to sixty without having served your country, and without leaving behind you any honourable recollections, you had better not have lived at all.

Jérôme never fulfilled the wishes of his brother, who always called him a little profligate. From his earliest years his conduct was often a source of vexation to his brother and his family. Westphalia will not soon forget that he was her King ; and his subjects did not without reason surname him "Heliogabalus in miniature."

The First Consul was harassed by the continual demands for money made on him by his brothers. To get rid of Joseph, who expended large sums at Mortfontaine, as Lucien did at Neuilly, he gave M. Collot the contract for victualling the navy, on the condition of his paying Joseph 1,500,000 francs a year out of his profits. I believe this arrangement answered Joseph's purpose very well ; but it was anything but advantageous to M. Collot. I think a whole year elapsed without his pocketing a single farthing. He obtained an audience of the First Consul, to whom he stated his grievances. His outlays he showed were enormous, and he could get no payment from the navy office. Upon which the Consul angrily interrupted him, saying, " Do you think I am a mere capuchin? Decrès must have 100,000 crowns, Duroc 100,000, Bourrienne 100,000 ; you must make the payments, and don't come here troubling me with your long stories. It is the business of my Ministers to give me accounts of such matters ; I will hear Decrès, and that's enough. Let me be teased no longer with these complaints ; I cannot attend to them." Bonaparte then very unceremoniously dismissed M. Collot. I learned afterwards that he did not get a settlement of the business until after a great deal of trouble. M. Collot once said to me, "If he had asked me for as much money as would have built a frigate he should have had it. All I want now is to be paid, and to get rid of the business." M. Collot had reason and honour on his side ; but there was nothing but shuffling on the other.

CHAPTER IX.

1802.

Proverbial falsehood of bulletins—M. Doublet—Creation of the Legion of
    Honour—Opposition to it in the Council and other authorities of the
    State—The partisans of an hereditary system—The question of the
    Consulship for life.

THE historian of these times ought to put no faith in the
bulletins, despatches, notes, and proclamations which have
emanated from Bonaparte, or passed through his hands.
For my part, I believe that the proverb, "As great a liar as
a bulletin," has as much truth in it as the axiom, two and
two make four.

The bulletins always announced what Bonaparte wished
to be believed true ; but to form a proper judgment on any
fact, counter-bulletins must be sought for and consulted.
It is well known, too, that Bonaparte attached great importance to the place whence he dated his bulletins ; thus,
he dated his decrees respecting the theatres and Hamburg
beef at Moscow.[1]

The official documents were almost always incorrect.
There was falsity in the exaggerated descriptions of his
victories, and falsity again in the suppression or palliation
of his reverses and losses. A writer, if he took his ma-
terials from the bulletins and the official correspondence
of the time, would compose a romance rather than a true

[1] This has been a common text for attacks on Napoleon, but *Erreurs* (tome i. p.
12) fairly remarks that with his centralised form of government the decrees daily required had to be daily signed, no matter where the Emperor was. The same with
his Ministers. Daru, in a paper not meant for publicity, sends from near Moscow a
long criticism on a plan for provisioning the great towns of France. See Sainte-
Beuve, *Causeries*, tome ix. p. 455.

history. Of this many proofs have been given in the present work.

Another thing which always appeared to me very remarkable was, that Bonaparte, notwithstanding his incontestable superiority, studied to depreciate the reputations of his military commanders, and to throw on their shoulders faults which he had committed himself. It is notorious that complaints and remonstrances, as energetic as they were well founded, were frequently addressed to General Bonaparte on the subject of his unjust and partial bulletins, which often attributed the success of a day to some one who had very little to do with it, and made no mention of the officer who actually had the command. The complaints made by the officers and soldiers stationed at Damietta compelled General Lanusse, the commander, to remonstrate against the alteration of a bulletin, by which an engagement with a body of Arabs was represented as an insignificant affair, and the loss trifling, though the General had stated the action to be one of importance, and the loss considerable. The misstatement, in consequence of his spirited and energetic remonstrances, was corrected.

Bonaparte took Malta, as is well known, in forty-eight hours. The empire of the Mediterranean, secured to the English by the battle of Aboukir, and their numerous cruising vessels, gave them the means of starving the garrison, and of thus forcing General Vaubois, the commandant of Malta, who was cut off from all communication with France, to capitulate. Accordingly on the 4th of September 1800 he yielded up the Gibraltar of the Mediterranean, after a noble defence of two years. These facts require to be stated in order the better to understand what follows.

On 22d February 1802 a person of the name of Doublet, who was the commissary of the French Government at Malta when we possessed that island, called upon me at the Tuileries. He complained bitterly that the letter which

he had written from Malta to the First Consul on the 2d
Ventôse, year VIII. (9th February 1800), had been altered
in the *Moniteur.* " I congratulated him," said M. Doublet,
" on the 18th Brumaire, and informed him of the state of
Malta, which was very alarming.   Quite the contrary was
printed in the *Moniteur,* and that is what I complain of.   It
placed me in a very disagreeable situation at Malta, where
I was accused of having concealed the real situation of the
island, in which I was discharging a public function that
gave weight to my words."   I observed to him that as I
was not the editor of the *Moniteur* it was of no use to apply
to me ; but I told him to give me a copy of the letter, and
I would mention the subject to the First Consul, and communicate the answer to him.   Doublet searched his pocket
for the letter, but could not find it.   He said he would
send a copy, and begged me to discover how the error
originated.   On the same day he sent me the copy of the
letter, in which, after congratulating Bonaparte on his
return, the following passage occurs :—" *Hasten to save
Malta with men and provisions: no time is to be lost.*"   For
this passage these words were substituted in the *Moniteur :*
" *His name inspires the brave defenders of Malta with fresh
courage ; we have men and provisions.*"

Ignorant of the motives of so strange a perversion, I
showed this letter to the First Consul.   He shrugged up
his shoulders and said, laughing, " Take no notice of
him, he is a fool ; give yourself no further trouble about
it."

It was clear there was nothing more to be done.   It
was, however, in despite of me that M. Doublet was played
this ill turn.   I represented to the First Consul the inconveniences which M. Doublet might experience from
this affair.   But I very rarely saw letters or reports published as they were received.   I can easily understand
how particular motives might be alleged in order to justify
such falsifications ; for, when the path of candour and

good faith is departed from, any pretext is put forward to excuse bad conduct. What sort of a history would he write who should consult only the pages of the *Moniteur ?*

After the vote for adding a second ten years to the duration of Bonaparte's Consulship he created, on the 19th of May, the order of the Legion of Honour. This institution was soon followed by that of the new nobility. Thus, in a short space of time, the *Concordat* to tranquillise consciences and re-establish harmony in the Church ; the decree to recall the emigrants ; the continuance of the Consular power for ten years, by way of preparation for the Consulship for life, and the possession of the Empire ; and the creation, in a country which had abolished all distinctions, of an order which was to engender prodigies, followed closely on the heels of each other. The Bourbons, in reviving the abolished orders, were wise enough to preserve along with them the Legion of Honour.

It has already been seen how, in certain circumstances, the First Consul always escaped from the consequences of his own precipitation, and got rid of his blunders by throwing the blame on others—as, for example, in the affair of the parallel between Cæsar, Cromwell, and Bonaparte. He was indeed so precipitate that one might say, had he been a gardener, he would have wished to see the fruits ripen before the blossoms had fallen off. This inconsiderate haste nearly proved fatal to the creation of the Legion of Honour, a project which ripened in his mind as soon as he beheld the orders glittering at the button-holes of the Foreign Ministers. He would frequently exclaim, "This is well ! These are the things for the people !"

I was, I must confess, a decided partisan of the foundation in France of a new chivalric order, because I think, in every well-conducted State, the chief of the Government ought to do all in his power to stimulate the honour of the citizens, and to render them more sensible to honorary distinctions than to pecuniary advantages. I tried, however, at the same time to warn the First Consul of his precipitancy. He heard me not ; but I must with equal frankness confess that on this occasion I was soon freed from all apprehension with respect to the consequences of the difficulties he had to encounter in the Council and in the other constituted orders of the State.

On the 4th of May 1801 he brought forward, for the first time officially, in the Council of State the question of the establishment of the Legion of Honour,[1] which on the 19th May 1802 was proclaimed a law of the State. The opposition to this measure was very great, and all the power of the First Consul, the force of his arguments, and the immense influence of his position, could procure him no more than 14 votes out of 24. The same feeling was displayed at the Tribunate, where the measure only passed by a vote of 56 to 38. The balance was about the same in the Legislative Body, where the votes were 166 to 110. It follows, then, that out of the 394 voters in those three separate bodies a majority only of 78 was obtained. Surprised at so feeble a majority, the First Consul said in the evening, " Ah ! I see very clearly the prejudices are still too strong. You were right ; I should have waited. It was not a thing of such urgency. But then, it must be owned, the speakers for the measure defended it badly. The strong minority has not judged me fairly."—" Be calm," rejoined I : " without doubt it would have been better to wait ; but the thing is done, and you will soon find that the taste for these distinctions is not near gone by. It is a taste which belongs to the nature of man. You may expect some extraordinary circumstances from this creation—you will soon see them."

In April 1802 the First Consul left no stone unturned to get himself declared Consul for life. It is perhaps at

[1] For details of the debates on the establishment of the Legion of Honour, see Mathieu Dumas (tome iii. p. 226), who was one of the commission for the preparation of the scheme, and one of the orators charged with its defence before the Corps Législatif.

this epoch of his career that he most brought into play
those principles of duplicity and dissimulation which are
commonly called Machiavellian.   Never were trickery,
falsehood, cunning, and affected moderation put into play
with more talent or success.

In the month of March hereditary succession and a
dynasty were in everybody's mouths.   Lucien was the
most violent propagator of these ideas, and he pursued
his vocation of apostle with constancy and address. It has
already been mentioned that, by his brother's confession,
he published in 1800 a pamphlet enforcing the same ideas ;
which work Bonaparte afterwards condemned as a premature development of his projects.   M. de Talleyrand,
whose ideas could not be otherwise than favourable to the
monarchical form of government, was ready to enter into
explanations with the Cabinets of Europe on the subject.
The words which now constantly resounded in every ear
were " stability and order," under cloak of which the
downfall of the people's right was to be concealed.   At
the same time Bonaparte, with the view of disparaging
the real friends of constitutional liberty, always called
them *idéologues*,[1] or terrorists.   Madame Bonaparte opposed with fortitude the influence of counsels which she
believed fatal to her husband.   He indeed spoke rarely,
and seldom confidentially, with her on politics or public
affairs.   " Mind your distaff or your needle," was with him

[1] I have classed all these people under the denomination of *idéologues*, which, besides, is what specially and literally fits them,—searchers after ideas (ideas generally
empty).   They have been made more ridiculous than even I expected by this application, a correct one, of the term *idéologie* to them.   The phrase has been successful, I believe, because it was mine (Napoleon in Iung's *Lucien*, tome ii. p. 243).
Napoleon welcomed every attack on this description of sage.   Much pleased with a
discourse by Royer Collard, he said to Talleyrand, " Do you know, Monsieur le
Grand Électeur, that a new and serious philosophy is rising in my university, which
may do us great honour and disembarrass us completely of the *idéologues*, slaying
them on the spot by reasoning ? "   (Merlet, *Littérature Française*, tome i. p. 138).
It is with something of the same satisfaction that Rénan, writing of 1848, says that
the finer dreams had been disastrous when brought into the domain of facts, and
that human concerns only began to improve when the *idéologues* ceased to meddle
with them (*Souvenirs*, p. 122).

a common phrase. The individuals who applied themselves with most perseverance in support of the hereditary
question were Lucien, Rœderer, Regnault de St. Jean
d'Angély, and Fontanes. Their efforts were aided by the
conclusion of peace with England, which, by re-establishing general tranquillity for a time, afforded the First Consul an opportunity of forwarding any plan.

While the First Consul aspired to the throne of France,
his brothers, especially Lucien, affected a ridiculous pride
and pretension. Take an almost incredible example of
which I was witness. On Sunday, the 9th of May, Lucien
came to see Madame Bonaparte, who said to him, " Why
did you not come to dinner last Monday ? "—" Because
there was no place marked for me: the brothers of Napoleon ought to have the first place after him."—" What am
I to understand by that ? " answered Madame Bonaparte.
"If you are the brother of Bonaparte, recollect what you
were. At my house all places are the same. Eugène
would never have committed such a folly." [1]

At this period, when the Consulate for life was only in
embryo, flattering counsels poured in from all quarters,
and tended to encourage the First Consul in his design of
grasping at absolute power.

Liberty rejected an unlimited power, and set bounds to
the means he wished and had to employ in order to gratify

[1] On such points there was constant trouble with the Bonapartist family, as will
be seen in Madame de Rémusat's *Memoirs.* For an instance, in 1802, where Joseph
insisted on his mother taking precedence of Josephine at a dinner in his house, when
Napoleon settled the matter by seizing Josephine's arm and leading her in first, to
the consternation of the party ; see *Rémusat,* tome i. p. 234. But Napoleon, right
in this case, had his own ideas on such points. " The place of the Princess Elisa,
the eldest of his sisters, had been put below that of Caroline, Queen of Naples.
Elisa was then only Princess of Lucca. The Emperor suddenly rose, and by a shift
to the right placed the Princess Elisa above the Queen. ' Now,' said he, ' do not forget that in the imperial family I am the only King ' (Iung's *Lucien,* tome ii. p. 231).
This rule he seems to have adhered to, for when he and his brothers went in the same
carriage to the Champ de Mai in 1815, Jérôme, titular King of Westphalia, had to
take the front seat, while his elder brother, Lucien, only bearing the Roman title of
Prince de Canino, sat on one of the seats of honour alongside Napoleon. Jérôme
was disgusted, and grumbled at a *King* having to give way to a mere Roman *Prince.*
See Iung's *Lucien,* tome ii. p. 190.

his excessive love of war and conquest. "The present state of things, this Consulate of ten years," said he to me, "does not satisfy me ; I consider it calculated to excite unceasing troubles." On the 7th of July 1801, he observed, "The question whether France will be a Republic is still doubtful : it will be decided in five or six years." It was clear that he thought this too long a term. Whether he regarded France as his property, or considered himself as the people's delegate and the defender of their rights, I am convinced the First Consul wished the welfare of France ; but then that welfare was in his mind inseparable from absolute power. It was with pain I saw him following this course. The friends of liberty, those who sincerely wished to maintain a Government constitutionally free, allowed themselves to be prevailed upon to consent to an extension of ten years of power beyond the ten years originally granted by the constitution. They made this sacrifice to glory and to that power which was its consequence ; and they were far from thinking they were lending their support to shameless intrigues. They were firm, but for the moment only, and the nomination for life was rejected by the Senate, who voted only ten years more power to Bonaparte, who saw the vision of his ambition again adjourned.

The First Consul dissembled his displeasure with that profound art which, when he could not do otherwise, he exercised to an extreme degree. To a message of the Senate on the subject of that nomination he returned a calm but evasive and equivocating answer, in which, nourishing his favourite hope of obtaining more from the people than from the Senate, he declared with hypocritical humility, "That he would submit to this new sacrifice if the wish of the people demanded what the Senate authorised." Such was the homage he paid to the sovereignty of the people, which was soon to be trampled under his feet !

An extraordinary convocation of the Council of State took place on Monday, the 10th of May. A communication was made to them, not merely of the Senate's consultation, but also of the Frst Consul's adroit and insidious reply. The Council regarded the first merely as a notification, and proceeded, to consider on what question the people should be consulted. Not satisfied with granting to the First Consul ten years of prerogative, the Council thought it best to strike the iron while it was hot, and not to stop short in the middle of so pleasing a work. In fine, they decided that the following question should be put to the people : "Shall the First Consul be appointed for life, and shall he have the power of nominating his successor?" The reports of the police had besides much influence on the result of this discussion, for they one and all declared that the whole of Paris demanded a Consul for life, with the right of naming a successor. The decisions on these two questions were carried as it were by storm. The appointment for life passed unanimously, and the right of naming the successor by a majority. The First Consul, however, formally declared that he condemned this second measure, which had not originated with himself. On receiving the decision of the Council of State the First Consul, to mask his plan for attaining absolute power, thought it advisable to appear to reject a part of what was offered him. He therefore cancelled that clause which proposed to give him the power of appointing a successor, and which had been carried by a small majority.

CHAPTER X.

1802.

General Bernadotte pacifies La Vendée and suppresses a mutiny at Tours
—Bonaparte's injustice towards him—A premeditated scene—Advice
given to Bernadotte, and Bonaparte disappointed—The First Consul's
residence at St. Cloud—His rehearsals for the Empire—His contempt
of mankind—Mr. Fox and Bonaparte—Information of plans of assassination—A military dinner given by Bonaparte—Moreau not of
the party—Effect of the *Sénatus-consultes* on the Consulate for life—
Journey to Plombières—Previous scene between Lucien and Josephine
—Theatrical representations at Neuilly and Malmaison—Loss of a
watch, and honesty rewarded—Canova at St. Cloud—Bonaparte's
reluctance to stand for a model.

HAVING arrived at nearly the middle of the career which I
have undertaken to trace, before I advance farther I must
go back for a few moments, as I have already frequently
done, in order to introduce some circumstances which
escaped my recollection, or which I purposely reserved,
that I might place them amongst facts analogous to them.
Thus, for instance, I have only referred in passing to a
man who, since become a monarch, has not ceased to
honour me with his friendship, as will be seen in the
course of my Memoirs, since the part we have seen him
play in the events of the 18th Brumaire. This man, whom
the inexplicable combination of events has raised to a
throne for the happiness of the people he is called to
govern, is Bernadotte.

It was evident that Bernadotte must necessarily fall into
a kind of disgrace for not having supported Bonaparte's
projects at the period of the overthrow of the Directory.
The First Consul, however, did not dare to avenge himself

openly; but he watched for every opportunity to remove Bernadotte from his presence, to place him in difficult situations, and to entrust him with missions for which no precise instructions were given, in the hope that Bernadotte would commit faults for which the First Consul might make him wholly responsible.

At the commencement of the Consulate the deplorable war in La Vendée raged in all its intensity. The organisation of the Chouans was complete, and this civil war caused Bonaparte much more uneasiness than that which he was obliged to conduct on the Rhine and in Italy; because, from the success of the Vendéans might arise a question respecting internal government, the solution of which was likely to be contrary to Bonaparte's views. The slightest success of the Vendéans spread alarm amongst the holders of national property; and, besides, there was no hope of reconciliation between France and England, her eternal and implacable enemy, as long as the flame of insurrection remained unextinguished.

The task of terminating this unhappy struggle was obviously a difficult one. Bonaparte therefore resolved to impose it on Bernadotte; but this general's conciliatory disposition, his chivalrous manners, his tendency to indulgence, and a happy mixture of prudence and firmness, made him succeed where others would have failed. He finally established good order and submission to the laws.

Some time after the pacification of La Vendée a rebellious disposition manifested itself at Tours amongst the soldiers of a regiment stationed there. The men refused to march until they received their arrears of pay. Bernadotte, as commander-in-chief of the army of the west, without being alarmed at the disturbance, ordered the fifty-second demi-brigade—the one in question—to be drawn up in the square of Tours, where, at the very head of the corps, the leaders of the mutiny were by his orders arrested without any resistance being offered. Carnot.

who was then Minister of War, made a report to the First Consul on this affair, which, but for the firmness of Bernadotte, might have been attended with disagreeable results. Carnot's report contained a plain statement of the facts, and of General Bernadotte's conduct. Bonaparte was, however, desirous to find in it some pretext for blaming him, and made me write these words on the margin of the report: " *General Bernadotte did not act discreetly in adopting such severe measures against the fifty-second demi-brigade, he not having the means, if he had been unsuccessful, of re-establishing order in a town the garrison of which was not strong enough to subdue the mutineers.*"

A few days after, the First Consul having learned that the result of this affair was quite different from that which he affected to dread, and being convinced that by Bernadotte's firmness alone order had been restored, he found himself in some measure constrained to write to the General, and he dictated the following letter to me :—

PARIS, 11*th Vendémiaire, year XI.*

CITIZEN-GENERAL—I have read with interest the account of what you did to re-establish order in the fifty-second demi-brigade, and also the report of General Liebert, dated the 5th Vendémiaire. Tell that officer that the Government is satisfied with his conduct. His promotion from the rank of Colonel to that of General of brigade is confirmed. I wish that brave officer to come to Paris. He has afforded an example of firmness and energy which does honour to a soldier.   (Signed)   BONAPARTE.

Thus in the same affair Bonaparte, in a few days, from the spontaneous expression of blame dictated by hate, was reduced to the necessity of declaring his approbation, which he did, as may be seen, with studied coldness, and even taking pains to make his praises apply to Colonel Liebert, and not to the general-in-chief.

Time only served to augment Bonaparte's dislike of Bernadotte. It might be said that the farther he advanced in his rapid march towards absolute power the more animosity he cherished against the individual who had refused to aid his first steps in his adventurous career. At the same time the persons about Bonaparte who practised the art of flattering failed not to multiply reports and insinuations against Bernadotte. I recollect one day, when there was to be a grand public levée, seeing Bonaparte so much out of temper that I asked him the cause of it. "I can bear it no longer," he replied impetuously. "I have resolved to have a scene with Bernadotte to-day. He will probably be here. I will open the fire, let what will come of it. He may do what he pleases. We shall see! It is time there should be an end of this."

I had never before observed the First Consul so violently irritated. He was in a terrible passion, and I dreaded the moment when the levée was to open. When he left me to go down to the *salon* I availed myself of the opportunity to get there before him, which I could easily do, as the *salon* was not twenty steps from the cabinet. By good luck Bernadotte was the first person I saw. He was standing in the recess of a window which looked on the square of the Carrousel. To cross the *salon* and reach the General was the work of a moment. "General!" said I, "trust me and retire!—I have good reasons for advising it!" Bernadotte, seeing my extreme anxiety, and aware of the sincere sentiments of esteem and friendship which I entertained for him, consented to retire, and I regarded this as a triumph; for, knowing Bernadotte's frankness of character and his nice sense of honour, I was quite certain that he would not submit to the harsh observations which Bonaparte intended to address to him. My stratagem had all the success I could desire. The First Consul suspected nothing, and remarked only one thing, which was that his victim was absent. When the levée was over he said to me, "What do you think of it, Bourrienne?—Bernadotte did not come."—"So much the better for him, General," was my reply. Nothing further happened. The

First Consul on returning from Josephine found me in the cabinet, and consequently could suspect nothing, and my communication with Bernadotte did not occupy five minutes. Bernadotte always expressed himself much gratified with the proof of friendship I gave him at this delicate conjuncture. The fact is, that from a disposition of my mind, which I could not myself account for, the more Bonaparte's unjust hatred of Bernadotte increased the more sympathy and admiration I felt for the noble character of the latter.[1]

The event in question occurred in the spring of 1802. It was at this period that Bonaparte first occupied St. Cloud, which he was much pleased with, because he found himself more at liberty there than at the Tuileries; which palace is really only a prison for royalty, as there a sovereign cannot even take the air at a window without immediately being the object of the curiosity of the public, who collect in large crowds. At St. Cloud, on the contrary, Bonaparte could walk out from his cabinet and prolong his promenade without being annoyed by petitioners. One of his first steps was to repair the cross road leading from St. Cloud to Malmaison, between which places Bonaparte rode in a quarter of an hour. This proximity to the country, which he liked, made staying at St. Cloud yet pleasanter to him. It was at St. Cloud that the

---

[1] All this part about Bernadotte is attacked in *Erreurs*, and it is evident that Bourrienne is influenced by his connection with that general. Bernadotte applied for the command in La Vendée which Bourrienne represents as forced on him. As for Napoleon not daring to attack Bernadotte openly, his treatment of Moreau, Pichegru, etc., shows that he told the truth when he, later, wrote to Joseph about Masséna : "I do not fear the generals, and I have no managements with them " (*Miot de Melito*, tome ii. p. 281). Bernadotte was not the important personage these Memoirs represent him to have been ; see *Erreurs*, tome i. p. 202 and tome ii. p. 113, etc. Indeed, Napoleon had little "management" for him. In 1800 or 1801 he tells Joseph, Bernadotte's great friend, "Understand that if this wrong-headed Southerner continues to jeer at the acts of my Government, instead of giving him the command he asks for, I will have him shot on the Place du Carrousel " (Iung's *Lucien*, tome ii. p. 107). Later on, too, the Emperor's order of the day after Wagram will be borne in mind, though of course the relative positions of the two men had then much altered.

First Consul made, if I may so express it, his first rehearsals of the grand drama of the Empire. It was there he began to introduce, in external forms, the habits and etiquette which brought to mind the ceremonies of sovereignty. He soon perceived the influence which pomp of ceremony, brilliancy of appearance, and richness of costume, exercised over the mass of mankind. "Men," he remarked to me a; this period, "well deserve the contempt I feel for them. I have only to put some gold lace on the coats of my virtuous republicans and they immediately become just what I wish them."

I remember one day, after one of his frequent sallies of contempt for human kind, I observed to him that although baubles might excite vulgar admiration, there were some distinguished men who did not permit themselves to be fascinated by their allurements ; and I mentioned the celebrated Fox by way of example, who, previous to the conclusion of the peace of Amiens, visited Paris, where he was remarked for his extreme simplicity. The First Consul said, "Ah! you are right with respect to him. Mr. Fox is a truly great man, and pleases me much."

In fact, Bonaparte always received Mr. Fox's visits with the greatest satisfaction ; and after every conversation they had together he never failed to express to me the pleasure which he experienced in discoursing with a man every way worthy of the great celebrity he had attained. He considered him a very superior man, and wished he might have to treat with him in his future negotiations with England. It may be supposed that Mr. Fox, on his part, never forgot the terms of intimacy, I may say of confidence, on which he had been with the First Consul. In fact, he on several occasions informed him in time of war of the plots formed against his life.[1] Less could not

---

[1] Bonaparte's friendship for Mr. Fox was perfectly sincere. It was a subject on which he often dwelt in his captivity at St. Helena :—

"'Fox,' said he, 'was sincere and honest in his intentions; had he lived there would have been a peace, and England would now be contented and happy. Fox

be expected from a man of so noble a character. I can likewise affirm, having more than once been in possession of proofs of the fact, that the English Government constantly rejected with indignation all such projects. I do not mean those which had for their object the overthrow of the Consular or Imperial Government, but all plans of assassination and secret attacks on the person of Bonaparte, whether First Consul or Emperor. I will here request the indulgence of the reader whilst I relate a circumstance which occurred a year before Mr. Fox's journey to Paris ; but as it refers to Moreau, I believe that the transposition will be pardoned more easily than the omission.

During the summer 1801 the First Consul took a fancy to give a grand military dinner at a restaurateur's. The restaurateur he favoured with his company was Véri, whose establishment was situated on the terrace of the

knew the true interests of your country. He was received with a sort of triumph in every city in France through which he passed. *Fêtes,* and every honour the inhabitants could confer, were spontaneously offered wherever he was known. It must have been a most gratifying sensation to him to be received in such a manner by a country which had been so long hostile to his own, particularly when he saw that they were the genuine sentiments of the people. Pitt probably would have been murdered. I liked Fox, and loved to converse with him. A circumstance occurred which, although accidental, must have been very flattering to him. As I paid him every attention, I gave orders that he should have free admission everywhere. One day he went with his family to see St. Cloud, in which there was a private cabinet of mine that had not been opened for some time and was never shown to strangers. By some accident Fox and his wife opened the door and entered. There he saw the statues of a number of great men, chiefly patriots, such as Sidney, Hampden, Washington, Cicero, etc., Lord Chatham, and amongst the rest his own, which was first recognised by his wife, who said, 'My dear, this is yours.' This little incident, although trifling and accidental, gained him great honour, and spread directly through Paris. The fact was that a considerable time before I had determined upon forming a collection of statues of the greatest men, and the most distinguished for their virtues, of all nations. I did not admire them the less because they were enemies, and had actually procured busts of some of the greatest enemies of France, amongst others that of Nelson. I was afterwards diverted from this intention by occurrences which did not allow me time to attend to the collecting of statues.'

"Napoleon then recounted the noble manner in which Fox had made known to him the proposal that had been made to assassinate him, which generous act he did not fail to compare with the treatment he now received, and with the attempts made upon his life by wretches paid by . . . in 1803, and landed in France in British men-of-war " (*Napoleon in Exile*).

Feuillans with an entrance into the garden of the Tuileries. Bonaparte did not send an invitation to Moreau, whom I met by chance that day in the following manner :—The ceremony of the dinner at Véri's leaving me at liberty to dispose of my time, I availed myself of it to go and dine at a restaurateur's named Rose, who then enjoyed great celebrity amongst the distinguished gastronomes. I dined in company with M. Carbonnet, a friend of Moreau's family, and two or three other persons. Whilst we were at table in the rotunda we were informed by the waiter who attended on us that General Moreau and his wife, with Lacuée and two other military men, were in an adjoining apartment. Suchet, who had dined at Véri's, where he said everything was prodigiously dull, on rising from the table joined Moreau's party. These details we learned from M. Carbonnet, who left us for a few moments to see the General and Madame Moreau.

Bonaparte's affectation in not inviting Moreau at the moment when the latter had returned a conqueror from the army of the Rhine, and at the same time the affectation of Moreau in going publicly the same day to dine at another restaurateur's, afforded ground for the supposition that the coolness which existed between them would soon be converted into enmity. The people of Paris naturally thought that the conqueror of Marengo might, without any degradation, have given the conqueror of Hohenlinden a seat at his table.

By the commencement of the year 1802 the Republic had ceased to be anything else than a fiction, or an historical recollection. All that remained of it was a deceptive inscription on the gates of the Palace. Even at the time of his installation at the Tuileries Bonaparte had caused the two trees of liberty which were planted in the court to be cut down ; thus removing the outward emblems before he destroyed the reality. But the moment the Senatorial decisions of the 2d and 4th of August were published it was evident to the dullest perceptions that the power of the First Consul wanted nothing but a name.

After these *Consultes* Bonaparte readily accustomed himself to regard the principal authorities of the State merely as neccessary instruments for the exercise of his power. Interested advisers then crowded round him. It was seriously proposed that he should restore the ancient titles, as being more in harmony with the new power which the people had confided to him than the republican forms. He was still of opinion, however, according to his phrase, that "the pear was not yet ripe," and would not hear this project spoken of for a moment. "All this," he said to me one day, "will come in good time ; but you must see, Bourrienne, that it is necessary I should, in the first place, assume a title, from which the others that I will give to everybody will naturally take their origin. The greatest difficulty is surmounted. There is no longer any person to deceive. Everybody sees as clear as day that it is only one step which separates the throne from the Consulate for life. However, we must be cautious. There are some troublesome fellows in the Tribunate, but I will take care of them."

Whilst these serious questions agitated men's minds the greater part of the residents at Malmaison took a trip to Plombières. Josephine, Bonaparte's mother, Madame Beauharnais-Lavallette, Hortense, and General Rapp, were of this party. It pleased the fancy of the jocund company to address to me a bulletin of the pleasant and unpleasant occurrences of the journey. I insert this letter merely as a proof of the intimacy which existed between the writers and myself. It follows, precisely as I have preserved it, with the exception of the *blots*, for which it will be seen they apologised.

An Account of the Journey to Plombières.
To the Inhabitants of Malmaison.

The whole party left Malmaison in tears, which brought on such dreadful headaches that all the amiable persons were quite overcome by the idea of the journey. Madame Bonaparte, *mère*, supported the fatigues of this memorable day with the greatest courage; but Madame Bonaparte, *Consulesse*, did not show any. The two young ladies who sat in the dormeuse, Mademoiselle Hortense and Madame Lavallette, were rival candidates for a bottle of Eau de Cologne; and every now and then the amiable M. Rapp made the carriage stop for the comfort of his poor little sick heart, which overflowed with bile: in fine, he was obliged to take to bed on arriving at Epernay, while the rest of the amiable party tried to drown their sorrows in champagne. The second day was more fortunate on the score of health and spirits, but provisions were wanting, and great were the sufferings of the stomach. The travellers lived on the hope of a good supper at Toul; but despair was at its height when, on arriving there, they found only a wretched inn, and nothing in it. We saw some odd-looking folks there, which indemnified us a little for spinach dressed in lamp-oil, and red asparagus fried with curdled milk. Who would not have been amused to see the Malmaison gourmands seated at a table so shockingly served!

In no record of history is there to be found a day passed in distress so dreadful as that on which we arrived at Plombières. On departing from Toul we intended to breakfast at Nancy, for every stomach had been empty for two days; but the civil and military authorities came out to meet us, and prevented us from executing our plan. We continued our route, wasting away, so that you might see us growing thinner every moment. To complete our misfortune, the dormeuse, which seemed to have taken a fancy to embark on the Moselle for Metz, barely escaped an overturn. But at Plombières we have been well compensated for this unlucky journey, for on our arrival we were received with all kinds of rejoicings. The town was illuminated, the cannon fired, and the faces of handsome women at all the windows give us reason to hope that we shall bear our absence from Malmaison with the less regret.

With the exception of some anecdotes, which we reserve for chit-chat on our return, you have here a correct account of our journey, which we, the undersigned, hereby certify.

JOSEPHINE BONAPARTE.
BEAUHARNAIS-LAVALLETTE.
HORTENSE BEAUHARNAIS.
RAPP.
BONAPARTE, *mère*.

The company ask pardon for the blots.
    21st Messidor.

It is requested that the person who receives this journal will show it to all who take an interest in the fair travellers.

This journey to Plombières was preceded by a scene which I should abstain from describing if I had not undertaken to relate the truth respecting the family of the First Cousul. Two or three days before her departure Madame Bonaparte sent for me. I obeyed the summons, and found her in tears. " What a man—what a man is that Lucien ! " she exclaimed in accents of grief. " If you knew, my friend, the shameful proposals he has dared to make to me ! ' You are going to the waters,' said he ; ' you must get a child by some other person since you cannot have one by him.' Imagine the indignation with which I received such advice. —'Well,' he continued, ' if you do not wish it, or cannot help it, Bonaparte must get a child by another woman, and you must adopt it, for it is necessary to secure an hereditary successor. It is for your interest ; you must know that.'—' What, sir ! ' I replied, ' do you imagine the nation will suffer a bastard to govern it ? Lucien ! Lucien ! you would ruin your brother ! This is dreadful ! Wretched should I be, were any one to suppose me capable of listening, without horror, to your infamous proposal ! Your ideas are poisonous ; your language horrible ! '—' Well, Madame,' retorted he, ' all I can say to that is, that I am really sorry for you ! ' "

The amiable Josephine was sobbing whilst she described this scene to me, and I was not insensible to the indignation which she felt. The truth is, that at that period Lucien, though constantly affecting to despise power for himself, was incessantly labouring to concentrate it in the hands of his brother ; and he considered three things necessary to the success of his views, namely, hereditary succession, divorce, and the Imperial Government.[1]

---

[1] This account of Lucien's conduct seems doubtful. Lucien had been one of the persons proposed to replace Napoleon in case of any disaster occurring at Marengo. And in suggesting the appearance of such a child, he would have been acting against

Lucien had a delightful house near Neuilly. Some
days before the deplorable scene which I have related he
invited Bonaparte and all the inmates at Malmaison to
witness a theatrical representation. *Alzire* was the piece
performed. Elisa played Alzire, and Lucien, Zamore.
The warmth of their declarations, the energetic expression of their gestures, the too faithful nudity of costume,
disgusted most of the spectators, and Bonaparte more
than any other. When the play was over he was quite indignant. "It is a scandal," he said to me in an angry
tone; "I ought not to suffer such indecencies—I will
give Lucien to understand that I will have no more of it."
When his brother had resumed his own dress, and came
into the *salon*, he addressed him publicly, and gave him
to understand that he must for the future desist from
such representations. When we returned to Malmaison
he again spoke of what had passed with dissatisfaction.
"What!" said he, "when I am endeavouring to restore
purity of manners, my brother and sister must needs exhibit themselves upon the boards almost in a state of nudity! It is an insult!"[1]

his own interests, and against the ambition which all his family felt; see also
Erreurs, tome ii. p. 117. He himself, speaking of the time when the Consul was
elected for a term of ten years only, says, "The eventual choice of a successor to
Napoleon had, for my misfortune, drawn on me the attention of certain political
circles; and it was that which alienated from me my brother's heart" (Iung's
Lucien, tome ii. p. 292). The position of the brothers of Napoleon at this time may
be understood by a later speech of Joseph's to Miot, "He (Napoleon) shall no
longer deceive me. I am sick of his tyranny, and of his vain promises, so often repeated and never fulfilled. I want all or nothing. Let him leave me a private individual, or else offer me a post *which assures me of power after him*" (*Miot de Melito*,
tome ii. p. 107). Lucien represents himself as rather the victim than the enemy of
Josephine. "I might have regretted having as enemy the citizeness Beauharnais,
become my sister-in-law, for it is on account of this hatred for me that she had not
the strength, or the wisdom, or the will to repress the antipathy of her husband for
me" (Iung's *Lucien*, tome ii. p. 213). His wife, the Princess de Canino, represents
Hortense saying to a third person that her mother, the ex-empress Josephine, had
not ceased to regret the fatality which had separated her from her brother-in-law
Lucien, and that she acknowledged she had made a mistake in her policy (Iung,
tome ii. p. 215).

[1] Lucien appears to have really acted well. See for details himself, in Iung's *Lucien*, tome ii. p. 256. There is probably some little jealousy in this account of Lucien's rival troupe. Madame Junot (tome ii. p. 105) says, "Lucien acquitted himself

Lucien had a strong predilection for theatrical exhibitions, to which he attached great importance. The fact is, he declaimed in a superior style, and might have competed with the best professional actors. It was said that the turban of Orosmane, the costume of America, the Roman toga, or the robe of the high priest of Jerusalem, all became him equally well; and I believe that this was the exact truth. Theatrical representations were not confined to Neuilly. We had our theatre and our company of actors at Malmaison; but there everything was conducted with the greatest decorum; and now that I have got behind the scenes, I will not quit them until I have let the reader into the secrets of our drama.

By the direction of the First Consul a very pretty little theatre was built at Malmaison. Our usual actors were Eugène Beauharnais, Hortense, Madame Murat, Lauriston, M. Didelot, one of the prefects of the Palace, some other individuals belonging to the First Consul's household, and myself. Freed from the cares of government, which we confined as much as possible to the Tuileries, we were a very happy colony at Malmaison; and, besides, we were young, and what is there to which youth does not add charms? The pieces which the First Consul most liked to see us perform were, *Le Barbier de Séville* and *Défiance et Malice.* In *Le Barbier* Lauriston played the part of Count Almaviva; Hortense, Rosina; Eugène, Basil; Didelot, Figaro; I, Bartholo; and Isabey, l'Éveillé. Our other stock pieces were, *Projets de Mariage, La Gageure,* the *Dépit Amoureux,* in which I played the part of

admirably, and declaimed to perfection. . . . Not so with Madame Bacciochi" (Elisa). "Her acting was irresistibly laughable. The First Consul found it so, and far from flying into a rage, as M. de Bourrienne represents, he did nothing but laugh during the whole play whenever his sister appeared on the stage, and when we returned to the drawing-room he exclaimed, 'I think we have seen Alzire beautifully parodied.'" Joseph Bonaparte, in meeting this attack, seems more concerned for the credit of the acting than for its decency. "The dresses were those of the Théâtre Français. They were no more indecent than those which the *élite* of France and of Europe delighted in seeing for many years at this national spectacle" (*Erreurs,* tome ii. p. 118).

the valet ; and *L'Impromptu de Campagne,* in which I en-
acted the Baron, having for my Baroness the young and
handsome Caroline Murat.

Hortense's acting was perfection, Caroline was mid-
dling, Eugène played very well, Lauriston was rather
heavy, Didelot passable, and I may venture to assert, without vanity, that I was not quite the worst of the company.
If we were not good actors it was not for want of good instruction and good advice.   Talma and Michot came to
direct us, and made us rehearse before them, sometimes
altogether and sometimes separately.   How many lessons
have I received from Michot whilst walking in the beautiful park of Malmaison !   And may I be excused for saying, that I now experience pleasure in looking back upon
these trifles, which are matters of importance when one is
young, and which contrasted so singularly with the great
theatre on which we did not represent fictitious characters ?   We had, to adopt theatrical language, a good supply of property.   Bonaparte presented each of us with a
collection of dramas very well bound ; and, as the patron
of the company, he provided us with rich and elegant
dresses.[1]

[1] While Bourrienne, belonging to the Malmaison company, considered that the
acting at Neuilly was indecent, Lucien, who refused to act at Malmaison, naturally
thought the Malmaison troupe was dull.   "Hortense and Caroline filled the principal parts.   They were very commonplace.   In this they followed the unfortunate
Marie Antoinette and her companions.   Louis XVI. not naturally polite, when seeing them act, had said that it was royally badly acted" (see Madame Campan's *Life
of Marie Antoinette,* tome i. p. 249).   "The First Consul said of his troupe that it
was sovereignly badly acted. . . . Murat, Lannes, and even Caroline ranted.
Elisa, who, having been educated at Saint Cyr, spoke purely and without accent, refused to act.   Junot acted well the drunken parts, and even the others he undertook.
The rest were decidedly bad.   Worse than bad—ridiculous" (Iung's *Lucien,* tome ii.
p. 256).   Rival actors are not fair critics.   Let us hear Madame Junot (tome ii. p.
103).   "The cleverest of our company was M. de Bourrienne.   He played the more
dignified characters in real perfection, and his talent was the more pleasing as it was
not the result of study, but of a perfect comprehension of his part."   And she goes
on to say that even the best professional actors might have learnt from him in some
parts.   The audience was not a pleasant one to face.   It was the First Consul's habit
to invite forty persons to dinner, and a hundred and fifty for the evening, and con
sequently to hear, criticise, and banter us without mercy" (*Memoirs of Duchesse
d'Abrantès,* tome ii. p. 106).

Bonaparte took great pleasure in our performances. He liked to see plays acted by persons with whom he was familiar. Sometimes he complimented us on our exertions. Although I was as much amused with the thing as others, I was more than once obliged to remind him that my occupations left me but little time to learn my parts. Then he would assume his coaxing manner and say, "Come, do not vex me! You have such a memory! You know that it amuses me. You see that these performances render Malmaison gay and animated; Josephine takes much pleasure in them. Rise earlier in the morning.—In fact, I sleep too much; is not that the case?—Come, Bourrienne, do oblige me. You make me laugh so heartily! Do not deprive me of this pleasure. I have not over much amusement, as you well know."—"Ah, truly! I would not deprive you of any pleasure. I am delighted to be able to contribute to your amusement." After a conversation of this sort I could not do less than set about studying my part.

At this period, during summer, I had half the Sunday to myself. I was, however, obliged to devote a portion of this precious leisure to pleasing Bonaparte by studying a new part as a surprise for him. Occasionally, however, I passed the time at Ruel. I recollect that one day, when I had hurried there from Malmaison, I lost a beautiful watch made by Breguet. It was four o'clock in the afternoon, and the road was that day thronged with people. I made my loss publicly known by means of the crier of Ruel. An hour after, as I was sitting down to table, a young lad belonging to the village brought me my watch. He had found it on the high road in a wheel rut. I was pleased with the probity of this young man, and rewarded both him and his father, who accompanied him. I related the circumstance the same evening to the First Consul, who was so struck with this instance of honesty that he directed me to procure information respecting the young man and his family. I learned that they were honest peasants. Bonaparte gave employment to three brothers of this family ; and, what was most difficult to persuade him to, he exempted the young man who brought me the watch from the conscription.

When a fact of this nature reached Bonaparte's ear it was seldom that he did not give the principal actor in it some proof of his satisfaction. Two qualities predominated in his character—kindness and impatience. Impatience, when he was under its influence, got the better of him ; it was then impossible for him to control himself. I had a remarkable proof of it about this very period.

Canova having arrived in Paris came to St. Cloud to model the figure of the First Consul, of whom he was about to make a colossal statue. This great artist came often, in the hope of getting his model to stand in the proper attitude ; but Bonaparte was so tired, disgusted, and fretted by the process, that he very seldom put himself in the required attitude, and then only for a short time. Bonaparte notwithstanding had the highest regard for Canova. Whenever he was announced the First Consul sent me to keep him company until he was at leisure to give him a sitting ; but he would shrug up his shoulders and say, "More modelling ! Good Heavens, how vexatious !" Canova expressed great displeasure at not being able to study his model as he wished to do, and the little anxiety of Bonaparte on the subject damped the ardour of his imagination. Everybody agrees in saying that he has not succeeded in the work, and I have explained the reason. The Duke of Wellington afterwards possessed this colossal statue, which was about twice his own height.

CHAPTER XI.

1802.

IT is a principle particularly applicable to absolute governments that a prince should change his ministers as
seldom as possible, and never except upon serious grounds.
Bonaparte acted on this principle when First Consul, and
also when he became Emperor. He often allowed unjust
causes to influence him, but he never dismissed a Minister
without cause ; indeed, he more than once, without any
reason, retained Ministers longer than he ought to have
done in the situations in which he had placed them.
Bonaparte's tenacity in this respect, in some instances,
produced very opposite results. For instance, it afforded
M. Gaudin[1] time to establish a degree of order in the
administration of Finance which before his time had never
existed ; and on the other hand, it enabled M. Decrès to
reduce the Ministry of Marine to an unparalleled state of
confusion.

Bonaparte saw nothing in men but helps and obstacles.
On the 18th Brumaire Fouché was a help. The First
Consul feared that he would become an obstacle ; it was
necessary, therefore, to think of dismissing him. Bona-

[1] Afterwards Duke of Gaeta.

parte's most sincere friends had from the beginning been
opposed to Fouché's having any share in the Government.
But their disinterested advice produced no other result
than their own disgrace, so influential a person had
Fouché become. How could it be otherwise? Fouché
was identified with the Republic by the death of the King,
for which he had voted ; with the Reign of Terror by his
sanguinary missions to Lyons and Nevers ; with the Consulate by his real though perhaps exaggerated services ;
with Bonaparte by the charm with which he might be
said to have fascinated him ; with Josephine by the
enmity of the First Consul's brothers. Who would
believe it? Fouché ranked the enemies of the Revolution amongst his warmest partisans. They overwhelmed
him with eulogy, to the disparagement even of the Head
of the State, because the cunning Minister, practising an
interested indulgence, set himself up as the protector of
individuals belonging to classes which, when he was pro-
consul, he had attacked in the mass. Director of public
opinion, and having in his hands the means at his pleasure
of inspiring fear or of entangling by inducements, it was
all in his favour that he had already directed this opinion.
The machinery he set in motion was so calculated that the
police was rather the police of Fouché than that of the
Minister of the General Police. Throughout Paris, and
indeed throughout all France, Fouché obtained credit
for extraordinary ability ; and the popular opinion was
correct in this respect, namely, that no man ever displayed such ability in making it be supposed that he
really possessed talent. Fouché's secret in this particular
is the whole secret of the greater part of those persons
who are called statesmen.

Be this as it may, the First Consul did not behold with
pleasure the factitious influence of which Fouché had possessed himself. For some time past, to the repugnance
which at bottom he had felt towards Fouché, were added

other causes of discontent. In consequence of having been deceived by secret reports and correspondence Bonaparte began to shrug up his shoulders with an expression of regret when he received them, and said, " Would you believe, Bourrienne, that I have been imposed on by these things ? All such denunciations are useless—scandalous. All the reports from prefects and the police, all the intercepted letters, are a tissue of absurdities and lies. I desire to have no more of them." He said so, but he still received them. However, Fouché's dismissal was resolved upon. But though Bonaparte wished to get rid of him, still, under the influence of the charm, he dared not proceed against him without the greatest caution. He first resolved upon the suppression of the office of Minister of Police in order to disguise the motive for the removal of the Minister. The First Consul told Fouché that this suppression, which he spoke of as being yet remote, was calculated more than anything else to give strength to the Government, since it would afford a proof of the security and internal tranquillity of France. Overpowered by the arguments with which Bonaparte supported his proposition, Fouché could urge no good reasons in opposition to it, but contented himself with recommending that the execution of the design, which was good in intention, should, however, be postponed for two years. Bonaparte appeared to listen favourably to Fouché's recommendation, who, as avaricious for money as Bonaparte of glory, consoled himself by thinking that for these two years the administration of the gaming tables would still be for him a Pactolus flowing with gold. For Fouché, already the possessor of an immense fortune, always dreamed of increasing it, though he himself did not know how to enjoy it. With him the ambition of enlarging the bounds of his estate of Pont-Carré was not less felt than with the First Consul the ambition of extending the frontier of France.

Not only did the First Consul not like Fouché, but it is perfectly true that at this time the police wearied and annoyed him. Several times he told me he looked on it as dangerous, especially for the possessor of power. In a Government without the liberty of the press he was quite right. The very services which the police had rendered to the First Consul were of a nature to alarm him, for whoever had conspired against the Directory in favour of the Consulate might also conspire against the Consulate in favour of any other Government. It is needless to say that I only allude to the political police, and not to the municipal police, which is indispensable for large towns, and which has the honourable mission of watching over the health and safety of the citizens.

Fouché, as has been stated, had been Minister of Police since the 18th Brumaire. Everybody who was acquainted with the First Consul's character was unable to explain the ascendency which he had suffered Fouché to acquire over him, and of which Bonaparte himself was really impatient. He saw in Fouché a centre around which all the interests of the Revolution concentrated themselves, and at this he felt indignant ; but, subject to a species of magnetism, he could not break the charm which enthralled him. When he spoke of Fouché in his absence his language was warm, bitter, and hostile. When Fouché was present, Bonaparte's tone was softened, unless some public scene was to be acted like that which occurred after the attempt of the 3d Nivôse.

The suppression of the Ministry of Police being determined on, Bonaparte did not choose to delay the execution of his design, as he had pretended to think necessary. On the evening of the 12th of September we went to Mortfontaine. We passed the next day, which was Monday, at that place, and it was there, far removed from Fouché, and urged by the combined persuasions of Joseph and Lucien, that the First Consul signed the decree of suppression. The next morning we returned to Paris. Fouché came to Malmaison, where we were, in the regular execution of his duties. The First Consul transacted business with him as usual without daring to tell him of his dismissal, and afterwards sent Cambacérès to inform him of it. After this act, respecting which he had hesitated so long, Bonaparte still endeavoured to modify his rigour. Having appointed Fouché a Senator, he said in the letter which he wrote to the Senate to notify the appointment :—

"Fouché, as Minister of Police, in times of difficulty, has by his talent, his activity, and his attachment to the Government done all that circumstances required of him. Placed in the bosom of the Senate, if events should again call for a Minister of Police the Government cannot find one more worthy of its confidence."

From this moment the departments of Justice and Police united were confided to the hands of Regnier.[1] Bonaparte's aversion for Fouché strangely blinded him with respect to the capabilities of his successor. Besides, how could the administration of justice, which rests on fixed, rigid, and unchangeable bases, proceed hand in hand with another administration placed on the quicksand of instantaneous decisions, and surrounded by stratagems and deceptions? Justice should never have anything to do with secret police, unless it be to condemn it.[2] What could be expected from Regnier, charged as he was with incompatible functions? What, under such

[1] Regnier, Claude Antoine (1746–1814), Grand Judge and Minister of Justice from 1802 to November 1813 ; the Ministry of Police was adjoined from 1802 to 1804, when it was again separated ; Duc de Massa, 1809 ; President of the Corps Législatif, 1813 to 1814. At this period the Senators were unable to hold any active office, so that on appointment a Senator was said to be " absorbed."

[2] M. Abrial, Minister of Justice, was called to the Senate at the same time as Fouché. Understanding that the assimilation of the two men was more a disgrace to Abrial than the mere loss of the Ministry, the First Consul said to M. Abrial : " In uniting the Ministry of Police to that of Justice I could not retain you in the Ministry, you are too upright a man to manage the police." Not a flattering speech for Regnier.—*Bourrienne.*

circumstances, could have been expected even from a man gifted with great talents? Such was the exact history of Fouché's disgrace. No person was more afflicted at it than Madame Bonaparte, who only learned the news when it was announced to the public. Josephine, on all occasions, defended Fouché against her husband's sallies. She believed that he was the only one of his Ministers who told him the truth. She had such a high opinion of the way in which Fouché managed the police that the first time I was alone with her after our return from Mortfontaine she said to me, "My dear Bourrienne, speak openly to me; will Napoleon know all about the plots from the police of Moncey, Duroc, Junot, and of Davoust? You know better than I do that these are only wretched spies. Has not Savary also eventually got his police? How all this alarms me. They take away all my supports, and surround me only with enemies."—"To justify your regrets we should be sure that Fouché has never been in agreement with Lucien in favour of the divorce."—"Oh, I do not believe that. Bonaparte does not like him, and he would have been certain to tell me of it when I spoke favourably to him of Fouché. You will see that his brothers will end by bringing him into their plan."

I have already spoken of Josephine's troubles, and of the bad conduct of Joseph, but more particularly of Lucien, towards her; I will therefore describe here, as connected with the disgrace of Fouché, whom Madame Bonaparte regretted as a support, some scenes which occurred about this period at Malmaison. Having been the confidant of both parties, and an involuntary actor in those scenes, now that twenty-seven years have passed since they occurred what motive can induce me to disguise the truth in any respect?

Madame Louis Bonaparte was *enceinte*. Josephine, although she tenderly loved her children, did not seem to behold the approaching event which the situation of her daughter indicated with the interest natural to the heart of a mother. She had long been aware of the calumnious reports circulated respecting the supposed connection between Hortense and the First Consul, and that base accusation cost her many tears. Poor Josephine paid dearly for the splendour of her station ! As I knew how devoid of foundation these atrocious reports were, I endeavoured to console her by telling her what was true, that I was exerting all my efforts to demonstrate their infamy and falsehood. Bonaparte, however, dazzled by the affection which was manifested towards him from all quarters, aggravated the sorrow of his wife by a silly vanity. He endeavoured to persuade her that these reports had their origin only in the wish of the public that he should have a child, so that these seeming consolations offered by self-love to Josephine's grief gave force to existing conjugal alarms, and the fear of divorce returned with all its horrors. Under the foolish illusion of his vanity Bonaparte imagined that France was desirous of being governed even by a bastard if supposed to be a child of his,—a singular mode truly of founding a new legitimacy !

Josephine, whose susceptibility appears to me even now excusable, well knew my sentiments on the subject of Bonaparte's founding a dynasty, and she had not forgotten my conduct when two years before the question had been agitated on the occasion of Louis XVIII.'s letters to the First Consul. I remember that one day, after the publication of the parallel of Cæsar, Cromwell, and Bonaparte, Josephine having entered our cabinet without being announced, which she sometimes did when from the good humour exhibited at breakfast she reckoned upon its continuance, approached Bonaparte softly, seated herself on his knee, passed her hand gently through his hair and over his face, and thinking the moment favourable, said to him in a burst of tenderness, "I entreat of you, Bonaparte, do not make yourself a King ! It is that wretch

Lucien who urges you to it. Do not listen to him!"
Bonaparte replied, without anger, and even smiling as he
pronounced the last words, "You are mad, my poor
Josephine. It is your old dowagers of the Faubourg St.
Germain, your Rochefoucaulds, who tell you all these
fables! . . . Come now, you interrupt me—leave me
alone." What Bonaparte said that day good-naturedly to
his wife I have often heard him declare seriously. I have
been present at five or six altercations on the subject.
That there existed, too, an enmity connected with this
question between the family of Beauharnais and the family of Bonaparte cannot be denied.

Fouché, as I have stated, was in the interest of Josephine, and Lucien was the most bitter of her enemies. One
day Rœderer inveighed with so much violence against
Fouché in the presence of Madame Bonaparte that she
replied with extreme warmth, "The real enemies of Bonaparte are those who feed him with notions of hereditary
descent, of a dynasty, of divorce, and of marriage!"
Josephine could not check this exclamation, as she knew
that Rœderer encouraged those ideas, which he spread
abroad by Lucien's direction. I recollect one day when
she had been to see us at our little house at Ruel: as I
walked with her along the high road to her carriage,
which she had sent forward, I acknowledged too unre-
servedly my fears on account of the ambition of Bonaparte, and of the perfidious advice of his brothers. "Madame," said I, "if we cannot succeed in dissuading the
General from making himself a King, I dread the future
for his sake. If ever he re-establishes royalty he will in
all probability labour for the Bourbons, and enable them
one day to re-ascend the throne which he shall erect.
No one, doubtless, without passing for a fool, can pretend
to say with certainty what series of chances and events
such a proceeding will produce; but common sense
alone is sufficient to convince any one that unfavourable

chances must long be dreaded. The ancient system being re-established, the occupation of the throne will then be only a family question, and not a question of government between liberty and despotic power. Why should not France, if it ceases to be free, prefer the race of her ancient kings? You surely know it. You had not been married two years when, on returning from Italy, your husband told me that he aspired to royalty. Now he is Consul for life. Would he but resolve to stop there ! He already possesses everything but an empty title. No sovereign in Europe has so much power as he has. I am sorry for it, Madame, but I really belive that, in spite of yourself, you will be made Queen or Empress."

Madame Bonaparte had allowed me to speak without interruption, but when I pronounced the words Queen and Empress she exclaimed, "My God ! Bourrienne, such ambition is far from my thoughts. That I may always continue the wife of the First Consul is all I desire. Say to him all that you have said to me. Try and prevent him from making himself King."—"Madame," I replied, "times are greatly altered. The wisest men, the strongest minds, have resolutely and courageously opposed his tendency to the hereditary system. But advice is now useless. He would not listen to me. In all discussions on the subject he adheres inflexibly to the view he has taken. If he be seriously opposed his anger knows no bounds ; his language is harsh and abrupt, his tone imperious, and his authority bears down all before him."— " Yet, Bourrienne, he has so much confidence in you that if you should try once more——" —" Madame, I assure you he will not listen to me. Besides, what could I add to the remarks I made upon his receiving the letters of Louis XVIII., when I fearlessly represented to him that being without children he would have no one to whom to bequeath the throne—that, doubtless, from the opinion which he entertained of his brothers, he could not desire to erect it for them?" Here Josephine again interrupted me by exclaiming, "My kind friend, when you spoke of children did he say anything to you? Did he talk of a divorce?"—"Not a word, Madame, I assure you."—"If they do not urge him to it, I do not believe he will resolve to do such a thing. You know how he likes Eugène, and Eugène behaves so well to him. How different is Lucien. It is that wretch Lucien, to whom Bonaparte listens too much, and of whom, however, he always speaks ill to me."—"I do not know, Madame, what Lucien says to his brother except when he chooses to tell me, because Lucien always avoids having a witness of his interviews with your husband, but I can assure you that for two years I have not heard the word 'divorce' from the General's mouth."—"I always reckon on you, my dear Bourrienne, to turn him away from it, as you did at that time."—"I do not believe he is thinking of it, but if it recurs to him, consider, Madame, that it will be now from very different motives. He is now entirely given up to the interests of his policy and his ambition, which dominate every other feeling in him. There will not now be any question of scandal, or of a trial before a court, but of an act of authority which complaisant laws will justify and which the Church perhaps will sanction."—"That's true. You are right. Good God! how unhappy I am." [1]

Such was the nature of one of the conversations I had with Madame Bonaparte on a subject to which she often recurred. It may not perhaps be uninteresting to endeavour to compare with this what Napoleon said at St.

---

[1] When Bourrienne complains of not knowing what passed between Lucien and Napoleon, we can turn to Lucien's account of Bourrienne, apparently about this very time. "After a stormy interview with Napoleon," says Lucien, "I at once went into the cabinet where Bourrienne was working, and found that unbearable busybody of a secretary, whose star had already paled more than once, which made him more prying than ever, quite upset by the time the First Consul had taken to come out of his bath. He must, or at least might, have heard some noise, for enough had been made. Seeing that he wanted to know the cause from me, I took up a newspaper to avoid being bored by his conversation" (Iung's *Lucien*, tome ii. p. 156).

Helena, speaking of his first wife.   According to the *Memorial* Napoleon there stated that when Josephine was at last constrained to renounce all hope of having a child, she often let fall allusions to a great political fraud, and at length openly proposed it to him.   I make no doubt Bonaparte made use of words to this effect, but I do not believe the assertion.   I recollect one day that Bonaparte, on entering our cabinet, where I was already seated, exclaimed in a transport of joy impossible for me to describe, "Well, Bourrienne, my wife is at last *enceinte!*" I sincerely congratulated him, more, I own, out of courtesy than from any hope of seeing him made a father by Josephine, for I well remembered that Corvisart, who had given medicines to Madame Bonaparte, had nevertheless assured me that he expected no result from them.   Medicine was really the only *political fraud* to which Josephine had recourse; and in her situation what other woman would not have done as much?   Here, then, the husband and the wife are in contradiction, which is nothing uncommon.   But on which side is truth?   I have no hesitation in referring it to Josephine.   There is indeed an immense difference between the statements of a woman entrusting her fears and her hopes to the sole confidant of her family secrets, and the tardy declaration of a man who, after seeing the vast edifice of his ambition levelled with the dust, is only anxious, in his compulsory retreat, to preserve intact and spotless the other great edifice of his glory.   Bonaparte should have recollected that Cæsar did not like the idea of his wife being even suspected.

CHAPTER XII.

1802.

CITIZEN FESCH, who, when we were forced to stop at Ajaccio
on our return from Egypt, discounted at rather a high
rate the General-in-Chief's Egyptian sequins, became
again the Abbé Fesch, as soon as Bonaparte by his Consular authority re-erected the altars which the Revolution
had overthrown. On the 15th of August 1802 he was consecrated Bishop, and the following year received the Cardinal's hat. Thus Bonaparte took advantage of one of the
members of his family being in orders to elevate him to
the highest dignities of the Church. He afterwards gave
Cardinal Fesch the Archbishopric of Lyons, of which place
he was long the titular.[1]

---

[1] Like Cambacérès, the Cardinal was a bit of a *gourmet*, and on one occasion had
invited a large party of clerical magnates to dinner. " By a coincidence two turbots
of singular beauty arrived as presents to his Eminence on the very morning of the
feast. To serve both would have appeared ridiculous, but the Cardinal was most
anxious to have the credit of both. He imparted his embarrassment to his *chef*.
' Be of good faith, your Eminence, was the reply, ' both shall appear and enjoy the
reception so justly their due.' The dinner was served : one of the turbots relieved
the soup. Delight was on every face—it was the moment of the *éprouvette positive*.
The *maître d'hôtel* advances ; two attendants raise the turbot and carry him off to
cut him up ; but one of them loses his equilibrium ; the attendants and the turbot
roll together on the floor. At this sad sight the assembled Cardinals became as pale
as death, and a solemn silence reigned in the *conclave*—it was the moment of the

The First Consul prided himself a good deal on his triumph, at least in appearance, over the scruples which the persons who surrounded him had manifested against the re-establishment of worship. He read with much self-satisfaction the reports made to him, in which it was stated that the churches were well frequented. Indeed, throughout the year 1802, all his attention was directed to the reformation of manners, which had become more dissolute under the Directory than even during the Reign of Terror.

In his march of usurpation the First Consul let slip no opportunity of endeavouring to obtain at the same time the admiration of the multitude and the approbation of judicious men. He was very fond of the arts, and was sensible that the promotion of industry ought to be the peculiar care of the head of the Government. It must, however, at the same time be owned that he rendered the influence of his protection null and void by the continual violations he committed on that liberty which is the animating principle of all improvement.

During the supplementary days of the year X., that is to say, about the beginning of the autumn of 1802, there was held at the Louvre an exhibition of the products of industry. The First Consul visited the exhibition, and as even at that period he had begun to attribute every good result to himself, he seemed proud of the high degree of perfection the manufacturing arts had attained in France. He was, above all, delighted with the admiration this exhibition excited among the numerous foreigners who resorted to Paris during the peace.[1]

éprouvette négative ; but the *maître d'hôtel* suddenly turns to one of the attendants, ' Bring another turbot,' said he, with the most perfect coolness. The second appeared, and the *éprouvette positive* was gloriously renewed." (Hayward's *Art of Dining*, p. 65.)

[1] See in *Chaptal* his account of his conducting Fox and Lord Cornwallis over this exhibition. Fox remarked on the absence of articles of common use, as compared with what he would have seen in England. Chaptal was struck with the remark, but, he says, eventually got a cutler and a watchmaker to produce, from the back of

In fact, throughout the year 1802 the capital presented
an interesting and animating spectacle. The appetite for
luxury and pleasure had insinuated itself into manners
which were no longer republican, and the vast number of
Russians and English who drove about everywhere with
brilliant equipages contributed not a little to this meta-
morphosis. All Paris flocked to the Carrousel on review
days, and regarded with eyes of delight the unusual
sight of rich foreign liveries and emblazoned carriages.
The parties at the Tuileries were brilliant and numerous,
and nothing was wanting but the name of levees. Count
Markoff, who succeeded M. de Kalitscheff as Russian ambassador ; the Marquis de Lucchesini, the Prussian ambassador ; and Lord Whitworth, the Minister from England, made numerous presentations of their countrymen
to the First Consul, who was well pleased that the Court
he was forming should have examples set by foreign
courtiers. Never since the meeting of the States-General
had the theatres been so frequented, or *fêtes* so magnificent ; and never since that period had Paris presented
so cheering an aspect. The First Consul, on his part,
spared no exertion to render the capital more and more
worthy the admiration of foreigners. The statue of the
Venus de Medicis, which had been robbed from the gallery of the Grand Duke of Tuscany, now decorated the
gallery of the Louvre, and near it was placed that of the
Velletrian Pallas, a more legitimate acquisition, since it
was the result of the researches of some French engineers
at Velletri. Everywhere an air of prosperity was per-
ceptible, and Bonaparte proudly put in his claim to be regarded as the author of it all. With what heartfelt satisfaction did he likewise cast his eye upon what he called
the grand thermometer of opinion, the price of the

their stalls, goods which Fox bought, and, surprised at their low price and good
quality, acknowledged that he had a very different opinion of French industries from
what he had expressed before (Chaptal, *De l'Industrie Française*, Paris, Renouard,
1819, tome ii. p. 92).

funds! For if he saw them doubled in value in consequence of the revolution of the 18th Brumaire, rising as
they did at that period from seven to sixteen francs, this
value was even more than tripled after the vote of Consulship for life and the *Sénatus-consulte* of the 4th of
August, when they rose to fifty-two francs.

While Paris presented so satisfactory an aspect the
departments were in a state of perfect tranquillity, and
foreign affairs had every appearance of security. The
Court of the Vatican, which since the *Concordat* may be
said to have become devoted to the First Consul, gave,
under all circumstances, examples of submission to the
wishes of France. The Vatican was the first Court which
recognised the erection of Tuscany into the Kingdom of
Etruria, and the formation of the Helvetic, Cisalpine, and
Batavian Republics. Prussia soon followed the example
of the Pope, which was successively imitated by the other
powers of Europe.

The whole of these new states, realms, or republics were
under the immediate influence of France. The Isle of
Elba, which Napoleon's first abdication afterwards rendered so famous, and Piedmont, divided into six departments, were also united to France, still called a Republic.
Everything now seemed to concur in securing his accession
to absolute power. We were now at peace with all the
world, and every circumstance tended to place in the hands
of the First Consul that absolute power which indeed was
the only kind of government he was capable of forming
any conception of. Indeed, one of the characteristic signs
of Napoleon's government, even under the Consular system, left no doubt as to his real intentions. Had he
wished to found a free Government it is evident that he
would have made the Ministers responsible to the country,
whereas he took care that there should be no reponsibility
but to himself. He viewed them, in fact, in the light of
instruments which he might break as he pleased. I found

this single index sufficient to disclose all his future designs. In order to make the irresponsibility of his Ministers to the public perfectly clear, he had all the acts of his Government signed merely by M. Maret, Secretary of State. Thus the Consulship for life was nothing but an Empire in disguise, the usufruct of which could not long satisfy the First Consul's ambition. His brothers influenced him, and it was resolved to found a new dynasty.

It was not in the interior of France that difficulties were likely first to arise on Bonaparte's carrying his designs into effect, but there was some reason to apprehend that foreign powers, after recognising and treating with the Consular Government, might display a different feeling, and entertain scruples with regard to a Government which had resumed its monarchical form. The question regarding the Bourbons was in some measure kept in the background as long as France remained a Republic, but the re-establishment of the throne naturally called to recollection the family which had occupied it for so many ages. Bonaparte fully felt the delicacy of his position, but he knew how to face obstacles, and had been accustomed to overcome them. He, however, always proceeded cautiously, as when obstacles induced him to defer the period of the Consulship for life.

Bonaparte laboured to establish in France not only an absolute government, but, what is still worse, a military one.[1] He considered a decree signed by his hand possessed

---

[1] This must not be taken too literally. " Except in the very rare cases of revolt, there was no instance under the Imperial Government in which the military chiefs commanded any but soldiers. . . . The new administrative organisation had taken away from the governors of towns and of provinces the higher police, with which they were invested under the *ancien régime.* Napoleon, when he re-established the general officers in their honorary rights, did not restore this power to them. Where a prefet arbitrarily decided on the interests, and even on the liberty of the most prominent citizens, the general, although covered with marks of the sovereign's approval, could not have had the humblest culprit arrested. In conflicts, frequent enough, between the military and the civil authority decision was almost always given in favour of the last " (Foy, *Hist. de la Péninsule,* tome i. p. 81). See, however, *Puymaigre,* p. 136, for the attention paid to military rank in the ballrooms.

of a magic virtue capable of transforming his generals into able diplomatists, and so he sent them on embassies, as if to show the Sovereigns to whom they were accredited that he soon meant to take their thrones by assault. The appointment of Lannes to the Court of Lisbon originated from causes which probably will be read with some interest, since they serve to place Bonaparte's character in its true light, and to point out, at the same time, the means he disdained not to resort to, if he wished to banish his most faithful friends when their presence was no longer agreeable to him.

Bonaparte had ceased to address Lannes in the second person singular; but that general continued the familiarity of *thee* and *thou* in speaking to Napoleon. It is hardly possible to conceive how much this annoyed the First Consul. Aware of the unceremonious candour of his old comrade, whose daring spirit he knew would prompt him to go as great lengths in civil affairs as on the field of battle, Bonaparte, on the great occasion of the 18th Brumaire, fearing his reproaches, had given him the command of Paris in order to ensure his absence from St. Cloud. After that time, notwithstanding the continually growing greatness of the First Consul, which, as it increased, daily exacted more and more deference, Lannes still preserved his freedom of speech, and was the only one who dared to treat Bonaparte as a comrade, and tell him the truth without ceremony. This was enough to determine Napoleon to rid himself of the presence of Lannes. But under what pretext was the absence of the conqueror of Montebello to be procured? It was necessary to conjure up an excuse; and in the truly diabolical machination resorted to for that purpose, Bonaparte brought into play that crafty disposition for which he was so remarkable.

Lannes, who never looked forward to the morrow, was as careless of his money as of his blood. Poor officers and soldiers partook largely of his liberality. Thus he had no fortune, but plenty of debts. When he wanted money, and this was not seldom, he used to come, as if it were a mere matter of course, to ask it of the First Consul, who, I must confess, never refused him. Bonaparte, though he well knew the general's circumstances, said to him one day, "My friend, you should attend a little more to appearances. You must have your establishment suitable to your rank. There is the Hôtel de Noailles—why don't you take it, and furnish it in proper style?" Lannes, whose own candour prevented him from suspecting the artful designs of others, followed the advice of the First Consul. The Hôtel de Noailles was taken and superbly fitted up. Odiot supplied a service of plate valued at 200,000 francs.

General Lannes having thus conformed to the wishes of Bonaparte came to him and requested 400,000 francs, the amount of the expense incurred, as it were, by his order. "But," said the First Consul, "I have no money."—"You have no money! What the devil am I to do, then?"—"But is there none in the Guard's chest? Take what you require, and we will settle it hereafter."

Mistrusting nothing, Lannes went to the treasurer of the Guards, who made some objections at first to the advance required, but who soon yielded on learning that the demand was made with the consent of the First Consul.

Within twenty-four hours after Lannes had obtained the 400,000 francs the treasurer received from the head commissary an order to balance his accounts. The receipt for the 400,000 francs advanced to Lannes, was not acknowledged as a voucher. In vain the treasurer alleged the authority of the First Consul for the transaction. Napoleon's memory had suddenly failed him; he had entirely forgotten all about it. In a word, it was incumbent on Lannes to refund the 400,000 francs to the Guards' chest; and, as I have already said, he had no property on earth, but debts in abundance. He repaired to General

Lefebvre, who loved him as his son, and to him he related all that had passed. " Simpleton," said Lefebvre, " why did you not come to me? Why did you go and get into debt with that —— ? Well, here are the 400,000 francs, take them to him, and let him go to the devil ! "

Lannes hastened to the First Consul. " What ! " he exclaimed, " is it possible you can be guilty of such baseness as this ? To treat me in such a manner ! To lay such a foul snare for me after all that I have done for you ; after all the blood I have shed to promote your ambition ! Is this the recompense you had in store for me ? You forget the 13th Vendémiaire, to the success of which I contributed more than you ! You forget Millesimo : I was colonel before you ! For whom did I fight at Bassano ? You were witness of what I did at Lodi and at Governolo, where I was wounded ; and yet you play me such a trick as this ! But for me, Paris would have revolted on the 18th Brumaire. But for me, you would have lost the battle of Marengo. I alone, yes, I alone, passed the Po, at Montebello, with my whole division. You gave the credit of that to Berthier, who was not there ; and this is my reward—humiliation. This cannot, this shall not be. I will—— " Bonaparte, pale with anger, listened without stirring, and Lannes was on the point of challenging him when Junot, who heard the uproar, hastily entered. The unexpected presence of this general somewhat reassured the First Consul, and at the same time calmed, in some degree, the fury of Lannes. " Well," said Bonaparte, " go to Lisbon. You will get money there ; and when you return you will not want any one to pay your debts for you." Thus was Bonaparte's object gained. Lannes set out for Lisbon, and never afterwards annoyed the First Consul by his familiarities, for on his return he ceased to address him with *thee* and *thou.*[1]

---

[1] Joseph Bonaparte asserts that Lannes never did address Napoleon in this familiar style, but says nothing in contradiction of the extraordinary story here

Having described Bonaparte's ill-treatment of Lannes I may here subjoin a statement of the circumstances which led to a rupture between the First Consul and me. So many false stories have been circulated on the subject that I am anxious to relate the facts as they really were.

Nine months had now passed since I had tendered my resignation to the First Consul. The business of my office had become too great for me, and my health was so much endangered by over-application that my physician, M. Corvisart, who had for a long time impressed upon me the necessity of relaxation, now formally warned me that I should not long hold out under the fatigue I underwent. Corvisart had no doubt spoken to the same effect to the First Consul, for the latter said to me one day, in a tone

related. We have heard Bourrienne's statements confirmed by several unprejudiced contemporaries, and everybody knows that poor Lannes was sent as a sort of exile to Lisbon.—*Editor of the 1836 edition.*

This explanation of Lannes being sent to Lisbon seems very far-fetched. Napoleon had readier and easier means of dealing with a presumptuous general. Meneval, allowing the wish to get rid of the familiarity of Lannes, gives a more likely story ; that Lannes, believing Napoleon to have promised to pay for the furniture of his house, tried to enforce payment by taking the money from the chest of the Guards. Napoleon was the most unlikely man in the world to advise any tampering with cash. See his extraordinary and almost pedantic insistance on adherence to the regular form for the issue of cash in *Beugnot*, tome i. p. 344 : "When I sign a payment order I lend this key (of the treasury), and it may be legally used ; but when I have not lent it, there is no other way of getting into the treasury but by breaking open the doors." Compare *Madame Junot*, tome ii. p. 184, where she denies the familiarity of Lannes ; see also tome iii. p. 215, alleging that Lannes took or was ready to take the treasure of the cathedral of Saragossa. In the case in question she only says that Lannes was not really so much to be blamed as was represented. In a previous note we have shown how Masséna was dealt with when he had appropriated money in Italy, but we may allude again to the subject for the sake of introducing a letter of Napoleon's which has an emphatic bearing as to the strictness he maintained in money matters.

"MY BROTHER—I have received your letter of the 27th of March [1806]. I have an accurate statement of the sums which M(asséna), S——, the paymaster, and the other officers have received. I have dismissed S——, who was at the bottom of this disgraceful business. It is adding absurdity to roguery to say that this money was a present from the new governments. Such an excuse is more revolting than the crime itself! Many bills are drawn upon me from Naples. Recollect that I have enormous expenses, and may be unable to meet them. I have directed the 2,900,000 francs, for which you told me a month ago that you had drawn upon me, to be paid. But take care that all is regularly passed through the Treasury. *There are forms from which I myself am not exempted.* The safety of the State depends upon them " (*Letters of Napoleon to Joseph*, English edition, vol. i. p. 98).

which betrayed but little feeling, "Why, Corvisart says you have not a year to live." This was certainly no very welcome compliment in the mouth of an old college friend, yet I must confess that the doctor risked little by the prediction.

I had resolved, in fact, to follow the advice of Corvisart; my family were urgent in their entreaties that I would do so, but I always put off the decisive step. I was loath to give up a friendship which had subsisted so long, and which had been only once disturbed : on that occasion when Joseph thought proper to play the spy upon me at the table of Fouché. I remembered also the reception I had met with from the conqueror of Italy ; and I experienced, moreover, no slight pain at the thought of quitting one from whom I had received so many proofs of confidence, and to whom I had been attached from early boyhood. These considerations constantly triumphed over the disgust to which I was subjected by a number of circumstances, and by the increasing vexations occasioned by the conflict between my private sentiments and the nature of the duties I had to perform. I was thus kept in a state of perplexity, from which some unforeseen circumstance alone could extricate me. Such a circumstance at length occurred, and the following is the history of my first rupture with Napoleon :—

On the 27th of February 1802, at ten at night, Bonaparte dictated to me a despatch of considerable importance and urgency, for M. de Talleyrand, requesting the Minister for Foreign Affairs to come to the Tuileries next morning at an appointed hour. According to custom, I put the letter into the hands of the office messenger that it might be forwarded to its destination.

This was Saturday. The following day, Sunday, M. de Talleyrand came as if for an audience about mid-day. The First Consul immediately began to confer with him on the subject of the letter sent the previous evening, and was astonished to learn that the Minister had not received it until the morning. He immediately rang for the messenger, and ordered me to be sent for. Being in a very bad humour, he pulled the bell with so much fury that he struck his hand violently against the angle of the chimney-piece. I hurried to his presence. "Why," he said, addressing me hastily, "why was not my letter delivered yesterday evening?"—"I do not know: I put it at once into the hands of the person whose duty it was to see that it was sent."—"Go and find the cause of the delay, and come back quickly." Having rapidly made my inquiries, I returned to the cabinet. "Well?" said the First Consul, whose irritation seemed to have increased. " Well, General, it is not the fault of anybody. M. de Talleyrand was not to be found, either at the office or at his own residence, or at the houses of any of his friends where he was thought likely to be." Not knowing with whom to be angry, restrained by the coolness of M. de Talleyrand, yet at the same time ready to burst with rage, Bonaparte rose from his seat, and proceeding to the hall, called the messenger and questioned him sharply. The man, disconcerted by the anger of the First Consul, hesitated in his replies, and gave confused answers. Bonaparte returned to his cabinet still more irritated than he had left it.

I had followed him to the hall, and on my way back to the cabinet I attempted to soothe him, and I begged him not to be thus discomposed by a circumstance which, after all, was of no great moment. I do not know whether his anger was increased by the sight of the blood which flowed from his hand, and which he was every moment looking at; but however that might be, a transport of furious passion, such as I had never before witnessed, seized him; and as I was about to enter the cabinet after him he threw back the door with so much violence that, had I been two or three inches nearer him, it must infallibly have struck me in the face. He accompanied this action, which was almost convulsive, with an appellation not to be borne; he

exclaimed before M. de Talleyrand, "Leave me alone ;
you are a —— fool." At an insult so atrocious I confess
that the anger which had already mastered the First Consul
suddenly seized on me. I thrust the door forward with
as much impetuosity as he had used in throwing it back,
and, scarcely knowing what I said, exclaimed, "You are a
hundredfold a greater fool than I am !" I then banged
the door and went upstairs to my apartment, which was
situated over the cabinet.

I was as far from expecting as from wishing such an
occasion of separating from the First Consul. But what
was done could not be undone ; and therefore, without
taking time for reflection, and still under the influence of
the anger that had got the better of me, I penned the
following positive resignation :—

GENERAL— *The state of my health no longer permits me to continue
in your service. I therefore beg you to accept my resignation.*

BOURRIENNE.

Some moments after this note was written I saw Bonaparte's saddle-horses brought up to the entrance of
the Palace. It was Sunday morning, and, contrary to
his usual custom on that day, he was going to ride out.
Duroc accompanied him. He was no sooner gone than I
went down into his cabinet, and placed my letter on his
table. On returning at four o'clock with Duroc Bonaparte
read my letter. "Ah ! ah !" said he, before opening it,
"a letter from Bourrienne." And he almost immediately
added, for the note was speedily perused, "He is in the
sulks.—*Accepted.*" I had left the Tuileries at the moment
he returned, but Duroc sent to me where I was dining the
following billet :—

*The First Consul desires me, my dear Bourrienne, to inform you
that he accepts your resignation, and to request that you will give me
the necessary information respecting your papers.*— *Yours,* DUROC.

P.S.—I will call on you presently.

Duroc came to me at eight o'clock the same evening. The First Consul was in his cabinet when we entered it. I immediately commenced giving my intended successor the necessary explanations to enable him to enter upon his new duties. Piqued at finding that I did not speak to him, and at the coolness with which I instructed Duroc, Bonaparte said to me in a harsh tone, "Come, I have had enough of this! Leave me." I stepped down from the ladder on which I had mounted for the purpose of pointing out to Duroc the places in which the various papers were deposited and hastily withdrew. I too had had quite enough of it!

I remained two more days at the Tuileries until I had suited myself with lodgings. On Monday I went down into the cabinet of the First Consul to take my leave of him. We conversed together for a long time, and very amicably. He told me he was very sorry I was going to leave him, and that he would do all he could for me. I pointed out several places to him; at last I mentioned the Tribunate. "That will not do for you," he said; "the members are a set of babblers and phrasemongers, whom I mean to get rid of. All the troubles of States proceed from such debatings. I am tired of them." He continued to talk in a strain which left me in no doubt as to his uneasiness about the Tribunate, which, in fact, reckoned among its members many men of great talent and excellent character.[1]

The following day, Tuesday, the First Consul asked me to breakfast with him. After breakfast, while he was conversing with some other person, Madame Bonaparte and Hortense pressed me to make advances towards obtaining a re-instalment in my office, appealing to me on the score of the friendship and kindness they had always shown me. They told me that I had been in the wrong, and that I had

[1] In 1802 the First Consul made a reduction of fifty members of the Tribunate, and subsequently the whole body was suppressed.—*Bourrienne.*

forgotten myself. I answered that I considered the evil beyond remedy ; and that, besides, I had really need of repose. The First Consul then called me to him, and conversed a considerable time with me, renewing his protestations of goodwill towards me.

At five o'clock I was going downstairs to quit the Tuileries for good when I was met by the office messenger, who told me that the First Consul wished to see me. Duroc, who was in the room leading to the cabinet, stopped me as I passed, and said, "He wishes you to remain. I beg of you not to refuse ; do me this favour. I have assured him that I am incapable of filling your office. It does not suit my habits ; and besides, to tell you the truth, the business is too irksome for me." I proceeded to the cabinet without replying to Duroc. The First Consul came up to me smiling, and pulling me by the ear, as he did when he was in the best of humours, said to me, "Are you still in the sulks?" and leading me to my usual seat he added, " Come, sit down."

Only those who knew Bonaparte can judge of my situation at that moment. He had at times, and when he chose, a charm in his manners which it was quite impossible to resist. I could offer no opposition, and I resumed my usual office and my accustomed labours. Five minutes afterwards it was announced that dinner was on table. "You will dine with me?" he said. "I cannot ; I am expected at the place where I was going when Duroc called me back. It is an engagement that I cannot break."—"Well, I have nothing to say, then. But give me your word that you will be here at eight o'clock."— "I promise you." Thus I became again the private secretary of the First Consul, and I believed in the sincerity of our reconciliation.

CHAPTER XIII.

1802–1803.

The *Concordat* and the Legion of Honour—The Council of State and the
Tribunate—Discussion on the word *subjects*—Chénier—Chabot de
l'Allier's proposition to the Tribunate—The *marked proof* of national
gratitude—Bonaparte's duplicity and self-command—Reply to the
Sénatus-consulte—The people consulted—Consular decree—The most,
or the least—M. de Vaublanc's speech—Bonaparte's reply—The address of the Tribunate—Hopes and predictions thwarted.

It may truly be said that history affords no example of an
empire founded like that of France, created in all its parts
under the cloak of a republic. Without any shock, and in
the short space of four years, there arose above the ruins
of the short-lived Republic a Government more absolute
than ever was Louis XIV.'s. This extraordinary change
is to be assigned to many causes; and I had the opportunity of observing the influence which the determined
will of one man exercised over his fellow-men.

The great object which Bonaparte had at heart was to
legitimate his usurpations by institutions. The *Concordat*
had reconciled him with the Court of Rome; the numerous
erasures from the emigrant list gathered round him a
large body of the old nobility; and the Legion of Honour,
though at first but badly received, soon became a general
object of ambition. Peace, too, had lent her aid in con-
solidating the First Consul's power by affording him
leisure to engage in measures of internal prosperity.

The Council of State, of which Bonaparte had made me
a member, but which my other occupations did not allow
me to attend, was the soul of the Consular Government.

Bonaparte felt much interest in the discussions of that body, because it was composed of the most eminent men in the different branches of administration; and though the majority evinced a ready compliance with his wishes, yet that disposition was often far from being unanimous. In the Council of State the projects of the Government were discussed from the first with freedom and sincerity, and when once adopted they were transmitted to the Tribunate, and to the Legislative Body. This latter body might be considered as a supreme Legislative Tribunal, before which the Tribunes pleaded as the advocates of the people, and the Councillors of State, whose business it was to support the law projects, as the advocates of the Government. This will at once explain the cause of the First Consul's animosity towards the Tribunate, and will show to what the Constitution was reduced when that body was dissolved by a sudden and arbitrary decision.

During the Consulate the Council of State was not only a body politic collectively, but each individual member might be invested with special power; as, for example, when the First Consul sent Councillors of State on missions to each of the military divisions where there was a Court of Appeal, the instructions given them by the First Consul were extensive, and might be said to be unlimited. They were directed to examine all the branches of the administration, so that their reports collected and compared together presented a perfect description of the state of France. But this measure, though excellent in itself, proved fatal to the State. The reports never conveyed the truth to the First Consul, or at least if they did, it was in such a disguised form as to be scarcely recognisable; for the Councillors well knew that the best way to pay their court to Bonaparte was not to describe public feeling as it really was, but as he wished it to be. Thus the reports of the Councillors of State only furnished fresh arguments in favour of his ambition.

I must, however, observe that in the discussions of the Council of State Bonaparte was not at all averse to the free expression of opinion. He, indeed, often encouraged it ; for although fully resolved to do only what he pleased, he wished to gain information ; indeed, it is scarcely conceivable how, in the short space of two years, Bonaparte adapted his mind so completely to civil and legislative affairs. But he could not endure in the Tribunate the liberty of opinion which he tolerated in the Council ; and for this reason—that the sittings of the Tribunate were public, while those of the Council of State were secret, and publicity was what he dreaded above all things. He was very well pleased when he had to transmit to the Legislative Body or to the Tribunate any proposed law of trifling importance, and he used then to say that he had thrown them a bone to gnaw.

Among the subjects submitted to the consideration of the Council and the Tribunate was one which gave rise to a singular discussion, the ground of which was a particular word, inserted in the third article of the treaty of Russia with France. This word seemed to convey a prophetic allusion to the future condition of the French people, or rather an anticipated designation of what they afterwards became. The treaty spoke of " the *subjects* of the two Governments." This term applied to those who still considered themselves citizens, and was highly offensive to the Tribunate. Chénier most loudly remonstrated against the introduction of this word into the dictionary of the new Government. He said that the armies of France had shed their blood that the French people might be citizens and not subjects. Chénier's arguments, however, had no effect on the decision of the Tribunate, and only served to irritate the First Consul. The treaty was adopted almost unanimously, there being only fourteen dissentient voices, and the proportion of black balls in the Legislative Body was even less.

Though this discussion passed off almost unnoticed, yet it greatly displeased the First Consul, who expressed his dissatisfaction in the evening. "What is it," said he, "these babblers want? They wish to be citizens—why did they not know how to continue so? My government must treat on an equal footing with Russia. I should appear a mere puppet in the eyes of foreign Courts were I to yield to the stupid demands of the Tribunate. Those fellows tease me so that I have a great mind to end matters at once with them." I endeavoured to soothe his anger, and observed, that one precipitate act might injure him. "You are right," he continued; "but stay a little, they shall lose nothing by waiting."

The Tribunate pleased Bonaparte better in the great question of the Consulate for life, because he had taken the precaution of removing such members as were most opposed to the encroachments of his ambition. The Tribunate resolved that a marked proof of the national gratitude should be offered to the First Consul, and the resolution was transmitted to the Senate. Not a single voice was raised against this proposition, which emanated from Chabot de l'Allier, the President of the Tribunate. When the First Consul came back to his cabinet after receiving the deputation of the Tribunate he was very cheerful, and said to me, "Bourrienne, it is a blank cheque that the Tribunate has just offered me; I shall know how to fill it up. That is my business."

The Tribunate having adopted the indefinite proposition of offering to the First Consul a *marked proof* of the national gratitude, it now only remained to determine what that proof should be. Bonaparte knew well what he wanted, but he did not like to name it in any positive way. Though in his fits of impatience, caused by the lingering proceedings of the Legislative Body and the indecision of some of its members, he often talked of mounting on horseback and drawing his sword, yet he so far controlled himself as to confine violence to his conversations with his intimate friends. He wished it to be thought that he himself was yielding to compulsion; that he was far from wishing to usurp permanent power contrary to the Constitution; and that if he deprived France of liberty it was all for her good, and out of mere love for her. Such deep-laid duplicity could never have been conceived and mantained in any common mind; but Bonaparte's was not a mind of the ordinary cast. It must have required extraordinary self-command to have restrained so long as he did that daring spirit which was so natural to him, and which was rather the result of his temperament than his character. For my part, I confess that I always admired him more for what he had the fortitude not to do than for the boldest exploits he ever performed.

In conformity with the usual form, the proposition of the Tribunate was transmitted to the Senate. From that time the Senators on whom Bonaparte most relied were frequent in their visits to the Tuileries. In the preparatory conferences which preceded the regular discussions in the Senate it has been ascertained that the majority was not willing that the *marked proof* of gratitude should be the Consulate for life; it was therefore agreed that the reporter should limit his demand to a temporary prolongation of the dignity of First Consul in favour of Bonaparte. The reporter, M. de Lacépède, acted accordingly, and limited the prolongation to ten years, commencing from the expiration of the ten years granted by the Constitution. I forget which of the Senators first proposed the Consulate for life; but I well recollect that Cambacérès used all his endeavours to induce those members of the Senate whom he thought he could influence to agree to that proposition. Whether from flattery or conviction I know not, but the Second Consul held out to his colleague, or rather his master, the hope of complete success. Bonaparte on hearing him shook his head with an

air of doubt, but afterwards said to me, " They will perhaps make some wry faces, but they must come to it at
last ! "

It was proposed in the Senate that the proposition of
the Consulate for life should take the priority of that of
the decennial prolongation ; but this was not agreed to ;
and the latter proposition being adopted, the other, of
course, could not be discussed.

There was something very curious in the *Sénatus-consulte* published on the occasion. It spoke in the name of
the French people, and stated that, " in testimony of their
gratitude to the Consuls of the Republic," the Consular
reign was prolonged for ten years ; but that the prolongation was limited to the First Consul only.

Bonaparte, though much dissatisfied with the decision
of the Senate, disguised his displeasure in ambiguous language. When Tronchet, then President of the Senate,
read to him, in a solemn audience, at the head of the
deputation, the *Sénatus-consulte* determining the proroga-
tion, he said in reply that he could not be certain of the
confidence of the people unless his continuance in the
Consulship were sanctioned by their suffrages. " The
interests of my glory and happiness," added he, " would
seem to have marked the close of my public life at the
moment when the peace of the world is proclaimed.
But the glory and the happiness of the citizen must yield
to the interests of the State and wishes of the public.
You, Senators, conceive that I owe to the people another
sacrifice. I will make it if the voice of the people commands what your suffrage authorises."

The true meaning of these words was not understood
by everybody, and was only manifest to those who were
initiated in the secret of Bonaparte's designs. He did not
accept the offer of the Senate, because he wished for
something more. The question was to be renewed and
to be decided by the people only ; and since the people

had the right to refuse what the Senate offered, they
possessed, for the same reason, the right to give what the
Senate did not offer.

The moment now arrived for consulting the Council of
State as to the mode to be adopted for invoking and collecting the suffrages of the people. For this purpose an
extraordinary meeting of the Council of State was summoned on the 10th of May. Bonaparte wished to keep
himself aloof from all ostensible influence ; but his two
colleagues laboured for him more zealously than he could
have worked for himself, and they were warmly supported
by several members of the Council. A strong majority
were of opinion that Bonaparte should not only be invested with the Consulship for life, but that he should be
empowered to nominate his successor. But he, still
faithful to his plan, affected to venerate the sovereignty
of the people, which he held in horror, and he promulgated the following decree, which was the first explanation of his reply to the Senate :—

The Consuls of the Republic, considering that the resolution of
the First Consul is an homage rendered to the sovereignty of the
People, and that the People, when consulted on their dearest interests, will not go beyond the limits of those interests, decree as follows :—First, that the French people shall be consulted on the
question whether Napoleon Bonaparte is to be made Consul for
life, etc.

The other articles merely regulated the mode of collecting the votes.

This decree shows the policy of the First Consul in a
new point of view, and displays his art in its fullest extent. He had just refused the less for the sake of getting the greater ; and now he had contrived to get the
offer of the greater to show off his moderation by accept-
ing only the less. The Council of State sanctioned the
proposition for conferring on the First Consul the right
of nominating his successor, and, of his own accord, the

First Consul declined this. Accordingly the Second Consul, when he, the next day, presented the decree to the Council of State, did not fail to eulogise this extreme moderation, which banished even the shadow of suspicion of any ambitious after-thought. Thus the Senate found itself out-manœuvred, and the decree of the Consuls was transmitted at once to the Legislative Body and to the Tribunate.

In the Legislative Body, M. de Vaublanc was distinguished among all the deputies who applauded the conduct of the Government; and it was he who delivered the apologetic harangue of the deputation of the Legislative Body to the First Consul. After having addressed the Government collectively he ended by addressing the First Consul individually—a sort of compliment which had not hitherto been put in practice, and which was far from displeasing him who was its object. As M. de Vaublanc's speech had been communicated beforehand to the First Consul, the latter prepared a reply to it which sufficiently showed how much it had gratified him. Besides the flattering distinction which separated him from the Government, the plenitude of praise was not tempered by anything like advice or comment. It was not so with the address of the Tribunate. After the compliments which the occasion demanded, a series of hopes were expressed for the future, which formed a curious contrast with the events which actually ensued. The Tribunate, said the address, required no guarantee, because Bonaparte's elevated and generous sentiments would never permit him to depart from those principles which brought about the Revolution and founded the Republic;—he loved real glory too well ever to stain that which he had acquired by the abuse of power;—the nation which he was called to govern was free and generous: he would respect and consolidate her liberty; he would distinguish his real friends, who spoke truth to him, from flatterers who might seek to deceive him. In short, Bonaparte would surround himself with the men who, having made the Revolution, were interested in supporting it.

To these and many other fine things the Consul replied, " This testimony of the affection of the Tribunate is gratifying to the Government. The union of all bodies of the State is a guarantee of the stability and happiness of the nation. The efforts of the Government will be constantly directed to the interests of the people, from whom all power is derived, and whose welfare all good men have at heart."

So much for the artifice of governments and the credulity of subjects! It is certain that, from the moment Bonaparte gained his point in submitting the question of the Consulate for life to the decision of the people, there was no longer a doubt of the result being in his favour. This was evident, not only on account of the influential means which a government always has at its command, and of which its agents extend the ramifications from the centre to the extremities, but because the proposition was in accordance with the wishes of the majority. The Republicans were rather shy in avowing principles with which people were now disenchanted ;—the partisans of a monarchy without distinction of family saw their hopes almost realised in the Consulate for life ;—the recollection of the Bourbons still lived in some hearts faithful to misfortune : but the great mass were for the First Consul, and his external acts in the new step he had taken towards the throne had been so cautiously disguised as to induce a belief in his sincerity. If I and a few others were witness to his accomplished artifice and secret ambition, France beheld only his glory, and gratefully enjoyed the blessings of peace which he had obtained for her. The suffrages of the people speedily realised the hopes of the First Consul, and thus was founded the CONSULATE FOR LIFE.

CHAPTER XIV.

1802–1803.

Departure for Malmaison—Unexpected question relative to the Bourbons
—Distinction between two opposition parties—New intrigues of
Lucien—Camille Jordan's pamphlet seized—Vituperation against the
liberty of the press—Revisal of the Constitution—New *Sénatus-con-
sulte*—Deputation from the Senate—Audience of the Diplomatic
Body—Josephine's melancholy—The discontented—Secret meetings—
Fouché and the police agents—The Code Napoléon—Bonaparte's
regular attendance at the Council of State—His knowledge of man-
kind, and the science of government—Napoleon's first sovereign act—
His visit to the Senate—The Consular procession—Polite etiquette—
The Senate and the Council of State—Complaints against Lucien—
The deaf and dumb assembly—Creation of senatorships.

WHEN nothing was wanting to secure the Consulate for
life but the votes of the people, which there was no doubt
of obtaining, the First Consul set off to spend a few days
at Malmaison.

On the day of our arrival, as soon as dinner was ended,
Bonaparte said to me, "Bourrienne, let us go and take a
walk." It was the middle of May, so that the evenings
were long. We went into the park: he was very grave,
and we walked for several minutes without his uttering a
syllable. Wishing to break silence in a way that would
be agreeable to him, I alluded to the facility with which
he had nullified the last *Sénatus-consulte*. He scarcely
seemed to hear me, so completely was his mind absorbed
in the subject on which he was meditating. At length,
suddenly recovering from his abstraction, he said, "Bourrienne, do you think that the pretender to the crown of
France would renounce his claims if I were to offer him a

good indemnity, or even a province in Italy?" Surprised
at this abrupt question on a subject which I was far from
thinking of, I replied that I did not think the pretender
would relinquish his claims; that it was very unlikely the
Bourbons would return to France as long as he, Bonaparte, should continue at the head of the Government,
though they would look forward to their ultimate return
as probable. "How so?" inquired he. "For a very
simple reason, General. Do you not see every day that
your agents conceal the truth from you, and flatter you in
your wishes, for the purpose of ingratiating themselves in
your favour? are you not angry when at length the truth
reaches your ear?"—"And what then?"—"Why, General,
it must be just the same with the agents of Louis XVIII.
in France. It is in the course of things, in the nature of
man, that they should feed the Bourbons with hopes of a
possible return, were it only to induce a belief in their
own talent and utility."—"That is very true! You are
quite right; but I am not afraid. However, something
might perhaps be done—we shall see." Here the subject
dropped, and our conversation turned on the Consulate
for life, and Bonaparte spoke in unusually mild terms of
the persons who had opposed the proposition. I was a
little surprised at this, and could not help reminding him
of the different way in which he had spoken of those who
opposed his accession to the Consulate. "There is nothing extraordinary in that," said he. "Worthy men may
be attached to the Republic as I have made it. It is a
mere question of form. I have nothing to say against
that; but at the time of my accession to the Consulate it
was very different. Then, none but Jacobins, terrorists,
and rogues resisted my endeavours to rescue France from
the infamy into which the Directory had plunged her.
But now I cherish no ill-will against those who have opposed me."

During the intervals between the acts of the different

bodies of the State, and the collection of the votes, Lucien renewed his intrigues, or rather prosecuted them with renewed activity, for the purpose of getting the question of hereditary succession included in the votes. Many prefects transmitted to M. Chaptal anonymous circulars which had been sent to them : all stated the ill effect produced by these circulars, which had been addressed to the principal individuals of their departments. Lucien was the originator of all this, though I cannot positively say whether his brother connived with him, as in the case of the pamphlet to which I have already alluded. I believe, however, that Bonaparte was not entirely a stranger to the business ; for the circulars were written by Rœderer at the instigation of Lucien, and Rœderer was at that time in favour at the Tuileries. I recollect Bonaparte speaking to me one day very angrily about a pamphlet which had just been published by Camille Jordan on the subject of the national vote on the Consulate for life. Camille Jordan did not withhold his vote, but gave it in favour of the First Consul ; and instead of requiring preliminary conditions, he contented himself, like the Tribunate, with enumerating all the guarantees which he expected the honour of the First Consul would grant. Among these guarantees were the cessation of arbitrary imprisonments, the responsibility of the agents of Government, and the independence of the judges. But all these demands were mere peccadilloes in comparison with Camille Jordan's great crime of demanding the liberty of the press.

The First Consul had looked through the fatal pamphlet, and lavished invectives upon its author. " How ! " exclaimed he, " am I never to have done with these firebrands ?—These babblers, who think that politics may be shown on a printed page like the world on a map ? Truly, I know not what things will come to if I let this go on. Camille Jordan, whom I received so well at Lyons, to think that he should ask for the liberty of the press !

Were I to accede to this I might as well pack up at once
and go and live on a farm a hundred leagues from Paris."
Bonaparte's first act in favour of the liberty of the press
was to order the seizure of the pamphlet in which Camille
Jordan had extolled the advantages of that measure. Publicity, either by words or writing, was Bonaparte's horror.
Hence his aversion to public speakers and writers.

Camille Jordan was not the only person who made unavailing efforts to arrest Bonaparte in the first steps of
his ambition. There were yet in France many men who,
though they had hailed with enthusiasm the dawn of the
French Revolution, had subsequently been disgusted by
its crimes, and who still dreamed of the possibility of
founding a truly Constitutional Government in France.
Even in the Senate there were some men indignant at the
usual compliance of that body, and who spoke of the necessity of subjecting the Constitution to a revisal, in order to
render it conformable to the Consulate for life.

The project of revising the Constitution was by no
means unsatisfactory to Bonaparte. It afforded him an
opportunity of holding out fresh glimmerings of liberty
to those who were too short-sighted to see into the future.
He was pretty certain that there could be no change but
to his advantage. Had any one talked to him of the wishes
of the nation he would have replied, "3,577,259 citizens
have voted. Of these how many were for me? 3,368,185.
Compare the difference! There is but one vote in forty-
five against me. I must obey the will of the people!"
To this he would not have failed to add, "Whose are the
votes opposed to me? Those of ideologists, Jacobins, and
peculators under the Directory." To such arguments
what could have been answered? It must not be supposed that I am putting these words into Bonaparte's
mouth. They fell from him oftener than once.[1]

---

[1] À propos of plebiscites, the following coincidence may be perhaps somewhat ir-
relevantly noted here. The votes given for the election of Napoleon's nephew in

As soon as the state of the votes was ascertained the Senate conceived itself under the necessity of repairing the only fault it had committed in the eyes of the First Consul, and solemnly presented him with a new *Senatus-consulte*, and a decree couched in the following terms :—

ARTICLE I.   The French people nominate and the Senate proclaim Napoleon Bonaparte Consul for life.

ARTICLE II.   A statue representing Peace, holding in one hand the laurel of victory, and in the other the decree of the Senate, shall commemorate to posterity the gratitude of the Nation.

ARTICLE III.   The Senate will convey to the First Consul the expression of the confidence, the love, and the admiration of the French people.

Bonaparte replied to the deputation from the Senate, in the presence of the Diplomatic Body, whose audience had been appointed for that day in order that the ambassadors might be enabled to make known to their respective Courts that Europe reckoned one King more.   In his reply he did not fail to introduce the high-sounding words "liberty and equality."   He commenced thus : "A citizen's life belongs to his country.   The French people wish that mine should be entirely devoted to their service.   I obey."

On the day this ceremony took place, besides the audience of the Diplomatic Body there was an extraordinary assemblage of general officers and public functionaries. The principal apartments of the Tuileries presented the appearance of a *fête*.   This gaiety formed a striking contrast with the melancholy of Josephine, who felt that every step of the First Consul towards the throne removed him farther from her.

She had to receive a party that evening, and though

1848 as president of the French Republic were 7,119,791, and those against were 1,119,000.   If the figures are *written* upon a piece of paper 7119791/1119, and it is held backwards to the light, the word "Empereur" will appear.   [The figures themselves have not been, however, verified by the annotator.]

greatly depressed in spirits she did the honours with her usual grace.

Let a Government be what it may, it can never satisfy every one. At the establishment of the Consulate for life, those who were averse to that change formed but a feeble minority. But still they met, debated, corresponded, and dreamed of the possibility of overthrowing the Consular Government.

During the first six months of the year 1802 there were meetings of the discontented, which Fouché, who was then Minister of the Police, knew and would not condescend to notice; but, on the contrary, all the inferior agents of the police contended for a prey which was easily seized, and, with the view of magnifying their services, represented these secret meetings as the effect of a vast plot against the Government. Bonaparte, whenever he spoke to me on the subject, expressed himself weary of the efforts which were made to give importance to trifles; and yet he received the reports of the police agents as if he thought them of consequence. This was because he thought Fouché badly informed, and he was glad to find him at fault; but when he sent for the Minister of Police the latter told him that all the reports he had received were not worth a moment's attention. He told the First Consul all, and even a great deal more than had been revealed to him, mentioning at the same time how and from whom Bonaparte had received his information.

But these petty police details did not divert the First Consul's attention from the great object he had in view. Since March 1802 he had attended the sittings of the Council of State with remarkable regularity. Even while we were at the Luxembourg he busied himself in drawing up a new code of laws to supersede the incomplete collection of revolutionary laws, and to substitute order for the sort of anarchy which prevailed in the legislation. The men who were most distinguished for legal knowledge had co-

operated in this laborious task, the result of which was
the code first distinguished by the name of the Civil Code,
and afterwards called the Code Napoléon. The labours
of this important undertaking being completed, a committee was appointed for the presentation of the code.
This committee, of which Cambacérès was the president,
was composed of MM. Portalis, Merlin de Douai, and
Tronchet. During all the time the discussions were pend-
ing, instead of assembling as usual three times a week,
the Council of State assembled every day, and the sittings,
which on ordinary occasions only lasted two or three hours,
were often prolonged to five or six. The First Consul
took such interest in these discussions that, to have an
opportunity of conversing upon them in the evening, he
frequently invited several members of the Council to dine
with him. It was during these conversations that I most
admired the inconceivable versatility of Bonaparte's genius,
or rather, that superior instinct which enabled him to
comprehend at a glance, and in their proper point of view,
legislative questions to which he might have been supposed
a stranger. Possessing as he did, in a supreme degree,
the knowledge of mankind, ideas important to the science
of government flashed upon his mind like sudden inspira-
tions.

Some time after his nomination to the Consulate for life,
anxious to perform a sovereign act, he went for the first
time to preside at the Senate. Availing myself that day
of a few leisure moments I went out to see the Consular
procession. It was truly royal. The First Consul had
given orders that the military should be ranged in the
streets through which he had to pass. On his first arrival
at the Tuileries, Napoleon had the soldiers of the Guard
ranged in a single line in the interior of the court, but he
now ordered that the line should be doubled, and should
extend from the gate of the Tuileries to that of the Luxembourg. Assuming a privilege which old etiquette had

confined exclusively to the Kings of France, Bonaparte now for the first time rode in a carriage drawn by eight horses. A considerable number of carriages followed that of the First Consul, which was surrounded by generals and *aides de camp* on horseback. Louis XIV. going to hold a bed of justice at the *Parlement* of Paris never displayed greater pomp than did Bonaparte in this visit to the Senate. He appeared in all the parade of royalty, and ten Senators came to meet him at the foot of the staircase of the Luxembourg.

The object of the First Consul's visit to the Senate was the presentation of five plans of *Senatus-consultes*. The other two Consuls were present at the ceremony, which took place about the middle of August.

Bonaparte returned in the same style in which he went, accompanied by M. Lebrun, Cambacérès remaining at the Senate, of which he was President. The five *Sénatus-consultes* were adopted, but a restriction was made in that which concerned the forms of the Senate. It was proposed that when the Consuls visited the Senate they should be received by a deputation of ten members at the foot of the staircase, as the First Consul had that day been received; but Bonaparte's brothers Joseph and Lucien opposed this, and prevented the proposition from being adopted, observing that the Second and Third Consuls being members of the Senate could not be received with such honours by their colleagues. This little scene of political courtesy, which was got up beforehand, was very well acted.

Bonaparte's visit to the Senate gave rise to a change of rank in the hierarchy of the different authorities composing the Government. Hitherto the Council of State had ranked higher in public opinion; but the Senate, on the occasion of its late deputation to the Tuileries, had for the first time received the honour of precedency. This had greatly displeased some of the Councillors of State, but

Bonaparte did not care for that. He instinctively saw that the Senate would do what he wished more readily than the other constituted bodies, and he determined to augment its rights and prerogatives even at the expense of the rights of the Legislative Body. These encroachments of one power upon another, authorised by the First Consul, gave rise to reports of changes in ministerial arrangements. It was rumoured in Paris that the number of the ministers was to be reduced to three, and that Lucien, Joseph, and M. de Talleyrand were to divide among them the different portfolios. Lucien helped to circulate these reports, and this increased the First Consul's dissatisfaction at his conduct. The letters from Madrid, which were filled with complaints against him, together with some scandalous adventures, known in Paris, such as his running away with the wife of a *limonadier*, exceedingly annoyed Bonaparte, who found his own family more difficult to govern than France.

France, indeed, yielded with admirable facility to the yoke which the First Consul wished to impose on her. How artfully did he undo all that the Revolution had done, never neglecting any means of attaining his object! He loved to compare the opinions of those whom he called the Jacobins with the opinions of the men of 1789; and even them he found too liberal. He felt the ridicule which was attached to the mute character of the Legislative Body, which he called his deaf and dumb assembly. But as that ridicule was favourable to him he took care to preserve the assembly as it was, and to turn it into ridicule whenever he spoke of it. In general, Bonaparte's judgment must not be confounded with his actions. His accurate mind enabled him to appreciate all that was good ; but the necessity of his situation enabled him to judge with equal shrewdness what was useful to himself.

What I have just said of the Senate affords me an opportunity of correcting an error which has frequently been

circulated in the chit-chat of Paris. It has erroneously
been said of some persons that they refused to become
members of the Senate, and among the number have been
mentioned M. Ducis, M. de La Fayette, and the Maréchal
de Rochambeau. The truth is, that no such refusals were
ever made. The following fact, however, may have contributed to raise these reports and give them credibility.
Bonaparte used frequently to say to persons in his *salon*
and in his cabinet, " You should be a Senator—a man like
you should be a Senator." But these complimentary
words did not amount to a nomination. To enter the Senate certain legal forms were to be observed. It was
necessary to be presented by the Senate, and after that
presentation no one ever refused to become a member of the
body, to which Bonaparte gave additional importance by
the creation of "Sénatoreries." [1] This creation took place
in the beginning of 1803.

[1] Districts presided over by a Senator.

CHAPTER XV.

1802.

PERHAPS one of the happiest ideas that ever were expressed was that of the Athenian who said, "I appeal from Philip drunk to Philip sober." The drunkenness here alluded to is not of that kind which degrades a man to the level of a brute, but that intoxication which is occasioned by success, and which produces in the heads of the ambitious a sort of cerebral congestion. Ordinary men are not subject to this excitement, and can scarcely form an idea of it. But it is nevertheless true that the fumes of glory and ambition occasionally derange the strongest heads; and Bonaparte, in all the vigour of his genius, was often subject to aberrations of judgment; for though his imagination never failed him, his judgment was frequently at fault.

This fact may serve to explain, and perhaps even to excuse the faults with which the First Consul has been most seriously reproached. The activity of his mind seldom admitted of an interval between the conception and the execution of a design ; but when he reflected coolly on the first impulses of his imperious will, his judgment discarded what was erroneous. Thus the blind obedience, which, like an epidemic disease, infected almost all who surrounded Bonaparte, was productive of the most fatal effects. The best way to serve the First Consul was never to listen to the suggestions of his first ideas, except on the field of battle, where his conceptions were as happy as they were rapid.[1] Thus, for example, MM. Maret, de Champagny, and Savary evinced a ready obedience to Bonaparte's wishes, which often proved very unfortunate, though doubtless dictated by the best intentions on their part. To this fatal zeal may be attributed a great portion of the mischief which Bonaparte committed. When the mischief was done, and past remedy, Bonaparte deeply regretted it. How often have I heard him say that Maret was animated by an *unlucky* zeal! This was the expression he made use of.

M. de Talleyrand was almost the only one among the ministers who did not flatter Bonaparte, and who really served both the First Consul and the Emperor. When Bonaparte said to M. de Talleyrand, "Write so and so, and send it off by a special courier," that minister was never in a hurry to obey the order, because he knew the character of the First Consul well enough to distinguish between what his passion dictated and what his reason would approve: in short, he appealed from Philip drunk to Philip sober. When it happened that M. de Talleyrand suspended the execution of an order Bonaparte never evinced the least displeasure. When, the day after he had received any hasty and angry order, M. de Talleyrand presented himself to the First Consul, the latter would say, "Well, did you send off the courier?"—"No," the minister would reply, "I took care not to do so before I showed you my letter." Then the First Consul would usually add, "Upon

[1] I have already mentioned how he frequently destroyed in the morning articles which he had dictated to me for the *Moniteur* over night.—*Bourrienne.*

second thoughts I think it would be best not to send it."
This was the way to deal with Bonaparte. When M. de
Talleyrand postponed sending off despatches, or when I
myself have delayed the execution of an order which I
knew had been dictated by anger, and had emanated
neither from his heart nor his understanding, I have heard
him say a hundred times, " It was right, quite right. You
understand me : Talleyrand understands me also. This
is the way to serve me : the others do not leave me time
for reflection : they are too precipitate." Fouché also
was one of those who did not on all occasions blindly obey
Bonaparte's commands. His other ministers, on the other
hand, when told to send off a courier the next morning,
would have more probably sent him off the same evening.
This was from zeal, but was not the First Consul right in
saying that such zeal was unfortunate?

Of Talleyrand and Fouché, in their connections with
the First Consul, it might be said that the one represented
the Constituent Assembly, with a slight perfume of the old
régime, and the other the Convention in all its brutality.
Bonaparte regarded Fouché as a complete personification
of the Revolution. With him, therefore, Fouché's influence was merely the influence of the Revolution. That
great event was one of those which had made the most
forcible impression on Bonaparte's ardent mind, and he
imagined he still beheld it in a visible form as long as
Fouché continued at the head of his police. I am now of
opinion that Bonaparte was in some degree misled as to
the value of Fouché's services as a minister. No doubt
the circumstance of Fouché being in office conciliated
those of the Revolutionary party who were his friends.
But Fouché cherished an undue partiality for them, because he knew that it was through them he held his place.
He was like one of the old Condottieri, who were made
friends of lest they should become enemies, and who owed
all their power to the soldiers enrolled under their banners.

Such was Fouché, and Bonaparte perfectly understood his
situation. He kept the chief in his service until he could
find an opportunity of disbanding his undisciplined followers. But there was one circumstance which confirmed
his reliance on Fouché. He who had voted the death of
the King of France, and had influenced the minds of those
who had voted with him, offered Bonaparte the best guarantee against the attempts of the Royalists for raising up in
favour of the Bourbons the throne which the First Consul
himself had determined to ascend. Thus, for different
reasons, Bonaparte and Fouché had common interests
against the House of Bourbon, and the master's ambition
derived encouragement from the supposed terror of the
servant.

The First Consul was aware of the existence in Paris of
a Royalist committee, formed for the purpose of corresponding with Louis XVIII. This committee consisted of
men who must not be confounded with those wretched
intriguers who were of no service to their employers, and
were not unfrequently in the pay of both Bonaparte and
the Bourbons. The Royalist committee, properly so
called, was a very different thing. It consisted of men
professing rational principles of liberty, such as the Marquis de Clermont Gallerande, the Abbé de Montesquiou,
M. Becquet, and M. Royer Collard. This committee had
been of long standing ; the respectable individuals whose
names I have just quoted acted upon a system hostile to
the despotism of Bonaparte, and favourable to what they
conceived to be the interests of France. Knowing the
superior wisdom of Louis XVIII., and the opinions which
he had avowed and maintained in the Assembly of the
Notables, they wished to separate that Prince from the
emigrants, and to point him out to the nation as a suitable
head of a reasonable Constitutional Government. Bonaparte, whom I have often heard speak on the subject,
dreaded nothing so much as these ideas of liberty, in con-

junction with a monarchy. He regarded them as reveries, called the members of the committee idle dreamers, but nevertheless feared the triumph of their ideas. He confessed to me that it was to counteract the possible influence of the Royalist committee that he showed himself so indulgent to those of the emigrants whose monarchical prejudices he knew were incompatible with liberal opinions. By the presence of emigrants who acknowledged nothing short of absolute power, he thought he might paralyse the influence of the Royalists of the interior; he therefore granted all such emigrants permission to return.

About this time I recollect having read a document, which had been signed, purporting to be a declaration of the principles of Louis XVIII. It was signed by M. d'André, who bore evidence to its authenticity. The principles contained in the declaration were in almost all points conformable to the principles which formed the basis of the charter. Even so early as 1792, and consequently previous to the fatal 21st of January, Louis XVI., who knew the opinions of M. de Clermont Gallerande, sent him on a mission to Coblentz to inform the Princes from him, and the Queen, that they would be ruined by their emigration. I am accurately informed, and I state this fact with the utmost confidence. I can also add with equal certainty that the circumstance was mentioned by M. de Clermont Gallerande in his Memoirs, and that the passage relative to his mission to Coblentz was cancelled before the manuscript was sent to press.

During the Consular Government the object of the Royalist committee was to seduce rather than to conspire. It was round Madame Bonaparte in particular that their batteries were raised, and they did not prove ineffectual. The female friends of Josephine filled her mind with ideas of the splendour and distinction she would enjoy if the powerful hand which had chained the Revolution should raise up the subverted throne. I must confess that I was myself, unconsciously, an accomplice of the friends of the throne ; for what they wished for the interest of the Bourbons I then ardently wished for the interest of Bonaparte.

While endeavours were thus made to gain over Madame Bonaparte to the interest of the royal family, brilliant offers were held out for the purpose of dazzling the First Consul.   It was wished to retemper for him the sword of the constable Duguesclin ; and it was hoped that a statue erected to his honour would at once attest to posterity his spotless glory and the gratitude of the Bourbons.   But when these offers reached the ears of Bonaparte he treated them with indifference, and placed no faith in their sincerity.   Conversing on the subject one day with M. de La Fayette he said, "They offer me a statue, but I must look to the pedestal.   They may make it my prison."   I did not hear Bonaparte utter these words ; but they were reported to me from a source, the authenticity of which may be relied on.

About this time, when so much was said in the Royalist circles and in the Faubourg St. Germain, of which the Hôtel de Luynes was the headquarters, about the possible return of the Bourbons, the publication of a popular book contributed not a little to direct the attention of the public to the most brilliant period of the reign of Louis XIV. The book was the historical romance of *Madame de la Vallière*, by Madame de Genlis, who had recently returned to France.   Bonaparte read it, and I have since understood that he was very well pleased with it, but he said nothing to me about it.   It was not until some time after that he complained of the effect which was produced in Paris by this publication, and especially by engravings representing scenes in the life of Louis XIV., and which were exhibited in the shop-windows.   The police received orders to suppress these prints ; and the order was implicitly obeyed ; but it was not Fouché's police.   Fouché saw the absurdity of interfering with trifles. I recollect that immediately after the creation of the Legion of Honour, it being summer, the young men of Paris indulged in the whim of wearing a carnation in a button-hole, which at a distance had rather a deceptive effect. Bonaparte took this very seriously. He sent for Fouché, and desired him to arrest those who presumed thus to turn the new order into ridicule. Fouché merely replied that he would *wait till the autumn ;* and the First Consul understood that trifles were often rendered matters of importance by being honoured with too much attention.

But though Bonaparte was piqued at the interest excited by the engravings of Madame de Genlis' romance he manifested no displeasure against that celebrated woman, who had been recommended to him by MM. de Fontanes and Fievée and who addressed several letters to him. As this sort of correspondence did not come within the routine of my business I did not see the letters ; but I heard from Madame Bonaparte that they contained a prodigious number of proper names, and I have reason to believe that they contributed not a little to magnify, in the eyes of the First Consul, the importance of the Faubourg St. Germain, which, in spite of all his courage, was a scarecrow to him.

Bonaparte regarded the Faubourg St. Germain as representing the whole mass of Royalist opinion ; and he saw clearly that the numerous erasures from the emigrant list had necessarily increased dissatisfaction among the Royalists, since the property of the emigrants had not been restored to its old possessors, even in those cases in which it had not been sold. It was the fashion in a certain class to ridicule the unpolished manners of the great men of the Republic compared with the manners of the nobility of the old Court. The wives of certain generals had several times committed themselves by their awkwardness. In many circles there was an affectation of treating with con-

tempt what are called the *parvenus;* those people who, to
use M. de Talleyrand's expression, do not know how to
walk upon a carpet. All this gave rise to complaints
against the Faubourg St. Germain ; while, on the other
hand, Bonaparte's brothers spared no endeavours to irritate him against everything that was calculated to revive
the recollection of the Bourbons.

Such were Bonaparte's feelings, and such was the state
of society during the year 1802. The fear of the Bourbons must indeed have had a powerful influence on the
First Consul before he could have been induced to take a
step which may justly be regarded as the most inconsiderate of his whole life. After suffering seven months to
elapse without answering the first letter of Louis XVIII.,
after at length answering his second letter in the tone of
a King addressing a subject, he went so far as to write to
Louis, proposing that he should renounce the throne of
his ancestors in his, Bonaparte's, favour, and offering him
as a reward for this renunciation a principality in Italy, or
a considerable revenue for himself and his family.[1]

---

[1] Napoleon seems to have always known, as with Cromwell and the Stuarts, that
if his dynasty failed the Bourbons *must* succeed him. "I remember," says Metternich, "Napoleon said to me, 'Do you know why Louis XVIII. is not now sitting opposite to you ? It is only because it is I who am sitting here. No other person
could maintain his position ; and if ever I disappear in consequence of a catastrophe
no one but a Bourbon could sit here'" (*Metternich*, tome i. p. 243). Further, he said
to Metternich, "The King overthrown, the Republic was master of the soil of
France. It is that which I have replaced. The old throne of France is buried
under its rubbish. I had to found a new one. The Bourbons could not reign over
this creation. My strength lies in my fortune. I am new, like the Empire ; there
is, therefore, a perfect homogeneity between the Empire and myself." "However,"
says Metternich, "I have often thought that Napoleon, by talking in this way, merely
sought to study the opinion of others, or to confuse it, and the direct advance which
he made to Louis XVIII. in 1804 seemed to confirm this suspicion. Speaking to me
one day of this advance he said, 'Monsieur's reply was grand ; it was full of fine tra-
ditions. There is something in legitimate rights which appeals to more than the
mere mind. If Monsieur had consulted his mind only he would have arranged with
me, and I should have made for him a magnificent future'" (*Metternich*, tome i.
p. 276). According to Iung's *Lucien* (tome ii. p. 421), the letter written and signed
by Napoleon, but never sent, another draft being substituted, is still in the French
archives. Metternich speaks of Napoleon making a direct advance to Louis XVIII.
in 1804. According to Colonel Iung (*Lucien Bonaparte*, tome ii. pp. 420–426) the
attempt was made through the King of Prussia in 1802, the final answer of Louis

The reader will recollect the curious question which the First Consul put to me on the subject of the Bourbons when we were walking in the park of Malmaison. To the reply which I made to him on that occasion I attribute the secrecy he observed towards me respecting the letter just alluded to. I am indeed inclined to regard that letter as the result of one of his private conferences with Lucien ; but I know nothing positive on the subject, and merely mention this as a conjecture. However, I had an opportunity of ascertaining the curious circumstances which took place at Mittau, when Bonaparte's letter was delivered to Louis XVIII.

That Prince was already much irritated against Bonaparte by his delay in answering his first letter, and also by the tenor of his tardy reply ; but on reading the First Consul's second letter the dethroned King immediately sat down and traced a few lines forcibly expressing his indignation at such a proposition. The note, hastily written by Louis XVIII. in the first impulse of irritation, bore little resemblance to the dignified and elegant letter which Bonaparte received, and which I shall presently lay before

being made on the 28th February 1803, as given in the text, but with a postscript of his nephew in addition, " With the permission of the King, my uncle, I adhere with heart and soul to the contents of this note.

"(Signed) LOUIS ANTOINE, Duc d'Angoulême."

The reader will remark that there is no great interval between this letter and the final break with the Bourbons by the death of the Duc d'Enghien. At this time, according to Savary (tome iii. p. 241), some of the Bourbons were receiving French pensions. The Prince de Conti, the Duchesse de Bourbon, and the Duchesse d'Orleans, when sent out of France by the Directory, were given pensions of from 20,000 to 25,000 francs each. They lived in Catalonia. When the French troops entered Spain in 1808 General Canclaux, a friend of the Prince de Conti, brought to the notice of Napoleon that the tiresome formalities insisted on by the pestilent clerks of all nations were observed towards these royal personages. Gaudin, the Minister of Finance, apparently on his own initiative, drew up a decree increasing the pensions to 60,000 francs, and doing away with the formalities. " *The Emperor signed at once, thanking the Minister of Finance.*" The reader, remembering the position of the French Princes then, should compare this action of Napoleon with the failure of the Bourbons in 1814 to pay the sums promised to Napoleon, notwithstanding the strong remonstrances made at Vienna to Talleyrand by Alexander and Lord Castlereagh. See *Talleyrand's Correspondence with Louis XVIII.*, tome ii. pp. 27, 28 ; or French edition, pp. 285, 288.

the reader. This latter epistle closed very happily with
the beautiful device of Francis I., "All is lost but honour."
But the first letter was stamped with a more chivalrous
tone of indignation. The indignant sovereign wrote it
with his hand supported on the hilt of his sword; but
the Abbé André, in whom Louis XVIII. reposed great
confidence, saw the note, and succeeded, not without some
difficulty, in soothing the anger of the King, and prevailing on him to write the following letter :—

I do not confound M. Bonaparte with those who have preceded
him. I esteem his courage and his military talents. I am grateful
for some acts of his government ; for the benefits which are conferred on my people will always be prized by me.

But he errs in supposing that he can induce me to renounce my
rights ; so far from that, he would confirm them, if they could possibly be doubtful, by the step he has now taken.

I am ignorant of the designs of Heaven respecting me and my
subjects ; but I know the obligations which God has imposed upon
me. As a Christian, I will fulfil my duties to my last breath—as
the son of St. Louis, I would, like him, respect myself even in
chains—as the successor of Francis I., I say with him—*Tout est
perdu fors l'honneur.*

MITTAU, 1802.

Louis.

Louis XVIII.'s letter having reached Paris, the Royalist
committee assembled, and were not a little embarrassed as
to what should be done. The meeting took place at Neuilly.
After a long deliberation it was suggested that the deliv-
ery of the letter should be entrusted to the Third Consul,
with whom the Abbé de Montesquiou had kept up acquaintance since the time of the Constituent Assembly.
This suggestion was adopted. The recollections of the
commencement of his career, under Chancellor Maupeou,
had always caused M. Lebrun to be ranked in a distinct
class by the Royalists. For my part, I always looked upon
him as a very honest man, a warm advocate of equality, and
anxious that it should be protected even by despotism,

which suited the views of the First Consul very well. The Abbé de Montesquiou accordingly waited upon M. Lebrun, who undertook to deliver the letter. Bonaparte received it with an air of indifference ; but whether that indifference were real or affected, I am to this day unable to determine. He said very little to me about the ill success of the negotiation with Louis XVIII. On this subject he dreaded, above all, the interference of his brothers, who created around him a sort of commotion which he knew was not without its influence, and which on several occasions had excited his anger.

The letter of Louis XVIII. is certainly conceived in a tone of dignity which cannot be too highly admired ; and it may be said that Bonaparte on this occasion rendered a real service to Louis by affording him the opportunity of presenting to the world one of the finest pages in the history of a dethroned King. This letter, the contents of which were known in some circles of Paris, was the object of general approbation to those who preserved the recollection of the Bourbons, and above all, to the Royalist committee. The members of that committee, proud of the noble spirit evinced by the unfortunate monarch, whose return they were generously labouring to effect, replied to him by a sort of manifesto, to which time has imparted interest, since subsequent events have fulfilled the predictions it contained.

CHAPTER XVI.

1802.

I SHALL now return to the circumstances which followed my first disgrace, of which I have already spoken. The day after that on which I had resumed my functions I went as usual to awaken the First Consul at seven in the morning. He treated me just the same as if nothing had happened between us ; and on my part I behaved to him just as usual, though I really regretted being obliged to resume labours which I found too oppressive for me. When Bonaparte came down into his cabinet he spoke to me of his plans with his usual confidence, and I saw, from the number of letters lying in the basket, that during the few days my functions had been suspended Bonaparte had not overcome his disinclination to peruse this kind of correspondence. At the period of this first rupture and reconciliation the question of the Consulate for life was yet unsettled. It was not decided until the 2d of August, and the circumstances to which I am about to refer happened at the end of February.

I was now restored to my former footing of intimacy with the First Consul, at least for a time; but I soon perceived that, after the scene which M. de Talleyrand had witnessed, my duties in the Tuileries were merely provisional, and might be shortened or prolonged according to circumstances. I saw at the very first moment that Bonaparte had sacrificed his wounded pride to the necessity (for such I may, without any vanity, call it) of employing my services. The forced preference he granted to me arose from the fact of his being unable to find any one able to supply my place; for Duroc, as I have already said, showed a disinclination to the business. I did not remain long in the dark respecting the new situation in which I stood. I was evidently still under quarantine; but the period of my quitting the port was undetermined.

A short time after our reconciliation the First Consul said to me, in a cajoling tone of which I was not the dupe, "My dear Bourrienne, you cannot do everything. Business increases, and will continue to increase. You know what Corvisart says. You have a family; therefore it is right you should take care of your health. You must not kill yourself with work; therefore some one must be got to assist you. Joseph tells me that he can recommend a secretary, one of whom he speaks very highly. He shall be under your direction; he can make out your copies, and do all that can consistently be required of him. This, I think, will be a great relief to you."—"I ask for nothing better," replied I, "than to have the assistance of some one who, after becoming acquainted with the business, may, some time or other, succeed me." Joseph sent M. de Meneval, a young man who, to a good education, added the recommendations of industry and prudence. I had every reason to be satisfied with him.

It was now that Napoleon employed all those devices and caresses which always succeeded so well with him, and which yet again gained the day, to put an end to the inconvenience caused to him by my retirement, and to retain me. Here I call every one who knew me as witnesses that nothing could equal my grief and despair to find myself obliged to again begin my troublesome work. My health had suffered much from it. Corvisart was a clever counsellor, but it was only during the night that I could carry out his advice. To resume my duties was to renounce all hope of rest, and even of health.[1]

I soon perceived the First Consul's anxiety to make M. de Meneval acquainted with the routine of business, and accustomed to his manner. Bonaparte had never pardoned me for having presumed to quit him after he had attained so high a degree of power ; he was only waiting for an opportunity to punish me, and he seized upon an unfortunate circumstance as an excuse for that separation which I had previously wished to bring about.

I will explain this circumstance, which ought to have obtained for me the consolation and assistance of the First Consul rather than the forfeiture of his favour. My rupture with him has been the subject of various misstatements, all of which I shall not take the trouble to correct ; I will merely notice what I have read in the Memoirs of the Duc de Rovigo, in which it is stated that I was accused of *peculation*. M. de Rovigo thus expresses himself :—

Ever since the First Consul was invested with the supreme power his life had been a continued scene of personal exertion. He had for his private secretary M. de Bourrienne, a friend and companion of his youth, whom he now made the sharer of all his labours. He frequently sent for him in the dead of the night, and particularly insisted upon his attending him every morning at seven. Bourrienne was punctual in his attendance with the public papers, which he had previously glanced over. The First Consul almost invariably read their contents himself ; he then despatched some business,

---

[1] There is considerable truth in this statement about the effect on his health. His successor, Meneval, without the same amount of work, broke down and had to receive assistance (*Meneval*, tome i. p. 149).

and sat down to table just as the clock struck nine. His breakfast, which lasted six minutes, was no sooner over than he returned to his cabinet, only left it for dinner, and resumed his close occupation immediately after, until ten at night, which was his usual hour for retiring to rest.

Bourrienne was gifted with a most wonderful memory ; he could speak and write many languages, and would make his pen follow as fast as words were uttered. He possessed many other advantages ; he was well acquainted with the administrative departments, was versed in the law of nations, and possessed a zeal and activity which rendered his services quite indispensable to the First Consul. I have known the several grounds upon which the unlimited confidence placed in him by his chief rested, but am unable to speak with equal assurance of the errors which occasioned his losing that confidence.

Bourrienne had many enemies ; some were owing to his personal character, a greater number to the situation which he held. Others were jealous of the credit he enjoyed with the Head of the Government ; others, again, discontented at his not making that credit subservient to their personal advantage. Some even imputed to him the want of success that had attended their claims. It was impossible to bring any charge against him on the score of deficiency of talent or of indiscreet conduct ; his personal habits were watched —it was ascertained that he engaged in financial speculations. An imputation could easily be founded on this circumstance. Peculation was accordingly laid to his charge.

This was touching the most tender ground, for the First Consul held nothing in greater abhorrence than unlawful gains. A solitary voice, however, would have failed in an attempt to defame the character of a man for whom he had so long felt esteem and affection ; other voices, therefore, were brought to bear against him. Whether the accusations were well founded or otherwise, it is beyond a doubt that all means were resorted to for bringing them to the knowledge of the First Consul.

The most effectual course that suggested itself was the opening a correspondence either with the accused party direct, or with those with whom it was felt indispensable to bring him into contact ; this correspondence was carried on in a mysterious manner, and related to the financial operations that had formed the grounds of a charge against him. Thus it is that, on more than one occasion, the very channels intended for conveying truth to the knowledge of a sovereign have been made available to the purpose of communicating false intelligence to him. To give an instance.

Under the reign of Louis XV., and even under the Regency, the Post Office was organized into a system of minute inspection, which did not indeed extend to every letter, but was exercised over all such as afforded grounds for suspicion. They were opened, and, when it was not deemed safe to suppress them, copies were taken, and they were returned to their proper channel without the least delay. Any individual denouncing another may, by the help of such an establishment, give great weight to his denunciation. It is sufficient for his purpose that he should throw into the Post Office any letter so worded as to confirm the impression which it is his object to convey. The worthiest man may thus be committed by a letter which he has never read, or the purport of which is wholly unintelligible to him.

I am speaking from personal experience. It once happened that a letter addressed to myself, relating to an alleged fact which had never occurred, was opened. A copy of the letter so opened was also forwarded to me, as it concerned the duties which I had to perform at that time; but I was already in possession of the original, transmitted through the ordinary channel. Summoned to reply to the questions to which such productions had given rise, I took that opportunity of pointing out the danger that would accrue from placing a blind reliance upon intelligence derived from so hazardous a source. Accordingly, little importance was afterwards attached to this means of information; but the system was in operation at the period when M. de Bourrienne was disgraced; his enemies took care to avail themselves of it; they blackened his character with M. de Barbé Marbois, who added to their accusations all the weight of his unblemished character. The opinion entertained by this rigid public functionary, and many other circumstances, induced the First Consul to part with his secretary (tome i. p. 418).

Peculation is the crime of those who make a fraudulent use of the public money. But as it was not in my power to meddle with the public money, no part of which passed through my hands, I am at loss to conceive how I can be charged with peculation! The Duc de Rovigo is not the author, but merely the echo, of this calumny; but the accusation to which his Memoirs gave currency afforded M. de Barbé Marbois an opportunity of adding one more to the many proofs he has given of his love of justice.

I had seen nothing of the Memoirs of the Duc de Rovigo except their announcement in the journals, when a
letter from M. de Barbé Marbois was transmitted to me
from my family.   It was as follows :—

SIR—My attention has been called to the enclosed article in a
recent publication.   The assertion it contains is not true, and I conceive it to be a duty both to you and myself to declare that I then was,
and still am, ignorant of the causes of the separation in question.—I
am, etc.

(Signed) MARBOIS.

I need say no more in my justification.   This unsolicited
testimony of M. de Marbois is a sufficient contradiction to
the charge of peculation which has been raised against me
in the absence of correct information respecting the real
causes of my rupture with the First Consul.

M. le Duc de Rovigo also observes that my enemies
were numerous.   My concealed adversaries were indeed
all those who were interested that the sovereign should
not have about him, as his confidential companion, a man
devoted to his glory and not to his vanity.   In expressing
his dissatisfaction with one of his ministers Bonaparte had
said, in the presence of several individuals, among whom
was M. Maret, " If I could find a second Bourrienne I
would get rid of you all."   This was sufficient to raise
against me the hatred of all who envied the confidence of
which I was in possession.

The failure of a firm in Paris in which I had invested a
considerable sum of money afforded an opportunity for
envy and malignity to irritate the First Consul against me.
Bonaparte, who had not yet forgiven me for wishing to
leave him, at length determined to sacrifice my services to
a new fit of ill-humour.

A mercantile house, then one of the most respectable in
Paris, had among its speculations undertaken some army
contracts.   With the knowledge of Berthier, with whom,

indeed, the house had treated, I had invested some money in this business. Unfortunately the principals were, unknown to me, engaged in dangerous speculations in the Funds, which in a short time so involved them as to occasion their failure for a heavy amount. This caused a rumour that a slight fall of the Funds, which took place at that period, was occasioned by the bankruptcy ; and the First Consul, who never could understand the nature of the Funds, gave credit to the report. He was made to believe that the business of the Stock Exchange was ruined. It was insinuated that I was accused of taking advantage of my situation to produce variations in the Funds, though I was so unfortunate as to lose not only my investment in the bankrupt house, but also a sum of money for which I had become bound, by way of surety, to assist the house in increasing its business. I incurred the violent displeasure of the First Consul, who declared to me that he *no longer required my services.* I might, perhaps have cooled his irritation by reminding him that he could not blame me for *purchasing* an interest in a contract, since he himself had stipulated for a *gratuity* of 1,500,000 francs for his brother Joseph out of the contract for victualling the navy.[1] But I saw that for some time past M. de Meneval had begun to supersede me, and the First Consul only wanted such an opportunity as this for coming to a rupture with me.

Such is a true statement of the circumstances which led to my separation from Bonaparte. I defy any one to adduce a single fact in support of the charge of peculation, or any transaction of the kind ; I fear no investigation of my conduct. When in the service of Bonaparte I caused many appointments to be made, and many names to be erased from the emigrant list before the *Sénatus-consulte* of the 6th Floréal, year X.; but I never counted upon

---

[1] Joseph Bonaparte contradicts this statement; but the practice was common in France, as it had once been in England.—*Editor of* 1836 *edition.*

gratitude, experience having taught me that it was an empty word.

The Duc de Rovigo attributed my disgrace to certain intercepted letters which injured me in the eyes of the First Consul. I did not know this at the time, and though I was pretty well aware of the machinations of Bonaparte's adulators, almost all of whom were my enemies, yet I did not contemplate such an act of baseness. But a spontaneous letter from M. de Barbé Marbois at length opened my eyes, and left little doubt on the subject. The following is the postscript to that noble peer's letter :—

I recollect that one Wednesday the First Consul, while presiding at a Council of Ministers at St. Cloud, opened a note, and, without informing us what it contained, hastily left the Board, apparently much agitated. In a few minutes he returned and told us that your functions had ceased.

Whether the sudden displeasure of the First Consul was excited by a false representation of my concern in the transaction which proved so unfortunate to me, or whether Bonaparte merely made that a pretence for carrying into execution a resolution which I am convinced had been previously adopted, I shall not stop to determine ; but the Duc de Rovigo having mentioned the violation of the secrecy of letters in my case, I shall take the opportunity of stating some particulars on that subject.

Before I wrote these Memoirs the existence in the Post Office of the cabinet, which had obtained the epithet of *black,* had been denounced in the chamber of deputies, and the answer was, that it *no longer* existed, which of course amounted to an admission that it *had* existed. I may therefore, without indiscretion, state what I know respecting it.

The " black cabinet " was established in the reign of Louis XV., merely for the purpose of prying into the scandalous gossip of the Court and the capital. The existence of this cabinet soon became generally known to every one. The numerous postmasters who succeeded each other, especially in latter times, the still more numerous Post Office clerks, and that portion of the public who are ever on the watch for what is held up as scandalous, soon banished all the secrecy of the affair, and none but fools were taken in by it. All who did not wish to be committed by their correspondence chose better channels of communication than the Post ; but those who wanted to ruin an enemy or benefit a friend long continued to avail themselves of the black cabinet, which, at first intended merely to amuse a monarch's idle hours, soon became a medium of intrigue, dangerous from the abuse that might be made of it.

Every morning, for three years, I used to peruse the portfolio containing the bulletins of the black cabinet, and I frankly confess that I never could discover any real cause for the public indignation against it, except inasmuch as it proved the channel of vile intrigue. Out of 30,000 letters, which daily left Paris to be distributed through France and all parts of the world, ten or twelve, at most, were copied, and often only a few lines of them.

Bonaparte at first proposed to send complete copies of intercepted letters to the ministers whom their contents might concern ; but a few observations from me induced him to direct that only the important passages should be extracted and sent. I made these extracts, and transmitted them to their destinations, accompanied by the following words : *" The First Consul directs me to inform you that he has just received the following information,"* etc. Whence the information came was left to be guessed at.

The First Consul daily received through this channel about a dozen pretended letters, the writers of which described their enemies as opponents of the Government, or their friends as models of obedience and fidelity to the constituted authorities. But the secret purpose of this vile correspondence was soon discovered, and Bonaparte gave orders that no more of it should be copied. I, however, suffered from it at the time of my disgrace, and was well-nigh falling a victim to it at a subsequent period.

The letter mentioned by M. de Marbois, and which was the occasion of this digression on the violation of private correspondence, derived importance from the circumstance that Wednesday, the 20th of October, when Bonaparte received it, was the day on which I left the Consular palace.

I retired to a house which Bonaparte had advised me to purchase at St. Cloud, and for the fitting up and furnishing of which he had promised to pay. We shall see how he kept this promise! I immediately sent to direct Landoire, the messenger of Bonaparte's cabinet, to place *all* letters sent to me in the First Consul's portfolio, because many intended for him came under cover for me. In consequence of this message I received the following letter from M. de Meneval :—

My DEAR BOURRIENNE—I cannot believe that the First Consul would wish that your letters should be presented to him. I presume you allude only to those which may concern him, and which come addressed under cover to you. The First Consul has written to citizens Lavallette and Mollien directing them to address their packets to him. I cannot allow Landoire to obey the order you sent.

The First Consul yesterday evening evinced great regret. He repeatedly said, "How miserable I am! I have known that man since he was seven years old." I cannot but believe that he will reconsider his unfortunate decision. I have intimated to him that the burden of the business is too much for me, and that he must be extremely at a loss for the services of one to whom he was so much accustomed, and whose situation, I am confident, nobody else can satisfactorily fill. He went to bed very low-spirited. I am, etc. (Signed) MENEVAL.

19 *Vendémiaire, an* X.
(21*st October* 1802.)

Next day I received another letter from M. Meneval as follows :—

I send you your letters. The First Consul prefers that you should break them open, and send here those which are intended for him. I enclose some German papers, which he begs you to translate.

Madame Bonaparte is much interested in your behalf; and I can assure you that no one more heartily desires than the First Consul himself to see you again at your old post, for which it would be difficult to find a successor equal to you, either as regards fidelity or fitness. I do not relinquish the hope of seeing you here again.

A whole week passed away in conflicts between the First Consul's friendship and pride. The least desire he manifested to recall me was opposed by his flatterers. On the fifth day of our separation he directed me to come to him. He received me with the greatest kindness, and after having good-humouredly told me that I often expressed myself with too much freedom—a fault I was never solicitous to correct—he added : "I regret your absence much. You were very useful to me. You are neither too noble nor too plebeian, neither too aristocratic nor too Jacobinical. You are discreet and laborious. You understand me better than any one else ; and, between ourselves be it said, we ought to consider this a sort of Court. Look at Duroc, Bessières, Maret. However, I am very much inclined to take you back ; but by so doing I should confirm the report that I cannot do without you."

Madame Bonaparte informed me that she had heard persons to whom Bonaparte expressed a desire to recall me observe, " What would you do ? People will say you cannot do without him. You have got rid of him now ; therefore think no more about him : and as for the English newspapers, he gave them more importance than they really deserved : you will no longer be troubled with them." This will bring to mind a scene which occurred at Malmaison on the receipt of some intelligence in the *London Gazette.*

I am convinced that if Bonaparte had been left to himself he would have recalled me, and this conviction is warranted by the interval which elapsed between his determination to part with me and the formal announcement of my dismissal. Our rupture took place on the 20th of October, and on the 8th of November following the First Consul sent me the following letter :—

CITIZEN BOURRIENNE, MINISTER OF STATE—I am satisfied with the services which you have rendered me during the time you have been with me ; but henceforth they are no longer necessary. I wish you to relinquish, from this time, the functions and title of my private secretary. I shall seize an early opportunity of providing for you in a way suited to your activity and talents, and conducive to the public service.

                              (Signed)   BONAPARTE.

If any proof of the First Consul's malignity were wanting it would be furnished by the following fact :—A few days after the receipt of the letter which announced my dismissal I received a note from Duroc ; but, to afford an idea of the petty revenge of him who caused it to be written, it will be necessary first to relate a few preceding circumstances.

When, with the view of preserving a little freedom, I declined the offer of apartments which Madame Bonaparte had prepared at Malmaison for myself and my family, I purchased a small house at Ruel : the First Consul had given orders for the furnishing of this house, as well as one which I possessed in Paris. From the manner in which the orders were given I had not the slightest doubt but that Bonaparte intended to make me a present of the furniture. However, when I left his service he applied to have it returned. As at first I paid no attention to his demand, as far as it concerned the furniture at Ruel, he directed Duroc to write the following letter to me :—

The First Consul, my dear Bourrienne, has just ordered me to send him this evening the keys of your residence in Paris, from which the furniture is not to be removed.

He also directs me to put into a warehouse whatever furniture you may have at Ruel or elsewhere which you have obtained from Government.

I beg of you to send me an answer, so as to assist me in the execution of these orders. You promised me to have everything settled before the First Consul's return. I must excuse myself in the best way I can.   (Signed)   DUROC.

24 *Brumaire, an X.*
(15th *November* 1802.)

Believing myself to be master of my own actions, I had formed the design of visiting England, whither I was called by some private business. However, I was fully aware of the peculiarity of my situation, and I was resolved to take no step that should in any way justify a reproach.

On the 11th of January I therefore wrote to Duroc :—

My affairs require my presence in England for some time. I beg of you, my dear Duroc, to mention my intended journey to the First Consul, as I do not wish to do anything inconsistent with his views. I would rather sacrifice my own interest than displease him. I rely on your friendship for an early answer to this, for uncertainty would be fatal to me in many respects.

The answer, which speedily arrived, was as follows :—

MY DEAR BOURRIENNE—I have presented to the First Consul the letter I just received from you. He read it, and said, " No ! " That is the only answer I can give you.   (Signed)   DUROC.

This monosyllable was expressive. It proved to me that Bonaparte was conscious how ill he had treated me ; and, suspecting that I was actuated by the desire of vengeance, he was afraid of my going to England, lest I should there take advantage of that liberty of the press which he had so effectually put down in France. He probably imagined that my object was to publish statements which would more effectually have enlightened the public respecting his government and designs than all the scandalous anecdotes, atrocious calumnies, and ridiculous fabrications of Pelletier,[1] the editor of the *Ambigu*. But Bonaparte was much deceived in this supposition ; and if there can remain any doubt on that subject, it will be removed on referring to the date of these Memoirs, and observing the time at which I consented to publish them.

I was not deceived as to the reasons of Bonaparte's unceremonious refusal of my application ; and as I well knew his inquisitorial character, I thought it prudent to conceal my notes. I acted differently from Camoens. He contended with the sea to preserve his manuscripts ; I made the earth the depository of mine. I carefully enclosed my most valuable notes and papers in a tin box, which I buried under ground.[2] A yellow tinge, the commencement of decay, has in some places almost obliterated the writing.

It will be seen in the sequel that my precaution was not useless, and that I was right in anticipating the persecution of Bonaparte, provoked by the malice of my enemies. On the 20th of April Duroc sent me the following note :—

I beg, my dear Bourrienne, that you will come to St. Cloud this morning. I have something to tell you on the part of the First Consul.   (Signed)   DUROC.

This note caused me much anxiety. I could not doubt but that my enemies had invented some new calumny ;

---

[1] Sometimes spelt as Peltier.

[2] This passage should be remarked by the reader. If Bourrienne was not carrying away documents to which he had no right, or if he had only been engaged in the ordinary correspondence of a private secretary, there was no possible reason for thus hiding documents. It will be noticed that he constantly quotes documents received by Napoleon when he was still secretary, and which he says were still in his possession. *Erreurs* (tome i. p. 261) naturally asks by what right he retained them. When Fouché left office in 1810 there was an amusing contest between him and Napoleon for the possession of certain correspondence, which Fouché declared he had destroyed, sticking to his assertion with great and almost daring pertinacity till he came to terms and produced them ; but the comparison is not flattering for Bourrienne.

but I must say that I did not expect such baseness as I experienced.

As soon as Duroc had made me acquainted with the business which the First Consul had directed him to communicate, I wrote on the spot the subjoined letter to Bonaparte :—

At General Duroc's desire I have this moment waited upon him, and he informs me that you have received notice that a deficit of 100,000 francs has been discovered in the Treasury of the Navy, which you require me to refund this day at noon.

Citizen First Consul, I know not what this means ! I am utterly ignorant of the matter. I solemnly declare to you that this charge is a most infamous calumny. It is one more to be added to the number of those malicious charges which have been invented for the purpose of destroying any influence I might possess with you.

I am in General Duroc's apartment, where I await your orders.

Duroc carried my note to the First Consul as soon as it was written. He speedily returned. "All's right !" said he. "He has directed me to say it was entirely a mistake !—that he is now convinced he was deceived !—that he is sorry for the business, and hopes no more will be said about it."

The base flatterers who surrounded Bonaparte wished him to renew his Egyptian extortions upon me ; but they should have recollected that the fusillade employed in Egypt for the purpose of raising money was no longer the fashion in France, and that the days were gone by when it was the custom to *grease the wheels of the revolutionary car.*[1]

---

[1] Bourrienne has defended himself with great success against a charge of misusing public money,—a charge which was not made against him. He has made no defence against the charge of using the information gained by him in his official capacity for private speculations ; he does not even seem to understand the gravity of such an accusation, for, in speaking of one of Ouvrard's projects for a speculation in Mexico, at a time when Bourrienne was still secretary, he says that he was to have had a share in the business. (See under 1805.) It never seems to strike him that a person in his confidential position ought not to have taken a share in an affair of the sort, especially in one distrusted by Napoleon. We may therefore take

for granted that he did so use his position. That he was partly unsuccessful was a misfortune which he shared with Talleyrand ; and his ill-success is no argument for his innocence. The story of his disgrace is told by Meneval thus : "The First Consul had made M. de Bourrienne Councillor of State on special service, and granted to him rights and privileges which made him an important personage. He corresponded directly with the ministers on some of the details of their work. Napoleon treated M. de Bourrienne familiarly, and often went out with him on foot or in a Boghei [1] to have a turn in the park of St. Cloud. M. de Bourrienne was very nearly independent, and did not eat or lodge in the palace. He had just bought a charming house at St. Cloud. He furnished it richly, and gave dinners, to which ministers, especially Fouché, senators, and councillors of state, etc., were invited. His expenses and his purchases were not in accordance with his fortune as known to the First Consul. Although their mutual relations seemed not to have altered, still the annoyance that the First Consul did not reveal to M. de Bourrienne was sometimes betrayed by reflections dropped before me. It seemed to me that the First Consul had special complaints against him which he had not sufficiently investigated.

"The unfortunate affair of the house of the brothers Coulon put an end to his irresolutions. It was the last drop in the cup. One Wednesday" (*the 20th October 1802, the date given by Bourrienne, was a Wednesday*) "I was at work in the cabinet of the First Consul when I saw him enter hurriedly. He asked me if M. de Bourrienne was at his desk, and on my saying he was, he called him from the threshold of the door. M. de Bourrienne came, a little upset by the animated air of the First Consul, who said to him in a severe tone, 'Give up to Meneval the papers and the keys which you have of mine and withdraw. Let me not find you here again.' After these few words he returned to the Council, slamming the door behind him. M. de Bourrienne, who had been overwhelmed by this sudden outburst, gave himself up to the greatest despair. I did all I could to calm him. I tried to make him accept consolations and hopes on which I hardly trusted, for a decision given in such a laconic and harsh manner left little hope. We exchanged some letters during the two or three days which followed this fatal scene, after which all connection between us ceased, by order of the First Consul.

"This explosion had been occasioned by the following occurrences :—About the time when I was called to the cabinet of the First Consul (*2d April 1802*), M. de Bourrienne, by his credit with the Minister of War, had obtained the contract for furnishing military equipments and harness. As his name could not appear, the contract was given to the brothers Coulon. M. de Bourrienne supplied the funds for starting the enterprise. A bank advanced 800,000 francs on a mortgage given by the brothers Coulon, but it required that M. de Bourrienne should guarantee it. The brothers Coulon failing soon afterwards, the bank enforced its claim on M. de Bourrienne, who disclaimed his liability with the Coulons. As the guarantee was created by private signed documents, secret contracts, and memoranda of accounts, all signed by Bourrienne, a suit ensued, which he lost at first, then gained on appeal, and finally lost in the Cour de Cassation. This business with which M. de Bourrienne had associated himself had much vexed the First Consul, who had an unconquerable repulsion for what is called *faire des affaires*. He was shocked at the cause and at the scandal of the suit. He never pardoned M. de Bourrienne. He often spoke to me of it at great length with real sorrow, which always degenerated into bitter complaint. He ended by taking his resolution ; he even congratulated himself on having broken the yoke. Without intending any comparison, he did what Louis XIV. did on the death of Mazarin. One day he said to me, 'I have abolished the

---

[1] A vehicle from which the Indian "buggy" takes its name?

title of private secretary. The name has too many inconveniences, I am obliged to recognise them. I desire that you will not take any other title than that of *attaché* to the First Consul'" (*Meneval*, tome i. p. 86).

This account of Meneval's will be found to be in fair agreement with the accounts of Bourrienne and of others (see *Savary*, tome i. p. 418, and *Erreurs*, tome ii. p. 11). And the account is to be the more accepted as Bourrienne acknowledges that he had nothing to complain of in the conduct of Meneval. We shall see that similar accusations were made against Bourrienne when he was at Hamburg. But while Meneval impeaches the moral character of Bourrienne, he corroborates his account of the important position held by the secretary; indeed, he almost increases our estimate of it when he speaks of Napoleon's satisfaction at having "broken the yoke."

CHAPTER XVII.

1803.

The First Consul's presentiments respecting the duration of peace—England's uneasiness at the prosperity of France—Bonaparte's real wish for war—Concourse of foreigners in Paris—Bad faith of England—Bonaparte and Lord Whitworth—Relative position of France and England—Bonaparte's journey to the seaboard departments—Breakfast at Compiègne—Father Berton—Irritation excited by the presence of Bouquet—Father Berton's derangement and death—Rapp ordered to send for me—Order countermanded.

THE First Consul never anticipated a long peace with England. He wished for peace merely because, knowing it to be ardently desired by the people, after ten years of war, he thought it would increase his popularity and afford him the opportunity of laying the foundation of his government. Peace was as necessary to enable him to conquer the throne of France as war was essential to secure it, and to enlarge its base at the expense of the other thrones of Europe. This was the secret of the peace of Amiens, and of the rupture which so suddenly followed, though that rupture certainly took place sooner than the First Consul wished. On the great questions of peace and war Bonaparte entertained elevated ideas; but in discussions on the subject he always declared himself in favour of war.[1] When told of the necessities of the people, of the advantages of peace, its influence on trade, the arts, national industry, and every branch of public

[1] Compare *Metternich* (tome ii. p. 249), where, speaking of the efforts made in 1808 by many French agents and officers to urge Napoleon to war with Austria, he says, "They too often end by carrying with them the strongest wills; and the Emperor's will is never strong when it is a question of opposing war."

prosperity, he did not attempt to deny the argument ; indeed, he concurred in it ; but he remarked, that all those advantages were only conditional, so long as England was able to throw the weight of her navy into the scale of the world, and to exercise the influence of her gold in all the Cabinets of Europe.   Peace must be broken ; since it was evident that England was determined to break it.   Why not anticipate her ?   Why allow her to have all the advantages of the first step?   We must astonish Europe !   We must thwart the policy of the Continent ! We must strike a great and unexpected blow.   Thus reasoned the First Consul, and every one may judge whether his actions agreed with his sentiments.

The conduct of England too well justified the foresight of Bonaparte's policy ; or rather England, by neglecting to execute her treaties, played into Bonaparte's hand, favoured his love for war, and justified the prompt declaration of hostilities in the eyes of the French nation, whom he wished to persuade that if peace were broken it would be against his wishes.   England was already at work with the powerful machinery of her subsidies, and the veil beneath which she attempted to conceal her negotiations was still sufficiently transparent for the lynx eye of the First Consul.   It was in the midst of peace that all those plots were hatched, while millions who had no knowledge of their existence were securely looking forward to uninterrupted repose.

Since the Revolution Paris had never presented such a spectacle as during the winter of 1802-3.   At that time the concourse of foreigners in the French capital was immense.   Everything wore the appearance of satisfaction, and the external signs of public prosperity.   The visible regeneration in French society exceedingly annoyed the British Ministry.   The English who flocked to the Continent discovered France to be very different from what she was described to be by the English papers.   This caused serious alarm on the other side of the Channel, and the English Government endeavoured by unjust complaints to divert attention from just dissatisfaction, which its own secret intrigues excited. The King of England sent a message to Parliament, in which he spoke of armaments preparing in the ports of France, and of the necessity of adopting precautions against meditated aggressions. This instance of bad faith highly irritated the First Consul, who one day, in a fit of displeasure, thus addressed Lord Whitworth in the *salon,* where all the foreign Ambassadors were assembled :

"What is the meaning of this ? Are you then tired of peace ? Must Europe again be deluged with blood ? Preparations for war indeed ! Do you think to overawe us by this ? You shall see that France may be conquered, perhaps destroyed, but never intimidated—never ! " [1]

The English Ambassador was astounded at this unexpected sally, to which he made no reply. He contented himself with writing to his Government an account of an interview in which the First Consul had so far forgotten himself,—whether purposely or not I do not pretend to say. [2]

---

[1] The tone of voice, the gesticulation, and whole manner of Bonaparte were so violent on this occasion that our Ambassador, fancying the First Consul was going to strike him, put his hand to the hilt of his sword. Lord Whitworth was a high-spirited man. Some time after, when Mr Canning asked him what he would have done had Bonaparte struck him, he replied, " I would have run him through the body in the midst of his Court ! "—*Editor of* 1836 *edition.*

[2] The following is Savary's description of this extraordinary scene :

"One of the receptions of the Consular Court was the occasion on which Bonaparte vented his displeasure on the conduct of England. He had just been reading the despatches of his Ambassador at the Court of London, who sent him a copy of the King's message to Parliament respecting alleged armaments in the ports of France.

"His mind being wholly biassed by the reflections to which the perusal of the despatches had given rise, he omitted going that day into the second *salon,* but went straight up to the Ambassadors. I was only at the distance of a few paces from him when, stopping short before the English Ambassador, he put the following hurried questions to him in a tone of anger : 'What does your Cabinet mean ? What is the motive for raising these rumours of armaments in our harbours? How ! Is it possible to impose in this manner upon the credulity of nations, or to be so ignorant of our real intentions ? If the actual state of things be known, it must be evident to all that there are only two transports fitting out for St. Domingo : that that island

That England wished for war there could be no doubt.
She occupied Malta, it is true, but she had promised to
give it up, though she never had any intention of doing
so. She was to have evacuated Egypt, yet there she still
remained ; the Cape of Good Hope was to have been surrendered, but she still retained possession of it. England
had signed, at Amiens, a peace which she had no intention
of maintaining. She knew the hatred of the Cabinets
of Europe towards France, and she was sure, by her
intrigues and subsidies, of arming them on her side
whenever her plans reached maturity. She saw France
powerful and influential in Europe, and she knew the
ambitious views of the First Consul, who, indeed, had
taken little pains to conceal them.

The First Consul, who had reckoned on a longer duration of the peace of Amiens, found himself at the
rupture of the treaty in an embarrassing situation. The
numerous grants of furloughs, the deplorable condition

engrosses all our attention, all our disposable means. Why then these complaints?
Can peace be already considered as a burden to be shaken off? Is Europe to be
again deluged in blood? Preparations making for war? To pretend to overawe us!
France may be conquered, perhaps destroyed, but never intimidated!'

"The Ambassador made a respectful bow, and gave no reply. The First Consul
left that part of the *salon ;* but whether he had been a little heated by this explosion
of ill-humour, or from some other cause, he ceased his round, and withdrew to his
own apartments. Madame Bonaparte followed. In an instant the *salon* was cleared
of company. The Ambassadors of Russia and England had retired to the embrasure
of a window, and were still conversing together after the apartments had been
cleared of visitors. ' Indeed,' said one to the other, ' you could hardly expect such
an attack ; how then could you be prepared to reply to it? All you have to do is to
give an account of it to your government ; in the meantime, let what has taken
place suggest to you the conduct you ought to pursue.'

"He took the advice. The communications became cold and reserved. England
had already formed her determination. A spirit of acrimony soon sprung up between the two Governments.

"An interchange of notes took place : categorical explanations were required ; the
demand for passports soon followed. The latter were immediately granted by the
First Consul. I was in his closet of St. Cloud when M. Maret was introduced, who
brought with him the corrected draft of the reply which was to accompany the
passports. He had it read out to him, and expressed himself in the kindest terms
respecting the personal character of Lord Whitworth, for whom he felt great regard.
He was quite satisfied that on this occasion the Ambassador had not at all
influenced the conduct of his government" (*Memoirs of the Duc de Rovigo*, tome i.
p. 456).

of the cavalry, and the temporary absence of artillery, in consequence of a project for refounding all the field-pieces, caused much anxiety to Bonaparte. He had recourse to the conscription to fill up the deficiencies of the army ; and the project of refounding the artillery was abandoned. Supplies of money were obtained from the large towns, and Hanover, which was soon after occupied, furnished abundance of good horses for mounting the cavalry.[1]

War had now become inevitable ; and as soon as it was declared the First Consul set out to visit Belgium and the seaboard departments to ascertain the best means of resisting the anticipated attacks of the English. In passing through Compiègne he received a visit from Father Berton, formerly principal of the military school of Brienne. He was then rector of the school of arts at Compiègne, a situation in which he had been placed by Bonaparte. I learned the particulars of this visit through Josephine. Father Berton, whose primitive simplicity of manner was unchanged since the time when he held us under the authority of his ferule, came to invite Bonaparte and Josephine to breakfast with him, which invitation was accepted. Father Berton had at that time living with him one of our old comrades of Brienne, named Bouquet ; but he expressly forbade him to show himself to Bonaparte or any one of his suite, because Bouquet, who had been a commissary at headquarters in Italy, was in disgrace with the First Consul.[2] Bouquet promised to observe Father

[1] Here Bourrienne appears to follow Savary, who (tome i. p. 467) draws an amusing picture of the irritation of Napoleon at finding that Marmont, as Inspector of Artillery, and Berthier, as War Minister, had so begun the conversion of the field artillery as to almost deprive him of guns at the very time war was declared with England. But this incredible story is totally denied by Marmont (tome ii. p. 208), who asks, "Was the First Consul a likely man to let one of his generals, and his Minister of War, change, modify, destroy, and reconstruct the artillery equipment without his order and without his approval ? He knew day by day the progress of my work."

[2] Bouquet had incurred Bonaparte's displeasure by the following dishonest transaction :—When the French had a second time taken Verona, Bouquet and a colonel of the army named Andrieux, went to the Monte-di-Pietàs in that city, and by representing that they had orders from their general to make an inventory of

Berton's injunctions, but was far from keeping his promise. As soon as he saw Bonaparte's carriage drive up, he ran to the door and gallantly handed out Josephine. Josephine, as she took his hand, said, "Bouquet, you have ruined yourself!" Bonaparte, indignant at what he considered an unwarrantable familiarity, gave way to one of his uncontrollable fits of passion, and as soon as he entered the room where the breakfast was laid, he seated himself, and then said to his wife in an imperious tone, "Josephine, sit there!" He then commenced breakfast, without telling Father Berton to sit down, although a third plate had been laid for him. Father Berton stood behind his old pupil's chair apparently confounded at his violence. The scene produced such an effect on the old man that he became incapable of discharging his duties at Compiègne. He retired to Rheims, and his intellect soon after became deranged. I do not pretend to say whether this alienation of mind was caused by the occurrence I have just related, and the account of which I received from Josephine. She was deeply afflicted at what had passed. Father Berton died insane. What I heard from Josephine was afterwards confirmed by the brother of Father Berton. The fact is, that in proportion as Bonaparte acquired power he was the more annoyed at the familiarity of old companions ; and, indeed, I must confess that their familiarity often appeared very ridiculous.

The First Consul's visit to the northern coast took place towards the end of the year 1803, at which time the English attacked the Dutch settlements of Surinam, Deme-

the property, induced the keeper to allow them to examine the place. The property in the Monte-di-Piétà amounted to 12,000,000, which the keeper never set eyes on after Bouquet's visit. The colonel absconded, but Bouquet was apprehended and about to be tried. The transaction, however, was found to involve so many persons that the captain appointed to conduct the trial thought right to ask the opinion of General Augereau as to the propriety of proceeding. What directions he gave I do not know, but I know very well that Bouquet in the meantime escaped from prison. Bonaparte was highly indignant at his conduct, and declared that had he been found guilty he would have allowed the sentence to be executed.

rara, and Essequibo, and a convention of neutrality was concluded between France, Spain, and Portugal. Rapp accompanied the First Consul, who attentively inspected the preparations making for a descent on England, which it was never his intention to effect, as will be shortly shown.[1]

On the First Consul's return I learned from Rapp that I had been spoken of during the journey, and in the following way :—Bonaparte, being at Boulogne, wanted some information which no one there could give him. Vexed at receiving no satisfactory answer to his inquiries he called Rapp, and said, "Do you know, Rapp, where Bourrienne is?"—"General, he is in Paris."—"Write to him to come here immediately, and send off one of my couriers with the letter." The rumour of the First Consul's sudden recollection of me spread like lightning, and the time required to write the letter and despatch the courier was more than sufficient for the efforts of those whom my return was calculated to alarm. Artful representations soon checked these spontaneous symptoms of a return to former feelings and habits. When Rapp carried to the First Consul the letter he had been directed to write the order was countermanded. However, Rapp advised me not to leave Paris, or if I did, to mention the place where I might be found, so that Duroc might have it in his power to seize on any favourable circumstance without delay. I was well aware of the friendship of both Rapp and Duroc, and they could as confidently rely on mine.

[1] See Madame de Rémusat on the extraordinary enthusiam with which Napoleon was received on these journeys. "The joy of the inhabitants of Amiens, . . . the crowd which pressed to see him, the blessings too universal to have been ordered, all this struck me so much that I could not restrain my tears. Madame Bonaparte herself burst into tears, and I saw the eyes of Bonaparte redden for an instant " (*Rémusat*, tome i. p. 239).

CHAPTER XVIII.

1803.

Vast works undertaken—The French and the Roman soldiers—Itinerary
    of Bonaparte's journeys to the coast—Twelve hours on horseback—
    Discussions in Council—Opposition of Truguet—Bonaparte's opinion
    on the point under discussion—Two divisions of the world—Europe a
    province—Bonaparte's jealousy of the dignity of France—The Eng-
    lishman in the dockyard of Brest—Public audience at the Tuileries—
    The First Consul's remarks upon England—His wish to enjoy the
    good opinion of the English people—Ball at Malmaison—Lines on
    Hortense's dancing—Singular motive for giving the ball.

AT the time of the rupture with England Bonaparte was,
as I have mentioned, quite unprepared in most branches
of the service ; yet everything was created as if by magic,
and he seemed to impart to others a share of his own incredible activity.   It is inconceivable how many things
had been undertaken and executed since the rupture of
the peace.   The north coast of France presented the appearance of one vast arsenal ; for Bonaparte on this occasion employed his troops like Roman soldiers, and made
the tools of the artisan succeed to the arms of the warrior.

On his frequent journeys to the coast Bonaparte usually
set off at night, and on the following morning arrived at
the post office of Chantilly, where he breakfasted.   Rapp,
whom I often saw when he was in Paris, talked incessantly
of these journeys, for he almost always accompanied the
First Consul, and it would have been well had he always
been surrounded by such men.   In the evening the First
Consul supped at Abbeville, and arrived early next day at
the bridge of Brique.   "It would require constitutions of
iron to go through what we do," said Rapp.   "We no

sooner alight from the carriage than we mount on horseback, and sometimes remain in our saddles for ten or
twelve hours successively. The First Consul inspects and
examines everything, often talks with the soldiers. How
he is beloved by them! When shall we pay a visit to
London with those brave fellows?"

Notwithstanding these continual journeys the First
Consul never neglected any of the business of government, and was frequently present at the deliberations of
the Council. I was still with him when the question
as to the manner in which the treaties of peace should be
concluded came under the consideration of the Council.
Some members, among whom Truguet was conspicuous,
were of opinion that, conformably with an article of the
Constitution, the treaties should be proposed by the Head
of the Government, submitted to the Legislative Body,
and after being agreed to promulgated as part of the laws.
Bonaparte thought differently. I was entirely of his
opinion, and he said to me, "It is for the mere pleasure of
opposition that they appeal to the Constitution, for if the
Constitution says so it is absurd. There are some things
which cannot become the subject of discussion in a public
assembly; for instance, if I treat with Austria, and my
Ambassador agrees to certain conditions, can those conditions be rejected by the Legislative Body? It is a monstrous absurdity! Things would be brought to a fine pass
in this way! Lucchesini and Markow would give dinners
every day like Cambacérès;[1] scatter their money about,
buy men who are to be sold, and thus cause our propositions to be rejected. This would be a fine way to manage matters!"

[1] Cambacérès had kept up his dinners in the worst times of the Revolution, and
the very crumbs from his table seem to have been good. Thus the unfortunate grand-
children of the Maréchal de Lévis, almost starved after the execution of their
mothers, Mesdames de Vintimille and de Béranger, "retained in their remembrances
of their mournful childhood the memory of the feasts to which they were invited by
the porter of Cambacérès, when they had the remains of the grand dinners" (*Emi-
grés*, par Forneron, tome i. p. 181). See also vol. i. of this work, pp.

When Bonaparte, according to his custom, talked to me in the evening of what had passed in the Council, his language was always composed of a singular mixture of quotations from antiquity, historical references, and his own ideas. He talked about the Romans, and I remember when Mr. Fox was at Paris that he tried to distinguish himself before that Foreign Minister, whom he greatly esteemed. In his enlarged way of viewing the world Bonaparte divided it into two large states, the East and the West : " What matters," he would often say, " that two countries are separated by rivers or mountains, that they speak different languages? With very slight shades of of variety France, Spain, England, Italy, and Germany, have the same manners and customs, the same religion, and the same dress. In them a man can only marry one wife ; slavery is not allowed ; and these are the great distinctions which divide the civilised inhabitants of the globe. With the exception of Turkey, Europe is merely a province of the world, and our warfare is but civil strife. There is also another way of dividing nations, namely, by land and water." Then he would touch on all the European interests, speak of Russia, whose alliance he wished for, and of England, the mistress of the seas. He usually ended by alluding to what was then his favourite scheme —an expedition to India.

When from these general topics Bonaparte descended to the particular interests of France, he still spoke like a sovereign ; and I may truly say that he showed himself more jealous than any sovereign ever was of the dignity of France, of which he already considered himself the sole representative. Having learned that a captain of the English navy had visited the dockyard of Brest, passing himself off as a merchant, whose passport he had borrowed, he flew into a rage because no one had ventured to arrest him.[1] Nothing was lost on Bonaparte, and he made

[1] See James' *Naval History* for an account of Sir Sidney Smith's daring exploit.

use of this fact to prove to the Council of State the necessity of increasing the number of commissary-generals of police. At a meeting of the Council he said, "If there had been a commissary of police at Brest he would have arrested the English captain and sent him at once to Paris. As he was acting the part of a spy I would have had him shot as such. No Englishman, not even a nobleman, or the English Ambassador, should be admitted into our dockyards. I will soon regulate all this." He afterwards said to me, "There are plenty of wretches who are selling me every day to the English without my being subjected to English spying." [1]

He had on one occasion said before an assemblage of generals, senators, and high officers of State, who were at an audience of the Diplomatic Body, "The English think that I am afraid of war, but I am not." And here the truth escaped him, in spite of himself. "My power will lose nothing by war. In a very short time I can have 2,000,-000 of men at my disposal. What has been the result of the first war? The union of Belgium and Piedmont to France. This is greatly to our advantage ; it will consolidate our system. France shall not be restrained by foreign fetters. England has manifestly violated the treaties! It would be better to render homage to the King of England, and crown him King of France at Paris, than to submit to the insolent caprices of the English Government. If, for the sake of preserving peace, at most for only two months longer, I should yield on a single point, the English would become the more treacherous and insolent, and would exact the more in proportion as we yield. But they little know me ! Were we to yield to

---

[1] During the short and hollow peace of Amiens Bonaparte sent over to England, as consuls and vice-consuls, a number of engineers and military men, who were instructed to *make plans of all the harbours and coasts of the United Kingdom.* They worked in secrecy, yet not so secretly but that they were soon suspected ; the facts were proved, and they were sent out of the country without ceremony.—*Editor of 1836 edition.*

England now, she would next prohibit our navigation in certain parts of the world. She would insist on the surrender of our ships. I know not what she would not demand; but I am not the man to brook such indignities. Since England wishes for war she shall have it, and that speedily!"

On the same day Bonaparte said a great deal more about the treachery of England. The gross calumnies to which he was exposed in the London newspapers powerfully contributed to increase his natural hatred of the liberty of the press; and he was much astonished that such attacks could be made upon him by English subjects when he was at peace with the English Government.

I had one day a singular proof of the importance which Bonaparte attached to the opinion of the English people respecting any misconduct that was attributed to him. What I am about to state will afford another example of Bonaparte's disposition to employ petty and roundabout means to gain his ends. He gave a ball at Malmaison when Hortense was in the seventh month of her pregnancy.[1] I have already mentioned that he disliked to see women in that situation, and above all could not endure to see them dance. Yet, in spite of this antipathy, he himself asked Hortense to dance at the ball at Malmaison. She at first declined, but Bonaparte was exceedingly importunate, and said to her in a tone of good-humoured persuasion, "Do, I beg of you; I particularly wish to see you dance. Come, stand up, to oblige me." Hortense at last consented. The motive for this extraordinary request I will now explain.

On the day after the ball one of the newspapers contained some verses on Hortense's dancing. She was exceedingly annoyed at this, and when the paper arrived at

---

[1] This refers to the first son of Louis and of Hortense, Napoléon Charles, the intended successor of Napoleon, who was born 1802, died 1807, elder brother of Napoleon III.

Malmaison she expressed displeasure at it. Even allowing for all the facility of our newspaper wits, she was
nevertheless at a loss to understand how the lines could
have been written and printed respecting a circumstance
which only occurred the night before. Bonaparte smiled,
and gave her no distinct answer. When Hortense knew
that I was alone in the cabinet she came in and asked me
to explain the matter; and seeing no reason to conceal
the truth, I told her that the lines had been written by
Bonaparte's direction before the ball took place. I added,
what indeed was the fact, that the ball had been prepared
for the verses, and that it was only for the appropriateness of their application that the First Consul had pressed
her to dance. He adopted this strange contrivance for
contradicting an article which appeared in an English
journal announcing that Hortense was delivered. Bonaparte was highly indignant at that premature announcement, which he clearly saw was made for the sole purpose
of giving credit to the scandalous rumours of his imputed
connection with Hortense. Such were the petty machinations which not unfrequently found their place in a mind
in which the grandest schemes were revolving.

CHAPTER XIX.

1803.

Mr. Pitt—Motive of his going out of office—Error of the English Government—Pretended regard for the Bourbons—Violation of the treaty
of Amiens—Reciprocal accusations—Malta—Lord Whitworth's departure—Rome and Carthage—Secret satisfaction of Bonaparte—
Message to the Senate, the Legislative Body, and the Tribunate—The
King of England's renunciation of the title of King of France—Complaints of the English Government—French agents in British ports
—Views of France upon Turkey—Observation made by Bonaparte
to the Legislative Body—Its false interpretation—Conquest of Hanover—The Duke of Cambridge caricatured—The King of England
and the Elector of Hanover—First address to the clergy—Use of the
word "Monsieur"—The Republican weeks and months.

ONE of the circumstances which foretold the brief duration
of the peace of Amiens was, that Mr. Pitt was out of office
at the time of its conclusion. I mentioned this to Bonaparte, and I immediately perceived by his hasty "What do
you say?" that my observation had been heard but not liked.
It did not, however, require any extraordinary shrewdness
to see the true motive of Mr. Pitt's retirement. That distinguished statesman conceived that a truce under the
name of a peace was indispensable for England ; but, intending to resume the war with France more fiercely than
ever, he for a while retired from office, and left to others
the task of arranging the peace ; but his intention was to
mark his return to the ministry by the renewal of the
implacable hatred he had vowed against France.   Still, I
have always thought that the conclusion of peace, however
necessary to England, was an error of the Cabinet of London.   England alone had never before acknowledged any
of the governments which had risen up in France since the
Revolution ; and as the past could not be blotted out, a

future war, however successful to England, could not take
from Bonaparte's Government the immense weight it had
acquired by an interval of peace.   Besides, by the mere fact
of the conclusion of the treaty England proved to all Europe
that the restoration of the Bourbons was merely a pretext,
and she defaced that page of her history which might have
shown that she was actuated by nobler and more generous
sentiments than mere hatred of France.   It is very certain that the condescension of England in treating with
the First Consul had the effect of rallying round him a
great many partisans of the Bourbons, whose hopes entirely depended on the continuance of war between Great
Britain and France.   This opened the eyes of the greater
number, namely, those who could not see below the sur-
face, and were not previously aware that the demonstrations of friendship so liberally made to the Bourbons by
the European Cabinets, and especially by England, were
merely false pretences, assumed for the purpose of dis-
guising, beneath the semblance of honourable motives,
their wish to injure France, and to oppose her rapidly-
increasing power.

When the misunderstanding took place, France and
England might have mutually reproached each other, but
justice was apparently on the side of France.   It was evident that England, by refusing to evacuate Malta, was
guilty of a palpable infraction of the treaty of Amiens,
while England could only institute against France what in
the French law language is called a suit or process of tendency.   But it must be confessed that this tendency on the
part of France to augment her territory was very evident,
for the Consular decrees made conquests more promptly
than the sword.   The union of Piedmont with France had
changed the state of Europe.   This union, it is true, was
effected previously to the treaty of Amiens ; [1] but it was not

---

[1] This is incorrect.   The *Sénatus-consulte* incorporating Piedmont with France
was dated 11th September 1802, six months after the peace of Amiens.

so with the states of Parma and Piacenza, Bonaparte having by his sole authority constituted himself the heir of the Grand Duke, recently deceased. It may therefore be easily imagined how great was England's uneasiness at the internal prosperity of France and the insatiable ambition of her ruler; but it is no less certain that, with respect to Malta, England acted with decidedly bad faith ; and this bad faith appeared in its worst light from the following circumstance :—It had been stipulated that England should withdraw her troops from Malta three months after the signing of the treaty, yet more than a year had elapsed, and the troops were still there. The order of Malta was to be restored as it formerly was ; that is to say, it was to be a sovereign and independent order, under the protection of the Holy See. The three Cabinets of Vienna, Berlin, and St. Petersburg were to guarantee the execution of the treaty of Amiens. The English Ambassador, to excuse the evasions of his Government, pretended that the Russian Cabinet concurred with England in the delayed fulfilment of the conditions of the treaty ; but at the very moment he was making that excuse a courier arrived from the Cabinet of St. Petersburg bearing despatches completely at variance with the assertion of Lord Whitworth. His lordship left Paris on the night of the 12th May 1803, and the English Government, unsolicited, sent passports to the French embassy in London. The news of this sudden rupture made the English consols fall four per cent., but did not immediately produce such a retrograde effect on the French funds, which were then quoted at fifty-five francs,—a very high point, when it is recollected that they were at seven or eight francs on the eve of the 18th Brumaire.

In this state of things France proposed to the English Government to admit of the mediation of Russia ; but as England had declared war in order to repair the error she committed in concluding peace, the proposition was of course rejected. Thus the public gave the First Consul credit for great moderation and a sincere wish for peace. Thus arose between England and France a contest resembling those furious wars which marked the reigns of King John and Charles VII. Our *beaux esprits* drew splendid comparisons between the existing state of things and the ancient rivalry of Carthage and Rome, and sapiently concluded that, as Carthage fell, England must do so likewise.

Bonaparte was at St. Cloud when Lord Whitworth left Paris. A fortnight was spent in useless attempts to renew negotiations. War, therefore, was the only alternative. Before he made his final preparations the First Consul addressed a message to the Senate, the Legislative Body, and the Tribunate. In this message he mentioned the recall of the English Ambassador, the breaking out of hostilities, the unexpected message of the King of England to his Parliament, and the armaments which immediately ensued in the British ports. "In vain," he said, "had France tried every means to induce England to abide by the treaty. She had repelled every overture, and increased the insolence of her demands. France," he added, "will not submit to menaces, but will combat for the faith of treaties, and the honour of the French name, confidently trusting that the result of the contest will be such as she has a right to expect from the justice of her cause and the courage of her people."

This message was dignified, and free from that vein of boasting in which Bonaparte so frequently indulged. The reply of the Senate was accompanied by a vote of a ship of the line, to be paid for out of the Senatorial salaries. With his usual address Bonaparte, in acting for himself, spoke in the name of the people, just as he did in the question of the Consulate for life. But what he then did for his own interests turned to the future interests of the Bourbons. The very treaty which had just been broken off gave rise to a curious observation. Bonaparte, though not yet a sovereign, peremptorily required the King of England to renounce the empty title of King of France, which was kept up as if to imply that old pretensions were not yet renounced. The proposition was acceded to, and to this circumstance was owing the disappearance of the title of King of France from among the titles of the King of England, when the treaty of Paris was concluded on the return of the Bourbons.

The first grievance complained of by England was the prohibition of English merchandise, which had been more rigid since the peace than during the war. The avowal of Great Britain on this point might well have enabled her to dispense with any other subject of complaint ; for the truth is, she was alarmed at the aspect of our internal prosperity, and at the impulse given to our manufactures. The English Government had hoped to obtain from the First Consul such a commercial treaty as would have proved a death-blow to our rising trade ; but Bonaparte opposed this, and from the very circumstance of his refusal he might easily have foreseen the rupture at which he affected to be surprised. What I state I felt at the time, when I read with great interest all the documents relative to this great dispute between the two rival nations, which eleven years afterwards was decided before the walls of Paris.

It was evidently disappointment in regard to a commercial treaty which created the animosity of the English Government, as that circumstance was alluded to, by way of reproach, in the King of England's declaration. In that document it was complained that France had sent a number of persons into the ports of Great Britain and Ireland in the character of commercial agents, which character, and the privileges belonging to it, they could only have acquired by a commercial treaty. Such was, in my opinion, the real cause of the complaints of England ; but as it would have seemed too absurd to make it the ground of a declaration of war, she enumerated other grievances, viz., the union of Piedmont and of the states of Parma and Piacenza with France, and the continuance of the French troops in Holland. A great deal was said about the views and projects of France with respect to Turkey, and this complaint originated in General Sebastiani's mission to Egypt.   On that point I can take upon me to say that the English Government was not misinformed.   Bonaparte too frequently spoke to me of his ideas respecting the East, and his project of attacking the English power in India, to leave any doubt of his ever having renounced them. The result of all the reproaches which the two Governments addressed to each other was, that neither acted with good faith.

The First Consul, in a communication to the Legislative Body on the state of France and on her foreign relations, had said, "England, single-handed, cannot cope with France." This sufficed to irritate the susceptibility of English pride, and the British Cabinet affected to regard it as a threat. However, it was no such thing. When Bonaparte threatened, his words were infinitely more energetic. The passage above cited was merely an assurance to France ; and if we only look at the vast efforts and sacrifices made by England to stir up enemies to France on the Continent, we may be justified in supposing that her anger at Bonaparte's declaration arose from a conviction of its truth. Singly opposed to France, England could doubtless have done her much harm, especially by assailing the scattered remnants of her navy ; but she could have done nothing against France on the Continent. The two powers, unaided by allies, might have continued long at war without any considerable acts of hostility.

The first effect of the declaration of war by England was the invasion of Hanover by the French troops under General Mortier. The telegraphic despatch by which this news was communicated to Paris was as laconic as correct, and contained, in a few words, the complete history of the expedition. It ran as follows : "The French are masters of the Electorate of Hanover, and the enemy's army are made prisoners of war." A day or two after the shop windows of the print-sellers were filled with caricatures on the English, and particularly on the Duke of Cambridge. I recollect seeing one in which the Duke was represented reviewing his troops mounted on a crab. I mention these trifles because, as I was then living entirely at leisure, in the Rue Hauteville, I used frequently to take a stroll on the Boulevards, where I was sometimes much amused with these prints ; and I could not help remarking, that in large cities such trifles have more influence on the public mind than is usually supposed.

The First Consul thought the taking of the prisoners in Hanover a good opportunity to exchange them for those taken from us by the English navy. A proposition to this effect was accordingly made ; but the English Cabinet was of opinion that, though the King of England was also Elector of Hanover, yet there was no identity between the two Governments, of both which George III. was the head. In consequence of this subtle distinction the proposition for the exchange of prisoners fell to the ground. At this period nothing could exceed the animosity of the two Governments towards each other ; and Bonaparte, on the declaration of war, marked his indignation by an act which no consideration can justify ; I allude to the order for the arrest of all the English in France—a truly barbarious measure ; for, can anything be more cruel and unjust than to visit individuals with the vengeance due to the Government whose subjects they may happen to be ? But Bonaparte, when under the influence of anger, was never troubled by scruples.

I must here notice the fulfilment of a remark Bonaparte often made use of to me during the Consulate. "You shall see, Bourrienne," he would say, "what use I will make of the priests."

War being declared, the First Consul, in imitation of the most Christian kings of olden times, recommended the success of his arms to the prayers of the faithful through the medium of the clergy. To this end he addressed a circular letter, written in royal style, to the Cardinals, Archbishops, and Bishops of France.

It was as follows :—

MONSIEUR—The motives of the present war are known throughout Europe. The bad faith of the King of England, who has violated his treaties by refusing to restore Malta to the order of St. John of Jerusalem, and attacked our merchant vessels without a previous declaration of war, together with the necessity of a just defence, forced us to have recourse to arms. I therefore wish you to order prayers to be offered up, in order to obtain the benediction of Heaven on our enterprises. The proofs I have received of your zeal for the public service give me an assurance of your readiness to conform with my wishes.

Given at St. Cloud, 18 Prairial, an XI. (7th June 1803).

(Signed)   BONAPARTE.

This letter was remarkable in more than one respect. It astonished most of his old brothers-in-arms, who turned it into ridicule ; observing that Bonaparte needed no praying to enable him to conquer Italy twice over. The First Consul, however, let them laugh on, and steadily followed the line he had traced out. His letter was admirably calculated to please the Court of Rome, which he wished should consider him in the light of another elder son of the Church. The letter was, moreover, remarkable for the use of the word "Monsieur," which the First Consul now employed for the first time in an act destined for publicity. This circumstance would seem to indicate that he considered Republican designations incompatible with the forms due to the clergy : the clergy were especially interested in the restoration of monarchy. It may, perhaps, be thought that I dwell too much on trifles ; but I lived long enough in Bonaparte's confidence to know the importance he attached to trifles. The First Consul restored the old names of the days of the week, while he allowed the names of the months, as set down in the Republican calendar, to remain. He commenced by ordering the *Moniteur* to be dated " Saturday," such a day of " Messidor." " See," said he one day, " was there ever such an inconsistency ? We shall be laughed at ! But I will do away with the Messidor. I will efface all the inventions of the Jacobins." [1]

The clergy did not disappoint the expectations of the First Consul. They owed him much already, and hoped for still more from him. The letter to the Bishops, etc., was the signal for a number of circulars full of eulogies on Bonaparte.

These compliments were far from displeasing to the First Consul, who had no objection to flattery though he despised those who meanly made themselves the medium of conveying it to him. Duroc once told me that they had all great difficulty in preserving their gravity when the curé of a parish in Abbeville addressed Bonaparte one day while he was on his journey to the coast. " Religion," said the worthy curé, with pompous solemnity, "owes to you all that it is, we owe to you all that we are ; and I, too, owe to you all that I am." [2]

---

[1] See the Republican Calendar at the end of the second volume.

[2] Not so fulsome as some of the terms used a year later when Napoleon was made Emperor. " I am what I am," was placed over a seat prepared for the Emperor. One phrase, " God made Napoleon and then rested," drew from Narbonne the sneer that it would have been better if the Deity had rested sooner. " Bonaparte," says Joseph de Maistre, " has had himself described in his papers as the ' Messenger of God.' Nothing more true. Bonaparte comes straight from heaven, *like a thunderbolt* " (Sainte-Beuve, *Causeries*, tome iv. p. 203).

CHAPTER XX.

1803.

Presentation of Prince Borghèse to Bonaparte—Departure for Belgium—Revival of a royal custom—The swans of Amiens—Change of formula in the acts of Government—Company of performers in Bonaparte's suite—Revival of old customs—Division of the Institute into four classes—Science and literature—Bonaparte's hatred of literary men—Ducis—Bernardin de Saint-Pierre—Chénier and Lemercier—Explanation of Bonaparte's aversion to literature—Lalande and his dictionary—Education in the hands of Government—M. de Roquelaure, Archbishop of Malines.

In the month of April 1803 Prince Borghèse, who was destined one day to become Bonaparte's brother-in-law by marrying the widow of Leclerc, was introduced to the First Consul by Cardinal Caprara.

About the end of June Bonaparte proceeded, with Josephine, on his journey to Belgium and the seaboard departments. Many curious circumstances were connected with this journey, of which I was informed by Duroc after the First Consul's return. Bonaparte left Paris on the 24th of June, and although it was not for upwards of a year afterwards that his brow was encircled with the imperial diadem, everything connected with the journey had an imperial air. It was formerly the custom, when the Kings of France entered the ancient capital of Picardy, for the town of Amiens to offer them in homage some beautiful swans. Care was taken to revive this custom, which pleased Bonaparte greatly, because it was treating him like a King. The swans were accepted, and sent to Paris to be placed in the basin of the Tuileries, in order to show the Parisians the royal homage which the First Consul received when absent from the capital.

It was also during this journey that Bonaparte began to
date his decrees from the places through which he passed.
He had hitherto left a great number of signatures in Paris,
in order that he might be present, as it were, even during
his absence, by the acts of his Government. Hitherto
public acts had been signed in the name of the Consuls of
the Republic. Instead of this formula, he substituted the
name of the Government of the Republic. By means of
this variation, unimportant as it might appear, the Government was always in the place where the First Consul
happened to be. The two other Consuls were now mere
nullities, even in appearance. The decrees of the Government, which Cambacérès signed during the campaign of
Marengo, were now issued from all the towns of France
and Belgium which the First Consul visited during his
six weeks' journey. Having thus centred the sole authority of the Republic in himself, the performers of the
theatre of the Republic became, by a natural consequence,
his ; and it was quite natural that they should travel in his
suite, to entertain the inhabitants of the towns in which
he stopped by their performances. But this was not all.
He encouraged the renewal of a host of ancient customs. He sanctioned the revival of the festival of Joan of
Arc at Orleans, and he divided the Institute into four
classes, with the intention of recalling the recollection of
the old academies, the names of which, however, he rejected, in spite of the wishes and intrigues of Suard and
the Abbé Morellet, who had gained over Lucien upon this
point.

However, the First Consul did not give to the classes of
the Institute the rank which they formerly possessed as
academies. He placed the class of sciences in the first
rank, and the old French Academy in the second rank.
It must be acknowledged that, considering the state of
literature and science at that period, the First Consul did
not make a wrong estimate of their importance.

Although the literature of France could boast of many men of great talent, such as La Harpe, who died during the Consulate, Ducis, Bernardin de Saint-Pierre, Chénier, and Lemercier, yet they could not be compared with Lagrange, Laplace, Monge, Fourcroy, Berthollet, and Cuvier, whose labours have so prodigiously extended the limits of human knowledge. No one, therefore, could murmur at seeing the class of sciences in the Institute take precedence of its elder sister. Besides, the First Consul was not sorry to show, by this arrangement, the slight estimation in which he held literary men. When he spoke to me respecting them he called them mere manufacturers of phrases. He could not pardon them for excelling him in a pursuit in which he had no claim to distinction. I never knew a man more insensible than Bonaparte to the beauties of poetry or prose.[1] A certain degree of vagueness, which was combined with his energy of mind, led him to admire the dreams of Ossian, and his decided character found itself, as it were, represented in the elevated thoughts of Corneille. Hence his almost exclusive predilection for these two authors. With this exception, the finest works in our literature were in his opinion merely arrangements of sonorous words, void of sense, and calculated only for the ear.

Bonaparte's contempt, or, more properly speaking, his dislike of literature, displayed itself particularly in the feeling he cherished towards some men of distinguished

[1] It is not true that Bonaparte was insensible to the beauties of poetry and prose. In his youth he was an enthusiastic admirer of J. J. Rousseau, whose finest works were familiar to him. In 1789, while still a youth, he wrote a compendium of the revolutions of Corsica, which was much esteemed by the Abbé Raynal. The abbé sent the work to Mirabeau, who, in reply, requested him to advise the young author to undertake a journey to Paris. Napoleon knew by heart, and often repeated, the finest passages in the tragedies of Corneille, Racine, and Voltaire. It cannot with strict justice be said that Napoleon hated Chénier. He was at first extremely partial to him. He had, however, subsequently reason to complain of him, though in the end he granted him a pension. Napoleon's connection with Arnault, Talma, David, Paesiello, Monti, and many other celebrated men of letters, musicians, and artists, is well known (*Joseph Bonaparte's Notes on Bourrienne in Erreurs*, vol. ii. p. 133).

literary talent. He hated Chénier, and Ducis still more.
He could not forgive Chénier for the Republican principles which pervaded his tragedies ; and Ducis excited in
him, as if instinctively, an involuntary hatred. Ducis, on
his part, was not backward in returning the Consul's animosity, and I remember his writing some verses which
were inexcusably violent, and overstepped all the bounds
of truth. Bonaparte was so singular a composition of
good and bad that to describe him as he was under one
or other of these aspects would serve for panegyric or
satire without any departure from truth. Bonaparte was
very fond of Bernardin Saint-Pierre's romance of *Paul and
Virginia,* which he had read in his boyhood. I remember
that he one day tried to read *Les Études de la Nature,* but
at the expiration of a quarter of an hour he threw down
the book, exclaiming, "How can any one read such silly
stuff? It is insipid and vapid ; there is nothing in it.
These are the dreams of a visionary ! What is nature ?
The thing is vague and unmeaning. Men and passions
are the subjects to write about—there is something there
for study. These fellows are good for nothing under any
government. I will, however, give them pensions, because I ought to do so, as Head of the State. They occupy
and amuse the idle. I will make Lagrange a Senator—
he has a head." [1]

[1] Sainte-Beuve says, " The persons who best knew Napoleon have remarked that
in the rapid literary education he had to improvise for himself when he had taken
possession of power, he began by much preferring Corneille : it was only later that
he got so far as to enjoy Racine, but he did reach that point. He began as every
one begins ; he ended as cultivated and well-informed intellects like to end "
(*Causeries,* tome i. p. 287). In another place Sainte-Beuve says, " Napoleon wrote
to his brother Joseph, then King of Naples, who was fond of literary men, ' You live
too much with literary and with scientific men. They are like coquettes, with whom
one should keep up an intercourse of gallantry, but of whom one should never
dream of making a wife or a minister.' This," says Sainte-Beuve, and other men
of letters need not be more touchy than he was, " this is true of many literary men,
and even of some of them whom in our time we have seen as ministers, but it is not
true of M. Guizot, nor of M. Thiers" (*Causeries,* tome i. p. 314). Again, " Napoléon, who, like his brothers, had been from the first a great admirer of the romance
of *Paul and Virginia,* said once to Bernardin de Saint-Pierre when he saw him,

Although Bonaparte spoke so disdainfully of literary men it must not be taken for granted that he treated them ill. On the contrary, all those who visited at Malmaison were the objects of his attention, and even flattery. M. Lemercier was one of those who came most frequently, and whom Bonaparte received with the greatest pleasure. Bonaparte treated M. Lemercier with great kindness ; but he did not like him. His character as a literary man and poet, joined to a polished frankness, and a mild but inflexible spirit of republicanism, amply sufficed to explain Bonaparte's dislike. He feared M. Lemercier and his pen ; and, as happened more than once, he played the part of a parasite by flattering the writer. M. Lemercier was the only man I knew who refused the cross of the Legion of Honour.

Bonaparte's general dislike of literary men was less the result of prejudice than circumstances. In order to appreciate or even to read literary works time is requsite, and time was so precious to him that he would have wished, as one may say, to shorten a straight line. He liked only those writers who directed their attention to positive and precise things, which excluded all thoughts of government and censures on administration. He looked with a jealous eye on political economists and lawyers ; in short, on all persons who in any way whatever meddled with legis-

---

'Monsieur Bernardin, when will you give us another *Paul and Virginia* or a *Chaumière Indienne ?* You should give us one every six months ' " (*Causeries,* tome vi. p. 446). Many essays in the *Causeries,* that, for instance, on Ducis (tome vi.), should be consulted to see that Bourrienne exaggerates a good deal here. " It was the period when Bonaparte (who had liked Ducis, and who had made many advances towards him during his stay in Paris after the first campaigns of Italy, going so far as to wish to take him with the expedition to Egypt) founded a new government, and sought to attach to it every one of distinction or of glory. How he failed with Ducis, who refused everything—Senate, Legion of Honour—has been often told " (*Causeries,* tome vi. p. 467). See also *Tableau de la Littérature Française,* 1800–1815, by Merlet, Paris, Hachette, 1884, tome i. p. 224, and *Meneval,* tome iii. p. 48, to the same effect. The literary men were difficult to deal with. One, pensioned by Napoleon, loudly complained of being *disgraced.* The Restoration cut off half his pension, and his fellow-writers congratulated him on losing half his disgrace (*Meneval,* tome iii. p. 158).

lation and moral improvements. His hatred of discussions on those subjects was strongly displayed on the occasion of the classification of the Institute. Whilst he permitted the reassembling of a literary class, to the number of forty, as formerly, he suppressed the class of moral and political science. Such was his predilection for things of immediate and certain utility that even in the sciences he favoured only such as applied to terrestrial objects. He never treated Lalande with so much distinction as Monge and Lagrange. Astronomical discoveries could not add directly to his own greatness ; and, besides, he could never forgive Lalande for having wished to include him in a dictionary of atheists precisely at the moment when he was opening negotiations with the court of Rome.

Bonaparte wished to be the sole centre of a world which he believed he was called to govern. With this view he never relaxed in his constant endeavour to concentrate the whole powers of the State in the hands of its Chief. His conduct upon the subject of the revival of public instruction affords evidence of this fact. He wished to establish 6000 bursaries, to be paid by Government, and to be exclusively at his disposal, so that thus possessing the monopoly of education, he could have parcelled it out only to the children of those who were blindly devoted to him. This was what the First Consul called the revival of public instruction. During the period of my closest intimacy with him he often spoke to me on this subject, and listened patiently to my observations. I remember that one of his chief arguments was this : "What is it that distinguishes men ? Education—is it not ? Well, if the children of nobles be admitted into the academies, they will be as well educated as the children of the revolution, who compose the strength of my government. Ultimately they will enter into my regiments as officers, and will naturally come in competition with those whom they regard as the plunderers of their families. I do not wish that !"

My recollections have caused me to wander from the journey of the First Consul and Madame Bonaparte to the seabord departments and Belgium. I have, however, little to add to what I have already stated on the subject. I merely remember that Bonaparte's military suite, and Lauriston and Rapp in particular, when speaking to me about the journey, could not conceal some marks of discontent on account of the great respect which Bonaparte had shown the clergy, and particularly to M. de Roquelaure, the Archbishop of Malines (or Mechlin). That prelate, who was a shrewd man, and had the reputation of having been in his youth more addicted to the habits of the world than to those of the cloister, had become an ecclesiastical courtier. He went to Antwerp to pay his homage to the First Consul, upon whom he heaped the most extravagant praises. Afterwards, addressing Madame Bonaparte, he told her that she was united to the First Consul by the *sacred bonds of a holy alliance.* In this harangue, in which unction was singularly blended with gallantry, surely it was a departure from ecclesiastical propriety to speak of *sacred bonds* and *a holy alliance* when every one knew that those bonds and that alliance existed only by a civil contract. Perhaps M. de Roquelaure merely had recourse to what casuists call a pious fraud in order to engage the married couple to do that which he congratulated them on having already done. Be this as it may, it is certain that this honeyed language gained M. de Roquelaure the Consul's favour, and in a short time after he was appointed to the second class of the Institute.[1]

[1] M. de Roquelaure (1721-1818) had been Bishop of Senlis and Aumônier du Roi. In 1802 he became Archbishop of Mechlin. In 1808 he resigned and was replaced by the better-known Abbé Pradt. He died in 1818. In his old age, retaining his strength, his memory stopped at the time when he was still Bishop of Senlis and almoner to the King. The Revolution he entirely forgot (*Meneval,* tome iii. p. 80).

CHAPTER XXI.

1804.

THE time was passed when Bonaparte, just raised to the
Consulate, only proceeded to the Temple to release the
victims of the "Loi des suspects" by his sole and immediate authority. This state prison was now to be filled by
the orders of his police. All the intrigues of Europe were
in motion. Emissaries came daily from England, who, if
they could not penetrate into the interior of France, remained in the towns near the frontiers, where they established correspondence, and published pamphlets, which
they sent to Paris by post, in the form of letters.

The First Consul, on the other hand, gave way, without
reserve, to the natural irritation which that power had
excited by her declaration of war. He knew that the most
effective war he could carry on against England would be
a war against her trade.

As a prelude to that piece of madness, known by
the name of the Continental system, the First Consul

adopted every possible preventive measure against the introduction of English merchandise.   Bonaparte's irritation against the English was not without a cause.   The intelligence which reached Paris from the north of France was not very consolatory.   The English fleets not only blockaded the French ports, but were acting on the offensive, and had bombarded Granville.   The mayor of the town did his duty, but his colleagues, more prudent, acted differently.   In the height of his displeasure Bonaparte issued a decree, by which he bestowed a scarf of honour on Letourneur, the mayor, and dismissed his colleagues from office as cowards unworthy of trust.   The terms of this decree were rather severe, but they were certainly justified by the conduct of those who had abandoned their posts at a critical moment.

I come now to the subject of the invasion of England, and what the First Consul said to me respecting it.   I have stated that Bonaparte never had any idea of realising the pretended project of a descent on England.   The truth of this assertion will appear from a conversation which I had with him after he returned from his journey to the north.   In this conversation he repeated what he had often before mentioned to me in reference to the projects and possible steps to which fortune might compel him to resort.

The peace of Amiens had been broken about seven months when, on the 15th of December 1803, the First Consul sent for me to the Tuileries.   His incomprehensible behaviour to me was fresh in my mind ; and as it was upwards of a year since I had seen him, I confess I did not feel quite at ease when I received the summons. He was perfectly aware that I possessed documents and data for writing his history which would describe facts correctly, and destroy the illusions with which his flatterers constantly entertained the public.   I have already stated that at that period I had no intention of the kind ;

but those who laboured constantly to incense him againt me might have suggested apprehensions on the subject. At all events the fact is, that when he sent for me I took the precaution of providing myself with a night-cap, conceiving it to be very likely that I should be sent to sleep at Vincennes. On the day appointed for the interview Rapp was on duty. I did not conceal from him my opinion as to the possible result of my visit. "You need not be afraid," said Rapp; "the First Consul merely wishes to talk with you." He then announced me.

Bonaparte came into the grand *salon* where I awaited him, and addressing me in the most good-humoured way said, "What do the gossips say of my preparations for the invasion of England?"—"There is a great difference of opinion on the subject, General," I replied. "Every one speaks according to his own views. Suchet, for instance, who comes to see me very often, has no doubt that it will take place, and hopes to give you on the occasion fresh proofs of his gratitude and fidelity."—"But Suchet tells me that you do not believe it will be attempted."—"That is true, I certainly do not."—"Why?"—"Because you told me at Antwerp, five years ago, that you would not risk France on the cast of a die—that the adventure was too hazardous—and circumstances have not altered since that time."—"You are right. Those who look forward to the invasion of England are blockheads. They do not see the affair in its true light. I can, doubtless, land in England with 100,000 men. A great battle will be fought, which I shall gain; but I must reckon upon 30,000 men killed, wounded, and prisoners. If I march on London, a second battle must be fought. I will suppose myself again victorious; but what should I do in London with an army diminished three-fourths and without the hope of reinforcements? It would be madness. Until our navy acquires superiority it is useless to think of such a project. The great assemblage of troops in the north has another object. My Government must be the first in the world, or it must fall." [1] Bonaparte then evidently wished it to be supposed that he entertained the design of invading England in order to divert the attention of Europe to that direction. [2]

From Dunkirk the First Consul proceeded to Antwerp, where also he had assembled experienced men to ascertain their opinions respecting the surest way of attempting a landing, the project of which was merely a pretence. The employment of large ships of war was, after long dis-

[1] Napoleon's conversation with M. Las Casas at St. Helena respecting the invasion of England is very different from the above. He speaks of a pitched battle, which would have decided the fate of England. "I should not have entered England," he said, "as a conqueror, but as a liberator." Bonaparte knew better than any one the difficulty of subduing a strong, powerful, and united nation. Some years after these feigned preparations against England he had evidence of this truth written in letters of blood in Spain. A combination of natural causes is always ruinous to the invading army. Napoleon must have been merely jesting at St. Helena when he said that four days would have enabled him to reach London, and that nature had made England one of our islands, like Oléron or Corsica. I find these words in my notes: "Remained with the First Consul from half-past eleven to one o'clock." During this hour and a half he said not a word bearing any resemblance to his assertions at St. Helena.—*Bourrienne.*

[2] It will probably always be impossible to say with certainty whether Napoleon really intended to attempt the invasion of England. It certainly cannot be described as an empty threat. The preparations were extraordinarily complete. The probability is, that if any chance had enabled him to cross the Channel he might have dared the stroke. But it is obvious that little reliance can be put on his statements at the time, which seem to have varied. If the expedition were intended, it was natural to try to throw doubt on the reality of the plan. If the troops were meant to be ready for a Continental war the more would the threat to England be dwelt on. In any case the effect of the preparations was very great on England; and contemporary accounts and caricatures are full of amusing descriptions of the frequent panics caused in the southern districts by rumours that the French had landed. The date given to this interview is in opposition to Meneval's statement that Napoleon did not see Bourrienne from his disgrace in 1802 till 1805 (*Meneval,* tome ii. p. 379). The Parisians of course had their jest, and the flat-bottomed boats of the flotilla were compared to walnut shells, and called *péniches.* In one piece Brunet, a comic actor, was seen on the stage eating walnuts, and throwing the shells into a tub of water. "What are you doing?" asked his companion. "Making *péniches,*" was the answer. For this the police punished him; but on the next night of the piece Brunet was found as before with his walnuts. This time he did not answer the question as to what he was doing till he was told, "Perhaps you don't know what you are about?" "Oh yes," said Brunet, "I know very well what I am about, but I know better than to tell" (*Junot,* vol. ii. p. 167). Marmont (tome ii. p. 211) asserts that Napoleon certainly intended to cross, and he tells us that Fulton repeatedly attempted to get Napoleon to experiment with steam. "The First Consul treated Fulton as a charlatan, and would not listen to him."

cussions, abandoned in favour of a flotilla.[1] After visiting Belgium, and giving directions there, the First Consul returned from Brussels to Paris by way of Maestricht,
Liége, and Soissons.

Before my visit to the Tuileries, and even before the
rupture of the peace of Amiens, certain intriguing speculators, whose extravagant zeal was not less fatal to the
cause of the Bourbons than was the blind subserviency of
his unprincipled adherents to the First Consul, had taken
part in some underhand manœuvres which could have no
favourable result. Amongst these great contrivers of petty
machinations the well-known Fauche Borel, the book-sel-
ler of Neufchâtel, had long been conspicuous. Fauche
Borel, whose object was to create a stir, and who wished
nothing better than to be noticed and paid, failed not to
come to France as soon as the peace of Amiens afforded
him the opportunity. I was at that time still with Bonaparte, who was aware of all these little plots, but who felt
no personal anxiety on the subject, leaving to his police
the care of watching their authors.

The object of Fauche Borel's mission was to bring
about a reconciliation between Moreau and Pichegru.
The latter general, who was banished on the 18th Fruc-
tidor 4th (September 1797), had not obtained the First
Consul's permission to return to France. He lived in
England, where he awaited a favourable opportunity for
putting his old projects into execution. Moreau was in
Paris, but no longer appeared at the levees or parties of
the First Consul, and the enmity of both generals against
Bonaparte, openly avowed on the part of Pichegru, and

---

[1] At this period a caricature [by Gillray ?] appeared in London, which was sent to
Paris, and strictly sought after by the police. One of the copies was shown to the
First Consul, who was highly indignant at it. The French fleet was represented by
a number of nut-shells. An English sailor, seated on a rock, was quietly smoking
his pipe, the whiffs of which were throwing the whole squadron into disorder.—
Bourrienne. Gillray's caricatures should be at the reader's side during the perusal
of this work, also *English Caricature and Satire on Napoleon I.*, by J. Ashton :
Chatto and Windus, 1884.

still disguised by Moreau, was a secret to nobody. But as everything was prosperous with Bonaparte he evinced contempt rather than fear of the two generals. His apprehensions were, indeed, tolerably allayed by the absence of the one and the character of the other. Moreau's name had greater weight with the army than that of Pichegru; and those who were plotting the overthrow of the Consular Government knew that that measure could not be attempted with any chance of success without the assistance of Moreau. The moment was inopportune; but, being initiated in some secrets of the British Cabinet, they knew that the peace was but a truce, and they determined to profit by that truce to effect a reconciliation which might afterwards secure a community of interests. Moreau and Pichegru had not been friends since Moreau sent to the Directory the papers seized in M. de Klinglin's carriage, which placed Pichegru's treason in so clear a light. Since that period Pichegru's name possessed no influence over the minds of the soldiers, amongst whom he had very few partisans, whilst the name of Moreau was dear to all who had conquered under his command.[1]

Fauche Borel's design was to compromise Moreau without bringing him to any decisive step. Moreau's natural indolence, and perhaps it may be said his good sense, induced him to adopt the maxim that it was necessary to let men and things take their course; for temporising policy is often as useful in politics as in war. Besides, Moreau was a sincere Republican; and if his habit of indecision had permitted him to adopt any resolution, it is quite certain that he would not then have assisted in the reestablishment of the Bourbons, as Pichegru wished.

What I have stated is an indispensable introduction to the knowledge of plots of more importance which preceded

---

[1] Pichegru had been actually transported to Sinnamarri [Guiana], along with the other unfortunate victims of the 18th Fructidor, but he had been fortunate enough to escape.

the great event that marked the close of the Consulship :
I allude to the conspiracy of Georges Cadoudal, Moreau,
and Pichegru, and that indelible stain on the character of
Napoleon,—the death of the Duc d'Enghien. Different
opinions have been expressed concerning Georges' conspiracy. I shall not contradict any of them. I will relate
what I learned and what I saw, in order to throw some
light on that horrible affair. I am far from believing what
I have read in many works, that it was planned by the
police in order to pave the First Consul's way to the
throne. I think that it was contrived by those who were
really interested in it, and encouraged by Fouché in order
to prepare his return to office.

To corroborate my opinion respecting Fouché's conduct
and his manœuvres I must remind the reader that about
the close of 1803 some persons conceived the project of
reconciling Moreau and Pichegru. Fouché, who was then
out of the Ministry, caused Moreau to be visited by men of
his own party, and who were induced, perhaps unconsciously, by Fouché's art, to influence and irritate the
general's mind. It was at first intended that the Abbé
David, the mutual friend of Moreau and Pichegru, should
undertake to effect their reconciliation ; but he, being
arrested and confined in the Temple, was succeeded by a
man named Lajolais, whom every circumstance proves to
have been employed by Fouché. He proceeded to London, and, having prevailed on Pichegru and his friends to
return to France, he set off to announce their arrival and
arrange everything for their reception and destruction.
Moreau's discontent was the sole foundation of this intrigue. I remember that one day, about the end of January 1804, I called on Fouché, who informed me that he
had been at St. Cloud, where he had had a long conversation
with the First Consul on the situation of affairs. Bonaparte told him that he was satisfied with the existing
police, and hinted that it was only to make himself of

consequence that he had given a false colouring to the picture. Fouché asked him what he would say if he told him that Georges and Pichegru had been for some time in Paris carrying on the conspiracy of which he had received information. The First Consul, apparently delighted at what he conceived to be Fouché's mistake, said, with an air of contempt, "You are well informed, truly! Regnier has just received a letter from London stating that Pichegru dined three days ago at Kingston with one of the King of England's ministers."

As Fouché, however, persisted in his assertion, the First Consul sent to Paris for the Grand Judge, Regnier, who showed Fouché the letter he had received. The First Consul triumphed at first to see Fouché at fault ; but the latter so clearly proved that Georges and Pichegru were actually in Paris that Regnier began to fear he had been misled by his agents, whom his rival paid better than he did. The First Consul, convinced that his old minister knew more than his new one, dismissed Regnier, and remained a long time in consultation with Fouché, who on that occasion said nothing about his reinstatement for fear of exciting suspicion. He only requested that the management of the business might be entrusted to Réal, with orders to obey whatever instructions he might receive from him. I will return hereafter to the arrest of Moreau and the other persons accused, and will now subjoin the account of a long interview which I had with Bonaparte in the midst of these important events.

On the 8th of March 1804, some time after the arrest but before the trial of General Moreau, I had an audience of the First Consul, which was unsought on my part. Bonaparte, after putting several unimportant questions to me as to what I was doing, what I expected he should do for me, and assuring me that he would bear me in mind, gave a sudden turn to the conversation, and said, "By the by, the report of my connection with Hortense is still

kept up : the most abominable rumours have been spread
as to her first child. I thought at the time that these reports had only been admitted by the public in consequence
of the great desire that I should not be childless. Since
you and I separated have you heard them repeated ? "—
"Yes, General, oftentimes ; and I confess I could not
have believed that this calumny would have existed so
long."—"It is truly frightful to think of! You know
the truth—you have seen all—heard all—nothing could
have passed without your knowledge ; you were in her
full confidence during the time of her attachment to
Duroc. I therefore expect, if you should ever write anything about me, that you will clear me from this infamous
imputation. I would not have it accompany my name
to posterity. I trust in you. You have never given credit
to the horrid accusation?"—"No, General, never." Napoleon then entered into a number of details on the previous life of Hortense ; on the way in which she conducted
herself, and on the turn which her marriage had taken.
"It has not turned out," he said, "as I wished : the union
has not been a happy one. I am sorry for it, not only
because both are dear to me, but because the circumstance
countenances the infamous reports that are current
among the idle as to my intimacy with her." He concluded the conversation with these words : —"Bourrienne, I sometimes think of recalling you ; but as there
is no good pretext for so doing, the world would say
that I have need of you, and I wish it to be known
that I stand in need of nobody." He again said a few
words about Hortense. I answered that it would fully
coincide with my conviction of the truth to do what he
desired, and that I would do it ; but that suppressing the
false reports did not depend on me.

Hortense, in fact, while she was Mademoiselle Beauharnais, regarded Napoleon with respectful awe. She trembled
when she spoke to him, and never dared to ask him a

favour. When she had anything to solicit she applied to me ; and if I experienced any difficulty in obtaining for her what she sought, I mentioned her as the person for whom I pleaded. " The little simpleton ! " Napoleon would say, " why does she not ask me herself : is the girl afraid of me ? " Napoleon never cherished for her any feeling but paternal tenderness. He loved her after his marriage with her mother as he would have loved his own child. During three years I was a witness to all their most private actions, and I declare that I never saw or heard anything that could furnish the least ground for suspicion, or that afforded the slightest trace of the existence of a culpable intimacy. This calumny must be classed among those with which malice delights to blacken the characters of men more brilliant than their fellows, and which are so readily adopted by the light-minded and unreflecting. I freely declare that did I entertain the smallest doubt with regard to this odious charge, of the existence of which I was well aware before Napoleon spoke to me on the subject, I would candidly avow it. He is no more : and let his memory be accompanied only by that, be it good or bad, which really belongs to it. Let not this reproach be one of those charged against him by the impartial historian. I must say, in concluding this delicate subject, that the principles of Napoleon on points of this kind were rigid in the utmost degree, and that a connection of the nature of that charged against him was neither in accordance with his morals nor his tastes.

I cannot tell whether what followed was a portion of his premeditated conversation with me, or whether it was the result of the satisfaction he had derived from ascertaining my perfect conviction of the purity of his conduct with regard to Hortense, and being assured that I would express that conviction. Be this as it may, as I was going out at the door he called me back, saying, " Oh ! I have forgotten something." I returned. "Bourrienne," said he, "do you still keep up your acquaintance with the Fauchers?"—"Yes, General; I see them frequently."—"You are wrong."—"Why should I not? They are clever, well-educated men, and exceedingly pleasant company, especially Cæsar. I derive great pleasure from their society; and then they are almost the only persons whose friendship has continued faithful to me since I left you. You know people do not care for those who can render them no service."—"Maret will not see the Fauchers."—"That may be, General; but it is nothing to me; and you must recollect that as it was through him I was introduced to them at the Tuileries, I think he ought to inform me of his reasons for dropping their acquaintance."—"I tell you again he has closed his door against them. Do you the same; I advise you." As I did not seem disposed to follow this advice without some plausible reason, the First Consul added, "You must know, then, that I learn from Cæsar all that passes in your house. You do not speak very ill of me yourself, nor does any one venture to do so in your presence. You play your rubber and go to bed. But no sooner are you gone than your wife, who never liked me, and most of those who visit at your house, indulge in the most violent attacks upon me. I receive a bulletin from Cæsar Faucher every day when he visits at your house; this is the way in which he requites you for your kindness, and for the asylum you afforded his brother.[1] But enough; you see I know all—farewell;" and he left me.

The grave having closed over these two brothers,[2] I shall merely state that they wrote me a letter the evening preceding their execution, in which they begged me to

---

[1] Constantine Faucher had been condemned in contumacy for the forgery of a public document.—*Bourrienne.*

[2] The Fauchers were twin brothers, distinguished in the wars of the Revolution, and made brigadier-generals at the same time on the field of battle. After the *Cent Jours* they refused to recognise the Bourbons, and were shot by sentence of court-martial at Bordeaux (Bouillet, *Dictionnaire d'Histoire*).

forgive their conduct towards me. The following is an extract from this letter :—

In our dungeon we hear our sentence of death being cried in the streets. To-morrow we shall walk to the scaffold ; but we will meet death with such calmness and courage as shall make our executioners blush. We are sixty years old, therefore our lives will only be shortened by a brief space. During our lives we have shared in common, illness, grief, pleasure, danger, and good fortune. We both entered the world on the same day, and on the same day we shall both depart from it. As to you, sir. . . .

I suppress what relates to myself.

The hour of the grand levee arrived just as the singular interview which I have described terminated. I remained a short time to look at this phantasmagoria. Duroc was there. As soon as he saw me he came up, and taking me into the recess of a window told me that Moreau's guilt was evident, and that he was about to be put on his trial. I made some observations on the subject, and in particular asked whether there were sufficient proofs of his guilt to justify his condemnation ? " They should be cautious," said I ; " it is no joke to accuse the conqueror of Hohenlinden." Duroc's answer satisfied me that he at least had no doubt on the subject. " Besides," added he, " when such a general as Moreau has been between two gendarmes he is lost, and is good for nothing more. He will only inspire pity." In vain I tried to refute this assertion so entirely contrary to facts, and to convince Duroc that Moreau would never be damaged by calling him " *brigand*," as was the phrase then, without proofs. Duroc persisted in his opinion. As if a political crime ever sullied the honour of any one ! The result has proved that I judged rightly.

No person possessing the least degree of intelligence will be convinced that the conspiracy of Moreau, Georges, Pichegru, and the other persons accused would ever have occurred but for the secret connivance of Fouché's police.

Moreau never for a moment desired the restoration of the Bourbons. I was too well acquainted with M. Carbonnet, his most intimate friend, to be ignorant of his private sentiments. It was therefore quite impossible that he could entertain the same views as Georges, the Polignacs, Rivière, and others; and they had no intention of committing any overt acts. These latter persons had come to the Continent solely to investigate the actual state of affairs, in order to inform the Princes of the House of Bourbon with certainty how far they might depend on the foolish hopes constantly held out to them by paltry agents, who were always ready to advance their own interests at the expense of truth. These agents did indeed conspire, but it was against the Treasury of London, to which they looked for pay.

Without entering into all the details of that great trial I will relate some facts which may assist in eliciting the truth from a chaos of intrigue and falsehood.

Most of the conspirators had been lodged either in the Temple or La Force, and one of them, Bouvet de Lozier, who was confined in the Temple, attempted to hang himself. He made use of his cravat to effect his purpose, and had nearly succeeded, when a turnkey by chance entered and found him at the point of death. When he was recovered he acknowledged that though he had the courage to meet death, he was unable to endure the interrogatories of his trial, and that he had determined to kill himself, lest he might be induced to make a confession. He did in fact confess, and it was on the day after this occurred that Moreau was arrested, while on his way from his country-seat of Grosbois to Paris.

Fouché, through the medium of his agents, had given Pichegru, Georges, and some other partisans of royalty, to understand that they might depend on Moreau, who, it was said, was quite prepared. It is certain that Moreau informed Pichegru that he (Pichegru) had been deceived, and that he had never been spoken to on the subject. Russillon declared on the trial that on the 14th of March the Polignacs said to some one, "Everything is going wrong—they do not understand each other. Moreau does not keep his word. We have been deceived." M. de Rivière declared that he soon became convinced they had been deceived, and was about to return to England when he was arrested. It is certain that the principal conspirators obtained positive information which confirmed their suspicions. They learned Moreau's declaration from Pichegru. Many of the accused declared that they soon discovered they had been deceived; and the greater part of them were about to quit Paris, when they were all arrested, almost at one and the same moment. Georges was going into La Vendée when he was betrayed by the man who, with the connivance of the police, had escorted him ever since his departure from London, and who had protected him from any interruption on the part of the police so long as it was only necessary to know where he was, or what he was about. Georges had been in Paris seven months before it was considered that the proper moment had arrived for arresting him.

The almost simultaneous arrest of the conspirators proves clearly that the police knew perfectly well where they could lay their hands upon them.[1]

[1] The *political crime* with which Moreau and Pichegru were charged, and which Bourrienne apparently believed was not of a nature to stain their characters, was an attempt on the life of the First Consul. There seems to be no doubt that whether or not Moreau entered into the conspiracy of Georges and Pichegru, he intimated his readiness to act if the First Consul were removed, and loss of power had hitherto in France meant loss of life. But it is quite certain that Moreau was for some time in possession of proofs of Pichegru's plot against the Directory in 1797, and that he concealed the fact till the plot had failed and Pichegru had been banished. We have a curious account of the calm way in which Napoleon acted in this arrest of Moreau, great mistake as it was. "Madame Bonaparte told me that Napoleon had passed almost all the night 'debout' (*walking, probably, as he often did in such cases*), considering the question whether he should arrest Moreau, and weighing the arguments for and against this measure, without a trace of personal feeling. Towards daybreak he sent for Berthier, and after a long interview he determined to send to Grosbois, where Moreau had retired" (*Rémusat*, tome i. p. 302). Too much stress has prob-

When Pichegru was required to sign his examination
he refused. He said it was unnecessary ; that, knowing
all the secret machinery of the police, he suspected that
by some chemical process they would erase all the writing
except the signature, and afterwards fill up the paper with
statements which he had never made. His refusal to sign
the interrogatory, he added, would not prevent him from
repeating before a court of justice the truth which he had
stated in answer to the questions proposed to him. Fear
was entertained of the disclosures he might make respecting his connection with Moreau, whose destruction was
sought for, and also with respect to the means employed
by the agents of Fouché to urge the conspirators to effect
a change which they desired.

On the evening of the 15th of February I heard of
Moreau's arrest, and early next morning I proceeded
straight to the Rue St. Pierre, where M. Carbonnet resided with his nephew. I was anxious to hear from him
the particulars of the general's arrest. What was my
surprise ! I had hardly time to address myself to the
porter before he informed me that M. Carbonnet and his
nephew were both arrested. "I advise you, sir," added
the man, "to retire without more ado, for I can assure
you that the persons who visit M. Carbonnet are watched."
—"Is he still at home?" said I. "Yes, sir ; they are
examining his papers."—"Then," said I, "I will go up."
M. Carbonnet, of whose friendship I had reason to be

ably been laid on Moreau's position, as if Napoleon feared a formidable rival in him.
Moreau had been more successful in his retreats than in other points of his career,
and Napoleon had certainly never from the first shown the least fear of the generals
who had been famous when he was in the junior ranks. His arrest of Moreau was
exactly a similar mistake to the trial of the Cardinal de Rohan by Louis XVI. in the
matter of the diamond necklace. In neither case were the difficulties and the effect
of a public trial understood by the Chief of the State. If the treatment of Masséna
by Napoleon is considered, it will be seen how little he was likely to fear such men as
Moreau or the already discredited Pichegru. Moreau himself said, in 1803, to an
Englishwoman (Lady Besborough ?), that he disapproved of the Government, but
was not afraid of Bonaparte, who "was a tyrant, but not an assassin ; " and that he
was not afraid of being banished, as he had the heart of the army (*Miss Berry's
Diary*, vol. ii. p. 235).

proud, and whose memory will ever be dear to me, was more distressed by the arrest of his nephew and Moreau than by his own. His nephew was, however, liberated after a few hours. M. Carbonnet's papers were sealed up, and he was placed in solitary confinement at St. Pélagie.

Thus the police, who previously knew nothing, were suddenly informed of all. In spite of the numerous police agents scattered over France, it was only discovered by the declarations of Bouvet de Lozier that three successive landings had been effected, and that a fourth was expected, which, however, did not take place, because General Savary was despatched by the First Consul with orders to seize the persons whose arrival was looked for. There cannot be a more convincing proof of the fidelity of the agents of the police to their old chief, and their combined determination of trifling with their new one.

CHAPTER XXII.

1804.

The events of 1804—Death of the Duc d'Enghien—Napoleon's arguments at St. Helena—Comparison of dates—Possibility of my having saved the Duc d'Enghien's life—Advice given to the Duc d'Enghien—Sir Charles Stuart—Delay of the Austrian Cabinet—Pichegru and the mysterious being—M. Massias—The historians of St. Helena—Bonaparte's threats against the emigrants and M. Cobentzel—Singular adventure of Davoust's secretary—The quartermaster—The brigand of La Vendée.

In order to form a just idea of the events which succeeded each other so rapidly at the commencement of 1804 it is necessary to consider them both separately and connectedly. It must be borne in mind that all Bonaparte's machinations tended to one object, the foundation of the French Empire in his favour; and it is also essential to consider how the situation of the emigrants, in reference to the First Consul, had changed since the declaration of war. As long as Bonaparte continued at peace the cause of the Bourbons had no support in foreign Cabinets, and the emigrants had no alternative but to yield to circumstances; but on the breaking out of a new war all was changed. The cause of the Bourbons became that of the powers at war with France; and as many causes concurred to unite the emigrants abroad with those who had returned but half satisfied, there was reason to fear something from their revolt, in combination with the powers arrayed against Bonaparte.

Such was the state of things with regard to the emigrants when the leaders and accomplices of Georges' conspiracy were arrested at the very beginning of 1804. The assassination of the Duc d'Enghien[1] took place on the 21st of March; on the 30th of April appeared the proposition of the Tribunate to found a Government in France under the authority of one individual; on the 18th of May came the *Sénatus-consulte,* naming Napoleon Bonaparte EMPEROR, and lastly, on the 10th of June, the sentence of condemnation on Georges and his accomplices. Thus the shedding of the blood of a Bourbon, and the placing of the crown of France on the head of a soldier of fortune were two acts interpolated in the sanguinary drama of Georges' conspiracy. It must be remembered, too, that during the period of these events we were at war with England, and on the point of seeing Austria and the Colossus of the north form a coalition against the new Emperor.

I will now state all I know relative to the death of the Duc d'Enghien. That unfortunate Prince, who was at Ettenheim, in consequence of a love affair, had no com-

---

[1] Louis Antoine Henri de Bourbon, Duc d'Enghien (1772-1804), son of the Duc de Bourbon, and grandson of the Prince de Condé, served against France in the army of Condé. When this force was disbanded he stayed at Ettenheim on account of a love affair with the Princesse Charlotte de Rohan-Rochefort. Arrested in the territory of Baden. he was taken to Vincennes, and after trial by court-martial shot in the moat, 21st May 1804. With him practically ended the house of Bourbon-Condé, as his grandfather died in 1818, leaving only the Duc de Bourbon, and the Princesse Louise Adelaide, Abbesse de Rémiremont, who died in 1824. The Duc de Bourbon, his father, was found in 1830 hung from a window at St. Leu. We have the following description of him :—" As to the Duc d'Enghien, I can still see him. Short, but well shaped, slender, he had the face of a hero and of a *mauvais sujet,* with the appearance and the physical details which please the French, and which he supported so well by his lightness, his grace, and his brilliant couragè, as well as by military talents to which the Republicans themselves did justice. His first words on my presentation were more worthy of a cornet of hussars than of a Prince fighting for the throne and for the altar. ' General,' said he, ' your son has quite an innocent air; but he will soon lose that in the society of the chevaliers of the Crown.' I paraphrase his coarser words " (*Puymaigre,* p. 16), where will also be found a more pleasing story of how the young Prince, after a long day, finding he could not pull off his boots, asked an old gentleman whether his boots hurt him. " Certainly, Monseigneur."—" Shall I take them off ? "—Monseigneur would not think of such a thing !—" Yes, because when I have pulled off your boots, I shall ask you to take off mine." This is a pleasanter version of the story of Charles the Bold of Burgundy and Commines, which Scott has used so well in *Quentin Durward.*

munication whatever with those who were concocting a
plot in the interior. Macchiavelli says that when the
author of a crime cannot be discovered we should seek
for those to whose advantage it turns. In the present
case Macchiavelli's advice will find an easy application, since
the Duke's death could be advantageous only to Bonaparte,
who considered it indispensable to his accession to the
crown of France. The motives may be explained, but can
they be justified? How could it ever be said that the Duc
d'Enghien perished as a presumed accomplice in the conspiracy of Georges?

Moreau was arrested on the 15th of February 1804, at
which time the existence of the conspiracy was known.
Pichegru and Georges were also arrested in February, and
the Duc d'Enghien not till the 15th of March. Now if the
Prince had really been concerned in the plot, if even he
had a knowledge of it, would he have remained at
Ettenheim for nearly a month after the arrest of his
presumed accomplices, intelligence of which he might
have obtained in the space of three days? Certainly not.
So ignorant was he of that conspiracy that when informed
at Ettenheim of the affair he doubted it, declaring that if
it were true his father and grandfather would have made
him acquainted with it. Would so long an interval have
been suffered to elapse before he was arrested? Alas!
cruel experience has shown that that step would have been
taken in a few hours.

The sentence of death against Georges and his accomplices was not pronounced till the 10th of June 1804, and
the Duc d'Enghien was shot on the 21st of March, before
the trials were even commenced. How is this precipitation to be explained? If, as Napoleon has declared,
the young Bourbon was an accomplice in the crime, why
was he not arrested at the time the others were? Why
was he not tried along with them, on the ground of his
being an actual accomplice; or of being compromised, by

communications with them ; or, in short, because his answers might have thrown light on that mysterious affair ? How was it that the name of the illustrious accused was not once mentioned in the course of that awful trial ?

It can scarcely be conceived that Napoleon could say at St. Helena, "Either they contrived to implicate the unfortunate Prince in their project, and so pronounced his doom, or, by omitting to inform him of what was going on, allowed him imprudently to slumber on the brink of a precipice ; for he was only a stone's cast from the frontier when they were about to strike the great blow in the name and for the interest of his family."

This reasoning is not merely absurd, it is atrocious. If the Duke was implicated by the confession of his accomplices, he should have been arrested and tried along with them. Justice required this. If he was not so implicated, where is the proof of his guilt ? Because some individuals, without his knowledge, plotted to commit a crime in the name of his family he was to be shot ! Because he was 130 leagues from the scene of the plot, and had no connection with it, he was to die ! Such arguments cannot fail to inspire horror. It is absolutely impossible any reasonable person can regard the Duc d'Enghien as an accomplice of Cadoudal ; and Napoleon basely imposed on his contemporaries and posterity by inventing such falsehoods, and investing them with the authority of his name.

Had I been then in the First Consul's intimacy I may aver, with as much confidence as pride, that the blood of the Duc d'Enghien would not have imprinted an indelible stain on the glory of Bonaparte. In this terrible matter I could have done what no one but me could even attempt, and this on account of my position, which no one else has since held with Bonaparte. I quite admit that he would have preferred others to me, and that he would have had more friendship for them than for me, supposing friendship to be compatible with the character of Bonaparte, but

I knew him better than any one else. Besides, among those who surrounded him I alone could have permitted myself some return to our former familiarity on account of our intimacy of childhood. Certainly, in a matter which permanently touched the glory of Bonaparte, I should not have been restrained by the fear of some transitory fit of anger, and the reader has seen that I did not dread disgrace. Why should I have dreaded it ? I had neither portfolio, nor office, nor salary, for, as I have said, I was only with Bonaparte as a friend, and we had, as it were, a common purse. I feel a conviction that it would have been very possible for me to have dissuaded Bonaparte from his fatal design, inasmuch as I positively know that his object, after the termination of the peace, was merely to frighten the emigrants, in order to drive them from Ettenheim, where great numbers, like the Duc d'Enghien, had sought refuge. His anger was particularly directed against a Baroness de Reith and a Baroness d'Ettengein, who had loudly vituperated him, and distributed numerous libels on the left bank of the Rhine. At that period Bonaparte had as little design against the Duc d'Enghien's life as against that of any other emigrant. He was more inclined to frighten than to harm him, and certainly his first intention was not to arrest the Prince, but, as I have said, to frighten the *émigrés*, and to drive them to a distance. I must, however, admit that when Bonaparte spoke to Rapp and Duroc of the emigrants on the other side of the Rhine he expressed himself with much irritability : so much so, indeed, that M. de Talleyrand,[1] dread-

---

[1] On this alleged warning by Talleyrand see the Baron Massias in *Erreurs* (tome ii. pp. 107 and 111). The Princesse de Rohan, the lady apparently alluded to, seems never to have known of this warning. Further, there is this to be said. If Talleyrand had remonstrated in the Council held before the arrest, the fact would have been known. He did not remonstrate ; see Bulwer, *Historical Characters*, p. 127, with its rather lame excuses for the silence. If he had really desired to warn the Prince there could have been no difficulty in doing so. Even men attached to Napoleon would have assisted Talleyrand in this. Thus, where Talleyrand's conduct *can* be proved, we find no action in favour of the Prince. We only have a vague state-

ing its effects for the Duc d'Enghien, warned that Prince, through the medium of a lady to whom he was attached, of his danger, and advised him to proceed to a greater distance from the frontier. On receiving this notice the Prince resolved to rejoin his grandfather, which he could not do but by passing through the Austrian territory. Should any doubt exist as to these facts it may be added that Sir Charles Stuart wrote to M. de Cobentzel to solicit a passport for the Duc d'Enghien ; and it was solely owing to the delay of the Austrian Cabinet that time was afforded for the First Consul to order the arrest of the unfortunate Prince as soon as he had formed the horrible resolution of shedding the blood of a Bourbon. This resolution could have originated only with himself, for who would have dared to suggest it to him ? The fact is, Bonaparte knew not what he did. His fever of ambition amounted to delirium ; and he knew not how he was losing himself in public opinion because he did not know that opinion, to gain which he would have made every sacrifice.

When Cambacérès (who, with a slight reservation, had voted[1] the death of Louis XVI.) warmly opposed in the

ment that he gave a warning, which no one received, and the sending of which is absolutely without corroboration. The Comte d'Artois (afterwards Charles X.), according to M. de Vitrolles, gives the following version of Talleyrand's conduct on the night of the execution :—"All that can be certainly known is that Talleyrand announced the consummation of this cruel murder with barbarous composure. He was at two in the morning at the house of Madame de Laval, reclining listlessly, as was his habit, in an arm-chair, when he drew his watch from his pocket, and, showing no kind of emotion in his voice or countenance, remarked, 'At this moment the last of the Condés has ceased to exist.'" It will be seen farther on—compare also *Savary*, tome ii.pp. 27–35—that effectual warning was given to whoever was the person expected to land on the Channel coast, and for whom Savary was waiting.

[1] In the Convention Cambacérès had nominally voted for the death of Louis XVI., but with a respite really intended to save him. Hence this sneer. Here it is to be remarked that if Napoleon had believed that Cambacérès had really been a regicide he would never have allowed him to be Consul with him. See his language to Dumas on this subject (*Mathieu Dumas*, tome iii. p. 316), allowing always for the circumstances that forced Fouché, a regicide, on him. It must be remembered that Napoleon, once arrived at power, had the greatest horror of the Revolution, that is, of the follies and bloodshed of the Revolution. "My last break with the Revolution" was his description of his abolition of the Tribunate. Again, "I will not bequeath France to the Revolution, from which I delivered her."

Council the Duc d'Enghien's arrest, the First Consul observed to him, "Methinks, Sir, you have *grown* very chary of Bourbon blood !"

Meanwhile the Duc d'Enghien was at Ettenheim, indulging in hope rather than plotting conspiracies. It is well known that an individual made an offer to the Prince de Condé to assassinate the First Consul, but the Prince indignantly rejected the proposition, and nobly refused to recover the rights of the Bourbons at the price of such a crime. The individual above-mentioned was afterwards discovered to be an agent of the Paris police, who had been commissioned to draw the Princes into a plot which would have ruined them, for public feeling revolts at assassination under any circumstances.

It has been alleged that Louis XVIII.'s refusal to treat with Bonaparte led to the fatal catastrophe of the Duc d'Enghien's death. The first correspondence between Louis XVIII. and the First Consul, which has been given in these Memoirs, clearly proves the contrary. It is certainly probable that Louis XVIII.'s refusal to renounce his rights should have irritated Bonaparte. But it was rather late to take his revenge two years after, and that too on a Prince totally ignorant of those overtures. It is needless to comment on such absurdities. It is equally unnecessary to speak of the mysterious being who often appeared at meetings in the Faubourg St. Germain, and who was afterwards discovered to be Pichegru.[1]

---

[1] Of this mysterious personage Savary gives the following particulars, collected from the evidence for the investigation of Georges' conspiracy :—

"Georges was considered as merely a principal instrument ; the question was, for whom, in whose name, he would have acted the day following that on which he should have despatched the First Consul. It was very naturally concluded that a more important personage was somewhere concealed, and waiting for the blow to be struck before he made himself known. An active search was set on foot. Georges' people, and those of the house in which he had lodged, were examined, but nothing was discovered. At length two of his servants, being separately interrogated, declared that every ten or twelve days there came to their master a gentleman whose name they did not know, about thirty-four or thirty-five years of age, who had light hair, was bald on the forehead, of middle height, and rather corpulent. They stated that he was always extremely well-dressed, both as to his linen

A further light is thrown on this melancholy catastrophe by a conversation Napoleon had, a few days after his elevation to the imperial throne, with M. Massias, the French Minister at the Court of the Grand Duke of Baden. This conversation took place at Aix-la-Chapelle. After some remarks on the intrigues of the emigrants Bonaparte observed, "You ought at least to have prevented the plots which the Duc d'Enghien was hatching at Ettenheim."— "Sire, I am too old to learn to tell a falsehood. Believe me, on this subject your Majesty's ear has been abused."— "Do you not think, then, that had the conspiracy of Georges and Pichegru proved successful, the Prince would have passed the Rhine, and have come post to Paris?"

M. Massias, from whom I had these particulars, added, "At this last question of the Emperor I hung down my head and was silent, for I saw he did not wish to hear the truth."

Now let us consider, with that attention which the importance of the subject demands, what has been said by the historians of St. Helena.

Napoleon said to his companions in exile that "the Duc d'Enghien's death must be attributed either to an excess of zeal for him (Napoleon), to private views, or to mysterious intrigues. He had been blindly urged on; he was, if he might say so, taken by surprise. The measure was precipitated, and the result predetermined."

and otherwise; that he must be a person of consequence, for their master always went to the door to receive him. When he was in the room everybody, Messrs. de Polignac and de Rivière, as well as the others, rose and did not sit down till he had again retired, and that whenever he came to see Georges they went together into a cabinet, where they remained alone till he went away, and then Georges attended him to the door.

"The description given of this mysterious person corresponded neither with the age of the Comte d'Artois nor the person of the Duc de Berri. Besides, the witnesses knew the latter personally, and declared it was not he. The Duc d'Angoulême was at Mittau with the King; the Duc de Bourbon was known to be in London. Attention was therefore directed to the Duc d'Enghien, who resided at Ettenheim on the ight bank of the Rhine" (*Memoirs of the Duke of Rovigo*, vol. ii. p. 42).

Rovigo subsequently corroborates the statement of M. de Bourrienne, that the mysterious person turned out to be Pichegru.

This he might have said ; but if he did so express himself, how are we to reconcile such a declaration with the state-ment of O'Meara?   How give credit to assertions so very opposite ? [1]

Napoleon said to M. de Las Casas :—

"One day when alone, I recollect it well, I was taking my coffee, half seated on the table at which I had just dined, when suddenly information was brought to me that a new conspiracy had been dis-covered.   I was warmly urged to put an end to these enormities ; they represented to me that it was time at last to give a lesson to those who had been day after day conspiring against my life ; that this end could only be attained by shedding the blood of one of them ; and that the Duc d'Enghien, who might now be convicted of form-ing part of this new conspiracy, and taken in the very act, should be that one.   It was added that he had been seen at Strasburg ; that it was even believed that he had been in Paris ; and that the plan was that he should enter France by the east at the moment of the explosion, whilst the Duc de Berri was disembarking in the west.   I should tell you," observed the Emperor, "that I did not even know precisely who the Duc d'Enghien was (the Revolution

[1] The following is the statement referred to :—

" It was discovered," said Napoleon , " by the confession of some of the conspira-tors, that the Duc d'Enghien was an accomplice, and that he was only waiting on the frontiers of France for the news of my assassination, upon receiving which he was to have entered France as the King's lieutenant. Was I to suffer that the Comte d'Artois should send a parcel of miscreants to murder me, and that a Prince of his House should hover on the borders of the country that I governed to profit by my assassination ? According to the laws of nature I was authorised to cause him to be assassinated in retaliation for the numerous attempts of the kind that he had before caused to be made against me. I gave orders to have him seized. He was tried and condemned by a law made long before I had any power in France. He was tried by a military commission formed of all the colonels of the regiments then in garrison at Paris. He was accused of having borne arms against the Republic, which he did not deny. When before the Tribunal he behaved with great bravery. When he arrived at Strasburg he wrote a letter to me in which he offered to discover everything if pardon were granted to him ; said that his family had lost their claims for a long time ; and concluded by offering his services to me. This letter was de-livered to Talleyrand, who concealed it until after his execution. Had the Comte d'Artois been in his place he would have suffered the same fate ; and were I now placed under similar circumstances I would act in a similar manner. As the po-lice," added Napoleon, " did not like to trust to the evidence of Mehée de la Touche alone, they sent Captain Rosey (a man in whose integrity they had every confi-dence) to Drake at Munich with a letter from Mehée, which procured him an in-terview, the result of which confirmed Mehée's statement, that he was concerned in a plot to *terrasser le premier Consul*, no matter by what means " (*Voice from St. Helena*).

having taken place when I was yet a very young man, and I having
never been at Court), and that I was quite in the dark as to where
he was at that moment.   Having been informed on those points I
exclaimed that if such were the case the Duke ought to be arrested,
and that orders should be given to that effect.   Everything had been
foreseen and prepared ; the different orders were already drawn up,
nothing remained to be done but to sign them, and the fate of the
young Prince was thus decided."

Napoleon next asserts that in the Duke's arrest and
condemnation all *the usual forms were strictly observed.*
But he has also declared that the death of that unfortunate Prince will be an eternal reproach to those who, carried
away by a criminal zeal, waited not for their Sovereign's
orders to execute the sentence of the court-martial.   He
would, perhaps, have allowed the Prince to live ; but yet
he said, "It is true I wished to make an example which
should deter."

It has been said that the Duc d'Enghien addressed a
letter to Napoleon, which was not delivered till after the
execution.   This is false and absurd !   How could that
Prince write to Bonaparte to offer him his services and to
solicit the command of an army ?   His interrogatory makes
no mention of this letter, and is in direct opposition to
the sentiments which that letter would attribute to him.
The truth is, no such letter ever existed.   The individual
who was with the Prince declared he never wrote it.   It
will never be believed that any one would have presumed
to withhold from Bonaparte a letter on which depended
the fate of so august a victim.

In his declarations to his companions in exile Napoleon
endeavoured either to free himself of this crime or to
justify it.   His fear or his susceptibility was such, that in
discoursing with strangers he merely said, that had he
known of the Prince's letter, which was not delivered to
him—God knows why !—until after he had breathed his
last, he would have pardoned him.   But at a subsequent
date he traced, with his own hand, his last thoughts,

which he supposed would be consecrated in the minds of his contemporaries, and of posterity. Napoleon, touching on the subject which he felt would be one of the most important attached to his memory, said that *if the thing were to do again he would act as he then did.* How does this declaration tally with his avowal, that *if he had received the Prince's letter he should have lived?* This is irreconcilable. But if we compare all that Napoleon said at St. Helena, and which has been transmitted to us by his faithful followers; if we consider his contradictions when speaking of the Duc d'Enghien's death to strangers, to his friends, to the public, or to posterity, the question ceases to be doubtful. Bonaparte wished to strike a blow which would terrify his enemies. Fancying that the Duc de Berri was ready to land in France, he despatched his *aide de camp* Savary, in disguise, attended by gendarmes, to watch the Duke's landing at Biville, near Dieppe. This turned out a fruitless mission. The Duke was warned in time not to attempt the useless and dangerous enterprise, and Bonaparte, enraged to see one prey escape him, pounced upon another. It is well known that Bonaparte often, and in the presence even of persons whom he conceived to have maintained relations with the partisans of the Bourbons at Paris, expressed himself thus: "I will put an end to these conspiracies. If any of the emigrants conspire they shall be shot. I have been told that Cobentzel harbours some of them. I do not believe this; but if it be true, Cobentzel shall be arrested and shot along with them. I will let the Bourbons know I am not to be trifled with."

The above statement of facts accounts for the suppositions respecting the probable influence of the Jacobins in this affair. It has been said, not without some appearance of reason, that to get the Jacobins to help him to ascend the throne Bonaparte consented to sacrifice a victim of the blood royal, as the only pledge capable of ensuring them against the return of the proscribed family. Be this as it may, there are no possible means of relieving Bonaparte from his share of guilt in the death of the Duc d'Enghien.

To the above facts, which came within my own knowledge, I may add the following curious story, which was related to me by an individual who himself heard it from the secretary of General Davoust.

Davoust was commanding a division in the camp of Boulogne, and his secretary when proceeding thither to join him met in the diligence a man who seemed to be absorbed in affliction. This man during the whole journey never once broke silence but by some deep sighs, which he had not power to repress. General Davoust's secretary observed him with curiosity and interest, but did not venture to intrude upon his grief by any conversation. The concourse of travellers from Paris to the camp was, however, at that time very great, and the inn at which the diligence stopped in the evening was so crowded that it was impossible to assign a chamber to each traveller. Two, therefore, were put into one room, and it so happened that the secretary was lodged with his mysterious travelling companion.

When they were alone he addressed him in a tone of interest which banished all appearance of intrusion. He inquired whether the cause of his grief was of a nature to admit of any alleviation, and offered to render him any assistance in his power. "Sir," replied the stranger, "I am much obliged for the sympathy you express for me—I want nothing. There is no possible consolation for me. My affliction can end only with my life. You shall judge for yourself, for the interest you seem to take in my misfortune fully justifies my confidence. I was quartermaster in the select gendarmerie, and formed part of a detachment which was ordered to Vincennes. I passed the night there under arms, and at daybreak was ordered down to the moat with six men. An execution was to take place. The prisoner was brought out, and I gave the word to fire. The man fell, and after the execution I learned that we had shot the Duc d'Enghien. Judge of my horror! . . . I knew the prisoner only by the name of the *brigand of La Vendée!* . . . I could no longer remain in the service—I obtained my discharge, and am about to retire to my family. Would that I had done so sooner!" The above has been related to me and other persons by Davoust's secretary, whom I shall not name.

Note.—At the time of the Duc d'Enghien's execution, General Murat, the First Consul's brother-in-law, was governor of Paris. The castle of Vincennes being within his military jurisdiction, many writers have held him up to that infamy which ought more properly to have fallen on other heads. Murat was a kind-hearted, humane man; though a soldier of fortune, and accustomed to scenes of carnage, he could see blood spilt only on the field, and shuddered at all civil executions or private acts of vengeance. Under his two immediate predecessors on that throne conspirators, and men called so, were hanged or shot by dozens at a time; but during the seven years that Murat was King of Naples he did not allow an execution of the kind, and he never could be brought to sign a death-warrant for any, the worst species of criminal, without the greatest difficulty. His feelings on these points amounted to a weakness. Being well aware of the reports against him he took every opportunity of contradicting them to the persons in his confidence; and to the last moment of his life he solemnly protested that he had done all he could to save the Duke. He denied that he appointed the eight officers who sat in judgment at Vincennes, and, without expressly naming them, he seemed to lay most of the blame on Fouché, Savary, and Hullin. He never spoke of the midnight trial and the execution in the ditch without horror. We have received this information from men of most honourable characters, and we give it a place here because we are convinced in our own minds of its veracity, and think it fair to rescue the fame of Murat, who, with all his faults, was one of the best men in the school he belonged to.

The end of Joachim Murat bore a striking resemblance to that of the Duc d'Enghien. He was tried by an incompetent military tribunal, and shot in the courtyard of an old castle in Calabria. Hence several authors have taken occasion to establish a visitation of Providence, and to declare that Murat, iniquitously tried and barbarously murdered, merited the fate he met at Pizzo on the 14th of October 1815 by what he had done at Vincennes on the 20th of March 1804.

In General Colletta's admirable history of the Kingdom of Naples there is a narrative of Murat's death, which was drawn up entirely from the accounts of eye and ear witnesses. One of the last things Joachim said to Captain Stratti, the commandant of the castle of Pizzo, was: "As for the tragedy of the Duc d'Enghien, which King Ferdinand is about to avenge with another tragedy, I had no part in it, and this I swear by that God in whose presence I must shortly appear."

Like the Duc d'Enghien, Murat refused to have his eyes bandaged, and he himself gave the word of command to his soldiers. These, the last words he spoke, were highly characteristic of the man—of his dauntless bravery and personal vanity. "Soldiers," he said, "spare my face—aim at my heart!" The volley was fired, and Joachim Murat fell dead, still holding in his hands the miniature portraits of his children (*Storia del Reame di Napoli dal 1734, sino al 1825*).—*Editor of 1836 Edition.*

CHAPTER XXIII.

1804.

General Ordener's mission—Arrest of the Duc d'Enghien—Horrible night-
scene—Harrel's account of the death of the Prince—Order for digging
the grave—The foster-sister of the Duc d'Enghien—Reading the
sentence—The lantern—General Savary—The faithful dog and the
police—My visit to Malmaison—Josephine's grief—The Duc d'Enghien's portrait and lock of hair—Savary's emotion—M. de Chateaubriand's resignation—M. de Chateaubriand's connection with Bonaparte—Madame Bacciocchi and M. de Fontanes—Cardinal Fesch—
Dedication of the second edition of the *Génie du Christianisme*—M.
de Chateaubriand's visit to the First Consul on the morning of the
Duc d'Enghien's death—Consequences of the Duc d'Enghien's death—
Change of opinion in the provinces—The Gentry of the Chateaux—
Effect of the Duc d'Enghien's death on foreign Courts—Remarkable
words of Mr. Pitt—Louis XVIII. sends back the insignia of the
Golden Fleece to the King of Spain.

I WILL now narrate more fully the sanguinary scene
which took place at Vincennes. General Ordener, commanding the mounted grenadiers of the Guard, received
orders from the War Minister to proceed to the Rhine, to
give instructions to the chiefs of the gendarmerie of New
Brissac, which was placed at his disposal. General Ordener sent a detachment of gendarmerie to Ettenheim,
where the Duc d'Enghien was arrested on the 15th of
March. He was immediately conducted to the citadel of
Strasburg, where he remained till the 18th, to give time
for the arrival of orders from Paris. These orders were
given rapidly, and executed promptly, for the carriage
which conveyed the unfortunate Prince arrived at the barrier at eleven o'clock on the morning of the 20th, where it
remained for five hours, and afterwards proceeded by the

exterior boulevards on the road to Vincennes, where it arrived at night. Every scene of this horrible drama was acted under the veil of night : the sun did not even shine upon its tragical close. The soldiers received orders to proceed to Vincennes at night. It was at night that the fatal gates of the fortress were closed upon the Prince. At night the Council assembled and tried him, or rather condemned him without trial. When the clock struck six in the morning the orders were given to fire, and the Prince ceased to exist.

Here a reflection occurs to me. Supposing one were inclined to admit that the Council held on the 10th of March had some connection with the Duc d'Enghien's arrest, yet as no Council was held from the time of the Duke's arrival at the barrier to the moment of his execution, it could only be Bonaparte himself who issued the orders which were too punctually obeyed. When the dreadful intelligence of the Duc d'Enghien's death was spread in Paris it excited a feeling of consternation which recalled the recollection of the Reign of Terror. Could Bonaparte have seen the gloom which pervaded Paris, and compared it with the joy which prevailed on the day when he returned victorious from the field of Marengo, he would have felt that he had tarnished his glory by a stain which could never be effaced.

About half-past twelve on the 22d of March I was informed that some one wished to speak with me. It was Harrel.[1] I will relate word for word what he communicated to me. Harrel probably thought that he was bound in gratitude to acquaint me with these details ; but he owed me no gratitude, for it was much against my will that he had encouraged the conspiracy of Céracchi, and received the reward of his treachery in that crime. The

---

[1] Harrel, who had been unemployed till the plot of Aréna and Céracchi on the 18th Vendémiaire an IX. (10th October 1800) which he had feigned to join, and had then revealed to the police (see *ante*), had been made Governor of Vincennes.

HENRI DE BOURBON

(DUC D'ENGHIEN)

following is Harrel's statement :—" On the evening of the day before yesterday, when the Prince arrived, I was asked whether I had a room to lodge a prisoner in ; I replied, No—that there were only my apartments and the Council-chamber. I was told to prepare instantly a room in which a prisoner could sleep who was to arrive that evening. I was also desired to dig a pit in the court-yard.[1] I replied that that could not be easily done, as the courtyard was paved. The moat was then fixed upon, and there the pit was dug. The Prince arrived at seven o'clock in the evening ; he was perishing with cold and hunger. He did not appear dispirited. He said he wanted something to eat, and to go to bed afterwards. His apartment not being yet sufficiently aired, I took him into my own, and sent into the village for some refreshment. The Prince sat down to table, and invited me to eat with him. He then asked me a number of questions respecting Vin-cennes—what was going on there, and other particulars. He told me that he had been brought up in the neigh-bourhood of the castle, and spoke to me with great free-dom and kindness. 'What do they want with me?' he said. 'What do they mean to do with me?' But these questions betrayed no uneasiness or anxiety. My wife, who was ill, was lying in the same room in an al-cove, closed by a railing. She heard, without being per-ceived, all our conversation, and she was exceedingly agitated, for she recognised the Prince, whose foster-sister she was, and whose family had given her a pension before the Revolution.

" The Prince hastened to bed, but before he could have fallen asleep the judges sent to request his presence in the Council-chamber. I was not present at his examina-

---

[1] This fact must be noted. Harrel is told to dig a trench before the sentence. Thus it was known that they had come to kill the Duc d'Enghien. How can this be answered ? Can it possibly be supposed that anyone, whoever it was, would have dared to give such an order in anticipation if the order had not been the carrying out of a formal command of Bonaparte ? That is incredible.—*Bourrienne.*

tion ; but when it was concluded he returned to his chamber, and when they came to read his sentence to him he was in a profound sleep. In a few moments after he was led out for execution. He had so little suspicion of the fate that awaited him that on descending the staircase leading to the moat he asked where they were taking him. He received no answer. I went before the Prince with a lantern. Feeling the cold air which came up the staircase he pressed my arm and said, 'Are they going to put me into a dungeon ? ' "

The rest is known. I can yet see Harrel shuddering while thinking of this action of the Prince's.

Much has been said about a lantern which it is pretended was attached to one of the Duc d'Enghien's button-holes. This is a pure invention. Captain Dautancourt, whose sight was not very good, took the lantern out of Harrel's hand to read the sentence to the victim, who had been condemned with as little regard to judicial forms as to justice. This circumstance probably gave rise to the story about the lantern to which I have just alluded. The fatal event took place at six o'clock on the morning of the 21st of March, and it was then daylight.

General Savary did not dare to delay the execution of the sentence, although the Prince urgently demanded to have an interview with the First Consul. Had Bonaparte seen the prince there can be little doubt but that he would have saved his life. Savary, however, thought himself bound to sacrifice his own opinions to the powerful faction which then controlled the First Consul ; and whilst he thought he was serving his master, he was in fact only serving the faction to which, I must say, he did not belong. The truth is, that General Savary can only be reproached for not having taken upon himself to suspend the execution, which very probably would not have taken place had it been suspended. He was merely an instrument, and regret on his part would, perhaps, have told more in his favour than his vain efforts to justify Bonaparte. I have just said that if there had been any suspension there would have been no execution ; and I think this is almost proved by the uncertainty which must have existed in the mind of the First Consul. If he had made up his mind all the measures would have been taken in advance, and if they had been, the carriage of the Duke would certainly not have been kept for five hours at the barriers. Besides, it is certain that the first intention was to take the Prince to the prison of the Temple.

From all that I have stated, and particularly from the non-suspension of the execution, it appears to me as clear as day that General Savary had received a formal order from Bonaparte for the Duc d'Enghien's death, and also a formal order that it should be so managed as to make it impossible to speak to Bonaparte again on the subject until all should be over. Can there be a more evident, a more direct proof of this than the digging of the grave beforehand? I have repeated Harrel's story just as he related it to me. He told it me without solicitation, and he could not invent a circumstance of this nature.[1]

General Savary was not in the moat during the execution, but on the bank, from whence he could easily see all that passed. Another circumstance connected with the Duc d'Enghien's death has been mentioned, which is true. The Prince had a little dog ; this faithful animal returned incessantly to the fatal spot in the moat. There are few who have not seen that spot. Who has not made a pilgrimage to Vincennes and dropped a tear where the victim fell? The fidelity of the poor dog excited so much interest that the police prevented any one from visiting the fatal spot, and the dog was no longer heard to howl over his master's grave.

I promised to state the truth respecting the death of the Duc d'Enghien, and I have done so, though it has cost me

[1] Harrel's antecedents should, however, be borne in mind.

some pain. Harrel's narrative, and the shocking circumstance of the grave being dug beforehand, left me no opportunity of cherishing any doubts I might have wished to entertain ; and everything which followed confirmed the view I then took of the subject. When Harrel left me on the 22d I determined to go to Malmaison to see Madame Bonaparte, knowing, from her sentiments towards the House of Bourbon, that she would be in the greatest affliction. I had previously sent to know whether it would be convenient for her to see me, a precaution I had never before observed, but which I conceived to be proper upon that occasion. On my arrival I was immediately introduced to her boudoir, where she was alone with Hortense and Madame de Rémusat. They were all deeply afflicted. "Bourrienne," exclaimed Josephine, as soon as she perceived me, "what a dreadful event ! Did you but know the state of mind Bonaparte is in ! He avoids, he dreads the presence of every one ! Who could have suggested to him such an act as this?" I then acquainted Josephine with the particulars which I had received from Harrel. " What barbarity !" she resumed. "But no reproach can rest upon me, for I did everything to dissuade him from this dreadful project. He did not confide the secret to me, but I guessed it, and he acknowledged all. How harshly he repelled my entreaties ! I clung to him ! I threw myself at his feet ! ' Meddle with what concerns you !' he exclaimed angrily. ' This is not women's business ! Leave me !' And he repulsed me with a violence which he had never displayed since our first interview after your return from Egypt. Heavens ! what will become of us ? "

I could say nothing to calm affliction and alarm in which I participated, for to my grief for the death of the Duc d'Enghien was added my regret that Bonaparte should be capable of such a crime. "What," said Josephine, " can be thought of this in Paris? He must be the object of universal imprecation, for even here his flatterers appear

astounded when they are out of his presence. How
wretched we have been since yesterday; and he! . . .
You know what he is when he is dissatisfied with himself.
No one dare speak to him, and all is mournful around us.
What a commission he gave to Savary! You know I do
not like the general, because he is one of those whose
flatteries will contribute to ruin Bonaparte. Well! I
pitied Savary when he came yesterday to fulfil a commission which the Duc d'Enghien had entrusted to him.
Here," added Josephine, " is his portrait and a lock of his
hair, which he has requested me to transmit to one who
was dear to him. Savary almost shed tears when he described to me the last moments of the Duke; then, endeavouring to resume his self-possession, he said: 'It is
in vain to try to be indifferent, Madame! It is impossible
to witness the death of such a man unmoved!'"

Josephine afterwards informed me of the only act of
courage which occurred at this period—namely, the resignation which M. de Chateaubriand had sent to Bonaparte.
She admired his conduct greatly, and said: "What a
pity he is not surrounded by men of this description! It
would be the means of preventing all the errors into which
he is led by the constant approbation of those about
him." Josephine thanked me for my attention in coming
to see her at such an unhappy juncture; and I confess
that it required all the regard I cherished for her to induce me to do so, for at that moment I should not have
wished to see the First Consul, since the evil was irrepara-
ble. On the evening of that day nothing was spoken of
but the transaction of the 21st of March, and the noble
conduct of M. de Chateaubriand. As the name of that celebrated man is for ever written in characters of honour in
the history of that period, I think I may with propriety
relate here what I know respecting his previous connection with Bonaparte.

I do not recollect the precise date of M. de Chateau-

briand's return to France ; I only know that it was about
the year 1800, for we were, I think, still at the Luxembourg.　However, I recollect perfectly that Bonaparte began to conceive prejudices against him ; and when I one
day expressed my surprise to the First Consul that M. de
Chateaubriand's name did not appear on any of the lists
which he had ordered to be presented to him for filling
up vacant places, he said : "He has been mentioned to
me, but I replied in a way to check all hopes of his obtaining any appointment.　He has notions of liberty and
independence which will not suit my system.　I would
rather have him my enemy than my forced friend.　At all
events, he must wait awhile ; I may, perhaps, try him first
in a secondary place, and, if he does well, I may advance
him."

The above is, word for word, what Bonaparte said the
first time I conversed with him about M. de Chateaubriand.　The publication of *Atala* and the *Génie du Christianisme* suddenly gave Chateaubriand celebrity, and attracted the attention of the First Consul.　Bonaparte,
who then meditated the restoration of religious worship
in France, found himself wonderfully supported by the
publication of a book which excited the highest interest,
and whose superior merit led the public mind to the consideration of religious topics.　I remember Madame Bacciocchi coming one day to visit her brother with a little
volume in her hand ; it was *Atala*.　She presented it to
the First Consul, and begged he would read it.　"What,
more romances !" exclaimed he.　"Do you think I have
time to read all your fooleries ?"　He, however, took the
book from his sister and laid it down on my desk.　Madame
Bacciocchi then solicited the erasure of M. de Chateaubriand's name from the list of emigrants.　"Oh ! oh !"
said Bonaparte, "it is Chateaubriand's book, is it ?　I will
read it, then.　Bourrienne, write to Fouché to erase his
name from the list."

Bonaparte at that time paid so little attention to what was doing in the literary world that he was not aware of Chateaubriand being the author of *Atala*. It was on the recommendation of M. de Fontanes that Madame Bacciocchi tried this experiment, which was attended by complete success. The First Consul read *Atala*, and was much pleased with it. On the publication of the *Génie du Christianisme* some time after, his first prejudices were wholly removed. Among the persons about him there were many who dreaded to see a man of M. de Chateaubriand's talent approach the First Consul, who knew how to appreciate superior merit when it did not excite his envy.

Our relations with the Court of the Vatican being renewed, and Cardinal Fesch appointed Ambassador to the Holy See, Bonaparte conceived the idea of making M. de Chateaubriand first secretary to the Embassy, thinking that the author of the *Génie du Christianisme* was peculiarly fitted to make up for his uncle's deficiency of talent in the capital of the Christian world, which was destined to become the second city of the Empire.

It was not a little extraordinary to see a man, previously a stranger to diplomatic business, stepping over all the intermediate degrees, and being at once invested with the functions of first secretary to an important Embassy. I oftener than once heard the First Consul congratulate himself on having made the appointment. I knew, though Bonaparte was not aware of the circumstance at the time, that Chateaubriand at first refused the situation, and that he was only induced to accept it by the entreaties of the heads of the clergy, particularly of the Abbé Émery, a man of great influence. They represented to the author of the *Génie du Christianisme* that it was necessary he should accompany the uncle of the First Consul to Rome ; and M. de Chateaubriand accordingly resolved to do so.

However, clouds gathered, I do not know from what cause, between the ambassador and his secretary. All I

know is, that on Bonaparte being informed of the circumstance he took the part of the Cardinal, and the friends of
M. de Chateaubriand expected to see him soon deprived
of his appointment, when, to the great astonishment of
every one, the secretary to the Roman Embassy, far from
being disgraced, was raised by the First Consul to the
rank of Minister Plenipotentiary to the Valais, with leave
to travel in Switzerland and Italy, together with the promise
of the first vacant Embassy.

This favour excited a considerable sensation at the Tuileries ; but as it was known to be the will and pleasure of
the First Consul all expression of opinion on the subject
was confined to a few quiet murmurs that Bonaparte had
done for the name of Chateaubriand what, in fact, he had
done only on account of his talent.   It was during the
continuance of this favour that the second edition of
the *Génie du Christianisme* was dedicated to the First
Consul.

M. de Chateaubriand returned to France previously to
entering on the fulfilment of his new mission. He remained
for some months in Paris, and on the day appointed for
his departure he went to take leave of the First Consul.
By a singular chance it happened to be the fatal morning
of the 21st of March, and consequently only a few hours
after the Duc d'Enghien had been shot. It is unnecessary
to observe that M. de Chateaubriand was ignorant of the
fatal event.   However, on his return home he said to his
friends that he had remarked a singular change in the appearance of the First Consul, and that there was a sort of
sinister expression in his countenance.   Bonaparte saw his
new minister amidst the crowd who attended the audience,
and several times seemed inclined to step forward to speak
to him, but as often turned away, and did not approach
him the whole morning.   A few hours after, when M.
de Chateaubriand mentioned his observations to some of
his friends, he was made acquainted with the cause of that

agitation which, in spite of all his strength of mind and self-command, Bonaparte could not disguise.

M. de Chateaubriand instantly resigned his appointment of Minister Plenipotentiary to the Valais. For several days his friends were much alarmed for his safety, and they called every morning early to ascertain whether he had not been carried off during the night. Their fears were not without foundation. I must confess that I, who knew Bonaparte well, was somewhat surprised that no serious consequence attended the anger he manifested on receiving the resignation of the man who had dedicated his work to him. In fact, there was good reason for apprehension, and it was not without considerable difficulty that Elisa succeeded in averting the threatened storm. From this time began a state of hostility between Bonaparte and Chateaubriand which only terminated at the Restoration.

I am persuaded, from my knowledge of Bonaparte's character, that though he retained implacable resentment against a returned emigrant who had dared to censure his conduct in so positive a manner, yet, his first burst of anger being soothed, that which was the cause of hatred was at the same time the ground of esteem. Bonaparte's animosity was, I confess, very natural, for he could not disguise from himself the real meaning of a resignation made under such circumstances. It said plainly, "You have committed a crime, and I will not serve your Government, which is stained with the blood of a Bourbon!" I can therefore very well imagine that Bonaparte could never pardon the only man who dared to give him such a lesson in the midst of the plenitude of his power. But, as I have often had occasion to remark, there was no unison between Bonaparte's feelings and his judgment.

I find a fresh proof of this in the following passage, which he dictated to M. de Montholon at St. Helena (*Mémoires*, tome iv. p. 248). "If," said he, "the royal confidence had not been placed in men whose minds were unstrung by too important circumstances, or who, renegades to their country, saw no safety or glory for their master's throne except under the yoke of the Holy Alliance; if the Duc de Richelieu, whose ambition was to deliver his country from the presence of foreign bayonets; if Chateaubriand, who had just rendered valuable services at Ghent; if they had had the direction of affairs, France would have emerged from these two great national crises powerful and redoubtable. Chateaubriand had received from Nature the sacred fire—his works show it! His style is not that of Racine but of a prophet. Only he could have said with impunity in the chamber of peers, 'that the redingote and cocked hat of Napoleon, put on a stick on the coast of Brest, would make all Europe run to arms.'[1]

The immediate consequences of the Duc d'Enghien's death were not confined to the general consternation which that unjustifiable stroke of state policy produced in the capital. The news spread rapidly through the provinces and foreign countries, and was everywhere accompanied by astonishment and sorrow. There is in the departments a

---

[1] Napoleon had been struck by the genius of Chateaubriand. Sainte-Beuve (*Chateaubriand*, tome i. p. 398), relating his progress from Ossian to Corneille, and from Corneille to Racine, says, " Notwithstanding all this, it may be said with certainty that he nowhere found poetry which fully answered his ideal, and which satisfied him : Chateaubriand alone offered him some resemblance to it. Thus, notwithstanding the insults he received from Chateaubriand, he always preserved a predilection for him, and rendered him justice." The same day on which the *Concordat* was proclaimed the *Moniteur* contained a graceful notice of the *Génie du Christianisme*. Chateaubriand was then full of admiration for the man he so bitterly attacked in 1814. Napoleon was then to him *the man who has dragged us back from the abyss*. Comparing the work of Napoleon to the restoration of the Temple of Jerusalem, Chateaubriand says that as an "obscure Israelite, I carry to-day my grain of sand." After the Restoration Chateaubriand, with the feelings of a French Royalist, accused Napoleon of a taste for bad literature. It was a strange return for the opinion Napoleon always had for him. Napoleon, on his side, was not unwilling to again employ Chateaubriand, but, as he said, wished to take him at his own estimation for him, and not at the price Chateaubriand set on himself. Chateaubriand disclaimed the exact words about the cocked hat Napoleon attributed to him. See Sainte-Beuve, *Chateaubriand et son Groupe Littéraire*, tome i. p. 279.

separate class of society, possessing great influence, and constituted entirely of persons usually called the " Gentry of the Chateaux," who may be said to form the provincial Faubourg St. Germain, and who were overwhelmed by the news. The opinion of the Gentry of the Châteaux was not hitherto unfavourable to the First Consul, for the law of hostages which he repealed had been felt very severely by them. With the exception of some families accustomed to consider themselves, in relation to the whole world, what they were only within the circle of a couple of leagues, that is to say, illustrious personages, all the inhabitants of the provinces, though they might retain some attachment to the ancient order of things, had viewed with satisfaction the substitution of the Consular for the Directorial government, and entertained no personal dislike to the First Consul. Among the Châteaux, more than anywhere else, it has always been the custom to cherish Utopian ideas respecting the management of public affairs, and to criticise the acts of the Government. It is well known that at this time there was not in all France a single old mansion surmounted by its two weathercocks which had not a system of policy peculiar to itself, and in which the question whether the First Consul would play the part of Cromwell or Monk was not frequently canvassed. In those innocent controversies the little news which the Paris papers were allowed to publish was freely discussed, and a confidential letter from Paris sometimes furnished food for the conversation of a whole week.

While I was with Bonaparte he often talked to me about the life in the Châteaux, which he considered as the happiest for men with sufficient income and exempt from ambition. He knew and could appreciate this sort of life, for he often told me the period of his life which he remembered with the greatest pleasure was that which he had passed in a château of the family of Boulat du

Colombier near Valence.[1] Bonaparte set great value on
the opinion of the Châteaux, because while living in the
country he had observed the moral influence which their
inhabitants exercise over their neighbourhood. He had
succeeded to a great degree in conciliating them, but the
news of the death of the Duc d'Enghien alienated from
him minds which were still wavering, and even those
which had already declared in his favour. That act of
tyranny dissolved the charm which had created hope from
his government and awakened affections which had as yet
only slumbered. Those to whom this event was almost
indifferent also joined in condemning it ; for there are
certain aristocratic ideas which are always fashionable in
a certain class of society. Thus for different causes this
atrocity gave a retrograde direction to public opinion,
which had previously been favourably disposed to Bonaparte throughout the whole of France.

The consequences were not less important, and might
have been disastrous with respect to foreign Courts. I
learned, through a channel which does not permit me to
entertain any doubt of the correctness of my information,
that as soon as the Emperor Alexander received the news
it became clear that England might conceive a well-
founded hope of forming a new coalition against France.
Alexander openly expressed his indignation. I also
learned with equal certainty that when Mr. Pitt was informed of the death of the French Prince he said, "Bonaparte has now done himself more mischief than we have
done him since the last declaration of war."[2] Pitt was
not the man to feel much concern for the death of any
one ; but he understood and seized all the advantages

[1] Compare with the passage where, in 1795, he wishes Bourrienne to buy for him,
in the beautiful valley of the Yonne, a small property to which he can retire. Then
came the Jour des Sections, and all the great dream of his ambition.

[2] The remark made on this murder by the astute cold-blooded Fouché is well
known. He said, "It was worse than a crime—it was a blunder ! "—(C'est plus
qu'un crime—c'est une faute).—Editor of 1836 Edition.

afforded to him by this great error of policy committed by the most formidable enemy of England. In all the Treasury journals published in London Bonaparte was never spoken of under any other name than that of the " assassin of the Duc d'Enghien."

The inert policy of the Cabinet of Vienna prevented the manifestation of its displeasure by remonstrances, or by any outward act. At Berlin, in consequence of the neighbourhood of the French troops in Hanover, the commiseration for the death of the Duc d'Enghien was also confined to the King's cabinet, and more particularly to the *salons* of the Queen of Prussia ; but it is certain that that transaction almost everywhere changed the disposition of sovereigns towards the First Consul, and that if it did not cause, it at least hastened the success of the negotiations which England was secretly carrying on with Austria and Prussia. Every Prince of Germany was offended by the violation of the Grand Duke of Baden's territory, and the death of a Prince could not fail everywhere to irritate that kind of sympathy of blood and of race which had hitherto always influenced the crowned heads and sovereign families of Europe ; for it was felt as an injury to all of them.

When Louis XVIII. learned the death of the Duc d'Enghien he wrote to the King of Spain, returning him the insignia of the Order of the Golden Fleece (which had also been conferred on Bonaparte), with the accompanying letter :—

SIRE, MONSIEUR, AND DEAR COUSIN—It is with regret that I send back to you the insignia of the Order of the Golden Fleece which his Majesty, your father, of glorious memory conferred upon me. There can be nothing in common between me and the great criminal whom audacity and fortune have placed on my throne, since he has had the barbarity to stain himself with the blood of a Bourbon, the Duc d'Enghien.

Religion might make me pardon an assassin, but the tyrant of my people must always be my enemy.

In the present age it is more glorious to merit a sceptre than to possess one.

Providence, for incomprehensible reasons, may condemn me to end my days in exile, but neither my contemporaries nor posterity shall ever have to say, that in the period of adversity I showed myself unworthy of occupying the throne of my ancestors.

LOUIS.

The death of the Duc d'Enghien was a horrible episode in the proceedings of the great trial which was then preparing, and which was speedily followed by the accession of Bonaparte to the Imperial dignity. It was not one of the least remarkable anomalies of the epoch to see the judgment by which criminal enterprises against the Republic were condemned pronounced in the name of the Emperor who had so evidently destroyed that Republic. This anomaly certainly was not removed by the subtlety, by the aid of which he at first declared himself Emperor of the Republic, as a preliminary to his proclaiming himself Emperor of the French. Setting aside the means, it must be acknowledged that it is impossible not to admire the genius of Bonaparte, his tenacity in advancing towards his object, and that adroit employment of suppleness and audacity which made him sometimes dare fortune, sometimes avoid difficulties which he found insurmountable, to arrive, not merely at the throne of Louis XVI., but at the reconstructed throne of Charlemagne.

Note.—Although the details of the death of the Duc d'Enghien are well known, some remarks may be made here. It is not evident what Napoleon gained by the step. From that moment he must have expected that the Royalists would turn from him, and it is strange that so many continued or afterwards consented to serve him. His proclaiming himself Emperor would have reassured the Republicans without shedding blood. He was quite capable of the execution, if he believed it necessary; but, as he himself said, "Great men are never cruel except from necessity," and here the necessity is not evident. If the reader compares the account of Madame de Rémusat (tome i. chap. v.), which agrees fairly with Bourrienne's account of what Josephine said to him (note especially the description in both of Savary's state), it will be seen that all Napoleon's actions are consonant with an intention to pardon the Prince at the last moment. His first anger was over, and he was not the man to uselessly act in private the foolish and ignoble part he did in repeating the following lines if he had intended the Prince to die:—

"Des Dieux que nous servons connais la différence :
Les tiens t'ont commandé le meurtre et la vengeance ;
Et le mien, quand ton bras vient de m'assassiner,
M'ordonne de te plaindre et de te pardonner."

(*Alzire*, Act V. Scene vii.)

(Know the difference between the Gods we serve. Thine have commanded thee murder and revenge, while, when thy arm drops from assassinating me, mine have ordered me to pity and pardon you.)

The most striking point of the whole matter is the implicit obedience that was paid to Napoleon's order, if such order were ever given to carry out the sentence without referring to him. In the very height of his power, when he wished to try such an unimportant personage as the Prince of Hatzfeld in Berlin in 1806, the men immediately around him determined this should not be done ; and they seemed to have taken for granted that if the Princess once saw Napoleon he was sure to pardon her husband. Why, we may ask, did not some person stir when they knew that such action would for ever constitute a claim on the Bourbons, who then were thought not far from the throne? Talleyrand, later, bore all the violent wrath of Napoleon without shrinking. He now at most kept silence. Savary, later, took on himself all the responsibility of evacuating Madrid after Baylen, knowing that the Emperor would storm. He was in command of the troops temporarily occupying Vincennes. With all his faults he was not the man to shrink from delaying the execution till Napoleon had been referred to. We know that Réal, one of the heads of the police, was ordered to go to Vincennes to examine the Prince. He would have found him at last fully aware of the danger of his position, and likely to make the appeal to the First Consul for which Napoleon may have been waiting ; an accident prevented him starting till too late. The extraordinary haste is strange, as no pressure seems to have been put on Napoleon, though the intended seizure of the Prince was known to many. It is easy for persons unacquainted with the difficulties of command to say that Napoleon was responsible for everything done ; but there is one theory which, if true, would explain all. Napoleon, the first burst of anger over, never intended to kill the Prince ; he meant to release him after obtaining some appeal from him damaging to his cause. The whole scene was prepared. Napoleon, left unsolicited, was to receive and comply with the appeal of the frightened Prince. But men around him wished to tie his hands, and bind him to the Revolutionary party. They did not understand how little he was made to play Monk's part : they dreaded his intentions and they forced his hand, just as the ministers of Elizabeth forced hers in the execution of Mary. Napoleon, with the words of mercy on his lips, finds that the Prince is dead ; he sees how vain it would be to disclaim the act, and he boldly accepts it. This was the view of Savary (see especially tome ii. p. 377). There is nothing unlikely about it. Such men as Talleyrand had everything then to dread from the return of the Bourbons ; they, not Napoleon, gained by the act. Talleyrand disclaimed any part in the matter, especially after his tenure of power, during the Provisional Government in 1814, had placed the records of the Foreign Office in his hands, and enabled him to destroy any incriminatory documents. Napoleon, while the evidence existed, and the event was fresh in the memory of men, accused Talleyrand of having advised the act. It is necessary to remember that Bourrienne was under obligations to Talleyrand at the time he wrote. The Princesse de Canino, the second wife of Lucien, says that she had seen a letter of Talleyrand to Napoleon tending to persuade him to try the Duc d'Enghien by a council of war. This letter, she says, was shown to Thiers, who refused to use it for his history, saying that to do so would be an act of ingratitude on his part towards Talleyrand, to whom he owed his political position (Iung's *Lucien*, tome ii. p. 432, note). Three days after the execution Talleyrand gave a ball, a proceeding in accordance with his answer to the question why, if he disapproved the act, he did not resign his post? "If *he* has committed a crime, that is no reason why *I* should commit a folly." For the men of the Revolution the murder was a gain; they made an accomplice of the man who hated their party, and whose intentions they doubted, while the act was in accordance with their conduct whenever, before or afterwards, they possessed power. For Napoleon the act was without object, and in utter contrast with his conduct in all previous and subsequent cases of the sort. One gain there was. Talleyrand, Fouché, or whoever was the author of the saying, "C'est pire qu'un crime, c'est une faute," was not quite right. "For humanity's sake," says Thiers (tome iv. p. 608), "one is sorry to say that the terror inspired by the First Consul acted efficaciously on the Bourbon Princes and the *émigrés*. . . . From this day plots of this sort ceased." See Savary's account in tome ii. p. 337, and Bulwer's (Lord Dalling) *Historical Sketches*, p. 126, both of which come to much the same conclusion as here expressed.

Some surprise has been expressed that so few attempts were made on the life of Napoleon. See, for example, the curious and not very creditable conversation of the Prince de Liechtenstein with Vitrolles in March 1814, when the Prince, forgetting the German subserviency, wondered that the acts of tyranny exercised on the nation and on individuals had never armed 'un bras vengeur,'" *i.e.*, an assassin (*Vitrolles*, tome i. p. 75). Napoleon himself always said that he knew any man who ventured his own life could take his. His safety was probably due to some simple precautions (see *D' Odeleben*, tome i. p. 163, copied in *Alison*, vol. x. p. 294), and also, quite as probably, to the absence, during the time of his power, of any of the great personal hatred affected, and perhaps felt, when he had fallen. The plots of the infernal machine and others, during the early days of the Consulate, were aimed at him as head of the Government, not as an individual. After Napoleon's fall from power it was natural that he should have a greater dread of attempts on his life. Dethroned Princes seldom live long. The Maubreuil affair, dealt with in this work under the year 1814, showed at least the possibility of an assassination, which would have been so convenient for many of the new adherents of the Bourbons.. We know that the Allies intended to remove Napoleon from Elba to some distant island (see the *Talleyrand Correspondence*, specially vol. i. p. 48); and it was practically certain that he would resist the attempt to consign him to the living tomb destined for him, when the struggle would offer many chances for his death. It might have been awkward to entrust such a mission to any of the regular and honourable officers of the allied fleets, and we find a plan laid before Talleyrand for seizing Napoleon on board his brig while coasting round Elba, which was to have been carried out by one of his own discontented officers. The plot was discovered by Napoleon, who seems to have had a probably not misplaced anxiety as to other attempts on his life. See the account of a very unfriendly writer (Iung's *Lucien*, tome iii. chap. ix.) On the whole it is difficult not to come to the conclusion that the real affection felt for Napoleon by the men immediately around him gave him a better safeguard than all the precautions of most sovereigns can procure for themselves.

If it be thought that Napoleon's anxiety was affected, it should be remembered that, putting aside some exclamations when in a rage, he ceased to express them when under the charge of English officers at St. Helena. His belief that a confinement there was intended to hasten his death cannot be thought unreasonable when we consider the hereditary disease of his family, the existence of which can hardly have been unknown to the allied Governments. Talleyrand had another explanation. Asked why some of the best French sovereigns had been attacked by assassins while none attempted the life of Napoleon, Talleyrand replied, "What else do you expect? there is no longer any religion in France" (*Vitrolles*, tome i. p. 58).

CHAPTER XXIV.

1804.

Pichegru betrayed—His arrest—His conduct to his old *aide de camp*—
Account of Pichegru's family, and his education at Brienne—Permission to visit M. Carbonnet—The prisoners in the Temple—Absurd
application of the word "brigand"—Moreau and the state of public
opinion respecting him—Pichegru's firmness—Pichegru strangled in
prison—Public opinion at the time—Report on the death of Pichegru.

I SHALL now proceed to relate what I knew at the time and
what I have since learnt of the different phases of the trial
of Georges, Pichegru, Moreau, and the other persons accused of conspiracy,—a trial to all the proceedings of
which I closely attended. From those proceedings I was
convinced that Moreau was no conspirator, but at the
same time I must confess that it is very probable the First
Consul might believe that he had been engaged in the
plot, and I am also of opinion that the real conspirators
believed Moreau to be their accomplice and their chief ;
for the object of the machinations of the police agents was
to create a foundation for such a belief, it being important
to the success of their scheme.

It has been stated that Moreau was arrested on the day
after the confessions made by Bouvet de Lozier ; Pichegru
was taken by means of the most infamous treachery that
a man can be guilty of. The official police had at last ascertained that he was in Paris, but they could not learn the
place of his concealment. The police agents had in vain
exerted all their efforts to discover him, when an old
friend, who had given him his last asylum, offered to deliver him up for 100,000 crowns. This infamous fellow

gave an exact description of the chamber which Pichegru occupied in the Rue de Chabanais, and in consequence of his information Comminges, commissary of police, proceeded thither, accompanied by some determined men. Precautions were necessary, because it was known that Pichegru was a man of prodigious bodily strength, and that besides, as he possessed the means of defence, he would not allow himself to be taken without making a desperate resistance. The police entered his chamber by using false keys, which the man who had sold him had the baseness to get made for them. A light was burning on his night table. The party of police, directed by Comminges, overturned the table, extinguished the light, and threw themselves on the general, who struggled with all his strength, and cried out loudly. They were obliged to bind him, and in this state the conqueror of Holland was removed to the Temple, out of which he was destined never to come alive.[1]

It must be owned that Pichegru was far from exciting the same interest as Moreau. The public, and more especially the army, never pardoned him for his negotiations with the Prince de Condé prior to the 18th Fructidor. However, I became acquainted with a trait respecting him while he was in Paris which I think does him much

[1] In *Erreurs* (tome ii. p. 69), a writer, apparently Réal himself, denies most of Bourrienne's account. Pichegru was betrayed by a man named Blanc, of the Bourse, who, agreeing to receive him, then betrayed him for 100,000 francs, which were paid. Blanc then had the audacity to ask for the Legion of Honour, and was ordered to leave Paris. He went to Hamburg, but did not stay there. Pichegru was seized without the light being extinguished; he kicked a gendarme in the stomach, and was himself wounded by a sword-thrust near the knee. At last he was bound and gagged, to stop his shouts. He was then carried, naked, tied, and gagged, and placed stretched on the floor of the cabinet of Réal, one of the chiefs of the police, where at last, worn out by his cries and fury, he answered the questions put to him. Thiers (tome iv. p. 575) gives a curious story of Pichegru, while trying to evade the police, going at night to the house of M. de Barbé Marbois, then Ministre du Trésor, one of the members of the Legislature who had been transported to Sinnamarri with Pichegru, after the 18th Fructidor, and who, like him, had escaped. Marbois, one of the most honourable of the Ministers, received him, and afterwards acknowledged to Napoleon what he had done. "The First Consul answered by a letter which was a noble approbation of his (Marbois') generous conduct."

honour.	A son of M. Lagrenée, formerly director of the French Academy at Rome, had been one of Pichegru's *aides de camp*.	This young man, though he had obtained the rank of captain, resigned on the banishment of his general, and resumed the pencil, which he had laid aside for the sword.	Pichegru, while he was concealed in Paris, visited his former *aide de camp*, who insisted upon giving him an asylum; but Pichegru positively refused to accept M. Lagrenée's offer, being determined not to commit a man who had already given him so strong a proof of friendship.	I learned this fact by a singular coincidence.	At this period Madame de Bourrienne wished to have a portrait of one of our children; she was recommended to M. Lagrenée, and he related the circumstance to her.

It was on the night of the 22d of February that Pichegru was arrested in the manner I have described. The deceitful friend who gave him up was named Le Blanc, and he went to settle at Hamburg with the reward of his treachery, I had entirely lost sight of Pichegru since we left Brienne, for Pichegru was also a pupil of that establishment; but, being older than either Bonaparte or I, he was already a tutor when we were only scholars, and I very well recollect that it was he who examined Bonaparte in the four first rules of arithmetic.

Pichegru belonged to an agricultural family of Franche-Comté.	He had a relation, a minim,[1] in that country. The minims, who had the charge of educating the pupils of the Military School of Brienne, being very poor, and their poverty not enabling them to hold out much inducement to other persons to assist them, they applied to the minims of Franche-Comté.	In consequence of this application Pichegru's relation, and some other minims, repaired to Brienne.	An aunt of Pichegru, who was a sister of the order of charity, accompanied them, and the care of the infirmary was entrusted to her.	This good woman

[1] A brother of the order founded by S. Francis de Paulo.

took her nephew to Brienne with her, and he was educated at the school gratuitously. As soon as his age permitted, Pichegru was made a tutor; but all his ambition was to become a minim. He was, however, dissuaded from that pursuit by his relation, and he adopted the military profession. There is this further remarkable circumstance in the youth of Pichegru, that, though he was older by several years than Bonaparte, they were both made lieutenants of artillery at the same time. What a difference in their destiny! While the one was preparing to ascend a throne the other was a solitary prisoner in the dungeon of the Temple.

I had no motive to induce me to visit either the Temple or La Force, but I received at the time circumstantial details of what was passing in those prisons, particularly in the former; I went, however, frequently to St. Pélagie, where M. Carbonnet was confined. As soon as I knew that he was lodged in that prison I set about getting an admission from Réal, who smoothed all difficulties. M. Carbonnet was detained two months in solitary confinement. He was several times examined, but the interrogatories produced no result, and, notwithstanding the desire to implicate him in consequence of the known intimacy between him and Moreau, it was at last found impossible to put him on trial with the other parties accused.

The Temple had more terrors than St. Pélagie, but not for the prisoners who were committed to it, for none of those illustrious victims of police machination displayed any weakness, with the exception of Bouvet de Lozier, who, being sensible of his weakness, wished to prevent its consequences by death. The public, however, kept their attention riveted on the prison in which Moreau was confined. I have already mentioned that Pichegru was conveyed thither on the night of the 22d of February; a fortnight later Georges was arrested, and committed to the same prison.

Either Réal or Desmarets, and sometimes both together, repaired to the Temple to examine the prisoners.   In vain the police endeavoured to direct public odium against the prisoners by placarding lists of their names through the whole of Paris, even before they were arrested.   In those lists they were styled " brigands," and at the head of " the brigands," the name of General Moreau shone conspicuously.   An absurdity without a parallel.   The effect produced was totally opposite to that calculated on ; for, as no person could connect the idea of a brigand with that of a general who was the object of public esteem, it was naturally concluded that those whose names were placarded along with his were no more brigands than he.

Public opinion was decidedly in favour of Moreau,[1] and every one was indignant at seeing him described as a brigand.   Far from believing him guilty, he was regarded as a victim fastened on because his reputation embarrassed Bonaparte ; for Moreau had always been looked up to as capable of opposing the accomplishment of the First Consul's ambitious views.   The whole crime of Moreau was his having numerous partisans among those who still clung to the phantom of the Republic, and that crime was unpardonable in the eyes of the First Consul, who for two years had ruled the destinies of France as sovereign master.   What means were not employed to mislead the opinion of the public respecting Moreau ?   The police published pamphlets of all sorts, and the Comte de Montgaillard was brought from Lyons to draw up a libel implicating him with Pichegru and the exiled Princes. But nothing that was done produced the effect proposed.

The weak character of Moreau is known.   In fact, he allowed himself to be circumvented by a few intriguers, who endeavoured to derive advantage from the influence of his name.   But he was so decidedly opposed to the re-establishment of the ancient system that he replied to one

[1] Little anticipating then that he was to die fighting against France !

of the agents who addressed him, "I cannot put myself at the head of any movement for the Bourbons, and such an attempt would not succeed. If Pichegru act on another principle—and even in that case I have told him that the Consuls and the Governor of Paris must disappear [1]—I believe that I have a party strong enough in the Senate to obtain possession of authority, and I will immediately make use of it to protect his friends ; public opinion will then dictate what may be fit to be done, but I will promise nothing in writing." Admitting these words attributed to Moreau to be true, they prove that he was dissatisfied with the Consular Goverment, and that he wished a change ; but there is a great difference between a conditional wish and a conspiracy.

The commander of the principal guard of the Temple was General Savary, and he had reinforced that guard by his select gendarmerie. The prisoners did not dare to communicate one with another for fear of mutual injury, but all evinced a courage which created no little alarm as to the consequences of the trial. Neither offers nor threats produced any confessions in the course of the interrogatories. Pichegru, in particular, displayed an extraordinary firmness, and Réal one day, on leaving the chamber where he had been examining him, said aloud in the presence of several persons, "What a man that Pichegru is ! "

Forty days elapsed after the arrest of General Pichegru when, on the morning of the 6th of April, he was found dead in the chamber he occupied in the Temple. Pichegru had undergone ten examinations ; [2] but he had made no

---

[1] The phrase here attributed on good authority to Moreau should be noted. The Consuls were to *disappear*. The King, the Girondists, Robespierre, etc., had *disappeared*. Whatever Moreau may have meant, the word was practically a recommendation for assassination, judicial or otherwise.

[2] The author of the observations on the trial of Pichegru, Georges, etc., in the collection entitled *Bourrienne et ses Erreurs,* is apparently one of the persons who was employed in instructing or preparing that extraordinary process, perhaps M. Réal himself. In adverting to the statement (*Erreurs,* tome ii. pp. 69-96) that

PICHEGRU.

confessions, and no person was committed by his replies. All his declarations, however, gave reason to believe that he would speak out, and that too in a lofty and energetic manner during the progress of the trial. "When I am before my judges," said he, "my language shall be conformable to truth and the interests of my country." What would that language have been? Without doubt there was no wish that it should be heard. Pichegru would have kept his promise, for he was distinguished for his firmness of character above everything, even above his qualities as a soldier; differing in this respect from Moreau, who allowed himself to be guided by his wife and mother-in-law, both of whom displayed ridiculous pretensions in their visits to Madame Bonaparte.

The day on which Réal spoke before several persons of Pichegru in the way I have related was the day of his last examination. I afterwards learned, from a source on which I can rely, that during his examination Pichegru, though careful to say nothing which could affect the other prisoners, showed no disposition to be tender of him who had sought and resolved his death, but evinced a firm resolution to unveil before the public the odious machinery of the plot into which the police had drawn him. He also

---

Pichegru underwent ten interrogatories, he remarks that the number is great, but that he knew of four. One, he says, took place in the presence of numerous witnesses, and that this precaution was adopted because it was suspected that Pichegru would refuse to sign his deposition. At the close of this examination M. Réal perceived an old translation of Xenophon lying on the general's table, which induced him to ask whether he wished to have books to read. "I should like one," said Pichegru. "What book do you want?" asked the Counsellor of State, and added, "Would you like travels?"—"Oh, no! I am tired of travels," was the answer, with a melancholy smile. "Well, then, what book would you have?"—"Seneca."— "Seneca!" said the prefect, with an allusion which was evidently quickly felt by the prisoner. "Why, general, the gamester does not ask for Seneca until the game is lost, and the game is not yet——" Pichegru did not allow the sentence to be finished, but said hastily, "Have the goodness to order a Seneca to be sent in to me." —"A French or a Latin one?" Pichegru hesitated, and after a moment's reflection said, "Let me have a Latin one, I can understand it still." The Seneca was sent, and the day after the suicide it was found on Pichegru's table. It was open, and turned down at the place where Seneca says that when public liberty must be despaired of, the upright man has nothing to do but to die.—*Editor of 1836 Edition.*

declared that he and his companions had no longer any
object but to consider of the means of leaving Paris, with
the view of escaping from the snares laid for them when
their arrest took place.   He declared that they had all of
them given up the idea of overturning the power of Bonaparte, a scheme into which they had been enticed by
shameful intrigues.   I am convinced the dread excited by
his manifestation of a resolution to speak out with the
most rigid candour hastened the death of Pichegru.   M.
Réal, who is still living, knows better than any one else
what were Pichegru's declarations, as he interrogated him.
I know not whether that gentleman will think fit, either
at the present or some future period, to raise the veil of
mystery which hangs over these events, but of this I am
sure, he will be unable to deny anything I advance.   There
is evidence almost amounting to demonstration that Pichegru was strangled in prison, and consequently all idea of
suicide must be rejected as inadmissible.   Have I positive
and substantive proof of what I assert?   I have not; but
the concurrence of facts and the weight of probabilities
do not leave me in possession of the doubts I should wish
to entertain on that tragic event.   Besides, there exists a
certain popular instinct, which is rarely at fault, and it
must be in the recollection of many, not only that the
general opinion favoured the notion of Pichegru's assassination, but that the pains taken to give that opinion another direction, by the affected exhibition of the body,
only served to strengthen it.[1]   He who spontaneously

[1] The following are a few extracts from the report of the examination of Pichegru's body, which took place on the 16th of April 1804:—

"The body had round the neck a black silk handkerchief, through which was
passed a stick about forty centimetres (nearly sixteen inches) long, and from four to
five (one and a half to two inches) in circumference, which after being twisted round
in the handkerchief, was stopped by the left cheek, against which one of its extremities rested, and which had produced a strangulation sufficient to occasion death."

A gendarme, named Sirot, next declares, "that being on duty as a sentinel outside of the Temple, near Pichegru's apartment, he several times heard a coughing
and spitting in the said apartment, and that he thought he could perceive from the
manner of the coughing and spitting that a person was suffering from oppression,

says, I have not committed such or such a crime, at least admits there is room for suspecting his guilt.

The truth is, the tide of opinion never set in with such force against Bonaparte as during the trial of Moreau; nor was the popular sentiment in error on the subject of the death of Pichegru, who was clearly strangled in the Temple by secret agents. The authors, the actors, and the witnesses of the horrible prison scenes of the period are the only persons capable of removing the doubts which still hang over the death of Pichegru ; but I must nevertheless contend that the preceding circumstances, the general belief at the time, and even probability, are in contradiction with any idea of suicide on the part of Pichegru. His death was considered necessary, and this necessity was its real cause.

but having heard nothing more of it, he did not think it necessary to give any alarm."

One Lapointe, who was orderly in the tower of the Temple, declares "that having slept from midnight until four in the morning he heard nothing."

Fauconnier declares "that at half-past seven in the morning citizen Popon, the turnkey on duty, informed him that he had lighted a fire in Pichegru's chamber, and that he was surprised at his not stirring." He added, "that he took the key of Pichegru's apartment at ten o'clock on the preceding night, after giving the general his supper ; that it remained in his pocket until he lighted the fire."

The following is Savary's account of Pichegru's death :—

"General Pichegru was lying on his right side ; he had put round his neck his own black silk cravat, which he had previously twisted like a small rope : this must have occupied him so long as to afford time for reflection had he not been resolutely bent on self-destruction. He appeared to have tied his cravat thus twisted about his neck, and to have at first drawn it as tight as he could bear it, then to have taken a piece of wood, of the length of a finger, which he had taken from a branch that yet lay in the middle of the room (part of a faggot, the relics of which were still in his fireplace); this he must have slipped between his neck and his cravat, on the right side, and turned round till the moment that reason forsook him. His head had fallen back on the pillow and compressd the little bit of stick, which had prevented the cravat from untwisting. In this situation apoplexy could not fail to supervene. His hand was still under his head and almost touched this little tourniquet " (*Memoirs of the Duc de Rovigo*, vol. ii. p. 78).

CHAPTER XXV.

1804.

Arrest of Georges—The fruiterer's daughter of the Rue de la Montagne
St. Geneviève—Louis Bonaparte's visit to the Temple—General
Lauriston—Arrest of Villeneuve and Barco—Villeneuve wounded—
Moreau during his imprisonment—Preparations for leaving the
Temple—Remarkable change in Georges—Addresses and congratula-
tions—Speech of the First Consul forgotten—Secret negotiations with
the Senate—Official proposition of Bonaparte's elevation to the
Empire—Sitting of the Council of State—Interference of Bonaparte
—Individual votes—Seven against twenty—*His* subjects and *his*
people—Appropriateness of the title of Emperor—Communications
between Bonaparte and the Senate—Bonaparte first called *Sire* by
Cambacérès—First letter signed by Napoleon as Emperor—Grand
levee at the Tuileries—Napoleon's address to the Imperial Guard—
Organic *Sénatus-consulte*—Revival of old formulas and titles—The
Republicanism of Lucien—The Spanish Princess—Lucien's clandes-
tine marriage—Bonaparte's influence on the German Princes—Intrigues of England—Drake at Munich—Project for overthrowing
Bonaparte's Government—Circular from the Minister for Foreign
Affairs to the members of the Diplomatic Body—Answers to that
circular.

GEORGES was arrested about seven o'clock, on the evening
of the 9th of March, with another conspirator, whose
name, I think, was Lèridan. Georges was stopped in a
cabriolet on the Place de l'Odéon, whither he had no
doubt been directed by the police agent, who was constantly about him. In not seizing him at his lodgings,
the object, probably, was to give more publicity to his
arrest, and to produce an effect upon the minds of the
multitude. This calculation cost the life of one man, and
had well-nigh sacrificed the lives of two, for Georges, who
constantly carried arms about him, first shot dead the

police officer who seized the horse's reins, and wounded another who advanced to arrest him in the cabriolet. Besides his pistols there was found upon him a poniard of English manufacture.

Georges lodged with a woman named Lemoine, who kept a fruiterer's shop in the Rue de la Montagne St. Geneviève, and on the evening of the 9th of March he had just left his lodging to go, it was said, to a perfumer's named Caron.[1] It is difficult to suppose that the circumstance of the police being on the spot was the mere effect of chance. The fruiterer's daughter was putting into the cabriolet a parcel belonging to Georges at the moment of his arrest. Georges, seeing the officers advance to seize him, desired the girl to get out of the way, fearing lest he should shoot her when he fired on the officers. She ran into a neighbouring house, taking the parcel along with her. The police, it may readily be supposed, were soon after her. The master of the house in which she had taken refuge, curious to know what the parcel contained, had opened it, and discovered, among other things, a bag containing 1000 Dutch sovereigns, from which he acknowledged he had abstracted a considerable sum. He and his wife, as well as the fruiterer's daughter, were all arrested ; as to Georges, he was taken that same evening to the Temple, where he remained until his removal to the Conciergerie when the trial commenced.

During the whole of the legal proceedings Georges and

[1] The author of the observations on the trial of Pichegru, Georges, etc., already quoted, admits the truth (vol. ii. p. 91) of the statement that Georges was expected by this Caron, who on the Restoration was appointed perfumer to the Duchesse d'Angoulême, and afterwards became one of the ushers of the chamber. He is described as a profligate hypocrite. His immoral excesses, however, did not prevent the Tartuffe from being remarkably devout. He was extremely attentive to religious ceremonies, and made masses be said to the Holy Ghost, to ascertain whether God approved of his giving an asylum to Georges. When Caron was examined this pious invocation gave not a little amusement to M. Réal : "What answer did the Holy Ghost give you?" said he. "None at all," replied the perfumer, quite coolly. "Why then did you resolve to give the asylum?" "Because," replied the pious peruquier, "silence is consent."—*Editor of* 1836 *edition.*

the other important prisoners were kept in solitary confinement. Immediately on Pichegru's death the prisoners were informed of the circumstance. As they were all acquainted with the general, and none believed the fact of his reported suicide, it may easily be conceived what consternation and horror the tragical event excited among them. I learned, and I was sorry to hear of it, that Louis Bonaparte, who was an excellent man, and, beyond all comparison, the best of the family, had the cruel curiosity to see Georges in his prison a few days after the death of Pichegru,[1] and when the sensation of horror excited by that event in the interior of the Temple was at its height, Louis repaired to the prison, accompanied by a brilliant escort of staff-officers, and General Savary introduced him to the prisoners. When Louis arrived, Georges was lying on his bed with his hands strongly bound by manacles. Lauriston, who accompanied Louis, related to me some of the particulars of this visit, which, in spite of his sincere devotedness to the First Consul, he assured me had been very painful to him.

After the arrest of Georges there were still some individuals marked out as accomplices in the conspiracy who had found means to elude the search of the police. The persons last arrested were, I think, Villeneuve, one of the principal confidants of Georges, Burban Malabre, who went by the name of Barco, and Charles d'Hozier. They were not taken till five days after the arrest of the Duc d'Enghien. The famous Commissioner Comminges, accompanied by an inspector and a detachment of *gendarmes d'Élite*, found Villeneuve and Burban Malabre in the house of a man named Dubuisson, in the Rue Jean Robert. This Dubuisson and his wife had sheltered some of the principal persons proscribed by the police. The Messieurs

---

[1] Joseph Bonaparte (*Erreurs*, tome ii. p. 138) discredits the visit of Louis to Georges. The alleged visit of the son of Louis, Louis Napoleon, to Orsini, when the latter was awaiting execution for his attempt to assassinate him, and its connection with the Italian war of 1859, may be remembered by the reader.

de Polignac and M. de Rivière had lodged with them.
When the police came to arrest Villeneuve and Burban
Malabre the people with whom they lodged declared that
they had gone away in the morning. The officers, however, searched the house, and discovered a secret door
within a closet. They called, and receiving no answer,
the gendarmerie had recourse to one of those expedients
which were, unfortunately, too familiar to them. They
fired a pistol through the door. Villeneuve, who went by
the name of Joyau, was wounded in the arm, which
obliged him and his companion to come from the place of
their concealment, and they were then made prisoners.

Moreau was not treated with the degree of rigour
observed towards the other prisoners. Indeed, it would
not have been safe so to treat him, for even in his prison
he received the homage and respect of all the military, not
excepting even those who were his guards. Many of
these soldiers had served under him, and it could not be
forgotten how much he was beloved by the troops he had
commanded. He did not possess that irresistible charm
which in Bonaparte excited attachment, but his mildness
of temper and excellent character inspired love and respect. It was the general opinion in Paris that a single
word from Moreau to the soldiers in whose custody he
was placed would in a moment have converted the gaoler-
guard into a guard of honour, ready to execute all that
might be required for the safety of the conqueror of
Hohenlinden. Perhaps the respect with which he was
treated and the indulgence of daily seeing his wife and
child were but artful calculations for keeping him within
the limits of his usual character. Besides, Moreau was so
confident of the injustice of the charge brought against
him that he was calm and resigned, and showed no disposition to rouse the anger of an enemy who would have
been happy to have some real accusation against him. To
these causes combined I always attributed the resignation,

and I may say the indifference, of Moreau while he was in prison and on his trial.

When the legal preparations for the trial were ended the prisoners of the Temple were permitted to communicate with each other, and, viewing their fate with that indifference which youth, misfortune, and courage inspired, they amused themselves with some of those games which usually serve for boyish recreation. While they were thus engaged the order arrived for their removal to the Conciergerie. The firmness of all remained unshaken, and they made their preparations for departure as if they were going about any ordinary business. This fortitude was particularly remarkable in Georges, in whose manner a change had taken place which was remarked by all his companions in misfortune.

For some time past the agents of Government throughout France had been instructed to solicit the First Consul to grant for the people what the people did not want, but what Bonaparte wished to take while he appeared to yield to the general will, namely, unlimited sovereign authority, free from any subterfuge of denomination. The opportunity of the great conspiracy just discovered, and in which Bonaparte had not incurred a moment's danger, as he did at the time of the infernal machine, was not suffered to escape ; that opportunity was, on the contrary, eagerly seized by the authorities of every rank, civil, ecclesiastical, and military, and a torrent of addresses, congratulations, and thanksgivings inundated the Tuileries. Most of the authors of these addresses did not confine themselves to mere congratulations ; they entreated Bonaparte to *consolidate his work,* the true meaning of which was that it was time he should make himself Emperor and establish hereditary succession. Those who on other occasions had shown an officious readiness to execute Bonaparte's commands did not now fear to risk his displeasure by opposing the opinion he had expressed in the Council of State on the discussion of the question of the Consulate for life. Bonaparte then said, "Hereditary succession is absurd. It is irreconcilable with the principle of the sovereignty of the people, and impossible in France."

In this scene of the grand drama Bonaparte played his part with his accustomed talent, keeping himself in the background and leaving to others the task of preparing the catastrophe. The Senate, who took the lead in the way of insinuation, did not fail, while congratulating the First Consul on his escape from the plots of foreigners, or, as they were officially styled, the daggers of England, to conjure him not to delay the completion of his work. Six days after the death of the Duc d'Enghien the Senate first expressed this wish. Either because Bonaparte began to repent of a useless crime, and felt the ill effect it must produce on the public mind, or because he found the language of the Senate somewhat vague, he left the address nearly a month unanswered, and then only replied by the request that the intention of the address might be more completely expressed. These negotiations between the Senate and the Head of the Government were not immediately published. Bonaparte did not like publicity except for what had arrived at a result ; but to attain the result which was the object of his ambition it was necessary that the project which he was maturing should be introduced in the Tribunate, and the tribune Curée had the honour to be the first to propose officially, on the 30th of April 1804, the conversion of the Consular Republic into an Empire, and the elevation of Bonaparte to the title of Emperor, with the rights of hereditary succession.

If any doubts could exist respecting the complaisant part which Curée acted on this occasion one circumstance would suffice to remove them ; that is, that ten days before the development of his proposition Bonaparte had caused the question of founding the Empire and establishing hereditary succession in his family to be secretly discussed in the Council of State. I learned from one of the Councillors of State all that passed on that occasion, and I may remark that Cambacérès showed himself particularly eager in the Council of State, as well as afterwards in the Senate, to become the exalted subject of him who had been his first colleague in the Consulate.

About the middle of April, the Council of State being assembled as for an ordinary sitting, the First Consul, who was frequently present at the sittings, did not appear. Cambacérès arrived and took the Presidency in his quality of Second Consul, and it was remarked that his air was more solemn than usual, though he at all times affected gravity.

The partisans of hereditary succession were the majority, and resolved to present an address to the First Consul. Those of the Councillors who opposed this determined on their part to send a counter-address; and to avoid this clashing of opinions Bonaparte signified his wish that each member of the Council should send him his opinion individually, with his signature affixed. By a singular accident it happened to be Berlier's task to present to the First Consul the separate opinions of the Council. Out of the twenty-seven Councillors present only seven opposed the question. Bonaparte received them all most graciously, and told them, among other things, that he wished for hereditary power only for the benefit of France; that the citizens would never be *his* subjects, and that the French people would never be *his* people. Such were the preliminaries to the official proposition of Curée to the Tribunate, and upon reflection it was decided that, as all opposition would be useless and perhaps dangerous to the opposing party, the minority should join the majority. This was accordingly done.

The Tribunate having adopted the proposition of Curée, there was no longer any motive for concealing the overtures of the Senate. Its address to the First Consul was therefore published forty days after its date : *the pear was then ripe.* This period is so important that I must not omit putting together the most remarkable facts which either came within my own observation, or which I have learned since respecting the foundation of the Empire.

Bonaparte had a long time before spoken to me of the title of Emperor as being the most appropriate for the new sovereignty which he wished to found in France. This, he observed, was not restoring the old system entirely, and he dwelt much on its being the title which Cæsar had borne. He often said, " One may be the Emperor of a republic, but not the King of a republic, those two terms are incongruous."

In its first address the Senate had taken as a text the documents it had received from the Government in relation to the intrigues of Drake, who had been sent from England to Munich. That text afforded the opportunity for a vague expression of what the Senate termed the necessities of France. To give greater solemnity to the affair the Senate proceeded in a body to the Tuileries, and one thing which gave a peculiar character to the preconcerted advances of the Senate was that Cambacérès, the Second Consul, fulfilled his functions of President on this occasion, and delivered the address to the First Consul.

However, the First Consul thought the address of the Senate, which, I have been informed, was drawn up by François de Neufchâteau, was not expressed with sufficient clearness ; he therefore, after suffering a little interval to elapse, sent a message to the Senate signed by himself, in which he said, " Your address has been the object of my earnest consideration." And though the address contained no mention of hereditary succession, he added, " You consider the hereditary succession of the supreme magistracy necessary to defend the French people against the plots of our enemies and the agitation arising from rival ambition.   At the same time several of our institutions appear to you to require improvement so as to ensure the triumph of equality and public liberty, and to offer to the nation and the Government the double guarantee they require."   From the subsequent passages of the message it will be sufficient to extract the following : " We have been constantly guided by this great truth : that the sovereignty dwells with the French people, and that it is for their interest, happiness, and glory that the Supreme Magistracy, the Senate, the Council of State, the Legislative Body, the Electoral Colleges, and the different branches of the Government, are and must be instituted." The omission of the Tribunate in this enumeration is somewhat remarkable.   It announced a promise which was speedily realised.

The will of Bonaparte being thus expressed in his message to the Senate, that body, which was created to preserve the institutions consecrated by the Constitution of the year VIII., had no alternative but to submit to the intentions manifested by the First Consul.   The reply to the message was, therefore, merely a counterpart of the message itself.   It positively declared that hereditary government was essential to the happiness, the glory, and the prosperity of France, and that that government could be confided only to Bonaparte and his family.   While the Senate so complaisantly played its part in this well-got-up piece, yet, the better to impose on the credulity of the multitude, its reply, like Bonaparte's message, resounded with the words liberty and equality.   Indeed, it was impudently asserted in that reply that Bonaparte's accession to hereditary power would be a certain guarantee for the liberty of the press, a liberty which Bonaparte held in the greatest horror, and without which all other liberty is but a vain illusion.[1]

---

[1] In the original motion as prepared by Curée the Imperial dignity was to be declared hereditary in the *family* of Napoleon.   Previous to being formally read before

By this reply of the Senate the most important step was performed.   There now remained merely ceremonies to regulate and formulas to fill up.   These various arrangements occasioned a delay of a fortnight.   On the 18th of May the First Consul was greeted for the first time by the appellation of *Sire* by his former colleague, Cambacérès, who at the head of the Senate went to present to Bonaparte the organic *Sénatus-consulte* containing the foundation of the Empire.   Napoleon was at St. Cloud, whither the Senate proceeded in state.   After the speech of Cambacérès, in which the old designation of Majesty was for the first time revived, the EMPEROR replied :—

All that can contribute to the welfare of the country is essentially connected with my happiness.   I accept the title which you believe to be conducive to the glory of the nation.   I submit to the sanction of the people the law of hereditary succession.   I hope that France will never repent the honours she may confer on my family.   At all events, my spirit will not be with my posterity when they cease to merit the confidence and love of the great nation.

Cambacérès next went to congratulate the Empress, and then was realised to Josephine the prediction which I had made to her three years before at Malmaison.

the Tribunate, the First Consul sent for the document, and when it was returned it was found that the word *family* was altered to *descendants*. Fabre, the President of the Tribunate, who received the altered document from Maret, seeing the effect the alteration would have on the brothers of Napoleon, and finding that Maret affected to treat the change as immaterial, took on himself to restore the original form, and in that shape it was read by the unconscious Curée to the Tribunate. On this curious passage see *Miot de Melito*, tome ii. p. 179. As finally settled the descent of the crown in default of Napoleon's children was limited to Joseph and Louis and their descendants, but the power of adoption was given to Napoleon. The draft of the *Sénatus-consulte* was heard by the Council of State in silence, and Napoleon tried in vain to get even the most talkative of the members now to speak. The Senate were not unanimous in rendering the *Sénatus-consulte.* The three votes given against it were said to have been Grégoire, the former constitutional Bishop of Blois, Garat, who as Minister of Justice had read to Louis XVI. the sentence of death, and Lanjuinais, one of the very few survivors of the Girondists (*Miot*, tome ii. pp. 182–183). Thiers (tome v. p. 125) says there was only one dissentient voice. For the fury of the brothers of Napoleon, who saw the destruction of all their ambitious hopes in any measure for the descent of the crown except in the *family*, see *Miot*, tome ii. p. 172, where Joseph is described as cursing the ambition of his brother, and desiring his death as a benefit for France and his family.

Bonaparte's first act as Emperor, on the very day of his elevation to the Imperial throne, was the nomination of Joseph to the dignity of Grand Elector, with the title of Imperial Highness. Louis was raised to the dignity of Constable, with the same title, and Cambacérès and Lebrun were created Arch-Chancellor and Arch-Treasurer of the Empire. On the same day Bonaparte wrote the following letter to Cambacérès, the first which he signed as Emperor, and merely with the name of Napoleon :—

CITIZEN CONSUL CAMBACÉRÈS—Your title has changed ; but your functions and my confidence remain the same. In the high dignity with which you are now invested you will continue to manifest, as you have hitherto done in that of Consul, that wisdom and that distinguished talent which entitle you to so important a share in all the good which I may have effected. I have, therefore, only to desire the continuance of the sentiments you cherish towards the State and me.

Given at the Palace of St. Cloud, 28th Floréal, an XII. (18th May 1804).　　　　　　　　　(Signed)　　NAPOLEON.
　　　　By the Emperor.
　　　　　　H. B. MARET.

I have quoted this first letter of the Emperor because it is characteristic of Bonaparte's art in managing transitions. It was to the *Citizen Consul* that the Emperor addressed himself, and it was dated according to the Republican calendar. That calendar, together with the delusive inscription on the coin, were all that now remained of the Republic. Next day the Emperor came to Paris to hold a grand levee at the Tuileries, for he was not the man to postpone the gratification that vanity derived from his new dignity and title. The assembly was more numerous and brilliant than on any former occasion. Bessières having addressed the Emperor on the part of the Guards, the Emperor replied in the following terms : "I know the sentiments the Guards cherish towards me. I repose perfect confidence in their courage and fidelity. I constantly see, with renewed pleasure, companions in arms who have escaped so many dangers, and are covered with so many honourable wounds. I experience a sentiment of satisfaction when I look at the Guards, and think that there has not, for the last fifteen years, in any of the four quarters of the world, been a battle in which some of them have not taken part."

On the same day all the generals and colonels in Paris were presented to the Emperor by Louis Bonaparte, who had already begun to exercise his functions of Constable. In a few days everything assumed a new aspect; but in spite of the admiration which was openly expressed the Parisians secretly ridiculed the new courtiers. This greatly displeased Bonaparte, who was very charitably informed of it in order to check his prepossession in favour of the men of the old Court, such as the Comte de Ségur, and at a later period Comte Louis de Narbonne.

To give all possible solemnity to his accession Napoleon ordered that the Senate itself should proclaim in Paris the organic *Sénatus-consulte*, which entirely changed the Constitution of the State. By one of those anomalies which I have frequently had occasion to remark, the Emperor fixed for this ceremony Sunday, the 30th Floréal. That day was a festival in all Paris, while the unfortunate prisoners were languishing in the dungeons of the Temple.

On the day after Bonaparte's accession the old formulas were restored. The Emperor determined that the French Princes and Princesses should receive the title of Imperial Highness; that his sisters should take the same title; that the grand dignitaries of the Empire should be called Serene Highnesses; that the Princes and titularies of the grand dignitaries should be addressed by the title of *Monseigneur;* that M. Maret, the Secretary of State, should have the rank of Minister; that the ministers should retain the title of Excellency, to which should be added that of Monseigneur in the petitions addressed to them; and that the title of Excellency should be given to the President of the Senate.

At the same time Napoleon appointed the first Marshals of the Empire, and determined that they should be called *Monsieur le Maréchal* when addressed verbally, and *Monseigneur* in writing. The following are the names of these sons of the Republic transformed into props of the Empire : Berthier, Murat, Moncey, Jourdan, Masséna, Augereau, Bernadotte, Soult, Brune, Lannes, Mortier, Ney, Davoust, and Bessières. The title of Marshal of the Empire was also granted to the generals Kellerman, Lefebvre, Pérignon, and Serrurier, as having served as commanders-in-chief.[1]

The reader cannot have failed to observe that the name of Lucien has not been mentioned among the individuals of Bonaparte's family on whom dignities were conferred. The fact is, the two brothers were no longer on good terms with each other. Not, as it has been alleged, because Lucien wished to play the part of a Republican, but because he would not submit to the imperious will of Napoleon in a circumstance in which the latter counted on his brother's docility to serve the interests of his policy. In the conferences which preceded the great change in the form of government it was not Lucien but Joseph who, probably for the sake of sounding opinion, affected an opposition, which was by some mistaken for Republicanism. With regard to Lucien, as he had really rendered great services to Napoleon on the 19th Brumaire at St. Cloud, and as he himself exaggerated the value of those services, he saw no reward worthy of his ambition but a throne independent of his brother. It is certain that

---

[1] A complete list of the Marshals of the first Empire will be found in the *Memoirs of the Duchesse d'Abrantès* (Madame Junot), English edition of 1883, at the end of the third volume. The Maréchaux *de l'Empire* created by Napoleon I. must not be confused with the Maréchaux *de France* of the monarchy before the Revolution and after the Restoration. Francis I. had first caused the title to be held for life, but it had been abolished in 1792. As some of Napoleon's generals were made Maréchaux de France under the Restoration and the monarchy of July, and as Duroc, Duc de Frioul, the Grand Maréchal du Palais, is often, for brevity's sake, called Maréchal, there is apt to be great confusion about this title.

when at Madrid he had aspired to win the good graces of a
Spanish Infanta, and on that subject reports were circulated with which I have nothing to do, because I never
had any opportunity of ascertaining their truth.   All I
know is that, Lucien's first wife being dead, Bonaparte
wished him to marry a German Princess, by way of forming the first great alliance in the family.¹ Lucien, however, refused to comply with Napoleon's wishes, and he
secretly married the wife of an agent, named, I believe,
Joubertou, who for the sake of convenience was sent to
the West Indies, where he died shortly after.   When Bonaparte heard of this marriage from the priest by whom
it had been clandestinely performed, he fell into a furious
passion, and resolved not to confer on Lucien the title of
French Prince, on account of what he termed his unequal
match. Lucien, therefore, obtained no other dignity than
that of Senator.   Jerôme, who pursued an opposite line

¹ According to Lucien himself, Napoleon wished him to marry the Queen of Etruria, Maria-Louise, daughter of Charles IV. of Spain, who had married, 1795, Louis de
Bourbon, Prince of Parma, son of the Duke of Parma, to whom Napoleon had given
Tuscany in 1801 as the Kingdom of Etruria.   Her husband had died in May 1803,
and she governed in the name of her son. Lucien, whose first wife, Anne Christine
Boyer, had died in 1801, had married his second wife, Alexandrine Laurence de Bles-
champs, who had married, but who had divorced, a M. Jouberthon.   When Lucien
had been ambassador in Spain in 1801, charged among other things with obtaining
Elba, the Queen, he says, wished Napoleon should marry an Infanta,—Donna Isa-
bella, her youngest daughter, afterwards Queen of Naples (*Iung*, tome ii. pp. 66 and
130), an overture to which Napoleon seems not to have made any answer.   As for
Lucien, he objected to his brother that the Queen was ugly, and laughed at Napoleon's representations as to her being " propre " ; but at last he acknowledged his
marriage with Madame Jouberthon.   This made a complete break between the
brothers, and on hearing of the execution of the Duc d'Enghien, Lucien said to his
wife, " Alexandrine, let us go ; he has tasted blood."   He went to Italy, and in 1810
tried to go to the United States.   Taken prisoner by the English, he was detained
first at Malta, and then in England, at Ludlow Castle and at Thorngrove, till 1814,
when he went to Rome.   The Pope, who ever showed a kindly feeling towards the
Bonapartes, made the ex- " Brutus " Bonaparte Prince de Canino and Duc de Musi-
gnano.   In 1815 he joined Napoleon, and on the final fall of the Empire he was in-
terned at Rome till the death of his brother.   He lived to have his hopes raised by
the Revolution of July 1830, and to be horrified, by his nephew, Louis Napoleon's
wild attempt on Strasburg in 1836.   He died at Viterbo, 1840.   See *Lucien Bonaparte*, by Iung : Paris, Charpentier, 1883, in which work note the curious account by
Lucien of Napoleon constantly dreaming of being attacked and dragged from his
palace by a mob of *sans-culottes* headed by Lucien (*Iung*, tome ii. p. 302).

of conduct, was afterwards made a King.   As to Lucien's Republicanism, it did not survive the 18th Brumaire, and he was always a warm partisan of hereditary succession.

But I pass on to relate what I know respecting the almost incredible influence which, on the foundation of the Empire, Bonaparte exercised over the powers which did not yet dare to declare war against him.   I studied Bonaparte's policy closely, and I came to this conclusion on the subject, that he was governed by ambition, by the passion of dominion, and that no relations, on a footing of equality, between himself and any other power, could be of long duration.   The other States of Europe had only to choose one of two things—submission or war.   As to secondary States, they might thenceforth be considered as fiefs of the French Government ; and as they could not resist, Bonaparte easily accustomed them to bend to his yoke.   Can there be a stronger proof of this arbitrary influence than what occurred at Carlsruhe, after the violation of the territory of Baden, by the arrest of the Duc d'Enghien ?   Far from venturing to make any observation on that violation, so contrary to the rights of nations, the Grand Duke of Baden was obliged to publish, in his own State, a decree evidently dictated by Bonaparte. The decree stated, that many individuals formerly belonging to the army of Condé having come to the neighbourhood of Carlsruhe, his Electoral Highness had felt it his duty to direct that no individual coming from Condé's army, nor indeed any French emigrant, should, unless he had permission previously to the peace, make a longer sojourn than was allowed to foreign travellers.   Such was already the influence which Bonaparte exercised over Germany, whose Princes, to use an expression which he employed in a later decree, were crushed by the grand measures of the Empire.

But to be just, without however justifying Bonaparte, I must acknowledge that the intrigues which England

fomented in all parts of the Continent were calculated to
excite his natural irritability to the utmost degree.   The
agents of England were spread over the whole of Europe,
and they varied the rumours which they were commissioned
to circulate, according to the chances of credit which the
different places afforded.   Their reports were generally
false ; but credulity gave ear to them, and speculators endeavoured, each according to his interest, to give them
support.   The headquarters of all this plotting was Munich, where Drake, who was sent from England, had the
supreme direction.   His correspondence, which was seized
by the French Government, was at first placed amongst
the documents to be produced on the trial of Georges,
Moreau, and the other prisoners ; but in the course of the
preliminary proceedings the Grand Judge received directions to detach them, and make them the subject of a
special report to the First Consul, in order that their publication beforehand might influence public opinion, and
render it unfavourable to those who were doomed to be
sacrificed.   The instructions given by Drake to his agents
render it impossible to doubt that England wished to
overthrow the Government of Bonaparte.   Drake wrote as
follows to a man who was appointed to travel through
France :—

The principal object of your journey being the overthrow of the
existing Government, one of the means of effecting it is to acquire
a knowledge of the enemy's plans.   For this purpose it is of the
highest importance to begin, in the first place, by establishing communications with persons who may be depended upon in the different Government offices, in order to obtain exact information of all
plans with respect to foreign or internal affairs.   The knowledge of
these plans will supply the best means of defeating them ; and failure is the way to bring the Government into complete discredit—
the first and most important step towards the end proposed.   Try to
gain over trustworthy agents in the different Government departments.   Endeavour, also, to learn what passes in the secret committee, which is supposed to be established at St. Cloud, and

composed of the friends of the First Consul.   Be careful to furnish
information of the various projects which Bonaparte may entertain
relative to Turkey and Ireland.   Likewise send intelligence respecting the movements of troops, respecting vessels and ship building,
and all military preparations.

Drake, in his instructions, also recommended that the
subversion of Bonaparte's Government should, for the
time, be the only object in view, and that nothing should
be said about the King's intentions until certain information could be obtained respecting his views ; but most of
his letters and instructions were anterior to 1804.   The
whole bearing of the seized documents proved what Bonaparte could not be ignorant of, namely, that England was
his constant enemy ; but after examining them, I was of
opinion that they contained nothing which could justify
the belief that the Government of Great Britain authorised any attempt at assassination.

When the First Consul received the report of the Grand
Judge relative to Drake's plots[1] against his Government he
transmitted a copy of it to the Senate, and it was in reply
to this communication that the Senate made those first
overtures which Bonaparte thought vague, but which,
nevertheless, led to the formation of the Empire.   Notwithstanding this important circumstance, I have not
hitherto mentioned Drake, because his intrigues for Bonaparte's overthrow appeared to me to be more immediately
connected with the preliminaries of the trial of Georges
and Moreau, which I shall notice in my next chapter.

At the same time that Bonaparte communicated to the

---

[1] These were not plots for assassination. Bonaparte, in the same way, had his
secret agents in every country of Europe, without excepting England. Alison (chap.
xxxvii. para. 39) says on this matter of Drake that, though the English agents were
certainly attempting a counter-revolution, they had no idea of encouraging the assassination of Napoleon, while " England was no match for the French police agents in
a transaction of this description, for the publication of Regnier revealed the mortifying fact that the whole correspondance both of Drake and Spencer Smith had been
regularly transmitted, as fast as it took place, to the police of Paris, and that their
principal correspondent in that city, M. Mehu de la Touche, was himself an agent of
the police, employed to tempt the British envoys into this perilous enterprise."

Senate the report of the Grand Judge, the Minister for
Foreign Affairs addressed the following circular letter to
the members of the Diplomatic Body:—

The First Consul has commanded me to forward to your Excellency a copy of a report which has been presented to him, respecting a conspiracy formed in France by Mr. Drake, his Britannic
Majesty's Minister at the Court of Munich, which, by its object as
well as its date, is evidently connected with the infamous plot now
in the course of investigation.

The printed copy of Mr. Drake's letters and authentic documents
is annexed to the report.   The originals will be immediately sent,
by order of the First Consul, to the Elector of Bavaria.

Such a prostitution of the most honourable function which can be
intrusted to a man is unexampled in the history of civilised nations.
It will astonish and afflict Europe as an unheard-of crime, which
hitherto the most perverse Governments have not dared to meditate.
The First Consul is too well acquainted with sentiments of the
Diplomatic Body accredited to him not to be fully convinced that
every one of its members will behold, with profound regret, the prof-
anation of the sacred character of Ambassador, basely transformed
into a minister of plots, snares, and corruption.

All the ambassadors, ministers, plenipotentiaries, envoys, ordinary or extraordinary, whatever might be their
denomination, addressed answers to the Minister for Foreign Affairs, in which they expressed horror and indignation at the conduct of England and Drake's machinations.
These answers were returned only five days after the Duc
d'Enghien's death ; and here one cannot help admiring
the adroitness of Bonaparte, who thus compelled all the
representatives of the European Governments to give official testimonies of regard for his person and Government.

CHAPTER XXVI.

1804.

Trial of Moreau, Georges, and others—Public interest excited by Moreau
—Arraignment of the prisoners—Moreau's letter to Bonaparte—Violence of the President of the Court towards the prisoners—Lajolais
and Rolland—Examinations intended to criminate Moreau—Remarkable observations—Speech written by M. Garat—Bonaparte's opinion
of Garat's eloquence—General Lecourbe and Moreau's son—Respect
shown to Moreau by the military—Different sentiments excited by
Georges and Moreau—Thuriot and *Tue-roi*—Georges' answers to the
interrogatories—He refuses an offer of pardon—Coster St. Victor—
Napoleon and an actress—Captain Wright—M. de Rivière and the
medal of the Comte d'Artois—Generous struggle between MM. de
Polignac—Sentence on the prisoners—Bonaparte's remark—Pardons and executions.

On the 28th of May, about ten days after Napoleon had
been declared Emperor, the trials of Moreau and others
commenced. No similar event that has since occurred
can convey an idea of the fermentation which then prevailed in Paris. The indignation excited by Moreau's
arrest was openly manifested, and braved the observation
of the police. Endeavours had been successfully made to
mislead public opinion with respect to Georges and some
others among the accused, who were looked upon as assassins in the pay of England, at least by that numerous portion of the public who lent implicit faith to declarations
presented to them as official. But the case was different
with regard to those individuals who were particularly the
objects of public interest, viz. MM. de Polignac, de
Rivière, Charles d'Hozier, and, above all, Moreau. The
name of Moreau towered above all the rest, and with respect to him the Government found itself not a little per-

plexed. It was necessary on the one hand to surround him with a guard sufficiently imposing, to repress the eagerness of the people and of his friends, and yet on the other hand care was required that this guard should not be so strong as to admit of the possibility of making it a rallying-point, should the voice of a chief so honoured by the army appeal to it for defence. A rising of the populace in favour of Moreau was considered as a very possible event,—some hoped for it, others dreaded it. When I reflect on the state of feeling which then prevailed, I am certain that a movement in his favour would infallibly have taken place had judges more complying than even those who presided at the trial condemned Moreau to capital punishment.

It is impossible to form an idea of the crowd that choked up the avenues of the Palace of Justice on the day the trials commenced. This crowd continued during the twelve days the proceedings lasted, and was exceedingly great on the day the sentence was pronounced. Persons of the highest class were anxious to be present.

I was one of the first in the Hall, being determined to watch the course of these solemn proceedings. The Court being assembled, the President ordered the prisoners to be brought in. They entered in a file, and ranged themselves on the benches each between two gendarmes. They appeared composed and collected, and resignation was depicted on the countenances of all except Bouvet de Lozier, who did not dare to raise his eyes to his companions in misfortune, whom his weakness, rather than his will, had betrayed. I did not recognise him until the President proceeded to call over the prisoners, and to put the usual questions respecting their names, professions, and places of abode. Of the forty-nine prisoners, among whom were several females, only two were personally known to me; namely, Moreau, whose presence on the prisoner's bench seemed to wring every heart, and

Georges, whom I had seen at the Tuileries in the First Consul's cabinet.

The first sitting of the Court was occupied with the reading of the act of accusation or indictment, and the voices of the ushers, commanding silence, could scarce suppress the buzz which pervaded the Court at the mention of Moreau's name.[1] All eyes were turned towards the conqueror of Hohenlinden, and while the Procureur Impérial read over the long indictment and invoked the vengeance of the law on an attempt against the head of the Republic, it was easy to perceive how he tortured his ingenuity to fasten apparent guilt on the laurels of Moreau. The good sense of the public discerned proofs of his innocence in the very circumstances brought forward against him. I shall never forget the effect produced—so contrary to what was anticipated by the prosecutors—by the reading of a letter addressed by Moreau from his prison in the Temple to the First Consul, when the judges appointed to interrogate him sought to make his past conduct the subject of accusation, on account of M. de Klinglin's papers having fallen into his hands. He was reproached with having too long delayed transmitting these documents to the Directory; and it was curious to see the Emperor Napoleon become the avenger of pretended offences committed against the Directory which he had overthrown.

In the letter here alluded to Moreau said to Bonaparte, then First Consul—

"In the short campaign of the year V. (from the 20th to the 23d of March 1797) we took the papers belonging to the staff of the enemy's army, and a number of documents were brought to me which

---

[1] Miot de Melito (tome ii. p. 192), who cannot be called an extreme partisan of Napoleon, acknowledging the excitement in favour of Moreau, attributes it, not to a belief in his innocence—the evidence was too strong for that—but to the striking contrast between the fortunes of the two generals ; see also tome ii. pp. 135, 136. The feeling for Moreau was certainly strong. "At the Théâtre Français some young men applauded loudly some lines which appeared to apply to Moreau, but the police arrested them" (*Puymaigre*, p. 108).

General Desaix, then wounded, amused himself by perusing. It appeared from this correspondence that General Pichegru had maintained communications with the French Princes. This discovery was very painful, and particularly to me, and we agreed to say nothing of the matter. Pichegru, as a member of the Legislative Body, could do but little to injure the public cause, since peace was established. I nevertheless took every precaution for protecting the army against the ill effects of a system of espionage. . . . The events of the 18th Fructidor occasioned so much anxiety that two officers, who knew of the existence of the correspondence, prevailed on me to communicate it to the Government. . . . I felt that, as a public functionary, I could no longer remain silent. . . . During the two last campaigns in Germany, and since the peace, distant overtures have been made to me, with the view of drawing me into connection with the French Princes. This appeared so absurd that I took no notice of these overtures. As to the present conspiracy, I can assure you I have been far from taking any share in it. I repeat to you, General, that whatever proposition to that effect was made me, I rejected it, and regarded it as the height of madness. When it was represented to me that the invasion of England would offer a favourable opportunity for effecting a change in the French Government, I invariably answered that the Senate was the authority to which the whole of France would naturally cling in the time of trouble, and that I would be the first to place myself under its orders. To such overtures made to a private individual, who wished to preserve no connection either with the army, of whom ninetenths have served under me, or any constituted authority, the only possible answer was a refusal. Betrayal of confidence I disdained. Such a step, which is always base, becomes doubly odious when the treachery is committed against those to whom we owe gratitude, or have been bound by old friendship.

"This, General, is all I have to tell you respecting my relations with Pichegru, and it must convince you that very false and hasty inferences have been drawn from conduct which, though perhaps imprudent, was far from being criminal." [1]

---

[1] This letter is, to say the least, curious. In at latest March 1797 Moreau became aware that Pichegru, the leader of one of the parties in the Legislative Body, and still possessing great influence with the army, was in communication with the Princes, that is, was conspiring with men facing Moreau in arms. It was not until after Pichegru's party was ruined by the *coup d'état* of the 18th Fructidor (4th September 1797) that Moreau revealed this fact to the Government, and only then when the step was forced on him by others. Moreau also acknowledges that it had been proposed to him to upset the Government during the expected absence of Napoleon in

Moreau fulfilled his duty as a public functionary by communicating to the Directory the papers which unfolded a plot against the Government, and which the chances of war had thrown into his hands. He fulfilled his duty as a man of honour by not voluntarily incurring the infamy which can never be wiped from the character of an informer. Bonaparte in Moreau's situation would have acted the same part, for I never knew a man express stronger indignation than himself against informers, until he began to consider everything a virtue which served his ambition, and everything a crime which opposed it.

The two facts which most forcibly obtruded themselves on my attention during the trial were the inveterate violence of the President of the Court towards the prisoners and the innocence of Moreau. But, in spite of the most insidious examinations which can be conceived, Moreau never once fell into the least contradiction. If my memory fail me not, it was on the fourth day that he was examined by Thuriot, one of the judges.[1] The result, clear as day to all present, was, that Moreau was a total stranger to all the plots, all the intrigues which had been set on foot in London. In fact, during the whole course of the trial, to

England, a step which would inevitably have ruined the French army in England. He says that he answered that he would put himself under the Senate; thus practically Moreau says, " Get rid of the Government without compromising me, and then I will act." He himself had taken an active part in establishing this very Government. A man who acts thus cannot complain if he be treated as a conspirator alongside the more daring men who were ready to take the dangers of the attempt of which Moreau was prepared to reap the advantages. That Moreau met Pichegru and Georges at night at the Madeleine is, surely rightly, taken by Thiers (tome v. p. 144) as proof that Moreau had some other object than, as he professed, the reconciliation of Pichegru with Napoleon. Georges undoubtedly intended assassination; see also *Savary*, tome ii. p. 94. Lanfrey's defence (tome iii. p. 385) is most lame; he adopts Rolland's correction of the phrase *il fallait faire disparaître les Consuls*, to *il faudrait qu'ils disparaissent*. Few persons can doubt what the disappearance of a ruler then meant in France.

[1] It is strange that Bourrienne does not acknowledge that he was charged by Napoleon with the duty of attending this trial of Moreau, and of sending in a daily report of the proceedings. If, says Meneval (tome iii. p. 29), these reports can yet be found, the public could judge of the difference of thoughts and language between the two versions Bourrienne has given of the trial.

which I listened with as much attention as interest, I did not discover the shadow of a circumstance which could in the least commit him, or which had the least reference to him. Scarcely one of the hundred and thirty-nine witnesses who were heard for the prosecution knew him, and he himself declared on the fourth sitting, which took place on the 31st of May, that there was not an individual among the accused whom he knew,—not one whom he had ever seen. In the course of the long proceedings, notwithstanding the manifest efforts of Thuriot to extort false admissions and force contradictions, no fact of any consequence was elicited to the prejudice of Moreau. His appearance was as calm as his conscience; and as he sat on the bench he had the appearance of one led by curiosity to be present at this interesting trial, rather than of an accused person, to whom the proceedings might end in condemnation and death. But for the fall of Moreau in the ranks of the enemy,—but for the foreign cockade which disgraced the cap of the conqueror of Hohenlinden, his complete innocence would long since have been put beyond doubt, and it would have been acknowledged that the most infamous machinations were employed for his destruction. It is evident that Lajolais, who had passed from London to Paris, and from Paris to London, had been acting the part of an intriguer rather than of a conspirator; and that the object of his missions was not so much to reconcile Moreau and Pichegru as to make Pichegru the instrument of implicating Moreau. Those who supposed Lajolais to be in the pay of the British Government were egregiously imposed on. Lajolais was only in the pay of the secret police; he was condemned to death, as was expected, but he received his pardon, as was agreed upon. Here was one of the disclosures which Pichegru might have made; hence the necessity of getting him out of the way before the trial. As to the evidence of the man named Rolland, it was clear to everybody that Moreau was right when he

said to the President, " In my opinion, Rolland is either
a creature of the police, or he has given his evidence under
the influence of fear." Rolland made two declarations :
the first contained nothing at all ; the second was in
answer to the following observations : " You see you stand
in a terrible situation ; you must either be held to be an
accomplice in the conspiracy, or you must be taken as
evidence. If you say nothing, you will be considered in
the light of an accomplice; if you confess, you will be
saved." This single circumstance may serve to give an
idea of the way the trials were conducted so as to criminate Moreau. On his part the general repelled the attacks,
of which he was the object, with calm composure and
modest confidence, though flashes of just indignation
would occasionally burst from him. I recollect the effect
he produced upon the Court and the auditors at one of
the sittings, when the President had accused him of the
design of making himself Dictator. He exclaimed, " *I*
Dictator ! What, make myself Dictator at the head of the
partisans of the Bourbons ! Point out my partisans ! My
partisans would naturally be the soldiers of France, of
whom I have commanded nine-tenths, and saved more
than fifty thousand. These are the partisans I should
look to ! All my *aides de camp,* all the officers of my
acquaintance, have been arrested ; not the shadow of a
suspicion could be found against any of them, and they
have been set at liberty. Why, then, attribute to me the
madness of aiming to get myself made Dictator by the aid
of the adherents of the old French Princes, of persons
who have fought in their cause since 1792 ? You allege
that these men, in the space of four-and-twenty hours,
formed the project of raising me to the Dictatorship ! It
is madness to think of it ! My fortune and my pay have
been alluded to ; I began the world with nothing ; I might
have had by this time fifty millions ; I have merely a
house and a bit of ground ; as to my pay, it is forty thou-

sand francs. Surely that sum will not be compared with my services ! "

During the trial Moreau delivered a defence, which I knew had been written by his friend Garat, whose eloquence I well remember was always disliked by Bonaparte. Of this I had a proof on the occasion of a grand ceremony which took place in the Place des Victoires, on laying the first stone of a monument which was to have been erected to the memory of Desaix, but which was never executed. The First Consul returned home in very ill-humour, and said to me, "Bourrienne, what a brute that Garat is ! What a stringer of words ! I have been obliged to listen to him for three-quarters of an hour. There are people who never know when to hold their tongues ! "

Whatever might be the character of Garat's eloquence or Bonaparte's opinion of it, his conduct was noble on the occasion of Moreau's trial ; for he might be sure Bonaparte would bear him a grudge for lending the aid of his pen to the only man whose military glory, though not equal to that of the First Consul, might entitle him to be looked upon as his rival in fame. At one of the sittings a circumstance occurred which produced an almost electrical effect. I think I still see General Lecourbe,[1] the worthy friend of Moreau, entering unexpectedly into the Court, leading a little boy. Raising the child in his arms, he exclaimed aloud, and with considerable emotion, "Soldiers, behold the son of your general ! " At this unexpected movement all the military present spontaneously rose and

---

[1] This action of Lecourbe, together with the part played in this trial by his brother, one of the judges, was most unfortunate, not only for Lecourbe but for France, which consequently lost the services of its best general of mountain warfare. His campaigns of Switzerland in 1799 on the St. Gothard against Suwarrow are well known. Naturally disgraced for the part he took with Moreau, he was not again employed till the *Cent Jours*, when he did good service, although he had disapproved of the defection of Ney from the Royalist cause. He died in 1815 ; his brother, the judge, had a most furious reception from Napoleon, who called him a prevaricating judge, and dismissed him from his office (*Rémusat*, tome ii. p. 8).

presented arms ; while a murmur of approbation from the spectators applauded the act. It is certain that had Moreau at that moment said but one word, such was the enthusiasm in his favour, the tribunal would have been broken up and the prisoners liberated. Moreau, however, was silent, and indeed appeared the only unconcerned person in Court. Throughout the whole course of the trial Moreau inspired so much respect that when he was asked a question and rose to reply the gendarmes appointed to guard him rose at the same time and stood uncovered while he spoke.

Georges was far from exciting the interest inspired by Moreau. He was an object of curiosity rather than of interest. The difference of their previous conduct was in itself sufficient to occasion a great contrast in their situation before the Court. Moreau was full of confidence and Georges full of resignation. The latter regarded his fate with a fierce kind of resolution. He occasionally resumed the caustic tone which he seemed to have renounced when he harangued his associates before their departure from the Temple. With the most sarcastic bitterness he alluded to the name and vote of Thuriot, one of the most violent of the judges, often terming him *Tue-roi ;* [1] and after pronouncing his name, or being forced to reply to his interrogatories, he would ask for a glass of brandy to wash his mouth.

Georges had the manners and bearing of a rude soldier ; but under his coarse exterior he concealed the soul of a hero. When the witnesses of his arrest had answered the questions of the President Hémart, this judge turned towards the accused, and inquired whether he had anything to say in reply.— " No."—" Do you admit the facts?"—" Yes." Here Georges busied himself in looking over the papers which lay before him, when Hémart

[1] Thuriot and the President Hémart both voted for the death of the King. Merlin, the imperial Procureur-Général, was one of the regicides.—*Bourrienne.*

warned him to desist, and attend to the questions. The following dialogue then commenced. "Do you confess having been arrested in the place designated by the witness?"—"I do not know the name of the place."—"Do you confess having been arrested?"—"Yes."—"Did you twice fire a pistol?"—"Yes."—"Did you kill a man?"—"Indeed I do not know."—"Had you a poniard?"—"Yes."—"And two pistols?"—"Yes."—"Who was in company with you?"—"I do not know the person."—"Where did you lodge in Paris?"—"Nowhere."—"At the time of your arrest did you not reside in the house of a fruiterer in the Rue de la Montagne St. Geneviève?"—"At the time of my arrest I was in a cabriolet. I lodged nowhere."—"Where did you sleep on the evening of your arrest?"—"Nowhere."—"What were you doing in Paris?"—"I was walking about."—"Whom have you seen in Paris?"—"I shall name no one; I know no one."

From this short specimen of the manner in which Georges replied to the questions of the President we may judge of his unshaken firmness during the proceedings. In all that concerned himself he was perfectly open; but in regard to whatever tended to endanger his associates he maintained the most obstinate silence, notwithstanding every attempt to overcome his firmness.

That I was not the only one who justly appreciated the noble character of Georges is rendered evident by the following circumstance. Having accompanied M. Carbonnet to the police, where he went to demand his papers, on the day of his removal to St. Pélagie, we were obliged to await the return of M. Réal, who was absent. M. Desmarets and several other persons were also in attendance. M. Réal had been at the Conciergerie, where he had seen Georges Cadoudal, and on his entrance observed to M. Desmarets and the others, sufficiently loud to be distinctly heard by M. Carbonnet and myself, "I have had an interview with Georges who is an extraordinary man. I told him that I was disposed to offer him a pardon if he would promise to renounce the conspiracy and accept of employment under Government. But to my arguments and persuasions he only replied, '*My comrades followed me to France, and I shall follow them to death.*' " In this he kept his word.

Were we to judge these memorable proceedings from the official documents published in the *Moniteur* and other journals of that period, we should form a very erroneous opinion. Those falsities were even the object of a very serious complaint on the part of Coster St. Victor, one of the accused.

After the speech of M. Gauthier, the advocate of Coster St. Victor, the President inquired of the accused whether he had anything further to say in his defence, to which he replied, "I have only to add that the witnesses necessary to my exculpation have not yet appeared. I must besides express my surprise at the means which have been employed to lead astray public opinion, and to load with infamy not only the accused but also their intrepid defenders. I have read with pain in the journals of to-day that the proceedings——" Here the President interrupting, observed that "these were circumstances foreign to the case." "Not in the least," replied Coster St. Victor ; "on the contrary, they bear very materially on the cause, since mangling and misrepresenting our defence is a practice assuredly calculated to ruin us in the estimation of the public. In the journals of to-day the speech of M. Gauthier is shamefully garbled, and I should be deficient in gratitude were I not here to bear testimony to the zeal and courage which he has displayed in my defence. I protest against the puerilities and absurdities which have been put into his mouth, and I entreat him not to relax in his generous efforts. It is not on his account that I make this observation ; he does not require it at my hands ; it is for myself, it is for the accused, whom such arts tend to injure in the estimation of the public."

Coster St. Victor had something chivalrous in his language and manners which spoke greatly in his favour ; he conveyed no bad idea of one of the Fiesco conspirators, or of those leaders of the Fronde who intermingled gallantry with their politics.

An anecdote to this effect was current about the period of the trial.   Coster St. Victor, it is related, being unable any longer to find a secure asylum in Paris, sought refuge for a single night in the house of a beautiful actress, formerly in the good graces of the First Consul ; and it is added that Bonaparte, on the same night, having secretly arrived on a visit to the lady, found himself unexpectedly in the presence of Coster St. Victor, who might have taken his life; but that only an interchange of courtesy took place betwixt the rival gallants.

This ridiculous story was doubtless intended to throw additional odium on the First Consul, if Coster St. Victor should be condemned and not obtain a pardon, in which case malignity would not fail to attribute his execution to the vengeance of a jealous lover.

I should blush to relate such stories, equally destitute of probability and truth, had they not obtained some credit at the time.   Whilst I was with Bonaparte he never went abroad during the night ; and it was not surely at a moment when the saying of Fouché, *" The air is full of poniards,"* was fully explained that he would have risked such nocturnal adventures.

Wright was heard in the sixth sitting, on the 2d of June, as the hundred and thirty-fourth witness in support of the prosecution.   He, however, refused to answer any interrogatories put to him, declaring that, as a prisoner of war, he considered himself only amenable to his own Government.

The Procureur-Général requested the President to order the examinations of Captain Wright on the 21st of May and at a later period to be read over to him ; which being done, the witness replied, that it was omitted to be stated that on these occasions the questions had been accompanied with the threat of transferring him to a military tribunal, in order to be shot, if he did not betray the secrets of his country.

In the course of the trial the most lively interest was felt for MM. de Polignac,[1] Charles d'Hozier, and de Rivière. So short a period had elapsed since the proscription of the nobility that, independently of every feeling of humanity, it was certainly impolitic to exhibit before the public the heirs of an illustrious name, endowed with that devoted heroism which could not fail to extort admiration even from those who condemned their opinions and principles.

The prisoners were all young, and their situation created universal sympathy. The greatest number of them disdained to have recourse to a denial, and seemed less anxious for the preservation of their own lives than for the honour of the cause in which they had embarked,—not with the view of assassination, as had been demonstrated, but for the purpose of ascertaining the true state of the public feeling, which had been represented by some factious intriguers as favourable to the Bourbons.

Even when the sword of the law was suspended over their heads the faithful adherents of the Bourbons dis-

---

[1] The eldest of the Polignacs, Armand (1771–1847), condemned to death, had that penalty remitted, but was imprisoned in Ham till permitted to escape in 1813. He became Duc de Richelieu in 1817. His younger brother, Jules (1780–1847), was also imprisoned and escaped. In 1814 he was one of the first to display the white flag in Paris. In 1829 he became Minister of Charles X., and was responsible for the *ordonnances* which cost his master his throne in 1830. Imprisoned, nominally for life, he was released in 1836, and after passing some time in England returned to France. The remission of the sentence of death on Prince Armand was obtained by the Empress Josephine. Time after time, urged on by Madame de Rémusat, she implored mercy from Napoleon, who at last consented to see the wife of the Prince. Unlike the Bourbon Louis XVIII., who could see Madame de Lavalette only to refuse the wretched woman's prayer for her husband, for Napoleon to grant the interview was to concede the pardon. The Prince escaped death, and his wife who had obtained the interview by applying to Madame de Rémusat, when she met her benefactress in the times of the Restoration, displayed a really grand forgetfulness of what had passed (see *Rémusat,* tome ii. chap. i.).

played on every occasion their attachment and fidelity to
the royal cause. I recollect that the Court was dissolved
in tears when the President adduced as a proof of the
guilt of M. de Rivière his having worn a medal of the
Comte d'Artois, which the prisoner requested to examine;
and, on its being handed to him by an officer, M. de
Rivière pressed it to his lips and his heart, then returning
it, he said that he only wished to render homage to the
Prince whom he loved.

The Court was still more deeply affected on witnessing
the generous fraternal struggle which took place during
the last sitting between the two De Polignacs. The
emotion was general when the eldest of the brothers, after
having observed that his always going out alone and during the day did not look like a conspirator anxious for
concealment, added these remarkable words which will
remain indelibly engraven on my memory: "I have now
only one wish, which is that, as the sword is suspended
over our heads, and threatens to cut short the existence
of several of the accused, you would, in consideration of
his youth if not of his innocence, spare my brother, and
shower down upon me the whole weight of your vengeance."

It was during the last sitting but one, on Friday the
8th of June, that M. Armand de Polignac made the above
affecting appeal in favour of his brother. The following
day, before the fatal sentence was pronounced, M. Jules
de Polignac addressed the judges, saying, "I was so
deeply affected yesterday, while my brother was speaking, as not fully to have attended to what I read in my
own defence: but being now perfectly tranquil, I entreat, gentlemen, that you will not regard what he urged
in my behalf. I repeat, on the contrary, and with more
justice, if one of us must fall a sacrifice, if there be yet
time, save him,—restore him to the tears of his wife; I
have no tie. Like him, I can meet death unappalled;—
too young to have tasted the pleasures of the world, I

cannot regret their loss."—"No, no," exclaimed his brother, "you are still in the outset of your career; it is I who ought to fall."

At eight in the morning the members of the Tribunal withdrew to the council-chamber. Since the commencement of the proceedings the crowd, far from diminishing, seemed each day to increase; this morning it was immense, and, though the sentence was not expected to be pronounced till a late hour, no one quitted the Court for fear of not being able to find a place when the Tribunal should resume its sitting.

Sentence of death was passed upon Georges Caudoudal, Bouvet de Lozier, Rusillon, Rochelle, Armand de Polignac, Charles d'Hozier, De Rivière, Louis Ducorps, Picot, Lajolais, Roger, Coster St. Victor, Deville, Gaillard, Joyaut, Burban, Lemercier, Jean Cadudol, Lelan, and Merille; while Jules de Polignac, Leridant, General Moreau,[1] Rolland, and Hisay were only condemned to two years' imprisonment.

This decree was heard with consternation by the assembly, and soon spread throughout Paris. I may well affirm it to have been a day of public mourning; even though it was Sunday every place of amusement was nearly deserted. To the horror inspired by a sentence of death passed so wantonly, and of which the greater number of the victims belonged to the most distinguished class of society, was joined the ridicule inspired by the condemnation of Moreau; of the absurdity of which no one seemed more sensible than Bonaparte himself, and respecting which he expressed himself in the most pointed terms. I am persuaded that every one who narrowly watched the proceedings of this celebrated trial must have been convinced that all means were resorted to in order that Moreau, once accused, should not appear entirely free from guilt.

[1] General Moreau's sentence was remitted, and he was allowed to go to America.

Bonaparte is reported to have said, "Gentlemen, I have no control over your proceedings; it is your duty strictly to examine the evidence before presenting a report to me. But when it has once the sanction of your signatures, woe to you if an innocent man be condemned."[1] This remark is in strict conformity with his usual language, and bears a striking similarity to the conversation I held with him on the following Thursday; but though this language might be appropriate from the lips of a sovereign whose ministers are responsible, it appears but a lame excuse in the mouth of Bonaparte, the possessor of absolute power.

The condemned busied themselves in endeavouring to procure a repeal of their sentence; the greatest number of them yielded in this respect to the entreaties of their friends, who lost no time in taking the steps requisite to obtain the pardon of those in whom they were most interested. Moreau at first also determined to appeal; but he relinquished his purpose before the Court of Cassation commenced its sittings.

As soon as the decree of the special Tribunal was delivered, Murat, Governor of Paris, and brother-in-law to the Emperor, sought his presence and conjured him in the most urgent manner to pardon all the criminals, observing that such an act of clemency would redound greatly to his honour in the opinion of France and all Europe, that it would be said the Emperor pardoned the attempt against the life of the First Consul, that this act of mercy

---

[1] This passage is taken from Savary (tome ii. p. 75), who often heard the Emperor say so to his Ministers. Any person who has held either a command or any executive post must know that Napoleon was strictly within his right in making his Ministers responsible in this manner. The cardinal error of Lanfrey and his school of critics is to consider that Napoleon could be responsible for all the acts of his administration. There is probably no one from whom any order, however contrary to their intentions, could not some time or other be obtained by any one able to wait for a moment of haste, or weariness, or misconception. Writers who would shrink from answering for the acts of their few servants cheerfully accuse Napoleon of every act done in France in his time, if the result be bad. They are less liberal with responsibility for the measures they are forced to approve of.

would shed more glory over the commencement of his reign than any security which could accrue from the execution of the prisoners. Such was the conduct of Murat; but he did not solicit, as has been reported, the pardon of any one in particular.

Those who obtained the imperial pardon were Bouvet de Lozier, who expected it from the disclosures he had made; Rusillon, de Rivière, Rochelle, Armand de Polignac, d'Hozier, Lajolais, who had beforehand received a promise to that effect, and Armand Gaillard.

The other ill-fated victims of a sanguinary police underwent their sentence on the 25th of June, two days after the promulgation of the pardon of their associates.

Their courage and resignation never forsook them even for a moment, and Georges,[1] knowing that it was rumoured he had obtained a pardon, entreated that he might die the first, in order that his companions in their last moments might be assured he had not survived them.

---

[1] Georges Cadoudal (1769-1804) was one of those strong characters not unfrequently found among conspirators. Napoleon would gladly have saved him or won him over, except for his determined attempts at assassination. He had been one of the chiefs in La Vendée, and when that rebellion had been put an end to in 1800, Napoleon had seen Georges alone, to the horror of his *aide de camp;* but he could not shake the gloomy resolution of the conspirator, or his firm attachment to the Royalist cause (*Thiers,* tome i. p. 209). Georges is even said to have afterwards regretted not having taken advantage of this opportunity to kill the First Consul. When condemned now he wrote, says Lavalette (tome ii. p. 26) a noble letter to Murat, the Governor of Paris, asking for the pardon of his accomplices. He did not ask for his own, but offered to be the first to throw himself on the English coast if life were granted to him. It was, he said, only changing the manner of his death, but in that way at least it would be useful to his country. Napoleon, says Madame de Rémusat (tome ii. p. 6), seemed struck by the firmness of the character of Georges and said, "If it were possible to save any of these assassins I would pardon Georges."

CHAPTER XXVII.

1804.

Clavier and Hémart—Singular proposal of Corvisart—M. Desmaisons—
Project of influencing the judges—Visit to the Tuileries—Rapp in attendance—Long conversation with the Emperor—His opinion on the
trial of Moreau—English assassins and Mr. Fox—Complaints against
the English Government—Bonaparte and Lacuée—Affectionate behaviour—Arrest of Pichegru—Method employed by the First Consul
to discover his presence in Paris—Character of Moreau—Measures of
Bonaparte regarding him—Lauriston sent to the Temple—Silence respecting the Duc d'Enghien—Napoleon's opinion of Moreau and
Georges—Admiration of Georges—Offers of employment and dismissal—Recital of former vexations—Audience of the Empress—Melancholy forebodings—What Bonaparte said concerning himself—
Marks of kindness.

THE judges composing the Tribunal which condemned
Moreau were not all like Thuriot and Hémart.   History
has recorded an honourable contrast to the general meanness of the period in the reply given by M. Clavier, when
urged by Hémart to vote for the condemnation of Moreau.
" Ah, Monsieur, if we condemn him, how shall we be able
to acquit ourselves ? " [1]   I have, besides, the best reason
for asserting that the judges were tampered with, from a
circumstance which occurred to myself.

Bonaparte knew that I was intimately connected with
M. Desmaisons, one of the members of the Tribunal, and
brother in-law to Corvisart ; he also knew that Desmaisons
was inclined to believe in Moreau's innocence, and favourable to his acquittal.   During the progress of the trial
Corvisart arrived at my house one morning at a very early
hour, in a state of such evident embarrassment that, be-

[1] Another version has it, " If we condemn him, who will acquit us ? "

fore he had time to utter a word, I said to him, "What is the matter? Have you heard any bad news?"

"No," replied Corvisart, "but I came by the Emperor's order. He wishes you to see my brother-in-law. 'He is,' said he to me, 'the senior judge, and a man of considerable eminence ; his opinion will carry with it great weight, and I know that he is favourable to Moreau ; he is in the wrong. Visit Bourrienne, said the Emperor, and concert with him respecting the best method of convincing Desmaisons of his error, for I repeat he is wrong,—he is deceived.' This is the mission with which I am entrusted."

"How," said I, with thorough astonishment, "how came you to be employed in this affair? Could you believe for one moment that I would tamper with a magistrate in order to induce him to exercise an unjust rigour?"

"No, rest assured," replied Corvisart, "I merely visited you this morning in obedience to the order of the Emperor ; but I knew beforehand in what manner you would regard the proposition with which I was charged. I knew your opinions and your character too well to entertain the smallest doubt in this respect, and I was convinced that I ran no risk in becoming the bearer of a commission which would be attended with no effect. Besides, had I refused to obey the Emperor, it would have proved prejudicial to your interest, and confirmed him in the opinion that you were favourable to the acquittal of Moreau. For myself," added Corvisart, "it is needless to affirm that I have no intention of attempting to influence the opinion of my brother-in-law ; and if I had, you know him sufficiently well to be convinced in what light he would regard such a proceeding."

Such were the object and result of Corvisart's visit, and I am thence led to believe that similar attempts must have been made to influence other members of the Tribunal.[1]

[1] "The judges had been pressed and acted on in a thousand ways by the hangers-on of the Palace, and especially by Réal, the natural intermediary between justice

But however this may be, prudence led me to discontinue visiting M. Desmaisons, with whom I was in habits of the strictest friendship.

About this period I paid a visit which occupies an important place in my recollections. On the 14th of June 1804, four days after the condemnation of Georges and his accomplices, I received a summons to attend the Emperor at St. Cloud. It was Thursday, and as I thought on the great events and tragic scenes about to be acted, I was rather uneasy respecting his intentions.

But I was fortunate enough to find my friend Rapp in waiting, who said to me as I entered, "Be not alarmed; he is in the best of humours at present, and wishes to have some conversation with you."

Rapp then announced me to the Emperor, and I was immediately admitted to his presence. After pinching my ear and asking his usual questions, such as, "What does the world say? How are your children? What are you about? etc.," he said to me, "By the by, have you attended the proceedings against Moreau?"—"Yes, Sire, I have not been absent during one of the sittings."—"Well, Bourrienne, are you of the opinion that Moreau is innocent?" —"Yes, Sire; at least I am certain that nothing has come out in the course of the trial tending to criminate him; I am even surprised how he came to be implicated in this conspiracy, since nothing has appeared against him which has the most remote connexion with the affair."—"I know your opinion on this subject; Duroc related to me the conversation you held with him at the Tuileries; experience has shown that you were correct; but how could I act otherwise? You know that Bouvet de Lozier hanged himself in prison, and was only saved by accident. Réal hurried to the Temple in order to interrogate him, and in

and the Government. Ambition, servility, fear, every motive capable of influencing them, had been used; even their humane scruples were employed" (*Lanfrey*, tome iii. p. 193, who goes on to say that the judges were urged to sentence Moreau to death in order that the Emperor might fully pardon him).

his first confessions he criminated Moreau, affirming that he had held repeated conferences with Pichegru. Réal immediately reported to me this fact, and proposed that Moreau should be arrested, since the rumours against him seemed to be well founded ; he had previously made the same proposition. I at first refused my sanction to this measure ; but after the charge made against him by Bouvet de Lozier, how could I act otherwise than I did ? Could I suffer such open conspiracies against the Government? Could I doubt the truth of Bouvet de Lozier's declaration, under the circumstances in which it was made ? Could I foresee that he would deny his first declaration when brought before the Court? There was a chain of circumstances which human sagacity could not penetrate, and I consented to the arrest of Moreau when it was proved that he was in league with Pichegru. Has not England sent assassins?"—"Sire," said I, "permit me to call to your recollection the conversation you had in my presence with Mr. Fox, after which you said to me, 'Bourrienne, I am very happy at having heard from the mouth of a man of honour that the British Government is incapable of seeking my life ; I always wish to esteem my enemies.' "— "Bah! you are a fool! Parbleu! I did not say that the English Minister sent over an assassin, and that he said to him, 'Here is gold and a poniard ; go and kill the First Consul.' No, I did not believe that ; but it cannot be denied that all those foreign conspirators against my Government were serving England, and receiving pay from that power. Have I agents in London to disturb the Government of Great Britain? I have waged with it honourable warfare ; I have not attempted to awaken a remembrance of the Stuarts amongst their old partisans. Is not Wright, who landed Georges and his accomplices at Dieppe, a captain in the British navy? But rest assured that, with the exception of a few babblers, whom I can easily silence, the hearts of the French people are with me ;—everywhere

public opinion has been declared in my favour, so that I
have nothing to apprehend from giving the greatest publicity to these plots, and bringing the accused to a solemn
trial.   The greater number of those gentlemen wished me
to bring the prisoners before a military commission, that
summary judgment might be obtained ; but I refused
my consent to this measure.   It might have been said
that I dreaded public opinion ; and I fear it not.   People
may talk as much as they please, well and good, I am not
obliged to hear them ; but I do not like those who are attached to my person to blame what I have done."

As I could not wholly conceal an involuntary emotion,
in which the Emperor saw something more than mere
surprise, he paused, took me by the ear, and, smiling in
the most affectionate manner, said, "I had no reference to
you in what I said, but I have to complain of Lacuée.'
Could you believe that during the trial he went about
clamouring in behalf of Moreau ?   He, my *aide de camp*—
a man who owes everything to me !   As for you, I have
said that you acted very well in this affair."—"I know not,
Sire, what has either been done or said by Lacuée, whom
I have not seen for a long time ; what I said to Duroc is
what history teaches in every page."—"By the by," resumed the Emperor, after a short silence, "do you know
that it was I myself who discovered that Pichegru was in
Paris.   Every one said to me, Pichegru is in Paris ; Fouché,
Réal, harped on the same string, but could give me no
proof of their assertion.   'What a fool you are,' said I to
Réal, 'when in an instant you may ascertain the fact.   Pichegru has a brother, an aged ecclesiastic, who resides in
Paris ; let his dwelling be searched, and should he be absent, it will warrant a suspicion that Pichegru is here ; if,
on the contrary, his brother should be at home, let him
be arrested : he is a simple-minded man, and in the first

---

¹ Lacuée was killed at the bridge of Guntzburg.   I believe that after this conversation he ceased to act as *aide de camp* to the Emperor.—*Bourrienne.*

moments of agitation will betray the truth.' Everything happened as I had foreseen, for no sooner was he arrested than, without waiting to be questioned, he inquired if it was a crime to have received his brother into his house. Thus every doubt was removed, and a miscreant in the house in which Pichegru lodged betrayed him to the police. What horrid degradation to betray a friend for the sake of gold."

Then reverting to Moreau, the Emperor talked a great deal respecting that general. "Moreau," he said, "possesses many good qualities; his bravery is undoubted; but he has more courage than energy; he is indolent and effeminate. When with the army he lived like a pasha; he smoked, was almost constantly in bed, and gave himself up to the pleasures of the table. His dispositions are naturally good; but he is too indolent for study; he does not read, and since he has been tied to his wife's apron-strings is fit for nothing. He sees only with the eyes of his wife and her mother, who have had a hand in all these late plots; and then, Bourrienne, is it not very strange that it was by my advice that he entered into this union? I was told that Mademoiselle Hulot was a creole, and I believed that he would find in her a second Josephine; how greatly was I mistaken! It is these women who have estranged us from each other, and I regret that he should have acted so unworthily. You must remember my observing to you more than two years ago that Moreau would one day run his head against the gate of the Tuileries; that he has done so was no fault of mine, for you know how much I did to secure his attachment.[1] You

---

[1] This seems to have been Napoleon's real opinion. "They will be sure to say that I am jealous of Moreau, that this is revenge, and a thousand pettinesses of that sort. *I*, jealous of Moreau! Good God! He owes the greater part of his glory to me. It was I who left him a fine army, while I only kept recruits for Italy" (*Rémusat*, tome i. p. 301). It must be remembered that Napoleon had only to leave Moreau unemployed in the campaign of 1800 to render him harmless. Moreau's fame, without the battles fought in the time Napoleon was in power—Hohenlinden, etc.—would not have been greater than that of Masséna, the victor of Zurich and, to most Republicans, the saviour of France from invasion.

cannot have forgotten the reception I gave him at Malmaison.   On the 18th Brumaire I conferred on him the
charge of the Luxembourg, and in that situation he fully
justified my choice.   But since that period he has behaved
towards me with the utmost ingratitude;—entered into
all the silly cabals against me, blamed all my measures,
and turned into ridicule the Legion of Honour.   Have
not some of the intriguers put it into his head that I regard him with jealousy? [1]   You must be aware of that.
You must also know as well as I how anxious the members
of the Directory were to exalt the reputation of Moreau.
Alarmed at my success in Italy, they wished to have in the
armies a general to serve as a counterpoise to my renown.
I have ascended the throne and he is the inmate of a
prison!   You are aware of the incessant clamouring
raised against me by the whole family, at which I confess
I was very much displeased ; coming from those whom I
had treated so well!   Had he attached himself to me, I
would doubtless have conferred on him the title of First
Marshal of the Empire ; but what could I do?   He constantly depreciated my campaigns and my government.
From discontent to revolt there is frequently only one
step, especially when a man of a weak character becomes
the tool of popular clubs ; and therefore when I was first
informed that Moreau was implicated in the conspiracy of
Georges I believed him to be guilty, but hesitated to issue
an order for his arrest till I had taken the opinion of my
Council.   The members having assembled, I ordered the
different documents to be laid before them, with an injunction to examine them with the utmost care, since they
related to an affair of importance, and I urged them candidly to inform me whether, in their opinion, any of the
charges against Moreau were sufficiently strong to en-

[1] Bonaparte was right in this respect, that the consciousness of his own superiority
over Moreau prevented him from being jealous of that general ; but he was certainly
jealous of the estimation in which he was held by the public, whether rightly or
wrongly.—*Bourrienne.*

danger his life. The fools! their reply was in the affirmative; I believe they were even unanimous! Then I had no alternative but to suffer the proceedings to take their course. It is unnecessary to affirm to *you*, Bourrienne, that Moreau never should have perished on a scaffold![1] Most assuredly I would have pardoned him; but with the sentence of death hanging over his head he could no longer have proved dangerous; and his name would have ceased to be a rallying-point for disaffected Republicans or imbecile Royalists. Had the Council expressed any doubts respecting his guilt I would have intimated to him that the suspicions against him were so strong as to render any further connection between us impossible; and that the best course he could pursue would be to leave France for three years, under the pretext of visiting some of the places rendered celebrated during the late wars; but that if he preferred a diplomatic mission I would make a suitable provision for his expenses; and the great innovator, Time, might effect great changes during the period of his absence. But my foolish Council affirmed to me that his guilt, as a principal, being evident, it was absolutely necessary to bring him to trial; and now his sen-

[1] This declaration is confirmed by M. de Rovigo, who defends Napoleon against the imputation of having wished that Moreau should suffer capital punishment.

"If," says he, "he was vexed at the result of the trial, on which point I am ignorant, it was no doubt merely because it deprived him of an opportunity to humble Moreau by pardoning him. He was not fond of revenging himself by capital punishments. After the condemnation of Georges and his people, he pardoned several of them at the first application. If I recollect rightly, there were seven pardoned in all. Would he have suffered the conqueror of Holland and the victor of Hohenlinden to perish? It would be unjust to think so.

"Did he leave Moreau to suffer the two years' confinement to which he was sentenced, and during which he might have found occasion to get rid of him had he harboured a thought of so doing? No; for on the night of the very day that Moreau solicited by letter permission to go to America, he granted him leave to depart.

"I was the person whom the First Consul sent to him in the Temple to communicate his consent, and to make arrangements with him for his departure. I gave him my own carriage, and the First Consul paid all the expenses of his journey to Barcelona. The general expressed a wish to see Madame Moreau; I went myself to fetch her, and brought her to the Temple" (*Memoirs of the Duc de Rovigo*, vol. ii. p. 99).

tence is only that of a pickpocket! What think you I ought to do? Detain him? He might still prove a rallying-point. No. Let him sell his property and quit France? Can I confine him in the Temple? it is full enough without him. Still, if this had been the only great error they had led me to commit——"

"Sire, how greatly you have been deceived!"

"Oh yes, I have been so; but I cannot see everything with my own eyes."

At this part of our conversation, of which I have suppressed my own share as much as possible, I conceived that the last words of Bonaparte alluded to the death of the Duc d'Enghien; and I fancied he was about to mention that event, but he again spoke of Moreau.

"He is very much mistaken," resumed the Emperor, "if he conceives I bore any ill-will towards him. After his arrest I sent Lauriston to the Temple, whom I chose because he was of an amiable and conciliating disposition; I charged him to tell Moreau to confess he had only seen Pichegru, and I would cause the proceedings against him to be suspended. Instead of receiving this act of generosity as he ought to have done, he replied to it with great haughtiness, so much was he elated that Pichegru had not been arrested; he afterwards, however, lowered his tone. He wrote to me a letter of excuse respecting his anterior conduct, which I caused to be produced on the trial. He was the author of his own ruin; besides, it would have required men of a different stamp from Moreau to conspire against me. Among the conspirators, for example, was an individual whose fate I regret; this Georges in my hands might have achieved great things. I can duly appreciate the firmness of character he displayed, and to which I could have given a proper direction. I caused Réal to intimate to him that, if he would attach himself to me, not only should he be pardoned, but that I would give him the command of a regiment. Perhaps I might even have

made him my *aide de camp*.   Complaints would have been
made, but, parbleu, I should not have cared.   Georges
refused all my offers ; he was as inflexible as iron.   What
could I do ? he underwent his fate, for he was a dangerous man ; circumstances rendered his death a matter of
necessity.   Examples of severity were called for, when
England was pouring into France the whole offscouring of
the emigration ; but patience, patience ! I have a long
arm, and shall be able to reach them, when necessary.
Moreau regarded Georges merely as a ruffian—I viewed
him in a different light.   You may remember the conversation I had with him at the Tuileries—you and Rapp
were in an adjoining cabinet.   I tried in vain to influence
him—some of his associates were affected at the mention
of *country* and of *glory ;* he alone stood cold and unmoved.
I addressed myself to his feelings, but in vain ; he was insensible to everything I said.   At that period Georges appeared to me little ambitious of power ; his whole wishes
seemed to centre in commanding the Vendeans.   It was
not till I had exhausted every means of conciliation that I
assumed the tone and language of the first magistrate.   I
dismissed him with a strong injunction to live retired—to
be peaceable and obedient—not to misinterpret the motives of my conduct towards himself—nor attribute to
weakness what was merely the result of moderation and
strength.   ' Rest assured,' I added, ' and repeat to your
associates, that while I hold the reins of authority there
will be neither chance nor salvation for those who dare to
conspire against me.'   How he conformed to this injunction the event has shown.   Réal told me that when Moreau
and Georges found themselves in the presence of Pichegru they could not come to any understanding, because
Georges would not act against the Bourbons.   Well, he
had a plan, but Moreau had none ; he merely wished for
my overthrow, without having formed any ulterior views
whatever.   This showed that he was destitute of even

common sense. Apropos, Bourrienne, have you seen Corvisart?"—"Yes, Sire."—"Well!"—"He delivered to me the message with which you entrusted him."—"And Desmaisons!—I wager that you have not spoken to him in conformity to my wishes."—"Sire, the estimation in which I hold Desmaisons deterred me from a course so injurious to him; for in what other light could he have considered what I should have said to him? I have never visited at his house since the commencement of the trial." —"Well! well! Be prudent and discreet, I shall not forget you." He then waved a very gracious salute with his hand, and withdrew into his cabinet.

The Emperor had detained me more than an hour. On leaving the audience-chamber I passed through the outer *salon*, where a number of individuals were waiting; and I perceived that an observance of etiquette was fast gaining ground, though the Emperor had not yet adopted the admirable institution of Court Chamberlains.

I cannot deny that I was much gratified with my reception; besides I was beginning to be weary of an inactive life, and was anxious to obtain a place, of which I stood in great need, from the losses I had sustained and the unjust resumption which Bonaparte had made of his gifts. Being desirous to speak of Napoleon with the strictest impartiality, I prefer drawing my conclusions from those actions in which I had no personal concern. I shall therefore only relate here, even before giving an account of my visit to the Empress on leaving the audience-chamber, the former conduct of Napoleon towards myself and Madame de Bourrienne, which will justify the momentary alarm with which I was seized when summoned to the Tuileries, and the satisfaction I felt at my reception. I had a proof of what Rapp said of the Emperor being in good-humour, and was flattered by the confidential manner in which he spoke to me concerning some of the great political secrets of his Government. On seeing me come out Rapp ob-

served, "You have had a long audience."—"Yes, not
amiss ; " and this circumstance procured for me a courtly
salutation from all persons waiting in the antechamber.[1]

I shall now relate how I spent the two preceding years.
The month after I tendered my resignation to the First
Consul, and which he refused to accept, the house at St.
Cloud belonging to Madame Deville was offered to me ; it
was that in which the Duc d'Angoulême and the Duc de
Berri were inoculated.   I visited this mansion, thinking it
might be suitable for my family ; but, notwithstanding the
beauty of its situation, it seemed far too splendid either
for my taste or my fortune.   Except the outer walls, it
was in a very dilapidated state, and would require numerous and expensive repairs.   Josephine, being informed
that Madame de Bourrienne had set her face against the
purchase, expressed a wish to see the mansion, and accompanied us for that purpose.   She was so much delighted with it that she blamed my wife for starting any
objections to my becoming its possessor.   " With regard
to the expense," Josephine replied to her, " ah, we shall
arrange that."   On our return to Malmaison she spoke of
it in such high terms that Bonaparte said to me, " Why
don't you purchase it, Bourrienne, since the price is so
reasonable ? "[2]

The house was accordingly purchased.   An outlay of
20,000 francs was immediately required to render it habit-
able.   Furniture was also necessary for this large mansion,

---

[1] That Bourrienne had any interview at this time with Napoleon is denied by the
Bonapartists, but all the account of this conversation is in accordance with other
records of Napoleon's feelings.   There is no doubt that Napoleon had been advised
that Moreau's condemnation was certain.   " I was," says Madame de Rémusat (tome
ii. p. 7), " at St. Cloud when the news of the sentence arrived.   Every one was overwhelmed with astonishment.   The Grand Judge (Regnier) had rashly assured the First
Consul of the condemnation of Moreau to death, and Bonaparte was so angry that he
could not conceal his state."   In another place (tome i. p. 305) she tells us that on
her husband advising Savary that the evidence would not convict Moreau, Savary
replied, " In that case the Grand Judge has made us commit a great folly.   It would
have been better to have employed a military commission."

[2] It was valued at 60,000 francs.

and orders for it were accordingly given.   But no sooner
were repairs begun than everything crumbled to pieces,
which rendered many additional expenses necessary.

About this period Bonaparte hurried forward the works
at St. Cloud, to which place he immediately removed.
My services being constantly required, I found it so
fatiguing to go twice or thrice a day from Ruël to St.
Cloud that I took possession of my new mansion, though
it was still filled with workmen.   Scarcely eight days had
elapsed from this period when Bonaparte intimated that
he no longer had occasion for my services.   When my
wife went to take leave Napoleon spoke to her in a flattering manner of my good qualities, my merit, and the
utility of my labours, saying that he was himself the most
unfortunate of the three, and that my loss could never be
replaced.   He then added, " I shall be absent for a month,
but Bourrienne may be quite easy ; let him remain in retirement, and on my return I shall reward his services,
should I even create a place on purpose for him."

Madame de Bourrienne then requested leave to retain
the apartments appropriated to her in the Tuileries till
after her accouchement, which was not far distant, to
which he replied, "You may keep them as long as you
please ; for it will be some time before I again reside in
Paris."

Bonaparte set out on his journey, and shortly afterwards I went with my family to visit Madame de Cou-
bertin, my cousin-german, who received us with her usual
kindness.   We passed the time of the First Consul's absence at her country seat, and only returned to St. Cloud
on the day Bonaparte was expected.

Scarcely a quarter of an hour had elapsed after his arrival when I received an intimation to give up, in twenty-
four hours, the apartments in the Tuileries, which he had
promised my wife should retain till after her confinement.
He reclaimed at the same time the furniture of Ruël,

which he presented to me two years before, when I purchased that small house on purpose to be near him.

I addressed several memorials to him on this subject,
stating that I had replaced the worn-out furniture with
new and superior articles; but this he wholly disregarded,
compelling me to give up everything, even to the greatest
trifle. It may be right to say that on his return the
Emperor found his table covered with information respecting my conduct in Paris, though I had not held the
smallest communication with any one in the capital, nor
once entered it during his absence.

After my departure for Hamburg, Bonaparte took possession of my stables and coach-house, which he filled
with horses. Even the very avenues and walks were converted into stabling. A handsome house at the entrance
to the park was also appropriated to similar purposes; in
fact, he spared nothing. Every thing was done in the true
military style; I neither had previous intimation of the
proceedings nor received any remuneration for my loss.
The Emperor seemed to regard the property as his own;
but though he all but ordered me to make the purchase,
he did not furnish the money that was paid for it. In
this way it was occupied for more than four years.

The recollection of those arbitrary and vexatious proceedings on the part of Bonaparte has led me farther than
I intended. I shall therefore return to the imperial residence of St. Cloud. On leaving the audience-chamber,
as already stated, I repaired to the apartments of the
Empress, who, knowing that I was in the Palace, had intimated her wishes for my attendance. No command
could have been more agreeable to me, for every one was
certain of a gracious reception from Josephine. I do not
recollect which of the ladies in waiting was in attendance
when my name was announced; but she immediately retired, and left me alone with Josephine. Her recent elevation had not changed the usual amenity of her disposi-

tion. After some conversation respecting the change in her situation, I gave her an account of what had passed between the Emperor and myself.

I faithfully related all that he had said of Moreau, observing that at one moment I imagined he was about to speak of the Duc d'Enghien, when he suddenly reverted to what he had been saying, and never made the slightest allusion to the subject.

Madame Bonaparte replied to me, "Napoleon has spoken the truth respecting Moreau. He was grossly deceived by those who believed they could best pay their court to him by calumniating that general. His silence on the subject of the Duc d'Enghien does not surprise me ; he says as little respecting it as possible, and always in a vague manner, and with manifest repugnance. When you see Bonaparte again be silent on the subject, and should chance bring it forward, avoid every expression in the smallest degree indicative of reproach ; he would not suffer it ; you would ruin yourself for ever in his estimation, and the evil is, alas ! without remedy. When you came to Malmaison I told you that I had vainly endeavoured to turn him from his fatal purpose, and how he had treated me. Since then he has experienced but little internal satisfaction ; it is only in the presence of his courtiers that he affects a calm and tranquil deportment ; but I perceive his sufferings are the greater from thus endeavouring to conceal them. By the by, I forgot to mention that he knew of the visit you paid me on the day after the catastrophe. I dreaded that your enemies, the greater number of whom are also mine, might have misrepresented that interview ; but, fortunately, he paid little attention to it. He merely said, 'So you have seen Bourrienne? Does he sulk at me? Nevertheless I must do something for him.' He has again spoken in the same strain, and repeated nearly the same expressions three days ago ; and since he has commanded your presence to-day, I have not a doubt but he has something in view for your advantage."—"May I presume to inquire what it is?"—"I do not yet know; but I would recommend to you, in the meantime, to be more strictly on your guard than ever; he is so suspicious, and so well informed of all that is done or said respecting himself. I have suffered so much since I last saw you; never can I forget the unkind manner in which he rejected my entreaties! For several days I laboured under a depression of spirits which greatly irritated him, because he clearly saw whence it proceeded. I am not dazzled by the title of Empress; I dread some evil will result from this step to him, to my children, and to myself. The miscreants ought to be satisfied; see to what they have driven us! This death embitters every moment of my life. I need not say to you, Bourrienne, that I speak this in confidence."—"You cannot doubt my prudence."—"No, certainly not, Bourrienne. I do not doubt it. My confidence in you is unbounded. Rest assured that I shall never forget what you have done for me, under various circumstances, and the devotedness you evinced to me on your return from Egypt.—Adieu, my friend. Let me see you soon again."

It was on the 14th of June 1804 that I had this audience of the Emperor, and afterwards attended the Empress.

On my return home I spent three hours in making notes of all that was said to me by these two personages; and the substance of these notes I have now given to the reader.

CHAPTER XXVIII.

1804.

Curious disclosures of Fouché—Remarkable words of Bonaparte respecting the protest of Louis XVIII.—Secret document inserted in the
Moniteur—Announcement from Bonaparte to Regnier—Fouché appointed Minister of Police—Error of Regnier respecting the conspiracy of Georges—Undeserved praise bestowed on Fouché—Indications of the return of the Bourbons—Variance between the words and
conduct of Bonaparte—The iron crown—Celebration of the 14th of
July—Church festivals and loss of time—Grand ceremonial at the
Invalides—Recollections of the 18th Brumaire—New oath of the Legion of Honour—General enthusiasm—Departure for Boulogne—Visits to Josephine at St. Cloud and Malmaison—Josephine and Madame
de Rémusat—Pardons granted by the Emperor—Anniversary of the
14th of July—Departure for the camp of Boulogne—General error
respecting Napoleon's designs—Cæsar's Tower—Distribution of the
crosses of the Legion of Honour—The military throne—Bonaparte's
charlatanism—Intrepidity of two English sailors—The decennial
prizes and the Polytechnic School—Meeting of the Emperor and
Empress—First negotiation with the Holy See—The Prefect of
Arras and Comte Louis de Narbonne—Change in the French Ministry.

LOUIS XVIII., being at Warsaw when he was informed
of the elevation of Napoleon to the Imperial dignity, addressed to the sovereigns of Europe a protest against that
usurpation of his throne. Fouché, being the first who
heard of this protest, immediately communicated the circumstance to the Emperor, observing that doubtless the
copies would be multiplied and distributed amongst the
enemies of his Government, in the Faubourg St. Germain,
which might produce the worst effects, and that he therefore deemed it his duty to inform him that orders might
be given to Regnier and Réal to keep a strict watch over
those engaged in distributing this document.

" You may judge of my surprise," added Fouché, "you who know so well that formerly the very mention of the Bourbons rendered Bonaparte furious, when, after perusing the protest, he returned it to me, saying, 'Ah, ah, so the Comte de Lille makes his protest ! Well, well, all in good time. I hold my right by the voice of the French nation, and while I wear a sword I will maintain it ! The Bourbons ought to know that I do not fear them ; let them, therefore, leave me in tranquillity. Did you say that the fools of the Faubourg St. Germain would multiply the copies of this protest of Comte de Lille ? Well, they shall read it at their ease. Send it to the *Moniteur,* Fouché ; and let it be inserted to-morrow morning.' " This passed on the 30th of June, and the next day the protest of Louis XVIII. did actually appear in that paper.

Fouché was wholly indifferent respecting the circulation of this protest ; he merely wished to show the Emperor that he was better informed of passing events than Regnier, and to afford Napoleon another proof of the inexperience and inability of the Grand Judge in police ; and Fouché was not long in receiving the reward which he expected from this step. In fact, ten days after the publication of the protest, the Emperor announced to Regnier the re-establishment of the Ministry of General Police.

The formula, *I pray God to have you in His holy keeping,* with which the letter to Regnier closed, was another step of Napoleon in the knowledge of ancient usages, with which he was not sufficiently familiar when he wrote Cambacérès on the day succeeding his elevation to the Imperial throne ; at the same time it must be confessed that this formula assorted awkwardly with the month of "Messidor," and the "twelfth year of the Republic ! "

The errors which Regnier had committed in the affair of Georges were the cause which determined Bonaparte to re-establish the Ministry of Police, and to bestow it on a

man who had created a belief in the necessity of that
measure, by a monstrous accumulation of plots and intrigues. I am also certain that the Emperor was swayed
by the probability of a war breaking out, which would
force him to leave France; and that he considered Fouché
as the most proper person to maintain the public tranquillity during his absence, and detect any cabals that
might be formed in favour of the Bourbons.

At this period, when Bonaparte had given the finishing
blow to the Republic, which had only been a shadow since
the 19th Brumaire, it was not difficult to foresee that the
Bourbons would one day remount the throne of their ancestors; and this presentiment was not, perhaps, without
its influence in rendering the majority greater in favour of
the foundation of the Empire than for the establishment of
a Consulate for life. The re-establishment of the throne
was a most important step in favour of the Bourbons, for
that was the thing most difficult to be done. But Bonaparte undertook the task; and, as if by the aid of a magic
rod, the ancient order of things was restored in the twink-
ling of an eye. The distinctions of rank—orders—titles—
the noblesse—decorations—all the baubles of vanity—in
short, all the burlesque tattooing which the vulgar regard
as an indispensable attribute of royalty, reappeared in an
instant. The question no longer regarded the form of
government, but the individual who should be placed at
its head. By restoring the ancient order of things, the
Republicans had themselves decided the question, and it
could no longer be doubted that when an occasion presented itself the majority of the nation would prefer the
ancient royal family, to whom France owed her civilisation, her greatness, and her power, and who had exalted
her to such a high degree of glory and prosperity.

It was not one of the least singular traits in Napoleon's
character that during the first year of his reign he retained
the *fête* of the 14th of July. It was not indeed strictly a

Republican *fête,* but it recalled the recollection of two
great popular triumphs,—the taking of the Bastille and
the first Federation.   This year the 14th of July fell on a
Saturday, and the Emperor ordered its celebration to be
delayed till the following day, because it was Sunday;
which was in conformity with the sentiments he delivered
respecting the *Concordat.*   "What renders me," he said,
"most hostile to the re-establishment of the Catholic worship is the number of festivals formerly observed.   A
saint's day is a day of indolence, and I wish not for that;
the people must labour in order to live.   I consent to four
holidays in the year, but no more ; if the gentlemen from
Rome are not satisfied with this, they may take their departure."

The loss of time seemed to him so great a calamity that
he seldom failed to order an indispensable solemnity to be
held on the succeeding holiday.   Thus he postponed the
Corpus Christi to the following Sunday.

On Sunday, the 15th of July 1804, the Emperor appeared for the first time before the Parisians surrounded
by all the pomp of royalty.   The members of the Legion
of Honour, then in Paris, took the oath prescribed by the
new Constitution, and on this occasion the Emperor and
Empress appeared attended for the first time by a separate and numerous retinue.

The carriages in the train of the Empress crossed the
garden of the Tuileries, hitherto exclusively appropriated
to the public ; then followed the cavalcade of the Emper-
or, who appeared on horseback, surrounded by his principal generals, whom he had created Marshals of the Empire.   M. de Ségur, who held the office of Grand Master
of Ceremonies, had the direction of the ceremonial to be
observed on this occasion, and with the Governor received the Emperor on the threshold of the Hôtel des
Invalides.   They conducted the Empress to a tribune
prepared for her reception, opposite the Imperial throne

which Napoleon alone occupied, to the right of the altar.
I was present at this ceremony, notwithstanding the repugnance I have to such brilliant exhibitions ; but as Duroc
had two days before presented me with tickets, I deemed
it prudent to attend on the occasion, lest the keen eye of
Bonaparte should have remarked my absence if Duroc had
acted by his order.

I spent about an hour contemplating the proud and
sometimes almost ludicrous demeanour of the new gran-
dees of the Empire ; I marked the manœuvring of the
clergy, who, with Cardinal Belloy at their head, proceeded
to receive the Emperor on his entrance into the church.
What a singular train of ideas was called up to my
mind when I beheld my former comrade at the school of
Brienne seated upon an elevated throne, surrounded by
his brilliant staff, the great dignitaries of his Empire—his
Ministers and Marshals ! I involuntarily recurred to the
19th Brumaire, and all this splendid scene vanished, when
I thought of Bonaparte stammering to such a degree that
I was obliged to pull the skirt of his coat to induce him to
withdraw.

It was neither a feeling of animosity nor of jealousy
which called up such reflections ; at no period of our career
would I have exchanged my situation for his ; but whoever can reflect, whoever has witnessed the unexpected
elevation of a former equal, may perhaps be able to conceive the strange thoughts that assailed my mind, for the
first time, on this occasion.

When the religious part of the ceremony terminated,
the church assumed, in some measure, the appearance of
a profane temple. The congregation displayed more devotion to the Emperor than towards the God of the Chris-
tians,—more enthusiasm than fervour. The mass had been
heard with little attention ; but when M. de Lacépède,
Grand Chancellor of the Legion of Honour, after pronouncing a flattering discourse, finished the call of the

Grand Officers of the Legion, Bonaparte covered, as did
the ancient kings of France when they held a bed of justice. A profound silence, a sort of religious awe, then
reigned throughout the assembly, and Napoleon, who did
not now stammer as in the Council of the Five Hundred,
said in a firm voice :—

"Commanders, officers, legionaries, citizens, soldiers; swear upon
your honour to devote yourselves to the service of the Empire—to
the preservation of the integrity of the French territory—to the defence of the Emperor, of the laws of the Republic, and of the property which they have made sacred—to combat by all the means
which justice, reason, and the laws authorise every attempt to re-
establish the feudal system ; in short, swear to concur with all your
might in maintaining liberty and equality, which are the bases of
all our institutions. Do you swear ? "

Each member of the Legion of Honour exclaimed, "*I
swear ;*" adding, "*Vive l'Empereur !* " with an enthusiam it
is impossible to describe, and in which all present joined.

What, after all, was this new oath ? It only differed
from that taken by the Legion of Honour, under the Consulate, in putting the defence of the Emperor before that
of the laws of the Republic ; and this was not merely a
form. It was, besides, sufficiently laughable and somewhat audacious, to make them swear to support *equality*
at the moment so many titles and monarchical distinctions
had been re-established.

On the 18th of July, three days after this ceremony,
the Emperor left Paris to visit the camp at Boulogne. He
was not accompanied by the Empress on this journey,
which was merely to examine the progress of the military
operations. Availing myself of the invitation Josephine
had given me, I presented myself at St. Cloud a few days
after the departure of Napoleon ; as she did not expect
my visit, I found her surrounded by four or five of the
ladies in waiting, occupied in examining some of the elegant productions of the famous Leroi and Madame

Despeaux ; for amidst the host of painful feelings experienced by Josephine she was too much of a woman not to devote some attention to the toilet.

On my introduction they were discussing the serious question of the costume to be worn by the Empress on her journey to Belgium to meet Napoleon at the Palace of Lacken, near Brussels. Notwithstanding those discussions respecting the form of hats, the colour and shape of dresses, etc., Josephine received me in her usual gracious manner. But not being able to converse with me, she said, without giving it an appearance of invitation but in a manner sufficiently evident to be understood, that she intended to pass the following morning at Malmaison.

I shortened my visit, and at noon next day repaired to that delightful abode, which always created in my mind deep emotion. Not an alley, not a grove but teemed with interesting recollections ; all recalled to me the period when I was the confidant of Bonaparte. But the time was past when he minutely calculated how much a residence at Malmaison would cost, and concluded by saying that an income of 30,000 livres would be necessary.

When I arrived Madame Bonaparte was in the garden with Madame de Rémusat, who was her favourite from the similarity of disposition which existed between them.[1]

Madame de Rémusat was the daughter of the Minister Vergennes, and sister to Madame de Nansouty, whom I had sometimes seen with Josephine, but not so frequently as her elder sister. I found the ladies in the avenue which leads to Ruel, and saluted Josephine by inquiring respecting the health of Her Majesty. Never can I forget the tone in which she replied : "Ah ! Bourrienne, I entreat

---

[1] Madame de Rémusat's *Memoirs* have been recently published by her grandson, M. Paul de Rémusat. Although Madame de Rémusat seems to have really liked Josephine, it is pleasant to think of her horror at finding herself to resemble the Empress in character. "Not a person of transcendent mind, with a neglected education, wanting in gravity and elevation of soul, incapable of prolonged feeling," such are some of her remarks on Josephine (*Rémusat*, tome i. p. 140).

that you will suffer me, at least here, to forget that I am an Empress." As she had not a thought concealed from Madame de Rémusat except some domestic vexations, of which probably I was the only confidant, we conversed with the same freedom as if alone, and it is easy to define that the subject of our discourse regarded Bonaparte.

After having spoken of her intended journey to Belgium, Josephine said to me, "What a pity, Bourrienne, that the past cannot be recalled! He departed in the happiest disposition : he has bestowed some pardons : and I am satisfied that but for those accursed politics he would have pardoned a far greater number. I would have said much more, but I endeavoured to conceal my chagrin because the slightest contradiction only renders him the more obstinate. Now, when in the midst of his army, he will forget everything. How much have I been afflicted that I was not able to obtain a favourable answer to all the petitions which were addressed to me. That good Madame de Montesson came from Romainville to St. Cloud to solicit the pardon of MM. de Rivière and de Polignac ; we succeeded in gaining an audience for Madame de Polignac ; . . . how beautiful she is ! Bonaparte was greatly affected on beholding her ; he said to her, 'Madame, since it was only my life your husband menaced, I may pardon him.' You know Napoleon, Bourrienne ; you know that he is not naturally cruel ; it is his counsellors and flatterers who have induced him to commit so many villainous actions. Rapp has behaved extremely well ; he went to the Emperor, and would not leave him till he had obtained the pardon of another of the condemned, whose name I do not recollect.[1] How much these Polignacs have interested me ! There will be then at least some families who will owe him gratitude ! Strive, if it be possible, to throw a veil over the past ; I am sufficiently miserable in my anticipations of the future.

---

[1] It was, I believe, De Rusillon.—*Bourrienne.*

Rest assured, my dear Bourrienne, that I shall not fail to exert myself during our stay in Belgium in your behalf, and inform you of the result. Adieu!"

During the festival in celebration of the 14th of July, which I have already alluded to, the Emperor before leaving the Hôtel des Invalides had announced that he would go in person to distribute the decorations of the Legion of Honour to the army assembled in the camp of Boulogne. He was not long before he fulfilled his promise. He left St. Cloud on the 18th and travelled with such rapidity that the next morning, whilst every one was busy with preparations for his reception, he was already at that port, in the midst of the labourers, examining the works. He seemed to multiply himself by his inconceivable activity, and one might say that he was present everywhere.

At the Emperor's departure it was generally believed at Paris that the distribution of the crosses at the camp of Boulogne was only a pretext, and that Bonaparte had at length gone to carry into execution the project of an invasion of England, which every body supposed he contemplated. It was, indeed, a pretext. The Emperor wished to excite more and more the enthusiasm of the army—to show himself to the military invested in his new dignity, to be present at some grand manœuvres, and dispose the army to obey the first signal he might give. How indeed, on beholding such great preparations, so many transports created, as it were, by enchantment, could any one have supposed that he did not really intend to attempt a descent on England? People almost fancied him already in London; it was known that all the army corps echelloned on the coast from Étaples to Ostend were ready to embark. Napoleon's arrival in the midst of his troops inspired them, if possible, with a new impulse. The French ports on the Channel had for a long period been converted into dockyards and arsenals, where works were carried on with that inconceivable activity which Napoleon knew so well how to inspire. An almost incredible degree of emulation prevailed amongst the commanders of the different camps, and it descended from rank to rank to the common soldiers and even to the labourers.

As every one was eager to take advantage of the slightest effects of chance, and exercised his ingenuity in converting them into prognostics of good fortune for the Emperor, those who had access to him did not fail to call his attention to some remains of a Roman camp which had been discovered at the *Tour d'Ordre*, where the Emperor's tent was pitched. This was considered an evident proof that the French Cæsar occupied the camp which the Roman Cæsar had formerly constructed to menace Great Britain. To give additional force to this allusion, the *Tour d'Ordre* resumed the name of Cæsar's Tower. Some medals of William the Conqueror, found in another spot, where, perhaps, they had been buried for the purpose of being dug up, could not fail to satisfy the most incredulous that Napoleon must conquer England.

It was not far from Cæsar's Tower that 80,000 men of the camps of Boulogne and Montreuil, under the command of Marshal Soult, were assembled in a vast plain to witness the distribution of the crosses of the Legion of Honour impressed with the Imperial effigy. This plain, which I saw with Bonaparte in our first journey to the coast, before our departure to Egypt, was circular and hollow, and in the centre was a little hill. This hill formed the Imperial throne of Bonaparte in the midst of his soldiers. There he stationed himself with his staff, and around this centre of glory the regiments were drawn up in lines and looked like so many diverging rays. From this throne, which had been erected by the hand of nature, Bonaparte delivered in a loud voice the same form of oath which he had pronounced at the Hôtel des Invalides a few days before. It was the signal for a general burst of enthusiasm, and Rapp, alluding to this ceremony, told me that he never saw the Emperor appear more pleased. How could he be otherwise? Fortune then seemed obedient to his wishes. A storm came on during this brilliant day, and it was apprehended that part of the flotilla would have suffered.[1] Bonaparte quitted the hill from which he had distributed the crosses and proceeded to the port to direct what measures should be taken, when upon his arrival the storm

---

[1] The following description of the incident when Napoleon nearly occasioned the destruction of the Boulogne flotilla was forwarded to the *Revue Politique et Littéraire* from a private memoir. The writer, who was an eye-witness, says:—

One morning, when the Emperor was mounting his horse, he announced that he intended to hold a review of his naval forces, and gave the order that the vessels which lay in the harbour should alter their positions, as the review was to be held on the open sea. He started on his usual ride, giving orders that everything should be arranged on his return, the time of which he indicated. His wish was communicated to Admiral Bruix, who responded with imperturbable coolness that he was very sorry, but that the review could not take place that day. Consequently not a vessel was moved. On his return back from his ride the Emperor asked whether all was ready. He was told what the Admiral had said. Twice the answer had to be repeated to him before he could realise its nature, and then, violently stamping his foot on the ground, he sent for the Admiral. The Emperor met him half-way. With eyes burning with rage, he exclaimed in an excited voice, " Why have my orders not been executed ? " With respectful firmness Admiral Bruix replied, " Sire, a terrible storm is brewing. Your Majesty may convince yourself of it ; would you without need expose the lives of so many men ? " The heaviness of the atmosphere and the sound of thunder in the distance more than justified the fears of the Admiral. " Sir," said the Emperor, getting more and more irritated, " I have given the orders once more ; why have they not been executed ? The consequences concern me alone. Obey ! " " Sire, I will not obey," replied the Admiral. " You are insolent ! " And the Emperor, who still held his riding-whip in his hand, advanced towards the Admiral with a threatening gesture. Admiral Bruix stepped back and put his hand on the sheath of his sword and said, growing very pale, " Sire, take care ! " The whole suite stood paralysed with fear. The Emperor remained motionless for some time, his hand lifted up, his eyes fixed on the Admiral, who still retained his menacing attitude. At last the Emperor threw his whip on the floor. M. Bruix took his hand off his sword, and with uncovered head awaited in silence the result of the painful scene. Rear-Admiral Magon was then ordered to see that the Emperor's orders were instantly executed. " As for you, sir," said the Emperor, fixing his eyes on Admiral Bruix, " you leave Boulogne within twenty-four hours and depart for Holland. Go ! " M. Magon ordered the fatal movement of the fleet on which the Emperor had insisted. The first arrangements had scarcely been made when the sea became very high. The black sky was pierced by lightning, the thunder rolled, and every moment the line of vessels was broken by the wind, and shortly after, that which the Admiral had foreseen came to pass, and the most frightful storm dispersed the vessels in such a way that it seemed impossible to save them. With bent head, arms crossed, and a sorrowful look in his face, the Emperor walked up and down on the beach, when suddenly the most terrible cries were heard. More than twenty gunboats filled with soldiers and sailors were being driven towards the shore, and the unfortunate men were vainly

ceased as if by enchantment. The flotilla entered the port safe and sound and he went back to the camp, where the sports and amusements prepared for the soldiers commenced, and in the evening the brilliant fireworks which were let off rose in a luminous column, which was distinctly seen from the English coast.

When he reviewed the troops he asked the officers, and often the soldiers, in what battles they had been engaged, and to those who had received serious wounds he gave the cross. Here, I think, I may appropriately mention a singular piece of charlatanism to which the Emperor had recourse, and which powerfully contributed to augment the enthusiasm of his troops. He would say to one of his *aides de camp*, "Ascertain from the colonel of such a regiment whether he has in his corps a man who has served in the campaigns of Italy or the campaigns of Egypt. Ascertain his name, where he was born, the particulars of his family, and what he has done. Learn his number in the ranks, and to what company he belongs, and furnish me with the information."

On the day of the review Bonaparte, at a single glance, could perceive the man who had been described to him. He would go up to him as if he recognised him, address him by his name, and say, "Oh! so you are here! You are a brave fellow—I saw you at Aboukir—how is your

fighting against the furious waves, calling for help which nobody could give them. Deeply touched by the spectacle and the heartrending cries and lamentations of the multitude which had assembled on the beach, the Emperor, seeing his generals and officers tremble with horror, attempted to set an example of devotion, and, in spite of all efforts to keep him back, he threw himself into a boat, saying, "Let me go! let me go! they must be brought out of this." In a moment the boat was filled with water. The waves poured over it again and again, and the Emperor was drenched. One wave larger than the others almost threw him overboard and his hat was carried away. Inspired by so much courage, officers, soldiers, seamen, and citizens tried to succour the drowning, some in boats, some swimming. But, alas! only a small number could be saved of the unfortunate men. The following day more than 200 bodies were thrown ashore, and with them the hat of the conqueror of Marengo. That sad day was one of desolation for Boulogne and for the camp. The Emperor groaned under the burden of an accident which he had to attribute solely to his own obstinacy. Agents were despatched to all parts of the town to subdue with gold the murmurs which were ready to break out into a tumult.

old father? What! have you not got the cross? Stay, I will give it you." Then the delighted soldiers would say to each other, "You see the Emperor knows us all; he knows our families; he knows where we have served." What a stimulus was this to soldiers, whom he succeeded in persuading that they would all some time or other become Marshals of the Empire!

Lauriston told me, amongst other anecdotes relating to Napoleon's sojourn at the camp at Boulogne, a remarkable instance of intrepidity on the part of two English sailors. These men had been prisoners at Verdun, which was the most considerable depot of English prisoners in France at the rupture of the peace of Amiens. They effected their escape from Verdun, and arrived at Boulogne without having been discovered on the road, notwithstanding the vigilance with which all the English were watched. They remained at Boulogne for some time, destitute of money, and without being able to effect their escape. They had no hope of getting aboard a boat, on account of the strict watch that was kept upon vessels of every kind. These two sailors made a boat of little pieces of wood, which they put together as well as they could, having no other tools than their knives. They covered it with a piece of sail-cloth. It was only three or four feet wide, and not much longer, and was so light that a man could easily carry it on his shoulders,—so powerful a passion is the love of home and liberty! Sure of being shot if they were discovered, almost equally sure of being drowned if they effected their escape, they, nevertheless, resolved to attempt crossing the Channel in their fragile skiff. Perceiving an English frigate within sight of the coast, they pushed off and endeavoured to reach her. They had not gone a hundred toises from the shore when they were perceived by the custom-house officers, who set out in pursuit of them, and brought them back again. The news of this adventure spread through the

camp, where the extraordinary courage of the two sailors
was the subject of general remark. The circumstance
reached the Emperor's ears. He wished to see the men,
and they were conducted to his presence, along with their
little boat. Napoleon, whose imagination was struck by
everything extraordinary, could not conceal his surprise
at so bold a project, undertaken with such feeble means
of execution. "Is it really true," said the Emperor to
them, "that you thought of crossing the sea in this?"—
"Sire," said they, "if you doubt it, give us leave to go,
and you shall see us depart."—"I will. You are bold and
enterprising men—I admire courage wherever I meet it.
But you shall not hazard your lives. You are at liberty ;
and more than that, I will cause you to be put on board
an English ship. When you return to London tell how I
esteem brave men, even when they are my enemies."
Rapp, who with Lauriston, Duroc, and many others were
present at this scene, were not a little astonished at the
Emperor's generosity. If the men had not been brought
before him, they would have been shot as spies, instead
of which they obtained their liberty, and Napoleon gave
several pieces of gold to each. This circumstance was one
of those which made the strongest impression on Napoleon, and he recollected it when at St. Helena, in one of
his conversations with M. de Las Casas.

No man was ever so fond of contrasts as Bonaparte.
He liked, above everything, to direct the affairs of war
whilst seated in his easy chair, in the cabinet of St. Cloud,
and to dictate in the camp his decrees relative to civil
administration. Thus, at the camp of Boulogne, he
founded the decennial premiums, the first distribution of
which he intended should take place five years afterwards,
on the anniversary of the 18th Brumaire, which was an
innocent compliment to the date of the foundation of the
Consular Republic. This measure also seemed to promise to the Republican calendar a longevity which it did

not attain.¹ All these little circumstances passed unobserved ; but Bonaparte had so often developed to me his theory of the art of deceiving mankind that I knew their true value. It was likewise at the camp of Boulogne that, by a decree emanating from his individual will, he destroyed the noblest institution of the Republic, the Polytechnic School, by converting it into a purely military academy. He knew that in that sanctuary of high study a Republican spirit was fostered ; and whilst I was with him he had often told me it was necessary that all schools, colleges, and establishments for public instruction should be subject to military discipline. I frequently endeavoured to controvert this idea, but without success.

It was arranged that Josephine and the Emperor should meet in Belgium. He proceeded thither from the camp of Boulogne, to the astonishment of those who believed that the moment for the invasion of England had at length arrived. He joined the Empress at the Palace of Lacken, which the Emperor had ordered to be repaired and newly furnished with great magnificence.

The Emperor continued his journey by the towns bordering on the Rhine. He stopped first in the town of Charlemagne,² passed through the three bishoprics, saw

¹ See the end of this volume.
² There are two or three little circumstances related by Mademoiselle Avrillion in connection with this journey that seem worth inserting here.

Mademoiselle Avrillion was the *femme de chambre* of Josephine, and was constantly about her person from the time of the first Consulship to the death of the Empress in 1814. In all such matters as we shall quote from them, her memoirs seem worthy of credit. According to Mademoiselle, the Empress during her stay at Aix la-Chapelle, drank the waters with much eagerness and some hope. As the theatre there was only supplied with some German singers who were not to Josephine's taste, she had part of a French operatic company sent to her from Paris. The amiable creole had always a most royal disregard of expense. When Bonaparte joined her, he renewed his old custom of visiting his wife now and then at her toilet, and according to Mademoiselle Avrillion, he took great interest in the subject of her dressing. She says, "It was a most extraordinary thing for us to see the man whose head was filled with such vast affairs enter into the most minute details of the female toilet, and of what dresses, what robes, and what jewels the Empress should wear on such and such an occasion. One day he daubed her dress with ink because he did not

on his way Cologne and Coblentz, which the emigration
had rendered so famous, and arrived at Mayence, where
his sojourn was distinguished by the first attempt at
negotiation with the Holy See, in order to induce the Pope
to come to France to crown the new Emperor, and consolidate his power by supporting it with the sanction of the
Church. This journey of Napoleon occupied three months,
and he did not return to St. Cloud till October. Amongst
the flattering addresses which the Emperor received in the
course of his journey I cannot pass over unnoticed the
speech of M. de la Chaise, Prefect of Arras, who said,
"God made Bonaparte, and then rested." This occasioned
Comte Louis de Narbonne, who was not yet attached to
the Imperial system, to remark "That it would have been
well had God rested a little sooner."

During the Emperor's absence a partial change took
place in the Ministry. M. de Champagny succeeded M.
Chaptal as Minister of the Interior. At the camp of Boulogne the pacific Joseph found himself, by his brother's

like it, and wanted her to put on another. Whenever he looked into her wardrobe
he was sure to throw everything topsy-turvy."

This characteristic anecdote perfectly agrees with what we have heard from other
persons. When the Neapolitan Princess di —— was at the Tuileries as *dame d'honneur* to Bonaparte's sister Caroline Murat, then Queen of Naples, on the grand occasion of the marriage with Maria Louisa, the Princess, to her astonishment, saw the
Emperor go up to a lady of the Court and address her thus: " This is the same gown
you wore the day before yesterday ! What's the meaning of this, madame ? This is
not right, madame ! "

Josephine never gave him a similar cause of complaint, but even when he was
Emperor she often made him murmur at the profusion of her expenditure under this
head. The next anecdote will give some idea of the quantity of dresses which she
wore for a day or so, and then gave away to her attendants, who appear to have
carried on a very active trade in them.

"While we were at Mayence the Palace was literally besieged by Jews, who continually brought manufactured and other goods to show to the followers of the Court ;
and we had the greatest difficulty to avoid buying them. At last they proposed that
we should barter with them ; and when Her Majesty had given us dresses that were
far too rich for us to wear ourselves, we exchanged them with the Jews for piece-
goods. The robes we thus bartered did not long remain in the hands of the Jews,
and there must have been a great demand for them among the belles of Mayence,
for I remember a ball there at which the Empress might have seen all the ladies of a
quadrille party dressed in her cast-off clothes,—I even saw German Princesses wearing them" (*Mémoires de Mademoiselle Avrillion*).

wish, transformed into a warrior, and placed in command
of a regiment of dragoons,[1] which was a subject of laughter
with a great number of generals.   I recollect that one day
Lannes, speaking to me of the circumstance in his usual
downright and energetic way, said, "He had better not
place him under my orders, for upon the first fault I will
put the scamp under arrest."

[1] Joseph was made colonel of the fourth regiment of the line, not of a dragoon
regiment (*Erreurs*, tome ii. p. 142).

CHAPTER XXIX.

1804.

ENGLAND was never so much deceived by Bonaparte as during the period of the encampment at Boulogne. The English really believed that an invasion was intended, and the Government exhausted itself in efforts for raising men and money to guard against the danger of being taken by surprise. Such, indeed, is the advantage always possessed by the assailant. He can choose the point on which he thinks it most convenient to act, while the party which stands on the defence, and is afraid of being attacked, is compelled to be prepared in every point. However, Napoleon, who was then in the full vigour of his genius and activity, had always his eyes fixed on objects remote from those which surrounded him, and which seemed to absorb his whole attention. Thus, during the journey of which I have spoken, the ostensible object of which was the organisation of the departments on the Rhine, he despatched two squadrons from Rochefort and Boulogne, one commanded by Missiessy, the other by Villeneuve. I shall not enter into any details about those squadrons ; I shall merely mention with respect to them that, while the Emperor was still in Belgium, Lauriston paid me a sudden and unexpected visit.[1] He was on his way to Toulon to take command of the troops which were to be embarked on Villeneuve's squadron, and he was not much pleased with the service to which he had been appointed.

Lauriston's visit was a piece of good fortune for me. We were always on friendly terms, and I received much information from him, particularly with respect to the manner in which the Emperor spent his time. "You can have no idea," said he, "how much the Emperor does, and the sort of enthusiasm which his presence excites in the army. But his anger at the contractors is greater than ever, and he has been very severe with some of them." These words of Lauriston did not at all surprise me, for I well knew Napoleon's dislike to contractors, and all men who had mercantile transactions with the army. I have often heard him say that they were a curse and a leprosy to nations ; that whatever power he might attain, he never would grant honours to any of them, and that of all aristocracies, theirs was to him the most insupportable. After his accession to the Empire the contractors were no longer the important persons they had been under the Directory, or even during the two first years of the Consulate. Bonaparte sometimes acted with them as he had before done with the Beys of Egypt, when he drew from them forced contributions.

[1] Lauriston, one of Napoleon's *aides de camp*, who was with him at the Military School of Paris, and who had been commissioned in the artillery at the same time as Napoleon, considered that he should have had the post of Grand Écuyer which Caulaincourt had obtained. He had complained angrily to the Emperor, and after a stormy interview was ordered to join the fleet of Villeneuve. In consequence he was at Trafalgar. On his return after Austerlitz his temporary disgrace was forgotten, and he was sent as governor to Venice. He became marshal under the Restoration. See *Meneval*, tome iii. p. 102, and *Savary*, tome ii. p. 239.

I recollect another somewhat curious circumstance respecting the visit of Lauriston, who had left the Emperor and Empress at Aix-la-Chapelle. Lauriston was the best educated of the *aides de camp*, and Napoleon often conversed with him on such literary works as he chose to notice. "He sent for me one day," said Lauriston, "when I was on duty at the Palace of Lacken, and spoke to me of the decennial prizes, and the tragedy of Carion de Nisas,[1] and a novel by Madame de Staël, which he had just read, but which I had not seen, and was therefore rather embarrassed in replying to him. Respecting Madame de Staël and her *Delphine*, he said some remarkable things. 'I do not like women,' he observed, 'who make men of themselves, any more than I like effeminate men. There is a proper part for every one to play in the world. What does all this flight of imagination mean? What is the result of it? Nothing. It is all sentimental metaphysics and disorder of the mind. I cannot endure that woman; for one reason, that I cannot bear women who make a set at me, and God knows how often she has tried to cajole me!'"

The words of Lauriston brought to my recollection the conversations I had often had with Bonaparte respecting Madame de Staël, of whose advances made to the First Consul, and even to the General of the Army of Italy, I had frequently been witness. Bonaparte knew nothing at first of Madame de Staël but that she was the daughter of M. Necker, a man for whom, as I have already shown, he had very little esteem. Madame de Staël had not been introduced to him, and knew nothing more of him than what fame had published respecting the young conqueror of Italy, when she addressed to him letters full of enthusi-

---

[1] Lauriston alluded to the tragedy of *Peter the Great*, which was twice represented before very tumultuous audiences. This piece was performed at the Théâtre Français in the first period of the Empire, but the Emperor prohibited the representation because the allusions were not taken in the sense he wished them to be, and which the author had hoped they would.—*Bourrienne*.

asm. Bonaparte read some passages of them to me, and, laughing, said, "What do you think, Bourrienne, of these extravagances. This woman is mad." I recollect that in one of her letters Madame de Staël, among other things, told him that they certainly were created for each other —that it was in consequence of an error in human institutions that the quiet and gentle Josephine was united to his fate—that nature seemed to have destined for the adoration of a hero such as he, a soul of fire like her own. These extravagances disgusted Bonaparte to a degree which I cannot describe. When he had finished reading these fine epistles he used to throw them into the fire, or tear them with marked ill-humour, and would say, " Well, here is a woman who pretends to genius—a maker of sentiments, and she presumes to compare herself to Josephine! Bourrienne, I shall not reply to such letters."

I had, however, the opportunity of seeing what the perseverance of a woman of talent can effect. Nothwithstanding Bonaparte's prejudices against Madame de Staël, which he never abandoned, she succeeded in getting herself introduced to him; and if anything could have disgusted him with flattery it would have been the admiration, or, to speak more properly, the worship, which she paid him; for she used to compare him to a god descended on earth,—a kind of comparison which the clergy, I thought, had reserved for their own use. But, unfortunately, to please Madame de Staël it would have been necessary that her god had been Plutus; for behind her eulogies lay a claim for two millions, which M. Necker considered still due to him on account of his good and worthy services. However, Bonaparte said on this occasion that whatever value he might set on the suffrage of Madame de Staël, he did not think fit to pay so dear for it with the money of the State. The conversion of Madame de Staël's enthusiasm into hatred is well known, as are also the petty vexations, unworthy of himself,

with which the Emperor harassed her in her retreat at
Coppet.[1]

Lauriston had arrived at Paris, where he made but a
short stay, some days before Caffarelli, who was sent on a
mission to Rome to sound the Papal Court, and to induce
the Holy Father to come to Paris to consecrate Bonaparte
at his coronation. I have already described the nature of
Bonaparte's ideas on religion. His notions on the subject
seemed to amount to a sort of vague feeling rather than
to any belief founded on reflection. Nevertheless, he had
a high opinion of the power of the Church; but not because he considered it dangerous to Governments, particularly to his own. Napoleon never could have conceived
how it was possible that a sovereign wearing a crown and

[1] Madame de Staël, with all her genius and worth, was certainly a vain woman;
but she was always high-minded, and we cannot help thinking that Bourrienne deals
rather harshly by her. The conduct of Bonaparte towards her was low-minded and
paltry in the extreme. Why has Bourrienne omitted to mention the unmanly manner in which she was suddenly exiled from France, and to give a copy of the brutal
letter to her, written at Bonaparte's orders by Savary, in which she was told, in
cruel mockery, that the air of France no longer suited her health? After her rupture with the First Consul Madame de Staël said that Bonaparte was nothing but a
Robespierre à cheval. This was her great offence. Bonaparte was always cut to
the quick by such epigrammatic sallies, and his resentment, even when its object
was a woman, was always implacable.—*Editor of 1836 edition.*

This passage is attacked in *Madame de Staël* (by A. Stevens, London, Murray,
1881), vol. i. p. 205. The debt claimed by her was paid by the Bourbons, but Bourrienne's account seems perfectly true. Napoleon's horror of such a whirlwind of
sentiment as Madame de Staël was most natural. The very damaging admissions
made by her biographer should be noted. "She acknowledged to him (Joseph)
sometimes, with regret, the violence of her language against Napoleon. . . . She
did not demand (!) the right to attack him publicly. . . . When the new
Napoleonic order appeared to be irreversibly established, she was not indisposed to
recognise what seemed to be invincible fate" (vol. i. p. 208). As for any improba-
bility of her throwing herself at Napoleon's head, see vol. ii. p. 95 for the spirit in
which she went to England : "If I discover there a noble character, I will sacrifice
my liberty." As for her extraordinary conceit and extravagant idea of her position,
see *Metternich*, tome iii. p. 505. When asked by the Police President of Vienna,
"Pray, Madame, are we to go to war about Herr Rocca?" she answered, "Why
not? Herr Rocca is my friend, and will be my husband!" It will be seen that
Metternich took much the same view of her as Napoleon did. When asked to obtain
the permission she so specially desired to perorate in the *salons* of Paris, he says (on
the same page), "My head, however, does not seem to be so easily turned, for I was
able to withstand her without difficulty. . . . Celebrity was a power to Madame
de Staël! The longer I live the more I mistrust this power."

a sword could have the meanness to kneel to a Pope, or to humble his sceptre before the keys of St. Peter. His spirit was too great to admit of such a thought. On the contrary, he regarded the alliance between the Church and his power as a happy means of influencing the opinions of the people, and as an additional tie which was to attach them to a Government rendered legitimate by the solemn sanction of the Papal authority. Bonaparte was not deceived. In this, as well as in many other things, the perspicacity of his genius enabled him to comprehend all the importance of a consecration bestowed on him by the Pope; more especially as Louis XVIII., without subjects, without territory, and wearing only an illusory crown, had not received that sacred unction by which the descendants of Hugh Capet become the eldest sons of the Church.

As soon as the Emperor was informed of the success of Caffarelli's mission, and that the Pope, in compliance with his desire, was about to repair to Paris to confirm in his hands the sceptre of Charlemagne, nothing was thought of but preparations for that great event, which had been preceded by the recognition of Napoleon as Emperor of the French on the part of all the States of Europe, with the exception of England.

On the conclusion of the *Concordat* Bonaparte said to me, "I shall let the Republican generals exclaim as much as they like against the Mass. I know what I am about; I am working for posterity." He was now gathering the fruits of his *Concordat*. He ordered that the Pope should be everywhere treated in his journey through the French territory with the highest distinction, and he proceeded to Fontainebleau to receive his Holiness. This afforded an opportunity for Bonaparte to re-establish the example of those journeys of the old Court, during which changes of ministers used formerly to be made. The Palace of Fontainebleau, now become Imperial, like all the old royal châteaux, had been newly furnished with a luxury and taste corresponding to the progress of modern art. The Emperor was proceeding on the road to Nemours when courtiers informed him of the approach of Pius VII. Bonaparte's object was to avoid the ceremony which had been previously settled. He had therefore made the pretext of going on a hunting-party, and was in the way as it were by chance when the Pope's carriage was arriving. He alighted from horseback, and the Pope came out of his carriage. Rapp was with the Emperor, and I think I yet hear him describing, in his original manner and with his German accent, this grand interview, upon which, however, he for his part looked with very little respect. Rapp, in fact, was among the number of those who, notwithstanding his attachment to the Emperor, preserved independence of character, and he knew he had no reason to dissemble with me. "Fancy to yourself," said he, "the amusing comedy that was played." After the Emperor and the Pope had well embraced they went into the same carriage ; and, in order that they might be upon a footing of equality, they were to enter at the same time by opposite doors. All that was settled ; but at breakfast the Emperor had calculated how he should manage, without appearing to assume anything, to get on the right-hand side of the Pope, and everything turned out as he wished. As to the Pope," said Rapp, " I must own that I never saw a man with a finer countenance or more respectable appearance than Pius VII." [1]

---

[1] The following is Savary's account of the meeting of the Pope and Napoleon :

"The Emperor went to meet the Pope on the road to Nemours. To avoid ceremony the pretext of a hunting party was assumed ; the attendants, with his equipages, were in the forest. The Emperor came on horseback, and in a hunting-dress, with his retinue. It was at the Half-Moon, on the top of the hill, that the meeting took place. There the Pope's carriage drew up : he got out at the left door in his white costume ; the ground was dirty; he did not like to step upon it with his white silk shoes, but was obliged to do so at last.

"Napoleon alighted to receive him. They embraced, and the Emperor's carriage, which had been purposely driven up, was advanced a few paces, as if from the carelessness of the driver ; but men were posted to hold the two doors open. At the moment of getting in the Emperor took the right door, and an officer of the

After the conference between the Pope and the Emperor at Fontainebleau, Pius VII. set off for Paris first. On the road the same honours were paid to him as to the Emperor. Apartments were prepared for him in the Pavilion de Flore in the Tuileries, and his bedchamber was arranged and furnished in the same manner as his chamber in the Palace of Monte-Cavallo, his usual residence in Rome. The Pope's presence in Paris was so extraordinary a circumstance that it was scarcely believed, though it had some time before been talked of. What, indeed, could be more singular than to see the Head of the Church in a capital where four years previously the altars had been overturned, and the few faithful who remained had been obliged to exercise their worship in secret! The Pope became the object of public respect and general curiosity. I was exceedingly anxious to see him, and my wish was gratified on the day when he went to visit the Imperial printing office, then situated where the Bank of France now is.

A pamphlet, dedicated to the Pope, containing the "Pater Noster," in one hundred and fifty different languages, was struck off in the presence of his Holiness. During this visit to the printing office an ill-bred young man kept his hat on in the Pope's presence. Several persons, indignant at this indecorum, advanced to take off the young man's hat. A little confusion arose, and the Pope, observing the cause of it, stepped up to the young man and said to him, in a tone of kindness truly patriarchal, "Young man, uncover, that I may give thee my blessing. An old man's blessing never yet harmed any one." This little incident deeply affected all who witnessed it. The countenance and figure of Pope Pius VII. commanded

court handed the Pope to the left; so that they entered the carriage by the two doors at the same time. The Emperor naturally seated himself on the right; and this first step decided, without negotiation, upon the etiquette to be observed during the whole time that the Pope was to remain in Paris."—*Memoirs of the Duc de Rovigo*, vol. ii. p. 111.

respect.   David's admirable portrait is a living likeness of him.

The Pope's arrival at Paris produced a great sensation in London, greater indeed there than anywhere else, notwithstanding the separation of the English Church from the Church of Rome.   The English Ministry now spared no endeavours to influence public opinion by the circulation of libels against Bonaparte.   The Cabinet of London found a twofold advantage in encouraging this system, which not merely excited irritation against the powerful enemy of England, but diverted from the British Government the clamour which some of its measures were calculated to create.   Bonaparte's indignation against England was roused to the utmost extreme, and in truth this indignation was in some degree a national feeling in France.

Napoleon had heard of the success of Caffarelli's negotiations previous to his return to Paris, after his journey to the Rhine.   On arriving at St. Cloud he lost no time in ordering the preparations for his coronation.   Everything aided the fulfilment of his wishes.   On 28th November the Pope arrived at Paris, and two days after, viz. on the 1st of December, the Senate presented to the Emperor the votes of the people for the establishment of hereditary succession in his family : for as it was pretended that the assumption of the title of Emperor was no way prejudicial to the Republic, the question of hereditary succession only had been proposed for public sanction. Sixty thousand registers had been opened in different parts of France,—at the offices of the ministers, the prefects, the mayors of the communes, notaries, solicitors, etc. France at that time contained 108 departments, and there were 3,574,898 voters.   Of these only 2569 voted against hereditary succession.   Bonaparte ordered a list of the persons who had voted against the question to be sent to him, and he often consulted it.   They proved to be not Royalist, but for the most part staunch Republicans.   To my knowledge many Royalists abstained from voting at all, not wishing to commit themselves uselessly, and still less to give their suffrages to the author of the Duc d'Enghien's death. For my part, I gave my vote in favour of hereditary succession in Bonaparte's family ; my situation, as may well be imagined, did not allow me to do otherwise.

Since the month of October the Legislative Body had been convoked to attend the Emperor's coronation. Many deputies arrived, and with them a swarm of those presidents of cantons who occupied a conspicuous place in the annals of ridicule at the close of the year 1804. They became the objects of all sorts of witticisms and jests. The obligation of wearing swords made their appearance very grotesque. As many droll stories were told of them as were ten years afterwards related of those who were styled the voltigeurs of Louis XIV. One of these anecdotes was so exceedingly ludicrous that, though it was probably a mere invention, yet I cannot refrain from relating it. A certain number of these presidents were one day selected to be presented to the Pope ; and as most of them were very poor they found it necessary to combine economy with the etiquette necessary to be observed under the new order of things. To save the expense of hiring carriages they therefore proceeded to the Pavilion de Flore on foot, taking the precaution of putting on gaiters to preserve their white silk stockings from the mud which covered the streets, for it was then the month of December. On arriving at the Tuileries one of the party put his gaiters into his pocket. It happened that the Pope delivered such an affecting address that all present were moved to tears, and the unfortunate president who had disposed of his gaiters in the way just mentioned drew them out instead of his handkerchief and smeared his face over with mud. The Pope is said to have been much amused at this mistake. If this anecdote should be thought too puerile to be repeated here, I may observe that it afforded no small merriment to Bonaparte, who made Michot the actor relate it to the Empress at Paris one evening after a Court performance.

Napoleon had now attained the avowed object of his ambition ; but his ambition receded before him like a boundless horizon. On the 1st of December, the day on which the Senate presented to the Emperor the result of the votes for hereditary succession, François de Neufchâteau delivered an address to him, in which there was no want of adulatory expressions. As President of the Senate he had had some practice in that style of speech-making ; and he only substituted the eulogy of the Monarchical Government for that of the Republican Government *a sempre bene*, as the Italians say.

If I wished to make comparisons I could here indulge in some curious ones. Is it not extraordinary that Fontainebleau should have witnessed, at the interval of nearly ten years, Napoleon's first interview with the Pope, and his last farewell to his army, and that the Senate, who had previously given such ready support to Bonaparte, should in 1814 have pronounced his abdication at Fontainebleau.

The preparations for the Coronation proved very advantageous to the trading classes of Paris. Great numbers of foreigners and people from the provinces visited the capital, and the return of luxury and the revival of old customs gave occupation to a variety of tradespeople who could get no employment under the Directory or Consulate, such as saddlers, carriage-makers, lacemen, embroiderers, and others. By these positive interests were created more partisans of the Empire than by opinion and reflection ; and it is but just to say that trade had not been so active for a dozen years before. The Imperial crown jewels were exhibited to the public at Biennais the jeweller's. The crown was of a light form, and, with its leaves of gold, it less resembled the crown of France than the antique crown of the Cæsars. These things were afterwards placed in the public treasury, together with the imperial insignia of Charlemagne, which Bonaparte had ordered to be brought from Aix-la-Chapelle. But while Bonaparte was thus priding himself in his crown and his imagined resemblance to Charlemagne, Mr. Pitt, lately recalled to the Ministry, was concluding at Stockholm a treaty with Sweden, and agreeing to pay a subsidy to that power to enable it to maintain hostilities against France. This treaty was concluded on the 3d of December, the day after the Coronation.[1]

[1] The details of the preparation for the Coronation caused many stormy scenes between Napoleon and his family. The Princesses, his sisters and sisters-in-law, were especially shocked at having to carry the train of the Imperial mantle of Josephine, and even when Josephine was actually moving from the altar to the throne the Princesses evinced their reluctance so plainly that Josephine could not advance, and an altercation took place which had to be stopped by Napoleon himself (*Rémusat*, tome ii. p. 71). For the details of the disputes between Napoleon and Joseph see *Miot de Melito*, tome ii. p. 221. Joseph was quite willing to himself give up appearing in a mantle with a train, but he wished to prevent his wife bearing the mantle of the Empress; and he opposed his brother on so many points that Napoleon ended by calling on him to either give up his position and retire from all politics, or else to fully accept the Imperial *régime*. How the economical Cambacérès used up the ermine he could not wear will be seen in *Junot*, tome iii. p. 195. Josephine herself was in the greatest anxiety as to whether the wish of the Bonaparte family that she should be divorced would carry the day with her husband. When she had gained her cause for the time, and after the Pope had engaged to crown her, she seems to have most cleverly managed to get the Pope informed that she was only united to Napoleon by a civil marriage. The Pope insisted on a religious marriage. Napoleon was angry, but could not recede, and the religious rite was performed by Cardinal Fesch the day, or two days, before the Coronation. The certificate of the marriage was carefully guarded from Napoleon by Josephine, and even placed beyond his reach at the time of the divorce. Such at least seems to be the most probable account of this mysterious and doubtful matter. Compare *Rémusat*, tome ii. p. 67; *Thiers*, tome v. p. 262, corrected by tome xi. p. 352; Cardinal Consalvi's *Memoirs*, and Jervis's *Gallican Church and the Revolution*, p. 448, and especially p. 451, where the opinion of the Abbé Emery as to the non-validity of this marriage is given. Metternich (tome i. p. 121) says concerning this, "For the Church this question did not exist, and therefore not for the Emperor (of Austria);" and he treats the matter as if there had been no religious marriage rite. "Indeed," he says, "otherwise the scheme of a divorce could not have been entertained for a moment." But the Austrian Court was deeply interested in this matter, and not likely to be too scrupulous. The fact that Cardinal Fesch maintained that the religious rite had been duly performed, and that thirteen of the Cardinals (not, however, including Fesch) were so convinced of the legality of the marriage that they refused to appear at the ceremony of marriage with Marie Louise, thus drawing down the

It cannot be expected that I should enter into a detail of the ceremony which took place on the 2d of December. The glitter of gold, the waving plumes, and richly-caparisoned horses of the Imperial procession ; the mule which preceded the Pope's *cortège*, and occasioned so much merriment to the Parisians, have already been described over and over again. I may, however, relate an anecdote connected with the Coronation, told me by Josephine, and which is exceedingly characteristic of Napoleon.

When Bonaparte was paying his addresses to Madame de Beauharnais, neither the one nor the other kept a carriage ; and therefore Bonaparte frequently accompanied her when she walked out. One day they went together to the notary Raguideau, one of the shortest men I think I ever saw in my life, Madame de Beauharnais placed great confidence in him, and went there on purpose to acquaint him of her intention to marry the young general of artillery,—the *protégé* of Barras. Josephine went alone into the notary's cabinet, while Bonaparte waited for her in an adjoining room. The door of Raguideau's cabinet did not shut close, and Bonaparte plainly heard him dissuading Madame de Beauharnais from her projected marriage. " You are going to take a very wrong step," said he, "and you will be sorry for it. Can you be so mad as to marry a young man who has nothing but his cloak and his sword ? " Bonaparte, Josephine told me, had never mentioned this to her, and she never supposed that he had heard what fell from Raguideau. " Only think, Bourrienne," continued she, " what was my astonishment when, dressed in the Imperial robes on the Coronation day, he desired that Raguideau might be sent for, saying that he wished to see him immediately ; and when Raguideau appeared, he said to him, ' Well, sir !

wrath of the Emperor, and becoming the " Cardinals Noirs," from being forbidden to wear their own robes, seems to leave no doubt that the religious rite had been duly performed. The marriage was only pronounced to be invalid in 1809 by the local canonical bodies, not by the authority of the Pope.

have I nothing but my cloak and my sword now?'"
Though Bonaparte had related to me almost all the circumstances of his life, as they occurred to his memory, he
never once mentioned this affair of Raguideau, which he
only seemed to have suddenly recollected on his Coronation day.[1]

The day after the Coronation all the troops in Paris
were assembled in the Champ de Mars, that the Imperial eagles might be distributed to each regiment, in
lieu of the national flags. I had stayed away from the
Coronation in the church of Notre Dame, but I wished to
see the military *fête* in the Champ de Mars, because I took
real pleasure in seeing Bonaparte amongst his soldiers.
A throne was erected in front of the Military School,
which, though now transformed into a barrack, must have
recalled to Bonaparte's mind some singular recollections
of his boyhood. At a given signal all the columns closed
and approached the throne. Then Bonaparte, rising, gave
orders for the distribution of the eagles, and delivered the
following address to the deputations of the different corps
of the army :—

"*Soldiers! behold your colours. These eagles will always
be your rallying-point! They will always be where your
Emperor may think them necessary for the defence of his
throne and of his people. Swear to sacrifice your lives to
defend them, and by your courage to keep them constantly
in the path of victory.—Swear!*"

It would be impossible to describe the acclamations

---

[1] The truth about this story seems to be that Raguideau went by appointment to
Josephine's house (she was not likely to go to his office) and there advised her against
the marriage, using the words attributed to him. He was disconcerted when introduced to Napoleon, who was standing at the window drumming on the panes.
When asked whether he had heard, Napoleon said, "Yes, he has spoken as an honest
man, and what he has said makes me esteem him. I hope he will continue to
manage your affairs, for he has inclined me to give him my confidence." Instead of
displaying himself as Emperor before Raguideau, Napoleon made him notary of the
civil list, and always treated him well.

Meneval, in upsetting Bourrienne's story, gives us a pleasanter one in telling us
that Napoleon did say, " Joseph, if our father saw us ! " (*Meneval*, tome i. p. 129).

which followed this address; there is something so seductive in popular enthusiasm that even indifferent persons cannot help yielding to its influence.   And yet the least reflection would have shown how shamefully Napoleon forswore the declaration he made to the Senate, when the organic *Sénatus-consulte* for the foundation of the Empire was presented to him at St. Cloud.   On that occasion he said, "The French people shall never be *my* people!" And yet the day after his Coronation his eagles were to be carried wherever they might be necessary for the defence of *his people*.

By a singular coincidence, while on the 2d of December 1804 Bonaparte was receiving from the head of the Church the Imperial crown of France, Louis XVIII., who was then at Colmar, prompted as it were by an inexplicable presentiment, drew up and signed a declaration to the French people, in which he declared that he then swore never to break the sacred bond which united his destiny to theirs, never to renounce the inheritance of his ancestors, or to relinquish his rights.

Note.—M. de Bourrienne's omission relative to the Imperial Coronation may be supplied by the following extracts :—

"The interior of the church of Notre Dame had been newly painted ; galleries and pews magnificently adorned had been erected, and they were thronged with a prodigious concourse of spectators.

"The Pope set out from the Tuileries, and proceeded along the quay to the archiepiscopal palace, whence he repaired to the choir by a private entrance.

"The Emperor set out with the Empress by the Carrousel.   The procession passed along the Rue St. Honoré to the Rue des Lombards, then the Pont au Change, the Palace of Justice, the court of Notre Dame, and entered the Archbishop's palace.

"It was a truly magnificent sight.   The procession was opened by the already numerous body of courtiers ; next came the Marshals of the Empire wearing their honours ; then the dignitaries and high officers of the Crown ; and lastly, the Emperor in a dress of state.   At the moment of his entering the cathedral there was a simultaneous shout of ' *Vive l'Empereur !* '

"The procession passed along the middle of the nave, and arrived at the choir facing the high altar.   This scene was not less imposing ; the galleries round the choir were filled with the handsomest women whom the best company could produce, and most of whom rivalled in the lustre of their beauty that of the jewels with which they were covered.

"His Holiness went to meet the Emperor at a tribune which had been placed in the middle of the choir ; there was another on one side for the Empress.   After saying a short prayer there they returned, and seated themselves on the throne at the end of the church facing the choir ; there they heard mass, which was said by the Pope. They went to make the offering, and came back ; they then descended from the platform of the throne, and walked in procession to receive the holy unction. The Emperor and Empress, on reaching the choir, replaced themselves at their tribunes, where the Pope performed the ceremony.

"He presented the crown to the Emperor, who received it, put it himself upon his head, took it off, placed it on that of the Empress, removed it again, and laid it on the cushion where it was at first. A smaller crown was immediately put upon the head of the Empress. All the arrangements had been made beforehand ; she was surrounded by her ladies ; everything was done in a moment, and nobody perceived the substitution which had taken place. The procession moved back to the platform. The Emperor there heard *Te Deum ;* the Pope himself went thither at the conclusion of the service, as if to say, *Ite, missa est.* The Testament was presented to the Emperor, who took off his glove, and pronounced his oath, with his hand upon the sacred book.

"He went back to the Archbishop's palace the same way as that he had come, and entered his carriage. The ceremony was very long ; the procession returned by a different route, and it was getting dusk when the Emperor arrived at the Tuileries."

The gossip of the *première femme de chambre* on the subject of the Coronation is amusing.

"A great many persons in the Palace sat up the whole of the night which preceded that great day. A fact which, though not important in itself, may serve to give an idea of the busy confusion in which we all were : I was obliged that day to have my head dressed at five o'clock in the morning. When, at the break of day, we entered the Empress's apartments, I was already dressed, *en grande toilette,* for the ceremony at the cathedral, whither I was to repair as soon as Her Majesty's toilet should be completed, having duties to perform there. As soon as the Empress was dressed I set out, having in my carriage her Imperial mantle and crown. . . . Arriving at Notre Dame a considerable time before the procession, I was conducted into an apartment which had been prepared for their Majesties. All the Imperal family were introduced therein successively as they arrived. I fastened on the Imperial mantle, and the Princesses put their toilets in fresh order. When everything was ready they formed in procession, and so went into the cathedral, where every one according to his or her rank took up a place which had been previously assigned. It was exactly like a theatrical representation, for all the parts had been studied beforehand, and we had even had several general rehearsals at the Palace, where, by the Emperor's orders, M. Isabey, the artist, had modelled a *sacre* in high relief, to serve as a guide. Messieurs the masters of the ceremonies played the part of prompters, they being charged with the duty of reminding each of the great personages figuring in the august ceremony as to where he was to go and what he was to do. I followed the procession with some other ladies of Her Majesty's household, and was so fortunate as to get placed in the gallery of the Empress, whence I saw perfectly all the ceremony in its greatest details ; but there already exist so many descriptions of it that I need not repeat what every one knows. And, in fine, who does not know that the Emperor put the crown on his head with his own hands, having first received the Pope's benediction and consecration, and that he afterwards crowned the Empress himself.

"On the day of the *sacre* the weather was cold and frosty ; we were all dressed as if for a well-heated drawing-room, and our only protection against the cold, our cachemere shawls, we were obliged to take off as we entered the gallery. I believe I never suffered so much from cold in all the days of my life ; but people do not enter the service of the great to enjoy their comforts, and this I perceived above all on that day, and in more ways than one. I set out in such a hurry, I had been so confused since the preceding day, that I forgot to take my breakfast ; and the pangs of hunger were added to the lively sufferings of cold. I never knew that while I was waiting to put on Her Majesty's mantle an excellent breakfast had been served up in the Archbishop's apartments for all the retinue. This was very unlucky, and when the beautiful sacred music of M. Lesueur was performed in the cathedral, I had good grounds for judging of the truth of the old proverb, *Ventre affamé n'a point d'oreilles.*

" When the ceremony was over their Majesties returned to their apartment. Never have I seen on any physiognomy such an expression of joy, content, and happiness as that which then animated the countenance of the Empress : her face was radiant. The crown just fixed on her forehead by her husband had settled her future lot, and seemed calculated to dissipate for ever those rumours of divorce which had long vexed her ears, and which had been repeated t) her even by the Emperor's own family. . . . On the return from Notre Dame I arrived at the Tuileries some time before their Majesties. Cold, hunger, and the bad night I had passed gave me such a headache that I was obliged to go to bed, and thus I saw nothing of the other ceremonies which took place that day. What I know is, that by the evening the Empress was completely exhausted—but, at last, she was a crowned Empress ! " (*Mémoires de Mademoiselle Avrillion*).

CHAPTER XXX.

1805.

My appointment as Minister Plenipotentiary at Hamburg—My interview
with Bonaparte at Malmaison—Bonaparte's designs respecting Italy—
His wish to revisit Brienne—Instructions for my residence in Hamburg—Regeneration of European society—Bonaparte's plan of making himself the oldest sovereign in Europe—Amédée Jaubert's mission
—Commission from the Emperor to the Empress—My conversation
with Madame Bonaparte.

I MUST now mention an event which concerns myself personally, namely, my appointment as Minister Plenipotentiary to the Dukes of Brunswick and Mecklenburg-
Schwerin, and to the Hanse towns.

This appointment took place on the 22d of March 1805.
Josephine, who had kindly promised to apprise me of
what the Emperor intended to do for me, as soon as she
herself should know his intentions, sent a messenger to
acquaint me with my appointment, and to tell me that the
Emperor wished to see me. I had not visited Josephine
since her departure for Belgium. The pomps and ceremonies of the Coronation had, I may say, dazzled me, and
deterred me from presenting myself at the Imperial Palace, where I should have been annoyed by the etiquette
which had been observed since the Coronation. I cannot
describe what a disagreeable impression this parade always
produced on me. I could not all at once forget the time
when I used without ceremony to go into Bonaparte's
chamber and wake him at the appointed hour. As to
Bonaparte, I had not seen him since he sent for me after
the condemnation of Georges, when I saw that my can-

dour relative to Moreau was not displeasing to him. Moreau had since quitted France without Napoleon's subjecting him to the application of the odious law which has only been repealed since the return of the Bourbons, and by virtue of which he was condemned to the confiscation of his property. Moreau sold his estate of Gros Bois to Berthier, and proceeded to Cadiz, whence he embarked for America. I shall not again have occasion to speak of him until the period of the intrigues into which he was drawn by the same influence which ruined him in France.

On the evening of the day when I received the kind message from Josephine I had an official invitation to proceed the next day to Malmaison, where the Emperor then was. I was much pleased at the idea of seeing him there rather than at the Tuileries, or even at St. Cloud. Our former intimacy at Malmaison made me feel more at my ease respecting an interview of which my knowledge of Bonaparte's character led me to entertain some apprehension. Was I to be received by my old comrade of Brienne, or by His Imperial Majesty ? I was received by my old college companion.

On my arrival at Malmaison I was ushered into the tent-room leading to the library. How I was astonished at the good-natured familiarity with which he received me ! This extraordinary man displayed, if I may employ the term, a coquetry towards me which surprised me, notwithstanding my past knowledge of his character. He came up to me with a smile on his lips, took my hand (which he had never done since he was Consul), pressed it affectionately, and it was impossible that I could look upon him as the Emperor of France and the future King of Italy. Yet I was too well aware of his fits of pride to allow his familiarity to lead me beyond the bounds of affectionate respect. "My dear Bourrienne," said he, "can you suppose that the elevated rank I have attained has altered my feelings towards you ? No. I do not attach importance to the glitter of

Imperial pomp; all that is meant for the people; but I must still be valued according to my deserts. I have been very well satisfied with your services, and I have appointed you to a situation where I shall have occasion for them. I know that I can rely upon you." He then asked with great warmth of friendship what I was about, and inquired after my family, etc. In short, I never saw him display less reserve or more familiarity and unaffected simplicity, which he did the more readily, perhaps, because his greatness was now incontestable.

"You know," added Napoleon, "that I set out in a week for Italy. I shall make myself King; but that is only a stepping-stone. I have greater designs respecting Italy. It must be a kingdom comprising all the Transalpine States, from Venice to the Maritime Alps.[1] The union of Italy with France can only be temporary; but it is necessary, in order to accustom the nations of Italy to live under common laws. The Genoese, the Piedmontese, the Venetians, the Milanese, the inhabitants of Tuscany, the Romans, and the Neapolitans, hate each other. None of them will acknowledge the superiority of the other, and yet Rome is, from the recollections connected with it, the natural capital of Italy. To make it so, however, it is necessary that the power of the Pope should be confined within limits purely spiritual. I cannot now think of this; but I will reflect upon it hereafter. At present I have only vague ideas on the subject, but they will be matured in time, and then all depends on circumstances. What was it told me, when we were walking like two idle fellows, as we were, in the streets of Paris, that I should one day be master of France—my wish—

---

[1] The statement that the union of Italy with France was only to be temporary should be remarked; it agrees with the promise made to Austria afterwards, in the treaty of Presburg, 26th December 1805, after Austerlitz, that the crowns of Italy and France were to be separated when Naples, the Ionian Islands, and Malta were evacuated by foreign armies. The present generation has seen this dream of the union of Italy realised, but the abortive attempt of 1848 has shown that Napoleon was right in the time he said he required for the completion of his plan.

merely a vague wish. Circumstances have done the rest. It is therefore wise to look into the future, and that I do. With respect to Italy, as it will be impossible with one effort to unite her so as to form a single power, subject to uniform laws, I will begin by making her French. All these little States will insensibly become accustomed to the same laws, and when manners shall be assimilated and enmities extinguished, then there will be an Italy, and I will give her independence. But for that I must have twenty years, and who can count on the future? Bourrienne, I feel pleasure in telling you all this. It was locked up in my mind. With you I think aloud."

I do not believe that I have altered two words of what Bonaparte said to me respecting Italy, so perfect, I may now say without vanity, was my memory then, and so confirmed was my habit of fixing in it all that he said to me. After having informed me of his vague projects Bonaparte, with one of those transitions so common to him, said, "By the by, Bourrienne, I have something to tell you. Madame de Brienne has begged that I will pass through Brienne, and I promised that I will. I will not conceal from you that I shall feel great pleasure in again beholding the spot which for six years was the scene of our boysh sports and studies." Taking advantage of the Emperor's good humour I ventured to tell him what happiness it would give me if it were possible that I could share with him the revival of all recollections which were mutually dear to us. But Napolean, after a moment's pause, said with extreme kindness, "Hark ye, Bourrienne, in your situation and mine this cannot be. It is more than two years since we parted. What would be said of so sudden a reconciliation? I tell you frankly that I have regretted you, and the circumstances in which I have frequently been placed have often made me wish to recall you. At Boulogne I was quite resolved upon it. Rapp, perhaps, has informed you of it. He liked you, and he assured me that he would be delighted at your return. But if upon reflection I changed my mind it was because, as I have often told you, I will not have it said that I stand in need of any one. No. Go to Hamburg. I have formed some projects respecting Germany in which you can be useful to me. It is there I will give a mortal blow to England. I will deprive her of the Continent,—besides, I have some ideas not yet matured which extend much farther. There is not sufficient unanimity amongst the nations of Europe. European society must be regenerated—a superior power must control the other powers, and compel them to live in peace with each other ; and France is well situated for that purpose. For details you will receive instructions from Talleyrand ; but I recommend you, above all things, to keep a strict watch on the emigrants. Woe to them if they become too dangerous ! I know that there are still agitators, —among them all the *Marquis de Versailles*, the courtiers of the old school. But they are moths who will burn themselves in the candle. You have been an emigrant yourself, Bourrienne ; you feel a partiality for them, and you know that I have allowed upwards of two hundred of them to return upon your recommendation. But the case is altered. Those who are abroad are hardened. They do not wish to return home. Watch them closely. That is the only particular direction I give you. You are to be Minister from France to Hamburg ; but your place will be an independent one ; besides your correspondence with the Minister for Foreign Affairs, I authorise you to write to me personally, whenever you have anything particular to communicate. You will likewise correspond with Fouché."

Here the Emperor remained silent for a moment, and I was preparing to retire, but he detained me, saying in the kindest manner, "What, are you going already, Bourrienne ? Are you in a hurry ? Let us chat a little longer. God knows when we may see each other again !" Then

after two or three moments' silence he said, "The more I
reflect on our situation, on our former intimacy, and our
subsequent separation, the more I see the necessity of your
going to Hamburg. Go, then, my dear fellow, I advise
you. Trust me. When do you think of setting out?—
"In May."—"In May? . . . Ah, I shall be in Milan then,
for I wish to stop at Turin. I like the Piedmontese ; they
are the best soldiers in Italy."—"Sire, the King of Italy
will be the junior of the Emperor of France ! "[1]—"Ah ! so
you recollect what I said one day at the Tuileries ; but,
my dear fellow, I have yet a devilish long way to go before
I gain my point."—"At the rate, Sire, at which you are
going you will not be long in reaching it."—"Longer than
you imagine. I see all the obstacles in my way ; but they
do not alarm me. England is everywhere, and the struggle
is between her and me. I see how it will be. The whole
of Europe will be our instruments ; sometimes serving one,
sometimes the other, but at bottom the dispute is wholly
between England and France.

"*À propos,*" said the Emperor, changing the subject,
for all who knew him are aware that this *à propos* was his
favourite, and, indeed, his only mode of transition ; *à
propos*, Bourrienne, you surely must have heard of the
departure of Jaubert,[2] and his mission. What is said on
the subject?"—"Sire, I have only heard it slightly alluded
to. His father, however, to whom he said nothing respecting the object of his journey, knowing I was intimate
with Jaubert, came to me to ascertain whether I could
allay his anxiety respecting a journey of the duration of

[1] I alluded to a conversation which I had with Napoleon when we first went to the
Tuileries. He spoke to me about his projects of royalty, and I stated the difficulties
which I thought he would experience in getting himself acknowledged by the old
reigning families of Europe. "If it comes to that," he replied, "I will dethrone them
all, and then I shall be the oldest sovereign among them."—*Bourrienne.*

[2] Amédée Jaubert had been with Napoleon in Egypt, and was appointed to the
Cabinet of the Consul as secretary interpreter of Oriental languages (see *Meneval*,
tome i. p. 81). He was sent on several missions to the East, and brought back, in
1818, goats from Thibet, naturalising in France the manufacture of cashmeres. He
became a peer of France under the Monarchy of July.

which he could form no idea. The precipitate departure
of his son had filled him with apprehension. I told him
the truth, viz., that Jaubert had said no more to me on
the subject than to him."—"Then you do not know where
he is gone?"—"I beg your pardon, Sire; I know very
well."—"How, the devil!" said Bonaparte, suddenly turning on me a look of astonishment. "No one, I declare,
has ever told me; but I guessed it. Having received a
letter from Jaubert dated Leipsic, I recollected what your
Majesty had often told me of your views respecting Persia
and India. I have not forgotten our conversation in
Egypt, nor the great projects which you unfolded to me
to relieve the solitude and sometimes the weariness of the
cabinet of Cairo. Besides, I long since knew your opinion
of Amédée, of his fidelity, his ability, and his courage. I
felt convinced, therefore, that he had a mission to the
Shah of Persia."—"You guessed right; but I beg of you,
Bourrienne, say nothing of this to any person whatever.
Secrecy on this point is of great importance. The English
would do him an ill turn, for they are well aware that
my views are directed against their possessions and their
influence in the East."—"I think, Sire, that my answer to
Amédée's worthy father is a sufficient guarantee for my
discretion. Besides, it was a mere supposition on my part,
and I could have stated nothing with certainty before
your Majesty had the kindness to inform me of the fact.
. . . Instead of going to Hamburg, if your Majesty
pleases, I will join Jaubert, accompany him to Persia, and
undertake half his mission."—"How! would you go with
him?"—"Yes, Sire; I am much attached to him. He is
an excellent man, and I am sure that he would not be
sorry to have me with him."—"But . . . stop, Bourrienne, . . . this, perhaps, would not be a bad idea.
You know a little of the East. You are accustomed to the
climate. You could assist Jaubert. . . . But. . . .
No. Jaubert must be already far off. I fear you could

not overtake him. And besides you have a numerous
family. You will be more useful to me in Germany. All
things considered, go to Hamburg—you know the country,
and, what is better you speak the language."

I could see that Bonaparte still had something to say
to me. As we were walking up and down the room he
stopped, and looking at me with an expression of sadness,
he said, "Bourrienne, you must, before I proceed to
Italy, do me a service. You sometimes visit *my wife*, and
it is right ; it is fit you should. You have been too long
one of the family not to continue your friendship with
her. Go to her.[1] Endeavour once more to make her
sensible of her mad extravagance. Every day I discover
new instances of it, and it distresses me. When I speak
to her on the subject I am vexed ; I get angry—she
weeps. I forgive her, I pay her bills—she makes fair
promises ; but the same thing occurs over and over
again.[2] If she had only borne me a child ! It is the tor-

---

[1] This employment of Bourrienne to remonstrate with Josephine is a complete answer to the charge sometimes made that Napoleon, while scolding, really encouraged
the foolish expenses of his wife, as keeping her under his control. Josephine was
incorrigible. "On the very day of her death," says Madame de Rémusat (tome ii.
p. 347), "she wished to put on a very pretty dressing-gown because she thought the
Emperor of Russia would perhaps come to see her. She died all covered with rib-
ons and rose-coloured satin." "One would not, sure, be frightful when one's dead !"
As for Josephine's great fault—her failure to give Napoleon an heir—he did not
always wish for one. In 1802, on his brother Jerôme jokingly advising Josephine to
give the Consul a little Cæsar, Napoleon broke out, "Yes, that he may end in the
same manner as that of Alexander ? Believe me, Messieurs, that at the present time
it is better not to have children : I mean when one is condemned to rule nations "
(*Iung*, tome ii. p. 131). The fate of the King of Rome shows that the exclamation
was only too true !

[2] The Emperor estimated the expenses of Malmaison to have been three or four
hundred thousand francs. He then calculated the amount of the sums which the
Empress Josephine must have received from him, and added, that with a little order
and regularity she might probably have left behind her fifty or sixty million
francs. "Her extravagance," said the Emperor, "vexed me beyond measure.
Calculator as I am, I would of course rather have given away a million francs
than have seen a hundred thousand squandered away." He informed me that having one day unexpectedly broken in upon Josephine's morning circle, he found a
celebrated milliner, whom he had expressly forbidden to go near the Empress, as she
was ruining her by extravagant demands. "My unlooked-for entrance," said he,
"occasioned great dismay in the academic sitting. I gave some orders unperceived

ment of my life not to have a child. I plainly perceive that my power will never be firmly established until I have one. If I die without an heir, not one of my brothers is capable of supplying my place. All is begun, but nothing

to the individuals in attendance, and on the lady's departure she was seized and conducted to the Bicêtre " (*Mémorial de Sainte Hélène*).

The story of the " celebrated milliner " arrested by Bonaparte is so amusingly told by Mademoiselle Avrillion, that we will find room for it here, and this we are the more inclined to do as the contrast between the conqueror of half Europe and the persecutor of a *marchande de modes* is most striking and as the whole scene shows how Bonaparte could play the part of the *tyran domestique.*

"On another day I was witness of a scene which I should be tempted to call ridiculous were it not for the respect I owe to their Majesties' memories. I will report it as I saw it; the reader will characterise it as he thinks fit. The Empress had been slightly indisposed ; one of the most famous *marchandes des modes* of the day, Mademoiselle Despeaux, had come to offer her services to her Majesty. She was waiting in the blue *salon* that joined the bedroom until she should be called for. At that very moment the Emperor came down to see the Empress, and the very first person that struck his eye in the blue *salon* through which he had to pass, was poor Mademoiselle Despeaux, armed with her band-boxes. 'Who are you ?' he angrily exclaimed. When, trembling all over, she had declared her name, he rushed like a madman into his wife's chamber, gesticulating and crying out. 'Who sent for this woman ? Who brought her here ? I insist upon knowing it.' Every one of us made an excuse for herself, and the fact was nobody had written to summon Mademoiselle Despeaux, who had come of her own accord. Knowing that the Empress was ill, she had fancied she might want some pretty *négligé* cap becoming to her delicate state. Our denials, however, only added fuel to the fire of the Emperor's rage. He shouted like a maniac : 'I *will* know who has done this! I will throw you all into prison !' Now, at the moment of all this fury the Empress was bound head and feet (that is to say, her *coiffeur* was dressing her hair, and she was taking a foot-bath). Women, hairdresser and all, instantly took to flight, and I was left alone in a small cabinet adjoining the bedchamber. I confess that if I had obeyed my first impulse I should have decamped like the rest, but reflecting on the situation in which the Empress found herself, I would not leave her all alone. The Emperor saw me, but did not say a word to me. A few moments after he came hastily out of the bedroom, nor had the Empress been able to calm him. As for herself, she was trembling and pale, and I found her countenance sorely troubled.

" Such was the scene of which I was a witness, and now for the consequences. As soon as the Emperor reached his own cabinet he sent to summon the Duc de Rovigo (Savary) whom he ordered instantly to have Mademoiselle Despeaux arrested by the gendarmes, and then shut up in prison. The Duke did all he could to prevent the Emperor from committing such an act of injustice, but his representations and prayers were in vain ; the Emperor was obstinate in his will—the Duke forced to obey, poor Mademoiselle Despeaux was arrested almost as soon as she got outside of the Palace, and carried to the greffe (a sort of police station), where she passed the night.

" In the meantime the Empress, having been informed of this arrest, repaired to the Emperor, who the next morning revoked his order and restored Mademoiselle Despeaux to liberty. It was quite time, poor thing ! for this unexpected act of rigour had caused such a revolution in that demoiselle's condition that she fell sick and had a dangerous illness " (*Mémoires de Mademoiselle Avrillion*).

is ended. God knows what will happen! Go and see Josephine, and do not forget my injunctions."

Then he resumed the gaiety which he had exhibited at intervals during our conversation, for clouds driven by the wind do not traverse the horizon with such rapidity as different ideas and sensations succeeded each other in Napoleon's mind. He dismissed me with his usual nod of the head, and seeing him in such good humour I said on departing, "Well, Sire, you are going to hear the old bell of Brienne. I have no doubt it will please you better than the bells of Ruel." He replied, "That's true—you are right. Adieu!"

Such are my recollections of this conversation, which lasted for more than an hour and a half. We walked about all the time, for Bonaparte was indefatigable in audiences of this sort, and would, I believe, have walked and talked for a whole day without being aware of it. I left him, and, according to his desire, went to see Madame Bonaparte, which indeed I had intended to do before he requested it.

I found Josephine with Madame de la Rochefoucauld, who had long been in her suite, and who a short time before had obtained the title of lady of honour to the Empress. Madame de la Rochefoucauld was a very amiable woman, of mild disposition, and was a favourite with Josephine. When I told the Empress that I had just left the Emperor, she, thinking that I would not speak freely before a third person, made a sign to Madame de la Rochefoucauld to retire. I had no trouble in introducing the conversation on the subject concerning which Napoleon had directed me to speak to Josephine, for, after the interchange of a few indifferent remarks, she herself told me of a violent scene, which had occurred between her and the Emperor two days before. " When I wrote to you yesterday," said she, "to announce your appointment, and to tell you that Bonaparte would recall you, I hoped that you would come to see me on quitting him, but I did not think that he would have sent for you so soon. Ah! how I wish that you were still with him, Bourrienne; you could make him hear reason. I know not who takes pleasure in bearing tales to him; but really I think there are persons busy everywhere in finding out my debts, and telling him of them."

These complaints, so gently uttered by Josephine, rendered less difficult the preparatory mission with which I commenced the exercise of my diplomatic functions. I acquainted Madame Bonaparte with all that the Emperor had said to me. I reminded her of the affair of the 1,200,000 francs which we had settled with half that sum. I even dropped some allusions to the promises she had made.

"How can I help it?" said she. "Is it my fault?" Josephine uttered these words in a tone of sincerity which was at once affecting and ludicrous. "All sorts of beautiful things are brought to me," she continued; "they are praised up; I buy them—I am not asked for the money, and all of a sudden, when I have got none, they come upon me with demands for payment. This reaches Napoleon's ears, and he gets angry. When I have money, Bourrienne, you know how I employ it. I give it principally to the unfortunate who solicit my assistance, and to poor emigrants. But I will try to be more economical in future. Tell him so if you see him again. But is it not my duty to bestow as much in charity as I can?"— "Yes, Madame; but permit me to say that nothing requires greater discernment than the distribution of charity. If you had always sat upon a throne you might have supposed that your bounty always fell into the hands of the deserving; but you cannot be ignorant that it oftener falls to the lot of intriguers than to the meritorious needy. I cannot disguise from you that the Emperor was very earnest when he spoke on this subject; and he desired me to tell you so."—"Did he reproach me with nothing else ? "—" No Madame. You know the influence you have over him with respect to everything but what relates to politics. Allow a faithful and sincere friend to prevail upon you seriously not to vex him on this point."— " Bourrienne, I give you my word. Adieu ! my friend."

In communicating to Josephine what the Emperor had said to me I took care not to touch a chord which would have awakened feelings far more painful to her than even the Emperor's harsh reproof on account of her extravagance. Poor Josephine ! how I should have afflicted her had I uttered a word of Bonaparte's regret at not having a child. She always had a presentiment of the fate that one day awaited her. Besides, Josephine told the truth in assuring me that it was not her fault that she spent as she did ; at least all the time I was with both of them, order and economy were no more compatible with her than moderation and patience with Napoleon. The sight of the least waste put him beside himself, and that was a sensation his wife hardly ever spared him. He saw with irritation the eagerness of his family to gain riches ; the more he gave, the more insatiable they appeared, with the exception of Louis, whose inclinations were always upright, and his tastes moderate. As for the other members of his family, they annoyed him so much by their importunity that one day he said, " Really to listen to them it would be thought that I had wasted the heritage of our father." [1]

[1] This story is often told, but generally the last words are said to have been, " *The inheritance of the late King our father.*"

CHAPTER XXXI.

1805.

VOLTAIRE says that it is very well to kiss the feet of
Popes provided their hands are tied. Notwithstanding the
slight estimation in which Bonaparte held Voltaire, he
probably, without being aware of this irreverent satire,
put it into practice. The Court of Rome gave him the opportunity of doing so shortly after his Coronation.   The
Pope, or rather the Cardinals, his advisers, conceiving that
so great an instance of complaisance as the journey of His
Holiness to Paris ought not to go for nothing, demanded
a compensation, which, had they been better acquainted
with Bonaparte's character and policy, they would never
have dreamed of soliciting.   The Holy See demanded the
restitution of Avignon, Bologna, and some parts of the
Italian territory which had formerly been subject to the
Papal dominion.   It may be imagined how such demands
were received by Napoleon, particularly after he had obtained all he wanted from the Pope.   It was, it must be

confessed, a great mistake of the Court of Rome, whose policy is usually so artful and adroit, not to make this demand till after the Coronation. Had it been made the condition of the Pope's journey to France perhaps Bonaparte would have consented to give up, not Avignon, certainly, but the Italian territories, with the intention of taking them back again. Be this as it may, these tardy claims, which were peremptorily rejected, created an extreme coolness between Napoleon and Pius VII. The public did not immediately perceive it, but there is in the public an instinct of reason which the most able politicians never can impose upon; and all eyes were opened when it was known that the Pope, after having crowned Napoleon as Emperor of France, refused to crown him as sovereign of the regenerated kingdom of Italy.

Napoleon left Paris on the 1st of April to take possession of the Iron Crown at Milan. The Pope remained some time longer in the French capital. The prolonged presence of His Holiness was not without its influence on the religious feelings of the people, so great was the respect inspired by the benign countenance and mild manners of the Pope. When the period of his persecutions arrived it would have been well for Bonaparte had Pius VII. never been seen in Paris, for it was impossible to view in any other light than as a victim the man whose truly evangelic meekness had been duly appreciated.

Bonaparte did not evince great impatience to seize the Crown of Italy, which he well knew could not escape him. He stayed a considerable time at Turin, where he resided in the Stupinis Palace, which may be called the St. Cloud of the Kings of Sardinia. The Emperor cajoled the Piedmontese. General Menou, who was made Governor of Piedmont, remained there till Napoleon founded the general government of the Transalpine departments in favour of his brother-in-law, the Prince Borghèse, of whom he would have found it difficult to make anything else than a

Roman Prince. Napoleon was still at Turin when the Pope passed through that city on his return to Rome. Napoleon had a final interview with His Holiness, to whom he now affected to show the greatest personal deference. From Turin Bonaparte proceeded to Alessandria, where he commenced those immense works on which such vast sums were expended. He had many times spoken to me of his projects respecting Alessandria, for, as I have already observed, all his great measures as Emperor were merely the execution of projects conceived at a time when his future elevation could have been only a dream of the imagination. He one day said to Berthier, in my presence, during our sojourn at Milan, after the battle of Marengo, " With Alessandria in my possession I should always be master of Italy. It might be made the strongest fortress in the world ; it is capable of containing a garrison of 40,000 men, with provisions for six months. Should insurrection take place, should Austria send a formidable force here, the French troops might retire to Alessandria, and stand a six months' siege. Six months would be more than sufficient, wherever I might be, to enable me to fall upon Italy, rout the Austrians, and raise the siege of Alessandria."

As he was so near the field of Marengo the Emperor did not fail to visit it, and to add to this solemnity he reviewed on the field all the corps of French troops which were in Italy. Rapp told me afterwards that the Emperor had taken with him from Paris the dress and the hat which he wore on the day of that memorable battle, with the intention of wearing them on the field where it was fought. He afterwards proceeded by the way of Casal to Milan.

There the most brilliant reception he had yet experienced awaited him. His sojourn at Milan was not distinguished by outward demonstrations of enthusiasm alone. M. Durazzo, the last Doge of Genoa, added another gem to the Crown of Italy by supplicating the

Emperor in the name of the Republic, of which he was
the representative, to permit Genoa to exchange her independence for the honour of becoming a department of
France.   This offer, as may be guessed, was merely a plan
contrived beforehand.   It was accepted with an air of
protecting kindness, and at the same moment that the
country of Andrea Doria was effaced from the list of
nations its last Doge was included among the number of
French Senators.   Genoa, which formerly prided herself
in her surname, the Superb, became the chief station of
the twenty-seventh military division.   The Emperor went
to take possession of the city in person, and slept in the
Doria Palace, in the bed where Charles V. had lain.   He
left M. le Brun at Genoa as Governor-General.

At Milan the Emperor occupied the Palace of Monza.
The old Iron Crown of the Kings of Lombardy was
brought from the dust in which it had been buried, and
the new Coronation took place in the cathedral at Milan,
the largest in Italy, with the exception of St. Peter's at
Rome.   Napoleon received the crown from the hands of
the Archbishop of Milan, and placed it on his head, exclaiming, "*Dieu me l'a donnée, gare à qui la touche.*"   This
became the motto of the Order of the Iron Crown, which
the Emperor founded in commemoration of his being
crowned King of Italy.

Napoleon was crowned in the month of May 1805 : and
here I cannot avoid correcting some gross and inconceivable errors into which Napoleon must have voluntarily
fallen at St. Helena.   The *Memorial* states " that the celebrated singer Madame Grassini attracted his attention at
the time of the Coronation."   Napoleon alleges that
Madame Grassini on that occasion said to him, " When I
was in the prime of my beauty and talent all I wished was
that you would bestow a single look upon me.   That wish
was not fulfilled, and now you notice me when I am no
longer worthy your attention."

I confess I am at a loss to conceive what could induce
Napoleon to invent such a story. He might have recollected his acquaintance with Madame Grassini at Milan
before the battle of Marengo. It was in 1800, and not in
1805, that I was first introduced to her, and I know that
I several times took tea with her and Bonaparte in the
General's apartments. I remember also another circumstance, which is, that on the night when I awoke Bonaparte to announce to him the capitulation of Genoa,
Madame Grassini also awoke. Napoleon was charmed
with Madame Grassini's delicious voice, and if his imperious duties had permitted it he would have listened
with ecstasy to her singing for hours together.

Whilst Napoleon was at Milan, priding himself on his
double sovereignty, some schemes were set on foot at
Vienna and St. Petersburg which I shall hereafter have
occasion to notice. The Emperor, indeed, gave cause for
just complaint by the fact of annexing Genoa to the
Empire within four months after his solemn declaration
to the Legislative Body, in which he pledged himself in
the face of France and Europe not to seek any aggrandisement of territory. The pretext of a voluntary offer on the
part of Genoa was too absurd to deceive any one. The
rapid progress of Napoleon's ambition could not escape
the observation of the Cabinet of Vienna, which began to
show increased symptoms of hostility. The change which
was effected in the form of the Government of the Cisalpine Republic was likewise an act calculated to excite
remonstrances on the part of all the powers who were not
entirely subject to the yoke of France. He disguised the
taking of Genoa under the name of a gift, and the possession of Italy under the appearance of a mere change of
denomination. Notwithstanding these flagrant outrages
the exclusive apologists of Napoleon have always asserted
that he did not wish for war, and he himself maintained
that assertion at St. Helena. It is said that he was always

attacked, and hence a conclusion is drawn in favour of his love of peace. I acknowledge Bonaparte would never have fired a single musket-shot if all the powers of Europe had submitted to be pillaged by him one after the other without opposition. It was in fact declaring war against them to place them under the necessity of breaking a peace, during the continuance of which he was augmenting his power, and gratifying his ambition, as if in defiance of Europe. In this way Napoleon commenced all the wars in which he was engaged, with the exception of that which followed the peace of Marengo, and which terminated in Moreau's triumph at Hohenlinden. As there was no liberty of the press in France he found it easy to deceive the nation. He was in fact attacked, and thus he enjoyed the pleasure of undertaking his great military expeditions without being responsible in the event of failure.

During the Emperor's stay in the capital of the new kingdom of Italy he received the first intelligence of the dissatisfaction of Austria and Russia. That dissatisfaction was not of recent date. When I entered on my functions at Hamburg I learned some curious details (which I will relate in their proper place) respecting the secret negotiations which had been carried on for a considerable time previously to the commencement of hostilities. Even Prussia was no stranger to the dissatisfaction of Austria and Russia ; I do not mean the King, but the Cabinet of Berlin, which was then under the control of Chancellor Hardenberg ; for the King of Prussia had always personally declared himself in favour of the exact observance of treaties, even when their conditions were not honourable. Be that as it may, the Cabinet of Berlin, although dissatisfied in 1805 with the rapid progress of Napoleon's ambition, was nevertheless constrained to conceal its discontent, owing to the presence of the French troops in Hanover.

On returning from Milan the Emperor ordered the erection of a monument on the Great St. Bernard in commemoration of the victory of Marengo. M. Denon, who accompanied Napoleon, told me that he made a useless search to discover the body of Desaix, which Bonaparte wished to be buried beneath the monument, and that it was at length found by General Savary. It is therefore certain that the ashes of the brave Desaix repose on the summit of the Alps.[1]

The Emperor arrived in Paris about the end of June, and instantly set off for the camp at Boulogne. It was now once more believed that the project of invading England would be accomplished. This idea obtained the greater credit because Bonaparte caused some experiments for embarkation to be made in his presence. These experiments, however, led to no result. About this period a fatal event but too effectually contributed to strengthen the opinion of the inferiority of our navy. A French

---

[1] On his return to Paris after the battle of Marengo, Napoleon resolved to perpetuate the memory of the conquest of Italy by erecting, in the hospital of the Great St. Bernard, a monument which should attest to future ages that glorious epoch in the history of our arms. He directed M. Denon to go and survey the spot, and to submit to him various plans; out of these he had selected one, and the building was just finished while the Emperor was at Milan. He resolved to have it solemnly inaugurated, and the remains of General Desaix, surrounded with the laurels amid which he had fallen, removed thither. A small column was formed of the deputations of different regiments of the army of Italy, and of a civil deputation of Italians, who were to proceed from Milan to the hospital of Mont St. Bernard. Everything was arranged when M. Denon came to inform the Emperor that the body of General Desaix was not to be found. The Emperor recollected the order which he had given to me on the field of battle at Marengo, and desired me to neglect no means for discovering what had been done with it. M. Denon assured me that he had made many inquiries without success. I begged him to come with me just for an hour, and conducted him straightway to the convent where I had caused the body of General Desaix to be deposited. The monastery had been secularised; one of the monks only was left there; at the first question he comprehended what I wanted; he took me into a little sacristy, contiguous to a chapel, and there I found the body of General Desaix, in the same place, and in the same state, in which I had left it some years before, after having had it embalmed, then put into a leaden coffin, then into one of copper, and lastly, the whole inclosed in a wooden one. M. Denon rejoiced at this discovery, for he was afraid that he should be obliged to perform the ceremony without the remains of the illustrious general who was the object of it. Since that time General Desaix has reposed in the church of Mont St. Bernard (*Memoirs of the Duc de Rovigo*, tome ii. p. 123).

squadron, consisting of fifteen ships, fell in with the English fleet commanded by Admiral Calder, who had only nine vessels under his command, and in an engagement, which there was every reason to expect would terminate in our favour, we had the misfortune to lose two ships. The invasion of England was as little the object of this as of the previous journey to Boulogne; all Napoleon had in view was to stimulate the enthusiasm of the troops, and to hold out those threats against England which he conceived necessary for diverting attention from the real motive of his hostile preparations, which was to invade Germany and repulse the Russian troops, who had begun their march towards Austria. Such was the true object of Napoleon's last journey to Boulogne.

I had been some time at Hamburg when these events took place, and it was curious to observe the effect they produced. But I must not forget one circumstance in which I am personally concerned, and which brings me back to the time when I was in Paris. My new title of Minister Plenipotentiary obliged me to see a little more of society than during the period when prudence required me to live as it were in retirement. I had received sincere congratulations from Duroc, Rapp, and Lauriston, the three friends who had shown the greatest readiness to serve my interests with the Emperor; and I had frequent occasion to see M. Talleyrand, as my functions belonged to his department. The Emperor, on my farewell audience, having informed me that I was to correspond directly with the Minister of the General Police, I called on Fouché, who invited me to spend some days at his estate of Pont-Carré. I accepted the invitation because I wanted to confer with him, and I spent Sunday and Monday, the 28th and 29th of April, at Pont-Carré.

Fouché, like the Emperor, frequently revealed what he intended to conceal; but he had such a reputation for cunning that this sort of indiscretion was attended by no

inconvenience to him. He was supposed to be such a
constant dissembler that those who did not know him well
looked upon the truth when he spoke it merely as an artful snare laid to entrap them. I, however, knew that
celebrated person too well to confound his cunning with
his indiscretion. The best way to get out of him more
than he was aware of was to let him talk on without interruption. There were very few visitors at Pont-Carré,
and during the two days I spent there I had several conversations with Fouché. He told me a great deal about
the events of 1804, and he congratulated himself on
having advised Napoleon to declare himself Emperor.
" I have no preference," says Fouché, " for one form of
government more than another. Forms signify nothing.
The first object of the Revolution was not the overthrow of
the Bourbons, but merely the reform of abuses and the
destruction of prejudices. However, when it was discovered that Louis XVI. had neither firmness to refuse
what he did not wish to grant, nor good faith to grant
what his weakness had led him to promise, it was evident
that the Bourbons could no longer reign over France ;
and things were carried to such a length that we were
under the necessity of condemning Louis XVI. and re-
sorting to energetic measures. You know all that passed
up to the 18th Brumaire, and after. We all perceived
that a Republic could not exist in France ; the question,
therefore, was to ensure the perpetual removal of the
Bourbons ; and I believed the only means for so doing
was to transfer the inheritance of their throne to another
family. Some time before the 18th Brumaire I had a conversation with Siéyès and Barras, in which it was proposed, in case of the Directory being threatened, to recall
the Duke of Orleans ; and I could see very well that
Barras favoured that suggestion, although he alluded to
it merely as a report that was circulated about, and recommended me to pay attention to it. Siéyès said noth-

ing, and I settled the question by observing, that if any such thing had been agitated I must have been informed of it through the reports of my agents. I added, that the restoration of the throne to a collateral branch of the Bourbons would be an impolitic act, and would but temporarily change the position of those who had brought about the Revolution. I rendered an account of this interview with Barras to General Bonaparte the first time I had an opportunity of conversing with him after your return from Egypt. I sounded him, and I was perfectly convinced that in the state of decrepitude into which the Directory had fallen he was just the man we wanted. I therefore adopted such measures with the police as tended to promote his elevation to the First Magistracy. He soon showed himself ungrateful, and instead of giving me all his confidence he tried to outwit me. He put into the hands of a number of persons various matters of police which were worse than useless. Most of their agents, who were my creatures, obeyed my instructions in their reports; and it often happened that the First Consul thought he had discovered, through the medium of others, information that came from me, and of the falsehood of which I easily convinced him. I confess I was at fault on the 3d Nivôse; but are there any human means of preventing two men, who have no accomplices, from bringing a plot to execution? You saw the First Consul on his return from the opera; you heard all his declamations. I felt assured that the infernal machine was the work of the Royalists. I told the Emperor this, and he was, I am sure, convinced of it; but he, nevertheless, proscribed a number of men on the mere pretence of their old opinions. Do you suppose I am ignorant of what he said of me and of my vote at the National Convention? Most assuredly it ill becomes him to reproach the Conventionists. It was that vote which placed the crown upon his head. But for the situation in which we

were placed by that event, which circumstances had rendered inevitable, what should we have cared for the chance
of seeing the Bourbons return? You must have remarked that the Republicans, who were not Conventionists, were in general more averse than we to the proceedings of the 18th Brumaire, as, for example, Bernadotte
and Moreau. I know positively that Moreau was averse
to the Consulate ; and that it was only from irresolution
that he accepted the custody of the Directory. I know
also that he excused himself to his prisoners for the duty
which had devolved upon him. They themselves told me
this."

Fouché entered further into many details respecting his
conduct, and the motives which had urged him to do what
he did in favour of the First Consul. My memory does
not enable me to report all he told me, but I distinctly
recollect that the impression made on my mind by what
fell from him was, that he had acted merely with a view
to his own interests. He did not conceal his satisfaction
at having outwitted Regnier, and obliged Bonaparte to recall him. That he set in motion every spring calculated
to unite the conspirators, or rather to convert the discontented into conspirators, is evident from the following
remarks which fell from him : " With the information I
possessed, had I remained in office it is probable that I
might have prevented the conspiracy ; but Bonaparte
would still have had to fear the rivalry of Moreau. He
would not have been Emperor, and we should still have
had to dread the return of the Bourbons, of which, thank
God, there is now no fear."

During my stay at Pont-Carré I said but little to Fouché
about my long audience with the Emperor. However, I
thought I might inform him that I was authorised to correspond directly with his Majesty. I thought it useless to
conceal this fact, since he would soon learn it through his
agents. I also said a few words about Bonaparte's regret

at not having children.   My object was to learn Fouché's opinion on this subject, and it was not without a feeling of indignation that I heard him say, "It is to be hoped the Empress will soon die.   Her death will remove many difficulties.   Sooner or later he must take a wife who will bear him a child ; for as long as he has no direct heir there is every chance that his death will be the signal for a Revolution.   His brothers are perfectly incapable of filling his place, and a new party would rise up in favour of the Bourbons ; which must be prevented above all things.   At present they are not dangerous, though they still have active and devoted agents.   Altona is full of them, and you will be surrounded by them.   I beg of you to keep a watchful eye upon them, and render me a strict account of all their movements, and even of their most trivial actions.   As they have recourse to all sorts of disguises, you cannot be too vigilant ; therefore it will be advisable, in the first place, to establish a good system of espionage ; but have a care of the spies who serve both sides, for they swarm in Germany."

This is all I recollect of my conversations with Fouché at Pont-Carré.   I returned to Paris to make preparations for my journey to Hamburg.

CHAPTER XXXII.

1805.

Capitulation of Sublingen—Preparations for war—Utility of commercial
information—My instructions—Inspection of the emigrants and the
journals—A pamphlet by Kotzebue—Offers from the Emperor of
Russia to Moreau—Portrait of Gustavus Adolphus by one of his
ministers—Fouché's denunciations—Duels at Hamburg—M. de Gimel
—The *Hamburg Correspondant*—Letter from Bernadotte.

I LEFT Paris on the 20th of May 1805. On the 5th of June
following I delivered my credentials to the Senate of Hamburg, which was represented by the Syndic Doormann
and the Senator Schutte. M. Reinhart, my predecessor,
left Hamburg on the 12th of June.[1]

The reigning Dukes of Mecklenburg-Schwerin and
Brunswick, to whom I had announced my arrival as accredited Minister to them, wrote me letters recognising
me in that character.

General Walmoden had just signed the capitulation of
Sublingen with Marshal Mortier, who had the command
in Hanover. The English Government refused to ratify
this, because it stipulated that the troops should be
prisoners of war. Bonaparte had two motives for relaxing
this hard condition. He wished to keep Hanover as a
compensation for Malta, and to assure the means of em-

---

[1] Comte Alexandre de Puymaigre, who was sent to Hamburg in 1811, says
(*Souvenirs*, p. 135), "In treating of the persons I knew at Hamburg, I recollect the
judgment which M. de Bourrienne pronounces on some of them in his *Memoirs*,
and I must allow that in general his assertions are well founded. This former companion of Napoleon has only forgotten to mention the opinion entertained of him in
this town. The fact is that he was believed to have made his money there, as also
was Marshal Brune. This belief was as strong as the esteem that was entertained
for Marshal Bernadotte, since, as the soldiers say, *promoted* King of Sweden."

barrassing and attacking Prussia, which he now began to
distrust. By advancing upon Prussia he would secure his
left, so that when convenient he might march northward.
Mortier, therefore, received orders to reduce the conditions
of the capitulation to the surrender of the arms, baggage,
artillery, and horses. England, which was making great
efforts to resist the invasion with which she thought herself threatened, expended considerable sums for the transport of the troops from Hanover to England. Her precipitation was indescribable, and she paid the most exor-
bitant charges for the hire of ships. Several houses in
Hamburg made fortunes on this occasion.

Experience has long since proved that it is not at their
source that secret transactions are most readily known.
The intelligence of an event frequently resounds at a distance, while the event itself is almost entirely unknown
in the place of its occurrence. The direct influence of
political events on commercial speculations renders mer-
chants exceedingly attentive to what is going on. All
who are engaged in commercial pursuits form a corpo-
ration united by the strongest of all bonds, common interest ; and commercial correspondence frequently presents
a fertile field for observation, and affords much valuable
information, which often escapes the inquiries of Government agents.

I resolved to form a connection with some of the mercantile houses which maintained extensive and frequent
communications with the Northern States. I knew that
by obtaining their confidence I might gain a knowledge
of all that was going on in Russia, Sweden, England, and
Austria. Among the subjects upon which it was desirable
to obtain information I included negotations, treaties, military measures—such as recruiting troops beyond the
amount settled for the peace establishment, movements of
troops, the formation of camps and magazines, financial
operations, the fitting-out of ships, and many other things,

which, though not important in themselves, frequently lead to the knowledge of what is important.

I was not inclined to place reliance on all public reports and gossiping stories circulated on the Exchange without close investigation ; for I wished to avoid transmitting home as truths what might frequently be mere stock-jobbing inventions. I was instructed to keep watch on the emigrants, who were exceedingly numerous in Hamburg and its neighbourhood, Mecklenburg, Hanover, Brunswick, and Holstein ; but I must observe that my inspection was to extend only to those who were known to be actually engaged in intrigues and plots.

I was also to keep watch on the state of the public mind, and on the journals which frequently give it a wrong direction, and to point out those articles in the journals which I thought censurable. At first I merely made verbal representations and complaints, but I could not always confine myself to this course. I received such distinct and positive orders that, in spite of myself, inspection was speedily converted into oppression. Complaints against the journals filled one-fourth of my despatches.

As the Emperor wished to be made acquainted with all that was printed against him, I sent to Paris, in May 1805, and consequently a very few days after my arrival in Hamburg, a pamphlet by the celebrated Kotzebue, entitled *Recollections of my Journey to Naples and Rome.* This publication, which was printed at Berlin, was full of indecorous attacks and odious allusions on the Emperor.

I was informed at that time, through a certain channel, that the Emperor Alexander had solicited General Moreau to enter his service, and take the command of the Russian infantry. He offered him 12,000 roubles to defray his travelling expenses. At a subsequent period Moreau unfortunately accepted these offers, and died in the enemy's ranks.

On the 27th of June M. Bouligny arrived at Hamburg. He was appointed to supersede M. d'Ocariz at Stockholm. The latter minister had left Hamburg on the 11th of June for Constantinople, where he did not expect to stay three months. I had several long conversations with him before his departure, and he did not appear to be satisfied with his destination. We frequently spoke of the King of Sweden, whose conduct M. d'Ocariz blamed. He was, he said, a young madman, who, without reflecting on the change of time and circumstances, wished to play the part of Gustavus Adolphus, to whom he bore no resemblence but in name. M. d'Ocariz spoke of the King of Sweden's camp in a tone of derision. That Prince had returned to the King of Prussia the cordon of the Black Eagle because the order had been given to the First Consul. I understood that Frederick William was very much offended at this proceeding, which was as indecorous and absurd as the return of the Golden Fleece by Louis XVIII. to the King of Spain was dignified and proper.[1] Gustavus Adolphus was brave, enterprising, and chivalrous, but inconsiderate and irascible. He called Bonaparte *Monsieur Napoléon.* His follies and reverses in Hanover were without doubt the cause of his abdication. On the 31st of October 1805 he published a declaration of war against France in language highly insulting to the Emperor.

Fouché overwhelmed me with letters. If I had attended to all his instructions I should have left nobody unmo-

[1] Of Gustavus IV. Napoleon spoke in the following terms at St. Helena:—

"That Prince," he said, "on his appearance in life announced himself as a hero, and terminated his career merely as a madman. He distinguished himself in his early days by some very remarkable traits. While yet under age he was seen to insult Catherine by the refusal of her granddaughter, at the very moment, too, when that great Empress, seated on her throne and surrounded by her Court, only waited for him to celebrate the marriage ceremony. At a later period he insulted Alexander in no less marked a way by refusing, after Paul's death, to allow one of the new Emperor's officers to enter his territory, and by answering to the official complaints addressed to him on the subject that Alexander ought not to be displeased that he, Gustavus, who still deplored the assassination of his father, should close the entrance of his States against one of those accused by the public voice of having immolated his (Alexander's)" (*Mémorial de Sainte Hélène*).

lested. He asked me for information respecting a man named Lazoret, of the department of Gard, a girl, named Rosine Zimbenni, having informed the police that he had been killed in a duel at Hamburg. I replied that I knew but of four Frenchmen who had been killed in that way ; one, named Clément, was killed by Tarasson; a second, named Duparc, killed by Lezardi; a third, named Sadremont, killed by Revel; and a fourth, whose name I did not know, killed by Lafond. This latter had just arrived at Hamburg when he was killed, but he was not the man sought for.

Lafond was a native of Brabant, and had served in the British army. He insulted the Frenchman because he wore the national cockade. A duel was the consequence, and the offended party fell. M. Reinhart, my predecessor, wished to punish Lafond, but the Austrian Minister having claimed him as the subject of his sovereign, he was not molested. Lafond took refuge in Antwerp, where he became a player.

During the first months which succeeded my arrival in Hamburg I received orders for the arrest of many persons, almost all of whom were designated as dangerous and ill-disposed men. When I was convinced that the accusation was groundless I postponed the arrest. The matter was then forgotten, and nobody complained.

A title, or a rank in foreign service, was a safeguard against the Paris inquisition. Of this the following is an instance. Count Gimel, of whom I shall hereafter have occasion to speak more at length, set out about this time for Carlsbad. Count Grote, the Prussian Minister, frequently spoke to me of him. On my expressing apprehension that M. de Gimel might be arrested, as there was a strong prejudice against him, M. Grote replied, "Oh ! there is no fear of that. He will return to Hamburg with the rank of an English colonel."

On the 17th of July there appeared in the *Correspondant*

an article exceedingly insulting to France. It had been inserted by order of Baron Novozilzow, who was at Berlin, and who had become very hostile to France, though it was said he had been sent from St. Petersburg on a specific mission to Napoleon. The article in question was transmitted from Berlin by an extraordinary courier, and Novozilzow in his note to the Senate said it might be stated that the article was inserted at the request of His Britannic Majesty. The Russian Minister at Berlin, M. Alopœus, despatched also an *estafette* to the Russian *chargé d'affaires* at Hamburg, with orders to apply for the insertion of the article, which accordingly appeared. In obedience to the Emperor's instructions, I complained of it, and the Senate replied that it never opposed the insertion of an official note sent by any Government; that insults would redound against those from whom they came; that the reply of the French Government would be published; and that the Senate had never deviated from this mode of proceeding.

I observed to the Senate that I did not understand why the *Correspondant* should make itself the trumpet of M. Novozilzow; to which the Syndic replied, that two great powers, which might do them much harm, had required the insertion of the article, and that it could not be refused.[1]

The hatred felt by the foreign Princes, which the death of the Duc d'Enghien had considerably increased, gave encouragement to the publication of everything hostile to Napoleon. This was candidly avowed to me by the Ministers and foreigners of rank whom I saw in Hamburg. The King of Sweden was most violent in manifesting the indignation which was generally excited by the death of the Duc d'Enghien. M. Wetterstadt, who had succeeded

---

[1] The circulation of the *Hamburg Correspondant* at that time was 27,000. At a later period it amounted to 60,000. It was a well-conducted and cheap journal, and was read in all parts of Germany. It was, at the time here alluded to, the most effective medium of publicity.—*Bourrienne.*

M. La Gerbielske in the Cabinet of Stockholm, sent to the Swedish Minister at Hamburg a long letter exceedingly insulting to Napoleon. It was in reply to an article inserted in the *Moniteur* respecting the return of the Black Eagle to the King of Prussia. M. Peyron, the Swedish Minister at Hamburg, who was very far from approving all that his master did, transmitted to Stockholm some very energetic remarks on the ill effect which would be produced by the insertion of the article in the *Correspondant.* The article was then a little modified, and M. Peyron received formal orders to get it inserted. However, on my representations the Senate agreed to suppress it, and it did not appear.

Marshal Bernadotte, who had the command of the French troops in Hanover, kept up a friendly correspondence with me unconnected with the duties of our respective functions.

On the occupation of Hanover Mr. Taylor, the English Minister at Cassel, was obliged to leave that place ; but he soon returned in spite of the opposition of France. On this subject the marshal furnished me with the following particulars :—

I have just received, my dear Bourrienne, information which leaves no doubt of what has taken place at Cassel with respect to Mr. Taylor. That Minister has been received in spite of the representations of M. Bignon, which, however, had previously been merely verbal. I know that the Elector wrote to London to request that Mr. Taylor should not return. In answer to this the English Government sent him back. Our Minister has done everything he could to obtain his dismissal; but the pecuniary interests of the Elector have triumphed over every other consideration. He would not risk quarrelling with the Court from which he expects to receive more than 12,000,000 francs. The British Government has been written to a second time, but without effect. The Elector himself, in a private letter, has requested the King of England to recall Mr. Taylor, but it is very probable that the Cabinet of London will evade this request.

Under these circumstances our troops have approached nearer to

Cassel.   Hitherto the whole district of Göttingen had been exempt
from quartering troops.   New arrangements, rendered necessary by
the scarcity of forage, have obliged me to send a squadron of
chasseurs à cheval to Munden, a little town four leagues from Cassel.
This movement excited some alarm in the Elector, who expressed a
wish to see things restored to the same footing as before.   He has
requested M. Bignon to write to me, and to assure me again that he
will be delighted to become acquainted with me at the waters of
Nemidorff, where he intends to spend some time.   But on this
subject I shall not alter the determination I have already mentioned
to you.—Yours, etc.,

(Signed)   BERNADOTTE.

STADE, 10*th Thermidor* (29th July, 1805).

CHAPTER XXXIII.

1805.

AT the beginning of August 1805 a treaty of alliance between Russia and England was spoken of. Some persons of consequence, who had the means of knowing all that was going on in the political world, had read this treaty, the principal points of which were communicated to me.

Article 1st stated that the object of the alliance was to restore the balance of Europe. By art. 2d the Emperor of Russia was to place 36,000 men at the disposal of England. Art. 3d stipulated that neither of the two powers would consent to treat with France, nor to lay down arms until the King of Sardinia should either be restored to his dominions or receive an equivalent indemnity in the northeast of Italy. By art. 4th Malta was to be evacuated by the English, and occupied by the Russians. By art. 5th the two powers were to guarantee the independence of the Republic of the Ionian Isles, and England was to pledge herself to assist Russia in her war against Persia. If this plan of a treaty, of the existence of which I was informed on unquestionable authority, had been brought to any result [1] it is impossible to calculate what might have been its consequences.

At that time an immediate Continental war was confidently expected by every person in the north of Europe; and it is very certain that, had not Napoleon taken the hint in time and renounced his absurd schemes at Boulogne, France would have stood in a dangerous situation.

M. Forshmann, the Russian *chargé d'affaires*, was intriguing to excite the north of Europe against France. He repeatedly received orders to obtain the insertion of irritating articles in the *Correspondant*. He was an active, intriguing, and spiteful little man, and a declared enemy of France; but fortunately his stupidity and vanity rendered him less dangerous than he wished to be. He was universally detested, and he would have lost all credit but that the extensive trade carried on between Russia and Hamburg forced the inhabitants and magistrates of that city to bear with a man who might have done them, individually, considerable injury.

The recollection of Duroc's successful mission to Berlin during the Consulate induced Napoleon to believe that that general might appease the King of Prussia, who complained seriously of the violation of the territory of Anspach, which Bernadotte, in consequence of the orders he received, had not been able to respect. Duroc remained about six weeks in Berlin.

The following letter from Duroc will show that the facility of passing through Hesse seemed to excuse the second violation of the Prussian territory; but there was a great difference between a petty Prince of Hesse and the King of Prussia.

I send you, my dear Bourrienne, two despatches, which I have received for you. M. de Talleyrand, who sends them, desires me

---

[1] The provisions in regard to Malta and Persia at once rendered this impossible.

to request that you will transmit General Victor's by a sure con-
veyance.

I do not yet know whether I shall stay long in Berlin. By the
last accounts I received the Emperor is still in Paris, and numerous
forces are assembling on the Rhine. The hopes of peace are van-
ishing every day, and Austria does everything to promote war.

I have received accounts from Marshal Bernadotte. He has
effected his passage through Hesse. Marshal Bernadotte was much
pleased with the courtesy he experienced from the Elector.

The junction of the corps commanded by Bernadotte
with the army of the Emperor was very important, and
Napoleon therefore directed the Marshal to come up with
him as speedily as possible, and by the shortest road. It
was necessary he should arrive in time for the battle of
Austerlitz. Gustavus, King of Sweden, who was always
engaged in some enterprise, wished to raise an army composed of Swedes, Prussians, and English ; and certainly a
vigorous attack in the north would have prevented Bernadotte from quitting the banks of the Elbe and the Weser,
and reinforcing the Grand Army which was marching on
Vienna. But the King of Sweden's coalition produced no
other result than the siege of the little fortress of Hameln.
Prussia would not come to a rupture with France, the
King of Sweden was abandoned, and Bonaparte's resentment against him increased. This abortive project of
Gustavus contributed not a little to alienate the affections
of his subjects, who feared that they might be the victims
of the revenge excited by the extravagant plans of their
King, and the insults he had heaped upon Napoleon, particularly since the death of the Duc d'Enghien.

On the 13th of September 1805 I received a letter from
the Minister of Police soliciting information about Swedish
Pomerania.

Astonished at not obtaining from the commercial Consuls at Lubeck and Stettin any accounts of the movements
of the Russians, I had sent to those ports, four days before the receipt of the Police Minister's letter, a confiden-

tial agent, to observe the Baltic : though we were only 64 leagues from Stralsund the most uncertain and contradictory accounts came to hand. It was, however, certain that a landing of the Russians was expected at Stralsund, or at Travemünde, the port of Lubeck, at the mouth of the little river Trave. I was positively informed that Russia had freighted a considerable number of vessels for those ports.

The hatred of the French continued to increase in the north of Europe. About the end of September there appeared at Kiel, in Denmark, a libellous pamphlet, which was bought and read with inconceivable avidity. This pamphlet, which was very ably written, was the production of some fanatic who openly preached a crusade against France. The author regarded the blood of millions of men as a trifling sacrifice for the great object of humiliating France and bringing her back to the limits of the old monarchy. This pamphlet was circulated extensively in the German departments united to France, in Holland, and in Switzerland. The number of incendiary publications which everywhere abounded indicated but too plainly that if the nations of the north should be driven back towards the Arctic regions they would in their turn repulse their conquerors towards the south ; and no man of common sense could doubt that if the French eagles were planted in foreign capitals, foreign standards would one day wave over Paris.

On the 30th of September 1805 I received, by an *estafette*, intelligence of the landing at Stralsund of 6000 Swedes, who had arrived from Stockholm in two ships of war.

About the end of September the Hamburg exchange on Paris fell alarmingly. The loss was twenty per cent. The fall stopped at seventeen below par. The speculation for this fall of the exchange had been made with equal imprudence and animosity by the house of Osy and Company. The head of that house, a Dutch emigrant, who had been settled at Hamburg about six years, seized every opportunity of manifesting his hatred of France. An agent of that rich house at Rotterdam was also very hostile to us, a circumstance which shows that if many persons sacrifice their political opinions to their interests there are others who endanger their interests for the triumph of their opinions.

On the 23d of October 1805 I received official intelligence of the total destruction of the first Austrian army. General Barbou, who was in Hanover, also informed me of that event in the following terms: " The first Austrian army has ceased to exist." He alluded to the brilliant affair of Ulm. I immediately despatched twelve *estafettes* to different parts; among other places to Stralsund and Husum. I thought that these prodigies, which must have been almost incredible to those who were unacquainted with Napoleon's military genius, might arrest the progress of the Russian troops, and produce some change in the movements of the enemy's forces. A second edition of the *Correspondant* was published with this intelligence, and 6000 copies were sold at four times the usual price.

I need not detain the reader with the details of the capitulation of Ulm, which have already been published, but I may relate the following anecdote, which is not generally known. A French general passing before the ranks of his men said to them, " Well, comrades, we have prisoners enough here."—" Yes indeed," replied one of the soldiers, "we never saw so many . . . collected together before." It was stated at the time, and I believe it, that the Emperor was much displeased when he heard of this, and remarked that it was "atrocious to insult brave men to whom the fate of arms had proved unfavourable."

In reading the history of this period we find that in whatever place Napoleon happened to be, there was the central point of action. The affairs of Europe were arranged at

his headquarters in the same manner as if he had been in
Paris.   Everything depended on his good or bad fortune.
Espionage, seduction, false promises, exactions,—all were
put in force to promote the success of his projects ; but
his despotism, which excited dissatisfaction in France, and
his continual aggressions, which threatened the independence of foreign States, rendered him more and more
unpopular everywhere.

The battle of Trafalgar took place while Napoleon was
marching on Vienna, and on the day after the capitulation
of Ulm.   The southern coast of Spain then witnessed an
engagement between thirty-one French and about an equal
number of English ships, and in spite of this equality of
force the French fleet was destroyed.[1]

This great battle afforded another proof of our naval
inferiority.   Admiral Calder first gave us the lesson which
Nelson completed, but which cost the latter his life.   According to the reports which Duroc transmitted to me,
courage gave momentary hope to the French ; but they
were at length forced to yield to the superior naval tactics of the enemy.   The battle of Trafalgar paralysed our
naval force, and banished all hope of any attempt against
England.[2]

The favour which the King of Prussia had shown to
Duroc was withdrawn when his Majesty received intelligence of the march of Bernadotte's troops through the
Margravate of Anspach.   All accounts concurred respecting the just umbrage which that violation of territory
occasioned to the King of Prussia.   The agents whom I
had in that quarter overwhelmed me with reports of the

---

[1] The actual forces present were 27 English ships of the line, and 33 Franco-Span-
ish ships of the line ; see James' *Naval History*, vol. iii. p. 459.

[2] On receiving the dismal news of the annihilation of his fleet at Trafalgar Bonaparte is reported to have said, " I cannot be everywhere."   Just as if he could have
changed the fate of the day—*he*, who knew nothing of naval tactics !   It has been
well remarked on this point that the presence of Bonaparte at Trafalgar would have
had about as much influence as Nelson mounted on horseback could have produced
in the land fights of Marengo and Austerlitz.—*Editor of* 1836 *edition*.

excesses committed by the French in passing through the
Margravate. A letter I received from Duroc contains the
following remarks on this subject:[1]

The corps of Marshal Bernadotte has passed through Anspach,
and by some misunderstanding this has been regarded at Berlin as
an insult to the King, a violence committed upon his neutrality.
How can it be supposed, especially under present circumstances,
that the Emperor could have any intention of insulting or committing violence upon his friend? Besides, the reports have been
exaggerated, and have been made by persons who wish to favour
our enemies rather than us. However, I am perfectly aware that
Marshal Bernadotte's 70,000 men are not 70,000 virgins. Be this
as it may, the business might have been fatal, and will, at all events,
be very injurious to us. Laforest and I are treated very harshly,
though we do not deserve it. All the idle stories that have been
got up here must have reached you. Probably Prussia will not forget that France was, and still may be, the only power interested in
her glory and aggrandisement.

At the end of October the King of Prussia, far from
thinking of war, but in case of its occurrence wishing to
check its disasters as far as possible, proposed to establish
a line of neutrality. This was the first idea of the Con-
federation of the North.[2] Duroc, fearing lest the Russians
should enter Hamburg, advised me, as a friend, to adopt
precautions. But I was on the spot; I knew all the move-

[1] The ignoble and ludicrous behaviour of Prussia at this time can be well seen in
the correspondence of Metternich (vol. ii. pp. 20–142). While Austria was urging her
to join the allies, and Russia was preparing to force her hand by violating her territory, Napoleon calmly marched his troops across her frontier. He had crushed Austria while Prussia was slowly preparing to march to attack the French. Finally,
Prussia had to cede Anspach and Neufchatel, Valengin, Cleves, etc., to France,
receiving in exchange Hanover, the possession of her ally the King of England. Napoleon did not even pay the empty compliment of waiting for the ratification of the
treaty by Prussia, but occupied the ceded districts at once. The whole affair is a
good instance of the shameless greed, irresolution, and jealousy of the Continental
powers which made it easy for Napoleon to crush them in detail. The reader, accustomed to hear of the so-called grand uprising of the Germans in 1813, when with
superior numbers they forced the young French recruits back from Germany, should
note how it was the French ever came to dominate over Germany.

[2] The "Confédération du Nord," which was projected in 1806, after the formation
of the Confédération du Rhin, was to have been composed of Prussia, Saxony,
Hesse, and the Hanse towns. The plan was never carried out.

ments of the little detached corps, and I was under no apprehension.

The editor of the *Hamburg Correspondant* sent me every evening a proof of the number which was to appear next day,—*a favour which was granted only to the French Minister.*[1] On the 20th of November I received the proof as usual, and saw nothing objectionable in it. How great, therefore, was my astonishment when next morning I read in the same journal an article personally insulting to the Emperor, and in which the legitimate sovereigns of Europe were called upon *to undertake a crusade against the usurper!* etc. I immediately sent for M. Doormann, first Syndic of the Senate of Hamburg. When he appeared his mortified look sufficiently informed me that he knew what I had to say to him. I reproached him sharply, and asked him how, after all I had told him of the Emperor's susceptibility, he could permit the insertion of such an article. I observed to him that this indecorous diatribe had no official character, since it had no signature ; and that, therefore, he had acted in direct opposition to a decree of the Senate, which prohibited the insertion in the journals of any articles which were not signed. I told him plainly that his imprudence might be attended with serious consequences. M. Doormann did not attempt to justify himself, but merely explained to me how the thing had happened.

---

[1] This is literally true. Metternich, writing in 1805, says that he has sent an article to the newspapers at Berlin and to M. de Höfer at Hamburg. "I do not know whether it has been accepted by the editors, for M. Bourrienne still exercises an authority so severe over these journals that they are always submitted to him before they appear, that he may erase or alter the articles which do not please him" (*Metternich*, tome ii. p. 96). In another place (tome ii. p. 227) he says "the newspapers are worth to Napoleon an army of 300,000 men, for such a force would not overlook the interior better, or frighten foreign powers more, than half a dozen of his paid pamphleteers." Sometimes the press was used to make it seem as if the assurances of the hostile powers were believed. Thus before the Ulm campaign the *Moniteur* solemnly announced : "The Russians continue their preparations *against the Persians*." The German papers themselves often took the French side : "Our journalists take up the cause of the tyrant and of the ' Grande Nation ' either from meanness, stupidity, fear, or for *gold*. I need only name Woltmann, Archenholz, Voss, and Bucholz " (*Memoirs of Perthes*, vol. i. p. 143).

On the 20th of November, at ten in the evening, M. Forshmann, the Russian *chargé d'affaires* who had in the course of the day arrived from the Russian headquarters, presented to the editor of the *Correspondant* the article in question. The editor, after reading the article, which he thought exceedingly indecorous, observed to M. Forshmann that his paper was already made up, which was the fact, for I had seen a proof. M. Forshmann, however, insisted on the insertion of the article. The editor then told him that he could not admit it without the approbation of the Syndic Censor. M. Forshmann immediately waited upon M. Doormann, and when the latter begged that he would not insist on the insertion of the article, M. Forshmann produced a letter written in French, which, among other things, contained the following: "You will get the enclosed article inserted in the *Correspondant* without suffering a single word to be altered. Should the censor refuse, you must apply to the directing Burgomaster, and, in case of his refusal, to General Tolstoy, who will devise some means of rendering the Senate more complying, and forcing it to observe an impartial deference."

M. Doormann, thinking he could not take upon himself to allow the insertion of the article, went, accompanied by M. Forshmann, to wait upon M. Von Graffen, the directing Burgomaster. MM. Doormann and Von Graffen earnestly pointed out the impropriety of inserting the article ; but M. Forshmann referred to his order, and added that the compliance of the Senate on this point was the only means of avoiding great mischief. The Burgomaster and the Syndic, finding themselves thus forced to admit the article, entreated that the following passage at least might be suppressed : "I know a certain chief, who, in defiance of all laws divine and human,—in contempt of the hatred he inspires in Europe, as well as among those whom he has reduced to be his subjects, keeps possession of a

usurped throne by violence and crime. His insatiable
ambition would subject all Europe to his rule. But the
time is come for avenging the rights of nations. . . ."
M. Forshmann again referred to his orders, and with some
degree of violence insisted on the insertion of the article
in its complete form. The Burgomaster then authorised
the editor of the *Correspondant* to print the article that
night, and M. Forshmann, having obtained that authority,
carried the article to the office at half-past eleven o'clock.

Such was the account given me by M. Doormann. I observed that I did not understand how the imaginary apprehension of any violence on the part of Russia should have
induced him to admit so insolent an attack upon the most
powerful sovereign in Europe, whose arms would soon
dictate laws to Germany. The Syndic did not dissemble
his fear of the Emperor's resentment, while at the same
time he expressed a hope that the Emperor would take into
consideration the extreme difficulty of a small power maintaining neutrality in the extraordinary circumstances in
which Hamburg was placed, and that the articles might
be said to have been presented almost at the point of the
Cossacks' spears. M. Doormann added that a refusal,
which would have brought Russian troops to Hamburg,
might have been attended by very unpleasant consequences
to me, and might have committed the Senate in a very different way. I begged of him, once for all, to set aside in
these affairs all consideration of my personal danger : and
the Syndic, after a conversation of more than two hours,
departed more uneasy in his mind than when he arrived,
and conjuring me to give a faithful report of the facts as
they had happened.

M. Doormann was a very worthy man, and I gave a
favourable representation of his excuses and of the readiness which he had always evinced to keep out of the *Correspondant* articles hostile to France ; as, for example, the
commencement of a proclamation of the Emperor of Ger-

many to his subjects, and a complete proclamation of the
King of Sweden. As it happened, the good Syndic escaped
with nothing worse than a fright ; I was myself astonished
at the success of my intercession. I learned from the
Minister for Foreign Affairs that the Emperor was furiously
indignant on reading the article, in which the French army
was outraged as well as he. Indeed, he paid but little
attention to insults directed against himself personally.
Their eternal repetition had inured him to them ; but at
the idea of his army being insulted he was violently enraged, and uttered the most terrible threats.

It is worthy of remark that the Swedish and English
Ministers, as soon as they read the article, waited upon the
editor of the *Correspondant,* and expressed their astonishment that such a libel should have been published. " Victorious armies," said they, " should be answered by cannon-
balls, and not by insults as gross as they are ridiculous."
This opinion was shared by all the foreigners at that time
in Hamburg.

CHAPTER XXXIV.

1805.

Difficulties of my situation at Hamburg—Toil and responsibility—Super-
    vision of the emigrants—Foreign Ministers—Journals—Packet from
    Strasburg—Bonaparte fond of narrating—GIULIO, an extempore rec-
    itation of a story composed by the Emperor.

THE brief detail I have given in the two or three preceding
chapters of the events which occurred previously to and
during the campaign of Austerlitz, with the letters of
Duroc and Bernadotte, may afford the reader some idea of
my situation during the early part of my residence in
Hamburg.   Events succeeded each other with such incredible rapidity as to render my labour excessive.   My
occupations were different, but not less laborious, than
those which I formerly performed when near the Emperor ; and, besides, I was now loaded with a responsibility
which did not attach to me as the private secretary of
General Bonaparte and the First Consul.   I had, in fact,
to maintain a constant watch over the emigrants in Altona,
which was no easy matter—to correspond daily with the
Minister for Foreign Affairs and the Minister of Police—
to confer with the foreign Ministers accredited at Hamburg
—to maintain active relations with the commanders of
the French army—to interrogate my secret agents, and
keep a strict surveillance over their proceedings ; it was,
besides, necessary to be unceasingly on the watch for
scurrilous articles against Napoleon in the *Hamburg Correspondant.*   I shall frequently have occasion to speak of
all these things, and especially of the most marked emi-

grants, in a manner less irregular, because what I have
hitherto said may, in some sort, be considered merely as
a summary of all the facts relating to the occurrences
which daily passed before my eyes.

In the midst of these multifarious and weighty occupations I received a packet with the Strasburg postmark at
the time the Empress was in that city. This packet had
not the usual form of a diplomatic despatch, and the su-
perscription announced that it came from the residence of
Josephine. My readers, I venture to presume, will not
experience less gratification than I did on a perusal of its
contents, which will be found at the end of this chapter ;
but before satisfying the curiosity to which I have perhaps
given birth, I may here relate that one of the peculiarities
of Bonaparte was a fondness of extempore narration ; and
it appears he had not discontinued the practice even after
he became Emperor.

In fact, Bonaparte, during the first year after his elevation to the Imperial throne, usually passed those evenings
in the apartments of the Empress which he could steal
from public business. Throwing himself on a sofa, he
would remain absorbed in gloomy silence, which no one
dared to interrupt. Sometimes, however, on the contrary,
he would give the reins to his vivid imagination and his
love of the marvellous, or, to speak more correctly, his
desire to produce effect, which was perhaps one of his
strongest passions, and would relate little romances, which
were always of a fearful description and in unison with
the natural turn of his ideas. During those recitals the
ladies-in-waiting were always present,—to one of whom I
am indebted for the following story, which she had written nearly in the words of Napoleon. "Never," said this
lady in her letter to me, " did the Emperor appear more
extraordinary. Led away by the subject, he paced the
salon with hasty strides ; the intonations of his voice varied
according to the characters of the personages he brought

on the scene; he seemed to multiply himself in order to play the different parts, and no person needed to feign the terror which he really inspired, and which he loved to see depicted in the countenances of those who surrounded him." In this tale I have made no alterations, as can be attested by those who, to my knowledge, have a copy of it. It is curious to compare the impassioned portions of it with the style of Napoleon in some of the letters addressed to Josephine.

GIULIO,

A STORY BY THE EMPEROR NAPOLEON I.

I.

In the city of Rome appeared a mysterious being who pretended to unveil the secrets of futurity, and who was enveloped in so much obscurity that even its sex was an object of doubt and discussion. Some, in relating the strange predictions which they had heard from the mouth of this being, described the form and the features of a woman, while others justified their terror by depicting a hideous monster.

The abode of this oracle was in one of the suburbs of Rome, in a deserted palace, where the delusions of superstition were a sufficient protection from popular curiosity. No one knew the period of the arrival of this singular being; everything connected with her existence was shrouded in impenetrable mystery. Nothing was spoken of in Rome but the Sibyl, the appellation by which she was generally known ; every one was anxious to consult the oracle, but few had courage to cross the threshold of her dwelling. On approaching it the greatest number of the curious were seized with a feeling of horror, which they could only attribute to a fatal presentiment, and fled as if forcibly repelled by an invisible hand.

II.

Camillo, a young Roman of a noble family, resolved to explore the retreat of the Sibyl, and entreated Giulio, his intimate friend, to be the companion of his adventure. Giulio, being of a timid and irresolute character, at first declined the invitation of his friend. It was not a dread of any unknown peril which produced this hesitation, but he shuddered at the idea of seeing the salutary veil withdrawn which concealed the future. At length, however, he yielded to the persuasions of his friend. The day was fixed, and together they proceeded to the fatal palace; the gate opened as of its own accord, and the two friends immediately entered. They wandered for some time through the deserted apartments, and at length found themselves in a gallery divided by a black curtain with this inscription : *If you wish to know your destiny, pass beyond this curtain; but prepare yourself by prayer.* Giulio experienced the most violent agitation, and sank involuntarily on his knees. Was he already under the influence of a mysterious power? In a few moments the youths, raising the curtain, drew their swords and penetrated into the sanctuary. A female approached them ;—she was young, perhaps even beautiful ; but her aspect defied and repelled all examination ; the cold immobility of death, strangely combined with the motions of life, formed the expression of her countenance. How find words to define or depict those supernatural beings, who doubtless inhabit regions where human language is unknown? Giulio shuddered, and turned away his eyes ; Camillo cast down his, and the Sibyl inquired the motive of their visit. Camillo answered her, but she listened not to his words, her whole attention seemed absorbed by Giulio ; she was agitated, trembled, extended one hand as if about to seize him, and suddenly stepped back. Camillo reiterated his request to be instructed in the secrets of his destiny ; she consented, and Giulio withdrew. After a short conference Camillo rejoined his friend, whom he found buried in a profound reverie. " Go," said he to him, smiling, " take courage, for I myself have learned nothing very awful ; the Sibyl promised that I should espouse your sister Giuliana (a thing already agreed on),—only she added that ' a trifling accident would for a short time retard our union ! '"

Giulio, in his turn, stepped beyond the fatal curtain, and Camillo remained in the gallery. Very soon he heard a fearful cry, and, recognising the voice of his friend, flew to his aid. Giulio was on his knees before the Sibyl, who, waving over his head a wand, pronounced these awful words : " Love without bounds ! Sacrilege ! Murder ! " Camillo, seized with horror, approached Giulio, who, pale and motionless, could not support himself.   To his interrogation he could obtain no reply from his friend, who vaguely repeated the fatal words, *Love without bounds!   Murder!   Sacrilege!*

[These words were pronounced in a lugubrious tone by Bonaparte.]

Camillo at length succeeded in conducting Giulio to his home, and the moment he could find a pretext for leaving him he flew to make another visit to the Sibyl: he had resolved to question and compel her to give an explanation of what she had said; but the place was deserted; the curtain, the inscription,—all had disappeared; there remained no trace of the magician, who was never seen again.

III.

Several weeks flew away; the marriage of Camillo was fixed, and Giulio seemed to have recovered his tranquillity.   His friend avoided speaking to him on the prediction, in the hope that the horrible scene would be gradually effaced from his memory.   On the day preceding that fixed for the marriage of Camillo the Marquis di Cosmo, the father of Giulio, fell from his horse, and though he received no serious injury, this accident delayed the nuptials.   Giulio, his sister, and Camillo, surrounded the couch of the marquis, deploring the delay of their happiness.   A sudden recollection darted into the mind of Camillo; he exclaimed aloud, " The prediction of the Sibyl is accomplished."   This exclamation threw Giulio into the greatest agitation; from that moment he shut himself up in his own apartment, and avoided all society.   He admitted only a venerable monk who had been his tutor, and with him he held long and mysterious conferences.   Camillo no longer sought entrance to the apartment of his friend; he perceived that he especially it was whom Giulio sought to avoid.

The day so anxiously anticipated at length arrived, and Camillo and Giuliana were united.   But Giulio did not attend the nuptials; he had left the paternal roof, and every attempt to discover his retreat proved unavailing.   His father was in despair, when about the termination of a month he received the following letter :—

My Father—Spare your useless search, my resolution is fixed.   Nothing can change it.   Dispose of your wealth; Giulio is dead to the world.

It grieves me to leave you ; but I must fly from a horrible destiny. Adieu !
forget the ill-fated

GIULIO.

This letter, which bore no date, was left by a stranger, who
departed the moment he had delivered it. The marquis interrogated the monk, who alone could enable him to recover
his fugitive son; but entreaties and threats proved equally ineffectual either to persuade or to intimidate the ecclesiastic.
He was not ignorant, he replied, of the designs of Giulio,
and for a long time opposed them ; but he had found him so
firmly resolved that he became at last convinced it was his
duty to acquiesce in his project ; he knew the place of his retreat, but declared that no power on earth could induce him
to betray secrets confided to him under the seal of confession.

IV.

Giulio had gone to Naples, and from thence had embarked
for Messina ; he intended to enter a Dominican monastery
recommended to him by his confessor. . The piety of Father
Ambrosio, the Superior of this monastery, was too sincere, and
his mind too enlightened, to take advantage of the disturbed
imagination of a youth, and Giulio in vain supplicated him to
dispense with his novitiate,—he would not consent. Giulio
was obliged to submit to this probation, but his resolution
remained unshaken ; he was under the dominion of a strange
delusion, and believed he had only the power to escape from
his destiny by embracing a monastic life. The image of the
Sibyl pursued him ; her words rung continually in his ear,
Love without bounds ! Sacrilege ! Murder ! The cloister seemed
to him to be the only refuge which could shield him from love
and from crime.   Unhappy youth ! as if the walls, the vows,
or the rules of a monastery, could counteract the decrees of
fate !

The year of his novitiate expired. Giulio pronounced the
vows ; he believed himself happy, and felt at least an abate-
ment of the torments that he had suffered. The idea of the
sacrifice he had consummated was not for a moment present to
his mind, to trouble or sadden his thoughts. But on the even-

ing of the solemn day on which he renounced the world for ever, at the moment when he was about to retire to his cell, he met one of the monks, who took his hand, and pressing it affectionately said to him, "Brother, it is for ever." The words *for ever* appalled Giulio. How marvellous the power of a word over a weak and superstitious mind! Giulio now for the first time seemed sensible of the extent of his sacrifice; he regarded himself as a being already dead, for time was no more. He became melancholy, and appeared to support with difficulty the weight of existence.

Father Ambrosio beheld with compassion the situation of the young man; it was sufficient to know that he was unhappy to create in the bosom of the Superior the tenderest interest in his behalf, and he thought that employment would prove best calculated to dispel his melancholy. Giulio was eloquent, and Ambrosio appointed him preacher to the monastery. His reputation rapidly spread, and crowds flocked from all parts to hear him. He was young and handsome, and, doubtless, the mystery which surrounded him imparted an additional charm to his words.

V.

The time approached for the celebration of a grand festival, at which the King of Naples and his whole Court were to be present. Giulio was appointed to pronounce the panegyric upon St. Thomas, the patron saint of the monastery, and the most splendid preparations were made for the occasion. The day arrived; immense crowds filled the church; Giulio could with difficulty make his way through them, in order to reach the pulpit, when in the midst of his exertions his cowl fell back and exposed his countenance to view. At the same moment he heard a voice exclaim, "Good God, how handsome!" Agitated and surprised, he involuntarily turned, and saw a female, whose eyes were fixed on him with the most penetrating expression. That moment sufficed to give a colour to the future existence of those two beings. Giulio delivered his sermon, and as soon as he found himself at liberty ran and shut himself up in his cell; but it was not to devote himself to his usual meditations. Pursued by the image of the unknown female, experiencing feelings altogether new to him,

restless, unhappy, he found no repose. Yet it seemed to him
that he only began to exist when he heard that voice, the tones
of which thrilled to the inmost recesses of his heart. He
durst not glance towards the future. Alas! of what avail
could it be? his destiny was fixed. Every morning when he
celebrated mass, every morning he beheld on the same spot a
veiled female ; he knew her, but durst not even indulge in the
wish to behold her features, though he eagerly fixed his gaze
on the veil. He watched all her motions ; he perceived, as it
were, the very pulsations of her heart, and his own responded
to them. Without resolution to tear himself from the dangerous indulgence, he trembled to analyse his sensations ; he
recoiled from the truth. His whole life seemed concentrated
in those few moments ; the rest of his days were an absolute
blank. He wished to fly. "If to-morrow she reappears in
the church," he at length said to himself, "I shall return
thither no more." Armed by this resolution he thought himself safe ; and he appeared to experience greater tranquillity.
Next day he repaired to the church somewhat earlier than
usual. She was not there. When the congregation had departed he approached the seat of the unknown, and saw her
prayer-book. He seized it, opened it, and upon the first leaf
read the name of Theresa. Now then, he could call her by her
name ; he could repeat it a thousand and a thousand times.
"Theresa! Theresa!" murmured he in a low voice, as if he
feared to be heard, though alone. Since she had not reappeared he need not scruple to return to the church. Days and
weeks flew away, and Theresa was still absent.

VI.

Theresa, the wife of an old man whom she loved as a father,
found her happiness in the fulfilment of her duties ; and
dreamed not that there existed a different species of existence
from that which she had hitherto experienced. She saw Giulio,
and her peace fled forever. In a soul ardent as Theresa's the
first serious passion she felt must decide the fate of her life.
She adored Giulio. Until this critical moment her husband
had been the confidant of all her thoughts ; but she spoke not
to him of Giulio. The reserve was painful, and seemed a

crime in her own eyes. She perceived that there was a danger
to be avoided, and abstained from attending mass. In the hope
of calming the agitation of her soul, Theresa determined to
have recourse to confession, and for this purpose returned to
the church of the Dominicans. Making choice of the hour
when she knew Giulio would be occupied, she approached the
confessional, and on her knees related all that she had felt
since the day of the festival of St. Thomas ; the delight she
had in beholding Giulio, the remorse consequent on that indulgence, and the courage with which she had relinquished it ;
but she feared that her resolution would soon fail. "What
ought I to do?" exclaimed she ; "have pity on a miserable
sinner!" Her tears fell in torrents—her agitation was extreme. Scarcely had she ceased speaking when a threatening
voice pronounced these words: "Unhappy woman! what sacrilege!" Giulio, for it was he himself that destiny had conducted to receive this avowal, at these words darted from the
confessional. Theresa, still on her knees, arrested his steps,
and seizing his robe supplicated him to retract his malediction :
she implored him in the name of his salvation—she implored
him in the name of love. Giulio replied but very feebly.
"Theresa, Theresa," cried he at last, "leave this place! very
soon my resolution will vanish." At these words Theresa
threw herself on his bosom, and encircled him with her arms.
"Tell me," she ejaculated, "oh! tell me that I am beloved
before I separate myself from thee!"

Giulio, agitated and taken by surprise, for a moment returned her caresses, and pressed her to his heart; but suddenly struck by a recollection of the prediction, he vowed to
fly from her for ever, and, without any explanation, exacted
from her a similar oath. Theresa, wholly abandoned to her
passion, scarcely comprehended the import of his words, and
consented to all that he dictated. What, in fact, imported to
her his language? it was sufficient that he loved her, she was
certain of seeing him again.

Giulio shuddered at the imprudence of which he had been
guilty; but it was too late to avoid the danger; he could not
escape from his destiny. He was already a prey to *love without bounds ;* the *sacrilege* was already committed. Had he not
avowed his passion, even within the very walls of that sacred

temple, where he had so recently pronounced the vows of
sanctity? and yet he had sworn to fly from Theresa for ever.
Strange inconsistency of the human heart! what ought to have
been his chastisement was his consolation.   But in this painful struggle the unfortunate Giulio saw only misery before him.
Theresa was less terrified.   She was a woman; Giulio had
declared that he loved her, and she could brave whatever else
of evil fate had in store.   With what delight she dwelt on
their brief interview!   One such hour teemed with more remembrances than a whole life without love.   She forgot her
determination to avoid Giulio ; she returned to the church,—
she again saw him, and he too seemed to have forgotten his
oath.   His whole existence was absorbed by his passion, and
when he beheld Theresa the universe disappeared from before
his eyes.   They avoided conversing together.   Giulio, in the
absence of Theresa, experienced the most bitter remorse; but
a single glance from her recalled the fatal charm which held
captive his soul.   At length he resolved to speak to her, and to
bid her an eternal adieu.

VII.

At the gate of the monastery stood a poor woman and her
child who were supported by Theresa.   Little Carlo often
followed her to church with her prayer-book, and performed
his devotions by her side.   Giulio, who dared not approach
Theresa, bade Carlo inform her that Father Giulio would attend her in the confessional at seven o'clock in the evening.
How wretchedly passed this day with Giulio ! he shuddered at
the idea of meeting Theresa alone.   He feared that he should
be wanting in resolution to say adieu ! he could never resolve
to do so.   He determined not to see her, but to write, and
Carlo was charged to deliver his letter to her as she entered
the church.   Theresa, on receiving this first message, was
much agitated.   Nevertheless, she failed not to repair to the
church at the appointed hour.   Carlo placed in her hand the
letter, which she opened with extreme emotion ; but how
great was her despair on reading its contents.

" Fly, imprudent woman, and no more sully by thy presence
the sanctity of this holy fane !   Banish a remembrance which

is the torment of my life. I never loved you! I will never see you more!"

This resolution pierced the heart of Theresa: she could have struggled against her remorse; but Giulio loved her not —he had never loved her!—her remorse was less bitter than those words! She was attacked by a violent fever, which threatened to deprive her of life; the name of Giulio often rose to her lips, but love protected it even in her delirium. His name was not betrayed; she only murmured from time to time in a low voice, "I never loved thee!"

Had Giulio in the meantime succeeded in recovering his tranquillity, or stifling his remorse? No, his sufferings were extreme. After having declared to Theresa that he never loved her, he wholly abandoned himself to his fatal passion. The sacrifice seemed to him sufficient,—so terrible had been the effort to write that letter! Oh, Theresa! if thou couldst know what it cost the unhappy Giulio, thine own grief would be forgotten in commiseration for his sufferings! Giulio was a prey to the most tormenting inquietude; three months had flown away, and he had heard no news of Theresa; time seemed still further to inflame his passion, and he now wholly avoided society. Having, on the plea of ill-health, obtained a dispensation from Father Ambrosio, he relinquished his public functions, shut himself up in his cell, or wandered during the night amongst the tombs of the brethren, thus encouraging the fatal morbidness of his feelings, having neither the strength of mind to subdue his passion nor yet to yield himself up to it. Distracted, above all, by the agonising pangs of suspense, which sap the springs of life, he could neither review the past with satisfaction nor look forward to the future with hope.

VIII.

The long and tedious malady of Theresa was succeeded by a state of weakness not less alarming; she thought her end approached, and wished to fulfil the last duties of religion. Her husband, who tenderly loved her, was convinced that some hidden sorrow was hurrying her to the tomb; but, respecting her silence, he forbore to question her on the subject. He entreated Father Ambrosio, who was held in great veneration, to visit Theresa. Ambrosio promised to comply with his request, but an unforeseen circumstance prevented him from fulfilling this promise; he directed Giulio to go in his stead to the house of Signor Vivaldi, the husband of Theresa, to administer consolation to a dying female. Alas! Giulio, himself the victim of despair, had only tears and sighs, instead of consolation, to offer. He would have excused himself, but Ambrosio refused to exempt him from this duty, and he therefore repaired to the residence of Vivaldi. He was conducted into a dimly-lighted apartment, where a numerous circle of sorrowing friends surrounded the bed of the patient. On his entrance every one withdrew, and Giulio was alone with the invalid. Agitated by an indefinable emotion, he remained immovable and irresolute. "Holy father," said the dying woman, "has Heaven mercy in store for a wretched sinner?" Scarcely were these words uttered when Giulio fell on his knees before the bed. "Theresa! Theresa!" he ejaculated. Who can depict the feelings of the lovers? Explanation was useless . . . they loved. Giulio related all that he had suffered for her, and accused himself as the cause of her sufferings. "Pardon! oh! pardon, Theresa. Giulio is thine for ever." These words re-animated Theresa; she could not speak, but she beheld Giulio, she heard his voice, she pressed his hand; to die thus appeared more sweet to her than life. Giulio folded her in his arms; he would have prolonged her life at the expense of his own: "Thou shalt live! thy lover is with thee! My Theresa! speak to me! am I not again to hear thee?" The sound of his voice seemed to re-animate the strength of Theresa: "I love you, Giulio! I love you!" murmured she. These words were life to him. What need had she to say more? The moments in which they conversed together flew rapidly away; the certainty of seeing each other again gave them courage to separate. Theresa recovered her health. Giulio visited her every day. A delightful intimacy reigned between them, and the lover appeared to forget his scruples and his remorse. Wholly engrossed by Theresa, he watched with the most tender interest the progress of her recovery; he durst not afflict her; he perceived that her life depended on him, and this pretext for continuing their intercourse he interpreted as a duty.

IX.

Two years had elapsed since he left Rome, and on the second anniversary of the fatal predictions of the Sibyl he sank into a gloomy reverie. Theresa longed to know the cause of his sadness : she had never questioned him on the subject ; but before she could share his sorrows it was necessary to know the cause whence they arose. Giulio related to her his interview with the Sibyl, and his flight from the paternal roof. In the course of this recital all his horrible feelings were revived, and he exclaimed in an accent of terror : *"Love ! Sacrilege ! Murder !"* The emotion of Theresa was extreme, but the word *love* threw a fatal spell over her heart and her imagination ; and when Giulio repeated *"Sacrilege ! Murder !"* she softly replied *"Love !"* thinking thus to calm the agitation of his spirit, because with her love was everything. Sometimes Giulio, led away by the violence of his passion, fixed on her a look which she dared not meet ; she felt his heart palpitate, his frame tremble, and a dangerous silence succeeded to those tumultuous emotions.

They were, however, happy, for they were not yet criminal. Giulio was obliged to be absent on an important mission, with which he was entrusted by Father Ambrosio. He had not courage to utter an adieu to Theresa, but he wrote to her, promising a speedy return. However, he was detained by numerous obstacles, and it was more than a month before he returned to Messina.

On his arrival he hastened to Theresa, whom he found alone on a terrace overlooking the shore, absorbed in thoughts of her lover. Never before had she appeared to him so beautiful, so seducing. He gazed on her for a moment in ecstasy, but not long could he resist the temptation of addressing her, of hearing her voice. He spoke ; she perceived him, and flew into his arms. In a delirium of passion Giulio at first responded to all her feelings ; but suddenly starting back with horror, he fell on his knees, and remained with his hands clasped, his eyes fixed, and in a state of the most dreadful agitation. His deadly paleness and the wild expression of his countenance rendered this scene truly dreadful to Theresa.

She durst not approach him, and for the first time could not share his emotions. "Theresa," said he at length, mournfully, "we must separate! you know not all you have to fear!" Theresa scarcely understood his words, but she saw his agitation, and endeavoured to calm it; but he again repulsed her. "In the name of Heaven," cried he, "approach me not!" She stood trembling and motionless. She knew only the tenderness of love, and was unacquainted with its madness. Giulio, impatient at her silence, abruptly started up: "To-morrow," he said, "my fate shall be decided;" and darted away without giving Theresa time to reply.

[The Emperor put extraordinary animation into the recitation of the dialogue in this scene. It is a mistake to say that he took lessons from Talma. He might perhaps have given them to Talma.]

X.

The next day Theresa received the following billet:—

"Theresa, I cannot again see you; I am unhappy in your presence. I know you cannot comprehend what I feel. Theresa, you must be mine, but it must be with your own free will. Never could I have the courage to take advantage of your weakness. Yesterday you saw it. I tore myself from your arms because you said not, 'I will be thine.' Reflect seriously; we are lost for ever! Oh, Theresa! eternal perdition! how terrible these words! even in thy arms they will interpose between me and happiness. For us there is no longer peace; death, the only refuge, is not a refuge for us. To-morrow, if you wish to see me—and you know the price—to-morrow send Carlo to church. If he bring your prayerbook that will indicate that you renounce Giulio; if not, then thou art mine for ever! *For ever* belongs to eternity; how dare I pronounce the words! Adieu."

Theresa, gentle and timid by nature, was overwhelmed with terror on perusing this letter; the words *eternal perdition* seemed to her a terrible malediction. "Giulio," she ejaculated, "we were happy! why could not that happiness satisfy you?" She knew not on what to resolve; to see him no more was impossible, and yet she exclaimed, "Remorse will pursue him without ceasing. Oh, Giulio! thou hast confided to

me thy destiny, and I ought to sacrifice myself for thee."
Carlo was ordered to carry the book to the church, and he
placed it on the seat usually occupied by Theresa.

Giulio, notwithstanding the violence of his passion, could
not resolve to possess Theresa without her own consent.
Cruel from his weakness, he wished to throw upon her the
whole responsibility of the crime. The church was empty
when Giulio saw the boy enter and deposit the book upon the
seat. No longer master of himself, he darted forward, seized
it, and giving it to Carlo, ordered him to carry it back to his
mistress. Long he stood rooted to the spot where he had
awaited the decree of his fate and that of Theresa. At length,
recovering from the tumult of his feelings, "I will see her!"
he murmured.

Carlo returned and delivered the book to Theresa, saying
Father Giulio had sent it. How great was the emotion of
Theresa! she knew that Giulio would return, and she waited
for him on the terrace where they had last parted. At length
he appeared, but sad and gloomy, and approached with a fal-
tering step. Theresa penetrated what was passing in his
mind, and shuddered at the idea of this interview. She had
assumed the fortitude to refuse; but on beholding her wor-
shipped lover so miserable she thought only of consoling him;
—she no longer hesitated or trembled, but approaching whis-
pered, " Giulio, I am thine!"

.   .   .   .   .

[Here Bonaparte made a long pause.]

Giulio, overwhelmed with remorse, now became gloomy
and morose, even in the presence of Theresa: her most tender
caresses had no longer the power to soften him. But the
love of Theresa was, on the contrary, increased by the sacrifice she had made. She secretly mourned the change that
had taken place in Giulio, but she forebore to complain, and
flattered herself with the hope that she should yet be able to
render him happy, and that he would forget everything but
her. Giulio, far, however, from returning her affection, accused her as the author of his misery: " Thou hast seduced,
thou hast destroyed me; but for thee my soul had still been
pure." His visits became less frequent, and at last wholly
ceased. Theresa demanded to see him: she constantly fre-

quented the church, and wrote to him daily. Her letters were
sent back unopened, and Giulio confined himself to his cell.
But it behoved Theresa to see him and confide to him a secret; alas! the secret that she would at no distant period
become a mother! what would be her fate should he persist
in abandoning her? Knowing that on the following Sunday
Giulio was to celebrate mass, she resolved not to neglect that
opportunity, on which more than life depended; and this idea
armed her with strength and courage.

XI.

Her whole attention during the two days which preceded
her expected interview with Giulio were employed in making
preparations for the flight she contemplated. The situation
of the monastery, on the sea-shore, would facilitate her project. She bestowed not a moment's consideration on the place
to which they should direct their flight. Giulio would decide that according to his pleasure: for except Giulio, all else
was indifferent to Theresa.

She had hired a small bark, and arranged everything with
so much prudence that no one suspected her design, so that
she had no fear of encountering any obstacles. The day so
impatiently expected at length arrived, and Theresa, enveloped in a long black veil, approached the altar. Giulio did
not recognise her, while she watched all his motions; and
when the congregation dispersed, she glided behind a column
which Giulio must pass on returning to the cloisters. On his
approach she perceived that he was more than ever a prey to
sorrow. His arms were folded across his breast, and his head
bent forward. He walked with the gloomy and lagging step
of a criminal. Theresa witnessed this with profound grief;
she would have sacrificed her own life to secure his repose,
but she durst no longer hesitate: the innocent being to whom
she would soon give birth, demanded of her a father. She
presented herself before Giulio. "Stop," she exclaimed, "I
must speak to you; you must listen to me! Never will I
leave you until you give me the key of the garden of the
monastery. I *must* have it. Oh, Giulio! it is not my life
alone that depends on you!" At these words Giulio believed

that a fearful apparition had arisen before him. "Wretched woman! what meanest thou? Depart! fly from this place!" But Theresa threw herself at his feet, and vowed that she would not stir until he had granted her request. All the efforts of Giulio to escape were ineffectual. Theresa seemed endowed with almost supernatural strength. "Swear," said she, "that you will meet me at midnight." As she spoke Giulio was startled at hearing a slight noise, and gave her the key. "At midnight," said he, and they separated.

XII.

Theresa repaired at the appointed time to the garden. The night was dark. She durst not call on Giulio for fear of discovery; but in a short time she heard approaching footsteps —they were those of Giulio. "Speak your purpose," said he, "the moments are precious. Cease to pursue a wretch who can never render you happy. Theresa, I adore you! without you life is an insupportable burden : yet even in your arms I experience the torments of remorse—torments which impoison our most rapturous moments. Thou hast witnessed my despair. How often have I reproached thee? Pardon me, adored Theresa! it is just I should punish myself. I renounce thee, and this sacrifice will expiate my crime." He ceased speaking, almost suffocated by his grief. Theresa endeavoured to console him by anticipating greater happiness for the future. "Giulio," said she, "had it been only for myself I would not have sought this interview. Like you, I fear not death ; but the pledge of our love demanded that I should see you. Come, then, Giulio, let us depart!—everything is prepared for our flight." Giulio, a prey to the most horrible feelings, suffered himself to be conducted by her ; a few moments and they would be united for ever. But suddenly disengaging himself from the arms of Theresa, "No," exclaimed he, "never!" and he plunged a poniard into her bosom.

[In pronouncing these words the Emperor, approaching the Empress, made the motion of drawing a dagger. The illusion was so great that the ladies shrieked with horror. Bonaparte, like a consummate actor, continued his recital without appearing to notice the effect he had produced.]

She fell, and Giulio was covered with her blood. Rooted to the spot, and with a wandering eye, he long contemplated his victim. Day began to dawn, and the bell of the monastery rang for matin service. Giulio raised the lifeless form of her who had so devotedly loved him and threw it into the sea. In a state of frenzy he rushed into the church. His blood-stained garments, and the dagger in his hand, declared him a murderer! He offered no resistance on being seized, and was never more seen!

[The Empress pressed Napoleon to relate the fate of Giulio. He replied—]

The secrets of the cloister are impenetrable.

[The story of Giulio is not fictitious. Previously to the Revolution an adventure of a similar kind occurred in a convent at Lyons, of which the documents fell into the hands of Bonaparte, and furnished him with the basis of this tale. I have frequently heard him relate such stories, which he always did in a dimly-lighted apartment in order to produce greater effect. I experienced more pleasure in reading Giulio from being able to recall to mind the varied tones of his voice, his action, his look, and the gestures with which he accompanied those improvisations. I can affirm that in no case whatever are words of Æschines more applicable: "What then would it have been had yourself heard him?"]